MY
LORD
OF
BELMONT

MY LORD OF BELMONT:

A BIOGRAPHY OF LEO HAID

DOM PASCHAL BAUMSTEIN, O.S.B.

LANEY·SMITH, INC.

Cum permissu Superiorum

Publishing coordinated by:
Laney-Smith, Inc.
1370 Briar Creek Road
Charlotte, North Carolina 28205

Distributed by:
The Archives of Belmont Abbey
100 Belmont-Mount Holly Road
Belmont, North Carolina 28012-2795

Manufactured in the United States of America
First printing: 1985   Second printing: 1995

Library of Congress Cataloging-in-Publication Data:

Baumstein, Paschal
    My Lord of Belmont: a biography of Leo Haid/Paschal Baumstein.
    p. cm.
    Originally published: Herald House, 1985.
    Includes bibliographical references and index.
    ISBN 0-9614976-5-3 (alk. paper)

    1. Haid, Leo. 1849-1924. 2. Benedictines-United States-Biography.
    3. Catholic Church-North Carolina-Bishops-Biography.
    I. Title.
    [BX4705.H215B38   1995]
    282'.092—dc20
    [B]   95-37460
                                                                   CIP

for

my mother

and for

Maryhelp

Belmont Abbey

I have taken the place for pity-sake—in favor of Faith—in order to give the few—all dispersed—Catholics a harbor of some stability.

—Archabbot Boniface Wimmer, O.S.B.
20 August 1884
(SVA: Letter To Joseph Amberger)

pREFACE

Leo Haid (1849-1924) was not typical of turn-of-the-century prelates in the Catholic Church. Obliged by powers beyond his own to live as both an active bishop in the domestic missions of the United States, and as a Benedictine monk and abbot who was vowed to stability and tied by preference to his cloister, he was a figure in conflict. This was not a struggle that would lend him happiness, but it did provide a remarkable backdrop for the active-contemplative questions that were so characteristic of the religious debates in American monasteries in his time.

His career was one of astounding successes. He is credited as the father of five monasteries, each with its own college or school. He ruled the Catholic Church in North Carolina—a state that boasted the most overwhelmingly Protestant citizenry in the Union—for the crucial three-and-a-half decades that preceded that territory's first diocese. But diocesan legitimacy was not granted until 1924. In the meantime the Holy See honored Haid repeatedly: he was abbot, bishop, Vicar Apostolic, Roman Count, Assistant at the Pontifical Throne, America's only Abbot-Ordinary. By the time of his death he was the Dean of both the American abbots and the American Catholic hierarchy. The Catholic Church in North Carolina grew under his leadership to its greatest numbers and strength in the history of the state. All of the schools he founded developed toward financial, popular, and educational distinction. Yet none of these were the standards by which this American Abbot-Bishop, with his heart firmly implanted in his monastery, evaluated success. Thus he believed to the end that his divided energies rendered him a failure.

The problem lay in the decision of the Holy See in 1887 that Leo Haid should reign over his bishopric without abandoning the demands of his monastery and monastic vows. This created an unusual, dual jurisdiction. Under this ruling, Leo Haid was bound by the duties of an active, missionary bishop, while by vow he held to the stability and observance of the monastic cloister. For his own taste—"a monk before I was either priest or bishop," as he phrased it— the hierarchy of values seemed obvious. But he seldom explained his standards to others, and in meeting the demands of his two jurisdictions, the priorities seemed horribly obscure. His career, for that reason, was always bifurcated in the perception of his respective constituencies, and his accomplishments (in his own eyes, at least) diminished.

What emerged from this disharmony and confusion, however, was a man who was far more distinguished than his regency. Always a theorist, Bishop Haid recorded detailed schemas regarding the principles by which his schools, monasteries, and episcopal jurisdiction were to be ruled. Through these somewhat abstract foundations for his practical duties, Haid surfaced as a man of surprising compassion and insight, possessed of an extraordinary optimism that maintained the essential, deeply spiritual, goodness of his subordinates and students. In the practical realm he was not a great success in dealing with the persons entrusted to his direction, particularly not with the priests of his diocese. Yet even when his efforts failed, they were noteworthy for the very unusual qualities Leo Haid brought to them. He ruled his diocese and his schools in the same manner as a monastery was governed: he was an *abbas*, a "father", prefering the authority of abbatial paternity over the power of episcopal jurisdiction and his legitimate prelacy. Out of this approach to leadership, rooted as it was in the theories he so carefully analyzed—and seen by some as a virtue, and by most of his contemporaries as a flaw—Leo Haid had a lasting impact on the character of the Catholic Church in his very Protestant domain, and on the abbey and college that survive him in the foothills of the North Carolina mountains.

This volume records the singular life and philosophy of this monk who found himself a bishop and college president in twentieth century America. Until now, his exceptional mind and heart have remained hidden—even to those at the institutions he founded—because of restrictions on his private papers. In opening these documents for the first time, in the interest of this project, the sixth Abbot of Belmont, Peter Stragand, O.S.B., has sought to offer a gift of considerable value to all of those still quietly influenced by Haid, to his monastery, his schools and colleges, and to the Catholic Church in the American South.

—Belmont Abbey
Solemnity of Maryhelp
24 May MCMLXXXV

acknowledgements

The Right Reverend Abbot of Belmont, Peter Nicholas Stragand, opened the archives of his abbey, its *nullius* 'diocese', and its various monastic and educational apostolates for the purposes of this project. Unrestricted access to these documents had never previously been allowed, and since then the holdings have returned to their earlier restrictions. I am deeply indebted to Abbot Peter for facilitating this project, and for his unfailing commitment to the value of history and the necessity of its careful preservation.

To the Reverend superiors and archivists of the American Cassinese Federation of the Order of Saint Benedict, Archabbey of Saint Vincent, Archdiocese of Baltimore, Abbey of Maryhelp, Dioceses of Richmond, Belmont Abbey *Nullius*, and Raleigh, Saint Benedict Motherhouse (Bristow, Virginia), Saint Benedict Priory (Richmond), and Benedictine Priory (Savannah), each of whom granted research privileges; to the Dioceses of Charlotte, Savannah, Superior, and Charleston, to Saint Bernard Abbey (Alabama), Saint Charles Seminary (Maryland), Saint John Abbey (Minnesota), Saint Anselm Abbey (Rome), Saint Anselm Abbey (New Hampshire), Saint Benedict Abbey (Kansas), Saint Leo Abbey (Florida), Saint Mary Abbey (New Jersey), the Redemptorists at the Provincial archives in New York, the University of Notre Dame (Indiana), the Sisters of the Blessed Sacrament for Indians and Colored People, and various individuals, seemingly endless in number, each of whom gave use of specific materials from their archival holdings; to the Most Reverend Joseph Federal, D.D., who donated Haid materials to the archives at Belmont; to Arthur L. Hite, Esquire, genealogist of the Haid family, with whom I have taken special joy in corresponding and working while unraveling the story of Abbot Leo; to each of these I offer thanks. In particular the Venerable Brother Philip Hurley, O.S.B., assistant archivist for the repository of the American Cassinese Federation and for Saint Vincent Archabbey, was an extraordinary resource, being not only proficient in his work but prompt as well.

The staff of the Abbot Vincent Taylor Library, on the campus of Belmont Abbey College, secured access to the various reference tools and instruments of research I required. They were gracious and courteous. I am particularly indebted to Mr. James R. Donoghue, also a member of the faculty and administrative staff at Belmont Abbey College. During his tenure as reference librarian his service was invaluable; subsequent to his promotion at the College, he donated hours of editorial counsel. This volume and its author were served immeasurably by this gentleman, his expertise, judgment, and good taste.

The Reverend David Kessinger, O.S.B., who preceeded me in the Abbey's archives, laid the groundwork for this project. Without the service, accuracy, and perseverance of Mrs. Martha S. Hendren the accessibility of the monastery's historical records would never have been achieved. The Reverend Colman Barry, O.S.B., historian of Saint John Abbey in Minnesota, graciously perused the text. The Reverend Ambrose Keefe, O.S.B., was helpful and informative, sharing his own research generously.

The Right Reverend Abbot-Ordinary Walter A. Coggin, O.S.B., Ph.D., D.D., is responsible for all the photography in this volume, often restoring to life images seemingly rendered useless by the passing years. Even more importantly, however, he has for more than a decade lent his guidance and insight to my weak efforts to inculcate the wisdom of Benedictine monasticism.

The Reverend Father Anselm Biggs, O.S.B., Ph.D., generously shared his expertise in Belmontana. It was Father Anselm who first introduced me to the riches of the Abbey's history. This scholarly monk and historian is possessed of a phenomenal memory and breadth of knowledge, talents that are complemented by his skills as a linguist and enriched by his faith and piety. When to him fell the task, by abbatial appointment, of evaluating my proposed text, his acute intellect and fraternal support were unfailing, and in every way beneficial.

In various times and ways, each of the monks of Belmont has assisted with this volume. Since approximately four hundred men have received the monastic habit in the course of the abbey's first century, however, the list does not follow. For this and all other sins of omission, I am sincerely sorry.

table of Contents

Chronology

1846	Boniface Wimmer establishes the first permanent Benedictine colony in the United States.
1847	John and Mary Hite immigrate to America.
1848	The Hites settle near the Benedictine monastery of Saint Vincent.
1849	The fourth child and third son, Michael, is born to the Hites. He is baptized at Saint Vincent Church.
1855	Erection of the American Cassinese Congregation of the Order of Saint Benedict is approved in Rome.
1861	John Hite dies. Mary Hite remarries. Michael Hite is enrolled in the monastery school at Saint Vincent.
1868	Michael Hite enters the Benedictine novitiate at Saint Vincent, taking the name "Leo" in religion.
1869	Frater Leo Hite professes his monastic vows, and changes the spelling of his patronym to "Haid".
1872	Frater Leo is admitted to solemn monastic vows, and is ordained a priest. He also begins teaching at Saint Vincent. Jeremiah Joseph O'Connell moves to the old Caldwell farm, in Gaston County, North Carolina.
1876	Saint Vincent accepts the Caldwell farm and establishes a monastery and school there.
1877	The Carolina monastery receives the name "Maryhelp" and the first chapel is constructed.
1878	Julius Pohl is assigned to Maryhelp.
1880	Felix Hintemeyer enters the monastery at Saint Vincent. The first permanent building at the North Carolina monastery is erected.
1884	The Holy See raises the Benedictine monastery of Maryhelp to the rank of an abbey.

1885	Leo Haid is elected, confirmed, and blessed as the first abbot of Maryhelp.
1886	Saint Mary's College is chartered by the state of North Carolina. The first wing of the College Building is erected.
1887	Haid is confirmed by the Holy See as Vicar Apostolic of North Carolina. Boniface Wimmer dies. Oswald Moosmueller is removed from Savannah.
1888	Abbot Leo is consecrated titular bishop of Messene and enthroned in the Pro-Cathedral of the Vicariate Apostolic of North Carolina. The Maryhelp Chapter accepts responsibility for the Benedictine missions in Florida. A new wing is added to the College Building at Saint Mary's. Walter Leahy leaves.
1889	Felix Hintemeyer is appointed Prior and Vicar General.
1890	The Seminary is opened to diocesan students. Francis Meyer is cured of typhoid fever after an urgent petition to the Virgin Mary. Leo Haid is elected *Praeses* of the American Cassinese Congregation.
1891	The Grotto of Our Lady of Lourdes is erected and blessed as a Pilgrimage Shrine. Another wing is added to the monastery. Nine counties of the Vicariate Apostolic are entrusted to the Order of Saint Benedict for fifty years.
1892	Construction begins on the new Abbey Church of Maryhelp. The Sisters of Mercy are welcomed to Belmont.
1893	Katharine Drexel makes the first of her many contributions to the missionary work of the Catholic Church in North Carolina. The first Mass is celebrated in the new Abbey Church. Saint Maur Priory in Bristow, Virginia, is created. A separate wing of the monastery is built for the brothers. Haid goes to Rome in an effort to limit the power of the Abbot Primate; he attends the congress of Abbots-President; he fulfills the obligations of the decennial visit *ad limina*.
1894	James Cardinal Gibbons blesses the new Abbey Church. Saint Leo Priory in Florida becomes the first of Maryhelp's daughterhouses to be granted canonical independence. The monastery in North Carolina is enlarged again. Jeremiah O'Connell dies. Saint Joseph Institute in Bristow is opened officially.

1897	Jubilee Hall is built at Maryhelp. Felix Hintemeyer is reportedly nominated to the See of Wilmington, Delaware.
1898	The College Building is completed.
1899	The water tower is razed by fire.
1900	The "Great Fire" destroys two-thirds of the College Building. Andrew Huemer dies. Haid's "missionary decade" begins.
1901	Willibald Baumgartner is removed from Richmond and sent to Europe to recruit candidates for the monastery.
1902	The Abbey's missions in Savannah are organized as a priory. Benedictine College opens there. Michael McInerney enters the Maryhelp novitiate.
1903	Haid undertakes his second decennial visit *ad limina* and embarks on the "Grand Tour".
1904	The library wing is appended to the Brothers' Building. Felix Hintemeyer is awarded an honorary doctorate by the Pontifical Athenaeum of Saint Anselm in Rome.
1906	Construction begins on Saint Leo Hall.
1909	Haid falls ill, and death is thought to be imminent. Diomede Falconio pontificates for the Solemnity of Saint Benedict. A prolonged rest is prescribed for the Abbot by his physicians. Thomas Oestreich is appointed rector of Saint Mary's College.
1910	Maryhelp accepts the new mission in Richmond. The Holy See creates the *Abbatia Nullius* of Belmont. Haid's silver abbatial jubilee is celebrated.
1911	Benedictine High School in Richmond opens. The petition for the erection of a new North Carolina diocese is not approved.
1912	Thomas Frederick Price is incardinated into the Archdiocese of Baltimore. The Perry Belmont controversy begins.
1913	The name of the College is changed to "Belmont Abbey College". The Warrenton Parish is given to the secular clergy, with the loss being made official the following year. The first Alumni Reunion is held at Belmont.

1914   Haid executes the third decennial visit *ad limina* and his second European tour. The Abbot is named an Assistant at the Pontifical Throne.

1919   Leo Haid is inscribed as a Count of the Apostolic Palace.

1922   Christopher Dennen and Michael Curley initiate the effort to terminate the Vicariate Apostolic of North Carolina. Typhoid fever assaults the inmates at Saint Joseph Institute. Julius Pohl is reassigned to Maryhelp.

1923   Haid celebrates his last jubilee.

1924   The fourth decennial visit *ad limina* is undertaken by Felix Hintemeyer. Hintemeyer, Haid, and Pohl die. Willibald Baumgartner is appointed Prior and Vicar General. Thomas Oestreich is removed as rector of the College. Vincent Taylor is elected and confirmed as the second Abbot Ordinary of Maryhelp. The Diocese of Raleigh is created.

author's note

1. In rendering quotations in this volume, I have ordinarily used a complete orthographic version of words that in the original were abbreviated. Clarity, consistency, and legibility seemed to demand this liberty.

2. Use of various articles by the author, first published in the journal *Crescat*, is by permission of the Southern Benedictine Society of North Carolina, Incorporated.

3. The maps used in this volume were supplied by the North Carolina Department of Cultural Resources.

4. The photographs in this volume are all reproduced from the resources of the Archives of the Southern Benedictine Society of North Carolina, Incorporated. They were prepared by The Right Reverend Abbot-Ordinary Walter A. Coggin, O.S.B. The photographs from the Haid obsequies were donated to the Archives by Bishop Joseph Federal.

PROLOGUE:

The Ideal of Benedict of Nursia

The word *monk* is taken from the Greek *monos,* meaning "alone". The modern inference of the term is not "solitary", however, but "apart" or "separated". Thus, while monks seek to abdicate their immediate roles in society, they do not hesitate to unite into appropriate aggregations, organized according to the demands of practicality, custom, or a formal "rule". Indeed, in the Benedictine tradition, the common, *cenobitical,* life is recognized as an integral part of the monastic charism.

The Benedictines take their name from Benedict of Nursia,[1] the sixth century father of Western monasticism. The Benedictine movement was spawned in young Benedict's desire for personal holiness, and was subsequently spread by fame, disciples, and Providence throughout the Catholic world. Benedict rejected the glamorous, if vice-prone, life of Rome and forsook the distractions of classical education in favor of the rigors of asceticism and prayer in an environment of solitude.[2] Yet as had been the case with several centuries of hermits before him, disciples were promptly attracted,[3] and eventually he was offered the abbacy of a monastery.[4]

Benedict proved more zealous in his new job than the monks had anticipated, however. And while a poisoned beverage did not succeed in killing the young abbot, it did at least encourage his resignation from office. Benedict indulged a few moments of verbal sanctimony, then retreated without further delay to the realm of religious solitude.

Nevertheless, many men heard of Benedict's integrity and his vision of monastic observance. These incipient monks attached themselves to the former abbot, and eventually at least a dozen monasteries came into existence, each with its own superior.[5] Benedict apparently took one of these posts himself, and during succeeding years refined his principles of monastic organization, observance, and governance,[6] creating the document now known as the *Regula Benedicti.*

In 529, he established a monastery atop the seven hundred foot Monte Cassino,[7] about eighty miles southeast of Rome. This was to become the motherhouse of Benedictine monasticism, and the showcase of Benedict's *Regula.* From this secluded site, Cassinese monasticism spread slowly to all of Europe, and eventually through most of the civilized world.

From the perspective of governance, there evolved through the centuries two principal types of monasteries. There were "priories", which were headed by a monk appointed for a temporary term of office, who was to be literally the *prior*; he was "before" the others; he was the "first" in the *statio,* the ordering of the monastic household. The other type of cenobitical arrangement was considered to be of higher rank, however, and this was the format associated with the Benedictine ideal. This type of monastery was designated an "abbey", so called because it was headed by an *abbas* ("abbot"), a "father". In Church law, the distinctions between a priory and an abbey were rather complicated, but for the monks the difference was pastoral rather than juridical in nature, and the Benedictines favored the familial atmosphere of an abbey, and the paternity of an *abbas*.

The "family" image used by the Benedictines also suggested a lasting relationship among the members, stable in character, and motivated by Providence. Just as the members of any family entered that body within the designs of the Deity, so too did the monks believe that they were "called" or had a "Divine vocation" to the vowed life of the monastery; indeed, their vocation was to a specific abbey, a particular monastic family. Thus the monks were not bound together because of their human or experiential commonality, but because in some mysterious way God had touched each one and "called" him to the abbey. This Providential character assigned to the familial bonds a solemn and sacred quality that encouraged the monk to cultivate the extraordinary and radical love for his "call"—with both its benisons and its blemishes—that came to exemplify the spirit of Benedict's monks.

The plan for Benedictine monastic life called for autonomous religious families, each governed by an abbot in consultation with his monks. Each of the abbeys enjoyed independence from other such institutions, and no intermonastic superstructure—what would later be called an "Order"—was recommended in the *Regula*. The monastery was to be as self-supporting as possible; farming was accepted as a given;[8] the house would have its own craftsmen,[9] library,[10] and supply officers.[11] And the good works the monks undertook were ideally to be executed in the environment of the monastic enclosure, called "cloister".[12] Visitors were welcomed, though they were guests of the monastery rather than of any individual monk,[13] and there was a keen awareness of the possibility that in these visitors, the young, the monks assembled, and primarily in the abbot, the voice of Christ might be heard.[14]

Benedictines took two mottos. The first was "Peace", reflecting the atmosphere of men who knew they were not to judge, engage in worldly affairs, or otherwise distract themselves from the art of drawing close to God.[15] The monks' peace proceeded from a type of goal-centered existence that sought to place all elements of life in the context of God and the manner of man's attainment of perfection according to Divine precepts. *Ut in omnibus glorificetur Deus* ("That in all things God may be glorified"), from the fifty-seventh chapter of the *Regula*, became their guiding principle.

It was an ambitious mode of existence, prudently saved by Benedict from continual frustration in the hands of succeeding generations of monks by the wise and practical tone with which he imbued his *Regula*. It proceeded first from his insistence on the value of a rightly ordered, well disciplined will.[16] He seldom mentioned attainment, but cast the monastery, instead, as a "school of the Lord's service,"[17] proposing that his monks were in process rather than at the level of perfection. Then he added a spirit of adaptability, that applied to everything from the horarium[18] to clothing.[19] The monks could be at peace, he suggested, so long as they sought to fulfill the three vows: *conversatio* (conversion of the manner of life to the monastic form),[20] stability (allegiance or adherence to the particular monastery and its observance), and obedience as detailed in the *Regula*.

The other motto of Benedict's monks covered less theoretical concerns: *Ora et labora*, it specified, "work and pray." These two elements—practiced in the context of *conversatio*, stability, and obedience—were the primary means of the Benedictine spiritual life. Work took all forms. There were agriculture,[21] household duties, [22] management positions;[23] the young had to be educated and trained;[24] craftsmen were to be encouraged in their work, too, so long as the integrity of the three vows was maintained.[25] Benedict did not provide for recreation, be it common, social, or extraordinary. Celebrations were discussed in the context only of liturgy. Distraction, in any medium, was unwelcome.

The prayer of the monks took two forms. Prayer in common, according to the *Regula*, was structured,[26] brief,[27] and sensitive to the liturgical calendar;[28] Scripture, especially psalms, was emphasized. The Divine Office, as the common prayer would come to be known, was solemn in character,[29] austere in form,[30] and viewed as a means, rather than an end, as a practical effort expended as part of the journey to God. Benedict called it the *opus dei*, the "work of God," and told the monks to prefer nothing above it,[31] and to vie with one another in hastening to the community's common prayer.[32]

The prayer of individuals was treated more sparingly in the *Regula*, though its mandate was no less clear. In both the public and private aspects of prayer, reading—called *lectio divina*—of Scripture and Patristics was emphasized as a font of meditation.[33]

On all levels, Benedict's *Regula* was a masterful document, permeated with discretion, moderation, adaptability, and psychological insight. These qualities allowed its vigorous promulgation throughout the world, but they also opened the portals of laxity and decline,[34] for adaptation was readily taken to extremes. That, in turn, would hurt the spirit and zeal of the monks, and finally the whole quality of monastic observance could be damaged. Thus as surely as the *Regula* provided fodder for a rather extraordinary golden age—indeed several golden ages of monasticism—those same qualities also sponsored an endless series of aberrations and monastic institutes with a decidedly perfunctory observance. The course charted by the *Regula Benedicti* never demonstrated the clarity that characterized its image among those outside the cloister.

Gregory the Great,[35] the first Roman Pontiff drawn from the Benedictines' own number, was the father of the broadening of Benedict's concept of monasticism. Gregory took these monks—who were supposed to do their good works in the environment of the cloister—and sent them to the English isles in 596, as missionaries.

These first Benedictine missionaries served as the impetus for the transition in Benedictinism which eventually carried it to the western hemisphere. Their general procedure was simple, involving the establishment of monastic centers to which the locals were to be initially attracted by architecture, ceremony, and the extraordinary lifestyle led by the monks. These cenobites broadened Benedictinism with their participation in the arts,[36] scholarship,[37] schools,[38] and other innovations in the character of monasticism. The missionary monks sought to evangelize by living as exemplars, presbyters, and bishops until a local clergy was developed. That process required, as a general principle, one century, after which the monastic life might be led again under a more primitive standard. This was not, of course, a rule, but it did become something of an ideal or goal through the succeeding generations of evangelical labor. By keeping in mind that a monastery's missionary activities were not perpetual in character, Benedictines could assuage the difficulties that attended the acceptance of immediate extra-claustral duties. The century-mark gave some legitimacy to those early compromises, too. But the primary value of the temporal boundary was the objective it erected before later generations of monks, suggesting an inevitable and laudable change that was to come. And there commonly emerged from the missionary period stable, well-supported, prestigious, often very powerful abbeys.

Pope Gregory II[39] sent English Benedictines, in 722, as missionaries to Thuringia and Hesse, and eventually to Bavaria and Westphalia as well. Primacy in this group belonged to Boniface of Crediton, who was supported by a variety of relatives and others. Among these were his nephews Willibald and Winnebald, their sister Walburga, and the beautiful Lioba, who was both cousin and confidante of Bishop Boniface.

The German missonaries generally took a different approach than had the apostles to England. On the continent, the virgin territory was larger; the heathens were less civilized,[40] and their needs different. Thus a greater tradition of preaching developed. The monks spread throughout the land, while only a few waited for natives to knock at the monastery door. The Germans were instructed in agricultural techniques by the monks, and the nuns fed and clothed the poor. In Germany the example was less liturgical and artistic than the English missionary work had been. In their new mission fields, the Benedictines became servants of the poor, providing corporal works of mercy as often as spiritual ones. But they also preached, taught,[41] and won converts. And yet, despite their revised missionary format, after their first century concluded, the Benedictines saw the number of monk-bishops start declining—as had been the pattern in previous areas the Order evangelized—and the more traditional standards of cloister and observance gradually took hold.

Through the next millennium, German monasticism variously grew strong, faded, revived; then the evanescence began again, until in the eighteenth century, the Order there neared extinction. But in the nineteenth century, the grand archabbey of Saint Michael at Metten was resurrected, and received novices. From that Bavarian abbey, in 1846, a new generation of missionary Benedictines set forth. Their destination was the United States of America, where Catholics were a minority, and where the Holy See had assigned the designation "mission territory".

For the nineteenth century move into the missions, it was not a Roman Pontiff who commissioned Benedictines for the apostolic work of the new territory, but a headstrong young cleric, with a rather minimal foundation in the monastic life. Though he had spent only two of his thirteen years of monastic profession in his own monastery, his ambition on behalf of the Order of Saint Benedict supplied for the deficiency of experience. Through this man, the Benedictines stretched toward North America. There, in only four decades, he guided five monasteries to abbatial rank.[42] This Benedictine apostle to the New World was Boniface Wimmer.[43] It was under his shadow and that of his principal abbey, Saint Vincent, that Leo Haid was born, professed the vows of the Order of Saint Benedict, and rose to his first prelacy. It was also at Saint Vincent that this young man learned and embraced the values of Benedict of Nursia, from which there would arise the unceasing conflicts that plagued his adult life.

MY
LORD
OF
BELMONT

Chapter 1:

michael hite

Diomede Falconio, Titular Archbishop of Larissa, and Apostolic Delegate to the United States, boarded train number thirty-seven at the Washington depot on Sunday evening, 16 October 1910. The Archbishop was accompanied by Owen Corrigan, auxiliary bishop of Baltimore, and by a valise of Papal documents pertinent to the journey. To accomodate the Delegate's mission, Belmont Township in Gaston County, North Carolina, had been added to the train's itinerary, and Southern Railway President W.W. Finley had personally made the bishops' travel arrangements.[1]

The train left Washington at forty-five minutes past ten o'clock that evening, stopped in Richmond where Father Edward Meyer, O.S.B., was added to the official party, then proceeded through the night toward the Carolinas. The clergymen reached the Belmont station as scheduled at twenty minutes past ten o'clock on Monday morning, and immediately entered a waiting automobile festooned in the Papal colors and those of Saint Mary's College.[2]

The prelates traveled north then, toward their destination. They detoured briefly to pass through the grounds of the Sisters of Mercy in Belmont, then continued on toward the Benedictine monastery of Maryhelp and the campus of Saint Mary's College. The Pope had sent his representative to the Carolina abbey to promulgate the *Bulla* issued on 8 June, erecting for the first time on the North American continent a Cathedral Abbey, territorially independent of all existing

3

diocesan boundaries. It was the highest rank a monastery could be granted.[3]

As the Delegate's car touched the abbey grounds, the monastery's bells began to peal and the college band started playing.[4] There was a grand arch welcoming the officials.[5] They passed beneath that, past the musicians in the pine grove, between the dutifully assembled rows of cheering students, and finally stopped at the abbey's porte cochere.[6] It was there that their host first stepped forward. He was an erect man in a monk's habit and episcopal zuchetto; his pectoral cross was gold, and studded with jewels, but his appearance was dominated by a fine-textured white beard which extended in length to mid-chest. This was Leo Haid, first abbot of Maryhelp, Titular Bishop of Messene, Vicar Apostolic of North Carolina, and now Abbot *Nullius* of Belmont. The abbot greeted the Pope's ambassador, and the Delegate in his turn acknowledged Haid with an inclination of the head, the extension of his hand, and the greeting, "My Lord of Belmont." The assembled monks and students responded with applause.

Haid had expended a quarter-century of effort to secure the future of his monastery. Lost as it was in a rural county of America's most Protestant state, Maryhelp had shown little promise. But this official visit and the *Bulla* to be read the following day legitimized his efforts. And Haid could not but have been aware that the unlikely choice of his monastery for these ecclesial distinctions was primarily a reflection of his own work and leadership.[7] He had guided the success of his abbey, created the area's first Catholic seminary, guided the college at Belmont, and fathered new monasteries in Florida, Savannah, Richmond, and northern Virginia. The abbot had also been named the bishop[8] for all of Catholic North Carolina and president of his branch of the Order of Saint Benedict.[9] Unquestionably, Haid's efforts had borne fruit. And the Lord of Belmont would be content, in those mid-October days of honors and festivities, to salute his abbey's elevation without any mention of the charges he knew were being brought against his administration by disaffected clergy in Carolina and the increasingly suspicious hierarchy of the Church in the United States.

At age sixty-one, the Abbot-Bishop of Belmont was still a man of distinguished presence and undaunted vigor. And the unanticipated resentment toward the *Nullius* was not to overshadow this resplendent moment of achievement. Apostolic Delegates were a rare sight in the Protestant South, and the presence of the regal Falconio at the promulgation of Belmont's greatest honor constituted a high personal tribute to Haid's stature. The moment was an impenetrable instant of satisfaction. The priests, the monks, the students and laity, none of them could impose on this scene the hostility that surrounded it. Here, in the company of the Pope's personal representative, Leo Haid stood in witness to the success of his painful transition from second-choice abbot, filled with insecurities, to abbot-bishop and Ordinary of two ecclesiastical Sees. Experience during twenty-five years in North Carolina had not taught him gently, but he had dealt with every commission Rome and Providence had imposed on him, and these latest tempests were to enjoy no more indulgence than had their predecessors. The *nullius* ceremonies progressed in every detail according to the abbot's wishes.

The man who governed the first abbey in the American South was not a Southerner by birth, having moved to Carolina only out of duty. Leo Haid was born in Unity Township, near Beatty, in western Pennsylvania, on 15 July 1849.[10] His parents were German-speaking immigrants. John, his father, was a native of Remischen, Luxemburg-Hollandin.[11] Trained as a cooper, John gave himself first to his craft, and only later took a bride, Mary Stetter, a Prussian girl, more than a decade his junior.[12] They had two children, Margaret and John, before leaving for America in 1847.[13]

In the New World, they lived briefly in Armstrong County, Pennsylvania,[14] but finally settled in Westmoreland County before the birth of their next child, Joseph, in 1848.[15] John Hite went to work immediately, to support his growing family. He drew a salary as a cooper, then augmented that income with work as a nurseryman.

The German settlement was substantial in Westmoreland County. It was heavily Catholic, too, with its priests being supplied by the local Benedictine monastery of Saint Vincent. The monks gave themselves generously in ministering to the immigrants' needs, bonded to these people by shared experience; for the Benedictines themselves were recent arrivals from Bavaria, having passed through customs in New York on 15 September 1846. But the monks had quickly established themselves in western Pennsylvania through agriculture, schools, and parishes. Indeed the church for Saint Vincent was firstly a parish church, so the future abbot of Maryhelp was baptized there, in the monastery-parish, by Father Celestine Englbrecht, O.S.B., on 17 August 1849. The boy was christened "Michael Hite".[16]

The early life of Michael is largely unrecorded. Part of the obscurity springs from the family name. At the time of Michael's birth, the family still consistently used "Hite". But as the children matured, variations appeared, apparently in an effort to appease American pronunciation. In the confusion, family records were lost and obscured. The children of John and Mary Hite became variously "Haid", "Hidt", and "Heid", as well as "Hite", and only through the diligence of Joseph's grandson Arthur, a proficient genealogist, was the Hite family in its several branches finally reconstructed a century later.[17]

Michael's birth was followed by that of Francis (1851), John Paul (1853), Augusto (1855), Mary Philomena (1857), Anna Barbara (1859), and William Ignatius (1861). Surprisingly, it was not Mrs. Hite, but her husband who died young. John's death, reportedly in a railroad accident,[18] occurred just before William Ignatius' birth. Despite his two employments, John Hite had little to leave his widow except a house filled with dependent children. But Mary remarried rather quickly, this time to Anthony Wilbert, a man about eighteen years her senior. Then in 1863, Mary Stetter Hite Wilbert bore one last child, Anthony Wilbert, Junior.[19]

After their marriage, the Wilberts relocated in Pittsburgh, where Mary worked as a domestic,[20] but it appears that young Michael was never part of his stepfather's household. For in 1861, already determined to set about his life's work, Michael Hite was enrolled in the scholasticate at Saint Vincent Abbey. He was twelve years old.[21]

In the scholasticate, an educational program for young priesthood candidates, Michael Hite studied classics primarily, but also took some commercial courses. The boys were taught discipline and ascetics, too; they lived on the monastery's grounds and worked on the abbey farm, but most of all they imbibed the flavor and content of the religious ethos that surrounded them. At so young an age, the boys were not expected to declare their preference for either the diocesan priesthood or the monastic, but Michael—baptized at the abbey, and educated there as well—seems to have set his mind from the beginning on the life of a monk-priest. In 1863 he declared his intentions, and on 12 September 1868, he received the habit of a Benedictine novice.[22]

By age nineteen, Michael Hite showed most of the features that would distinguish his appearance throughout his life. Only the beard was missing.[23] He had matured with large, strikingly limped, brown eyes that distracted attention from his aquiline nose.[24] The boy was still painfully thin in those days, and his angular frame made him seem taller than he really was. But his wide hands and long fingers already moved with a fluidity and grace that softened his appearance. His voice was more powerful than rich, but a flair for dramatics and interpretive speech transformed it into an effective instrument. His hair was unruly and looked unkempt.[25]

In the monastery, Michael received Pope Saint Leo the Great as his patron saint, and was henceforth termed "Leo".[26] Until ordination, his title was "frater". As a novice monk, Frater Leo was instructed in the Benedictine *Regula*, the observance of Saint Vincent Abbey, monastic history, Gregorian chant, liturgy, Latin, psalmody, and related subjects. He followed a strict monastic horarium and was carefully supervised, instructed and corrected by the Magister. Hite found himself serving as a field laborer, a table waiter. He assisted the sick and infirm. The novitiate was supposed to teach the tools of the art of monasticism by instilling a great and unquenchable thirst for God. The desire for God was approached then, though the traditional Benedictine media of prayer, work, and virtue, of humility and love, poverty and faith. Though he had lived in the shadow of Saint Vincent all his life, dwelled beside the monks for seven years, it was not until Michael Hite became Frater Novice Leo in 1868, donning the monastic habit and committing himself to the cenobitical regimen at Saint Vincent, that he formally entered the fourteen hundred year old Benedictine tradition.

Pennsylvania Benedictines

The Abbey of Saint Vincent was not just ruled by Boniface Wimmer, its abbot, it was inspired by him. His character was stamped on every aspect of Benedictine life there. For Abbot Boniface had not just brought the traditions of Benedict's monks to a new country; he had also labeled them with a spirit as adventurous as was his own.

Originally a secular priest of Regensburg, Wimmer had won admission to the first novitiate class at Saint Michael Abbey, Metten, Bavaria, after the monastery was restored in 1830 by Ludwig I. Father Boniface was the second of five novices, each of whom came from the diocesan clergy, to pronounce his vows. Wimmer possessed unbounded energy, resilience and vision. And though his stubbornness and self-will would receive more attention than any sanctity he may have shown, his legacy as a monastic builder is indisputable.

When Boniface Wimmer set out to establish the Benedictine Order in the United States, he decided to use priestly ministry to the immigrant Germans as his primary medium of contact. His plan also called for the establishment of schools as a lasting apostolate for his monasteries. Stability would be lent to the Benedictine presence, he resolved, through strong abbeys that owned land, staffed their schools, lived the Benedictine life, and insured a degree of self-sufficiency through the existence of both ordained and non-ordained monks, both in quantity, at each foundation. His success was extraordinary. And even though time and monastic theology would not always treat his ambitions kindly, that he secured his ends stands unimpugned.[27]

Nevertheless, throughout his abbatial career, Boniface Wimmer had to fight for his standards of monastic life. His followers regularly chastised him for the apparent primacy given to apostolic endeavors over more cloistered responsibilities. The abbot was also charged with stealing the best professors from the schools and sending them into his fledgling foundations. His houses were suspected—though generally exonerated—of being lax. Although the list of accusations is substantial, the criticisms do not always note that Wimmer was clearly in the tradition of Benedictine missionaries: the first century was filled with activity and growth; he insisted on such features as an emphasis on culture and the arts in his schools;[28] through his seminary he sought to promote and establish a native clergy.[29] Nevertheless, he was in the German, not the English, tradition of missionary Benedictines: his monks went out to the people.

The monastic vision of Boniface Wimmer required a high level of activity. And depending as it did on missionary contact, the monks were called upon to be away from the motherhouse for long periods of time, often years. This was a problem for monks, even missionary monks, and Abbot Boniface magnified it by proving a tremendous success. His followers spread throughout the country, establishing some of the largest monasteries of modern times. Many of these had schools, too. Thus, in addition to the regular pastoral travels of missionaries, monks also had to be sent for studies, as preparation for the classroom. The better one was at his work, the more likely it was that he would soon be transferred to new foundations that needed zealous missionaries for their large territories, or experienced teachers to establish the most recent Benedictine school or college.

The growth and breadth of Wimmer's dream were so staggering that Pius IX erected the American children of Wimmer as a separate congregation within the Order of Saint Benedict at the early date of 24 August 1855. Having its own federation was a tremendous advantage for Wimmer's concept of monasticism, because it permitted the new American monasteries to be confirmed in their particular, Wimmer-inspired character and identity, with minimal influence from European monastics. This aided in establishing in North America the otherwise disjointed Order.

Of course the Benedictines were already free of much of the internal hierarchy that characterized some religious Orders. Monasteries in the Order of Saint Benedict were each constituted as independent polities. There was no international superior for the Benedictines. Indeed, when the office of "Abbot Primate" was created, it was not endowed with powers, as much as with precedence. The primate did not *rule*; at best he *coordinated* the "Confederation" of Benedictine monasteries. Within the Confederation, the Holy See could erect any number of congregations. These groupings consisted of independent monasteries linked by factors such as origin, location, or other common elements. Each congregation had a *praeses*, or president, who coordinated dealings with Rome. The monasteries of a congregation conducted visitations—scrutinies of the observance in a particular abbey—but there was no central authority within the Order that dictated norms or requirements.

With the erection of his new American congregation, under the patronage of the Holy Guardian Angels, Wimmer won some valuable concessions including his personal appointment to a life term as *praeses*; he was also to acquire for his monasteries the privileges of the Cassinese Congregation of Benedictines. By replacing his Bavarian statutes with those of the monasteries gathered around Montecassino, the Order's primary See, he secured the American Cassinese Congregation, as the new division was known, as a more viable and coordinated ecclesial entity. And with himself as the congregation's head, he was assured of maximum influence in realizing his dreams.

Accordingly, the American Cassinese Congregation, under Abbot Boniface, was established from the beginning as a broadly based enterprise of diversified interests—as multifarious as the vision of Wimmer himself. Thus the monks were not just priests and schoolmasters; the abbot also emphasized, for example, the arts. So he sent monks to study painting in Bavaria; he sought musicians for his cloister; and men proficient in these areas were spread among Wimmer's monasteries to foster artistic values and performances.

Perhaps worst of all, in terms of stability, were not the artists, however, but the craftsmen. These men, mostly non-ordained monks, the Brothers, were usually spared duties in the parishes, and only on occasion were they assigned to the schools. But with their skills for cooking, farming, masonry, construction, tailoring, and countless other tasks, they were always in demand, and thus they were forever being transferred from one of Wimmer's young monasteries to another.

The monasticism of Boniface Wimmer was breathless. It spread at a fantastic rate. Vocations came from Europe and America; young men entered the novitiate in Pennsylvania, then spread the values of

Benedict—and Abbot Wimmer—throughout these broad, American fields of labor.

Wimmer himself was a hearty Bavarian, thick and sturdy looking, with deep lines in his brow and a full white beard that stopped abruptly at breast level with a perfectly trimmed horizontal line. Wimmer was bombastic and forceful. He wore the mitre as a symbol of authority, of course, but also as a reminder of power. And he would vent that power according to demand and necessity. He was hated or loved, idolized or despised. There was no median level with Boniface Wimmer. He would fight with bishops; he would fight with monks. But he usually won, and just in case a poor loser tried to appeal to Rome, the abbot cultivated a firm cadre of supportive prelates in or near the Curia to fight for his positions. He was known as the "farmer abbot," but he was recognized primarily as prelate and *praeses,* and anyone who challenged him knew that effort would require a mighty struggle.

Although the abbot of Saint Vincent was not known for his gentleness, his deeply pastoral concern was above question. Despite the flair for bombast, his apostolic character was never obscured. Abbot Boniface was genuinely devoted to his work; some thought him a tyrant and an egomaniac; he was unquestionably self-willed and liberal in his treatment of traditional Benedictinism. At the same time, however, he so obviously enjoyed what he did that he inspired great love, affection and admiration. In the forty-one years of his service in America, of the hundreds of men who were drawn to enter the monastic life, apparently as many were drawn by the excitement and oversized presence of Abbot Boniface Wimmer, O.S.B., as by the more traditional longings of the soul for the monastic values and commitment. And even those who disliked the Pennsylvania abbot gave him credit for his wholehearted pursuit of the principles of his monastic insight.[30]

WImmeR's monk

Because the Hites lived in the shadow of Wimmer's abbey, Michael from his earliest days was aware of Abbot Boniface and his monks. The Benedictines' church was always the Hites' parish, and Johnny, Joseph, and Michael, as children, assisted at the liturgies and solemnities there. As a student, the vision of Wimmer sharpened for young Michael, and the enthusiasm of those fervent missionary days in Saint Vincent's history infected his zealous and idealistic spirit. He fell in love with the larger-than-life presence of Boniface Wimmer and his dreams. Then, as a scholastic, Michael lived on the monastery grounds and was drawn even more under the influence and attraction monasticism—and Wimmer himself—held.

But in 1868, when Hite entered the monastic life, the dreams and ideals could easily have been shattered, for the perspective was radically altered, *de facto*. Life in the monastery seldom lent the clarity an outsider's view accommodated. And Frater Leo would have known, from *within* the cloister, the full complement of issues that existed in nineteenth century monasticism. This realization of the complexity of cloistered life often hit young monks with a frightening ferocity. It could threaten weaker novices; it tended to enth.all and intoxicate the mediocre candidates. But for some—usually the more mature young men—the impact could constitute a challenge in the most positive sense. Nevertheless, regardless of the type of effect, all novices found that they had to discover means of coping with the internal issues of the monastery. And the manner of this coping colored the future of the novice in a way he could neither escape nor evade.

At Saint Vincent in the 1860's, the issues that could not but influence novitiate idealism centered primarily on this active character with which Wimmer had imbued American monasticism. His emphasis on active, essentially priestly, endeavors seemed in the eyes of many to undercut the monastic character of the house. The balance between *ora* and *labora* was always delicate, and a problem that was only compounded by extraclaustral assignments. Thus Wimmer's expansionism provoked a continuous debate in Pennsylvania regarding Benedictine integrity. And since novices grappled with integrity as one of their special problems,[31] Hite would have been particularly susceptible to the undercurrents of his new vocation.

And yet with the budding adaptability and strength of will that would function throughout his life, Frater Leo seems to have dealt efficiently with this challenge: Hite simply gave himself totally to the guidance of Wimmer. To the extent that there were factions within Saint Vincent,[32] Frater Leo was definitely aligned from the beginning with the abbot. And even with maturation in the monastic life, there came no compromise of his affinity for the charismatic archabbot of Pennsylvania.

This immersion in personal loyalty to the founder of American monasticism gave Hite a strong identity with Wimmer's missionary spirit.[33] It also influenced the values Leo, as an abbot himself, would communicate to his own monasteries. The positive relationship with Wimmer, furthermore, solidified in Hite the qualities of professional optimism, idealism, and enthusiasm which underscored his future monastic and apostolic activity. The impact Wimmer had on Hite, and the fierce loyalty the younger monk maintained toward his monastic father, were all the more amazing because the two men were never especially close. Wimmer, well known as he was for naming his opponents to positions of leadership, entrusted no office expressive of particular confidence to Father Leo; neither did the abbot give any evidence of favor or recognition of promise. Hite was not Wimmer's first choice for the Carolina abbacy; indeed, on the first ballot Leo Hite's name did not appear as anyone's nominee for the office.

The early years of Hite's monastic life passed in the ordinary sequence and with little distinction. On 17 September 1869, Frater Leo pronounced his monastic vows of stability, *conversatio*, and obedience. It was at this point that he made the change in his cognomen: occasional variations notwithstanding, he became "Leo Haid".[34]

The period following the monk's first profession of vows was known as the "clericate". During this time the newly professed monk concentrated on his studies for priesthood. Since Saint Vincent had its own seminary, Haid remained at the Westmoreland abbey. His mother and stepfather occasionally visited him there, but it would have been extraordinary for the cleric to visit them in Pittsburgh even though he was enrolled in some commercial courses in the city.[35]

A young monk's clericate lasted for a minimum period of three years, after which an application might be made for solemn vows. This second profession constituted a permanent commitment, and was permitted only after careful scrutiny by the monastic Chapter and after the approbation of the abbot had been granted. Despite solemn vows the monk would remain in the clericate, however, pending ordination to priesthood. Whereas in these early days at Saint Vincent the brothers lived the established monastic routine from the time of their vows, the cleric-monks did not enter into what would be their ordinary regimen until after the reception of Major Orders. Regular assignments, be they educational, parochial or otherwise, seldom preceded priestly ordination.

Frater Leo Haid professed his solemn monastic vows in Saint Vincent Church on 5 October 1872. Soon afterwards, he was ordained to Minor Orders. And on 21 December of that same year, at the hands of Bishop Michael Domenec, C.M., he was ordained to the priesthood,[36] and took his place among the fathers in the monastic *statio*—the ordering of the monks according to their response to the "call" of God.

Haid had already entered upon some of the duties that ordinarily followed on priesthood, however. For at the beginning of the Michaelmas term at Saint Vincent College that year, Haid had commenced his service in the classroom and undertaken the chaplaincy of the college. Like all of the monk-professors, Father Leo taught whatever subjects were assigned him—his training, after all, was generally undistinguished from that of most of the other fathers. Thus, in his first year Haid found himself listed as a professor of English grammar, commercial law, bookkeeping, spelling, and reading.

His success in the classroom and his popularity among the boys studying at Saint Vincent was immediate, and his duties in the schools went uninterrupted for the next thirteen years. Indeed, Haid was never assigned to a parish or daughterhouse. He may have performed some interim service as a priestly assistant, but he was primarily a school monk.

In 1873 he found composition and elocution appended to his teaching load, and he undertook service with the dramatics society at Saint Vincent. In 1875, history was added to his classroom duties. Subsequently, through the years, he found himself instructing in penmanship, political economy, civil government, English post-graduate studies, and the various commercial courses offered at the time.[37] He also wrote plays. His *Major John Andre* was published and widely circulated,[38] and his *Saint Hermenegild of Spain* was only slightly less popular among the pious tastes of the Catholic schools of the period.

During these years, Father Leo matured into an edifying, if inconspicuous, young religious. He had the solid health to maintain the hectic pace his duties required of him, and Abbot Boniface, characteristically, rewarded extraordinary service with an ever increasing quantity of responsibilities. Haid's incredible capacity for work and his growing popularity secured his position as a school-monk. Moreover, Father Leo was wholly and unquestionably dedicated to Wimmer and his ideal, to Saint Vincent and to her schools. But none of these factors won advancement for Haid. It was charism that the young priest exhibited, not leadership; and Wimmer neither promoted Father Leo nor tested him in the Benedictine missions. Haid, for his part, did not volunteer for any of the three abbeys that achieved independence during his time as a monk of Saint Vincent, and he gave every evidence of being contented in the work of the schools, where he could remain near his mentor, Abbot Boniface.[39]

The abbot was apparently satisfied with this arrangement, too. Given the turmoil which so frequently surrounded him, loyal sons among his more gifted monks never seemed particularly bountiful in Wimmer's monastery. But circumstances conspired against Haid's life in the schools at Saint Vincent, and the simple peace with which he finished the spring term in 1885 was never to be restored to him.

The Monasteries Of 1884

Boniface Wimmer enjoyed a prolific paternity. After thirty years in America, he was responsible for the existence of three hundred fifty Benedictine monks at twelve monasteries (three of which were abbeys), seventy parochial churches and five schools.[40] In 1881, Wimmer began to envision a new abbey, however, and by 1883, when he was the proud possessor of the honorific title of "archabbot", and the privilege of wearing the *cappa magna,* his vision swelled toward the creation of two new abbeys at once. As usual, the course of this effort was circuitous.

The first of these abbeys was to be fashioned from the priory and parish in Newark, New Jersey. Though its location was too urban to suit Wimmer, he did believe the monastery had promise. To contribute to the potential of the new abbey in Newark, he intended to attach the foundations in Elizabeth, New Jersey, and Wilmington, Delaware, as dependencies.[41]

At the General Chapter of the American Cassinese Congregation, held at Saint Vincent in the summer of 1881, Wimmer had introduced a resolution calling for a petition to Rome, asking that Saint Mary, in Newark, be elevated to the rank of an abbey. Wimmer's resolution was worded craftily, so that while approving Newark's independence, the capitulars would endorse in the same effort the concept of even more abbeys. It read

> The rather large number of dependent priories of Saint Vincent renders it difficult to govern them well. Therefore it seems best to establish several independent houses. To begin at least with one: Saint Mary's, in Newark, New Jersey; it should be raised to such a rank, because the Right Reverend Bishops of the See have already earnestly expressed the wish of having such a community.[42]

As so often happened, however, Wimmer had misread the tenor of his monks. It was not a good year for expansionism. The Cassinese congregation was on the verge in 1881 of one of its greatest disputes over the active character of American monasticism, and Wimmer found his resolution defeated.

Undaunted, however, Abbot Boniface began considering that not only New Jersey should be an abbey, but perhaps as many as four others, as well, one each in the West (Chicago, Wetaug), Southeast (Baltimore, Richmond, North Carolina), South (Alabama), and Pennsylvania (Saint Mary's, Erie).[43]

While Wimmer's ambitions were unrealistic in the face of the conditions of the scattered missions he sought to liberate from the motherhouse, he had correctly—if belatedly—recognized the excessive commitments for which Saint Vincent was accountable. And this, rather than expansionism, was an argument that would appeal to the capitulars: already in his seventies, and tired by fifty years in religion, Abbot Boniface was no longer able, it seemed, to supervise a national network of dependent monasteries; his vigor was declining. Unfortunately, while this argument constituted grounds for relieving the abbot of some of his dependencies, it did not really justify canonical independence for these scattered, unstable foundations.[44]

In 1882, opposition to monastic expansionism was too strong for Wimmer to make a fresh push for abbeys. But in the spring of 1883, the wily patriarch began sampling opinions and pushing his new strategy, only to find himself distracted by poor health and the elaborate preparations, celebrations, and honors that marked his golden jubilee of monastic profession.[45]

The ambitions for 1883, which envisioned (by this time) two new abbeys, did not die, however, amid these diversions. Newark, with its two dependencies, remained at the head of Wimmer's list. The second proposed foundation was now to be a union of three southern missions: Virginia, North Carolina, and Georgia. Wimmer decided that the monastery in Garibaldi, North Carolina would hold the abbatial rank. It was not necessarily the most promising or even the most important of the three sites; rather, it was the most centrally located, lying approximately three hundred miles from each of the other foundations, according to Wimmer's estimate.[46]

North Carolina, Wimmer theorized, could not support itself. The whole state had about two thousand Catholics, not one of whom, he thought, lived near the monastery.[47] The foundation had only one brick building and two of wood, with facilities for six priests, eight brothers, and sixty students.[48] In the fall of 1883, however, the school had only fifteen students, and even lowering the fee for board and tuition from one hundred eighty to one hundred fifty dollars gave little help to the sagging enrollment.[49] Wimmer was certain, nonetheless, that the monastery of Maryhelp was the "foothold for the Catholic Church in the whole state."[50]

Savannah, however, was a very promising foundation. It had seven hundred acres—two hundred more than North Carolina—that were fertile fields for rice and cotton. In addition to the farm there was parochial work and a small institute for young black males.[51] Both Savannah and Richmond could boast of having a contingent of interested, supportive, local Catholics. And Richmond, though it lacked a farm, had a strong, successful, debt-free parish[52] that could contribute one thousand dollars a year to Garibaldi.[53]

To promote his new abbeys, Wimmer first consulted his two fellow Cassinese abbots. Alexius Edelbrock, of Saint John in Minnesota, proved favorable to the Wimmer plan.[54] And Innocent Wolf, of the abbey in Kansas, evaded the question, but did not explicitly object.[55]

On 8 June 1883, Wimmer addressed Henry Northrop, Catholic bishop of Charleston, South Carolina, who was also acting as Vicar Apostolic of North Carolina, requesting endorsement of the proposed Southern abbey. The Pennsylvania monastery promised continued support for Maryhelp, despite its changed status, and Wimmer deftly tied the whole future of monastic life in Carolina to the issue of independence.

> After mature deliberation I came to the conclusion, that for the success of Maryhelp it is necessary to raise that house to the rank of a small abbey. As conditions are now, the Prior, the Fathers and the Brothers do not consider themselves permanently attached to the monastery. They are therefore, not taking the same interest in its prosperity, as they would, if they regarded [it] as their home. In a community under an abbot things will be different, especially in College matters.[56]

Northrop responded promptly and enthusiastically.

> I certainly and with a very glad heart say: God speed the work. I give my approval and blessing and assure you I will do whatever I can to my best judgment to further your plans and help you and the Order to which religion and the Vicariate owe already a great deal.[57]

Finally, his health restored, festivities ended, and with the endorsements of his Chapter, the episcopal Ordinaries, and the Cassinese abbots in hand, Wimmer petitioned Rome on 18 June 1884 for the erection of the monasteries in Newark, New Jersey and Garibaldi, North Carolina, as abbeys. Subsequently, in July, three additional letters were sent to Rome, just as the Holy See began to ponder Wimmer's latest ambitions for the Benedictine Order in America.

The July letters went to prelates who could promote Wimmer's cause in the Curia. One message went to the sixty-six year old

Joannes Cardinal Simeoni, Prefect of De Propaganda Fide.[58] The United States, being a mission territory, fell under the Propaganda's interest. A second missive enlisted the aid of Cardinal Bartolini, protector of the Order of Saint Benedict. Wimmer also addressed his Roman procurator, Abbot Pucci-Sisti,[59] to fight any idea that the time was not "ripe" for a North Carolina abbey.[60]

Submitting the two petitions together was a risky move, since it could seem imprudent and ambitious. And given the way Rome labored over such requests, it would have been unreasonable to assume Carolina could sneak through as a companion for the more promising house in New Jersey. But Wimmer's experience in Church intricacies was masterfully displayed in his petition regarding Carolina. Giving a marvelous illusion of candor, the abbot freely admitted to Simeoni that the request for Garibaldi's abbey was "premature," but how much greater, he pondered, might be the danger of delay?[61] *Petitio principii* is fallacious, of course, but not always a failure. And Wimmer was confident that his petition was "very strongly explained."[62] It might have been more accurate to say it was "cleverly" explained, but it was successful nonetheless. In late September the archabbot received unofficial notification by cable that his petitions had been approved.

Pucci-Sisti wrote soon afterwards, however, to advise Wimmer that the formal documents were not to be written immediately, and the period of delay could not be estimated.[63] October passed, November, Christmas, a new year began, and still the Roman documents did not appear. Without them, no abbots could be elected, no new communities formed. Wimmer was impatient, but impeded from action.[64]

Then, on 14 January 1885, the archabbot's seventy-sixth birthday, he received the two bulls of erection.[65] Garibaldi's was dated 19 December 1884.[66]

Northrop responded to the news with his customary warmth and optimism:

> I hope indeed that in spite of the poverty and poor prospects, the Abbey of Saint Mary's will flourish to the great good of religion in North Carolina and to the prosperity of the Order. I am most anxious to see it succeed...[67]

Wimmer was elated. He had two simultaneously created abbeys. Two communities needed to be formed then—each with at least ten monks—and each house was to have a duly elected abbot as its head. Wasting no time, Archabbot Boniface wrote the one hundred fifteen capitulars of Saint Vincent on 20 January 1885:

> Because by the Apostolic Briefs of December 19, 1884, two abbeys were erected, one at Saint Mary's, Newark, New Jersey; the other in North Carolina; Pastors and Abbots have to be provided by a canonical election. Therefore, since you are, as far as We know, free from any impediment of censure, We, Boniface Wimmer, Archabbot of Saint Vincent and President of the American Cassinese Congregation, invite, call and summon you herewith to the election which is to be held in accordance with the Sacred Canons and the Statutes of our Congregation in the monastery of Saint Vincent, February 11, 1885, at eight o'clock forenoon. We request that you be here in good time on the preceeding day, or if legitimately excused, to appoint a procurator. We admonish you and demand that you inform Us within ten days of the receipt of this summons.[68]

The monks of Saint Vincent journeyed to their motherhouse in February of 1885 from their assignments through the eastern two-thirds of the country. Of the one hundred fifteen capitulars, sixty-four were there in person; the rest were represented by proxies, except for eight who had failed to properly designate a procurator. In the election Chapter, after a resolution was passed allowing all the capitulars—regardless of future affiliation—to vote in each election, one monk stormed out. There were, finally, one hundred six possible votes to be cast for the abbots of Saint Mary in Newark and Maryhelp in Garibaldi.[69]

The election process began on 11 February with Mass, celebrated by Saint Vincent's prior, Michael Hofmayer. There followed prayers to the Holy Ghost, entreating presence, guidance, and protection in the deliberations that were to follow. Each capitular then took an oath testifying that he would follow the Spirit's guidance and endorse the worthiest candidate, abandoning personal wants or prejudices in favor of the guidance of Providence. James Zilliox, Hilary Pfraengle, and Andrew Hintenach[70] were then selected as tellars for the abbatial election.[71]

Saint Mary in New Jersey, as the senior monastery, was the first to have an abbot provided. On the first ballot thirteen men received votes, the thirty-five year old Zilliox earning a plurality of forty-seven votes. On the second ballot, Zilliox exceeded the minimum for election, garnering sixty-two votes. He accepted the office, received the applause of his confreres, and the Chapter adjourned for the *opus dei* and luncheon.[72]

The monks reconvened the Chapter at two o'clock, and proceeded to the election of an abbot for Maryhelp. With one vote to spare, there was an absolute majority, and thus an election, on the first ballot. Father Oswald Moosmueller was elected first abbot of Maryhelp.[73]

Since Father Oswald was not present, no acceptance address followed. Moosmueller was at his mission assignment in Savannah,

Father Paul Wenkmann serving as his proxy at Saint Vincent. Accordingly, Wimmer dismissed the monks, and at four o'clock, sent a telegram to Bishop William Gross, C.SS.R, in Savannah, asking that news of the proceedings be communicated to the abbot-elect. The capitulars, confident in the promise of the two monks they had elected abbots, wasted no time in leaving the motherhouse, and returning to their missions and assignments.[74]

The archabbot was extremely pleased. Zilliox, a native of Newark, was a deeply spiritual man who, despite a less than hearty constitution, had filled various responsible posts in the Wimmer administration. Abbot-elect James had also been a leader of the opposition to Wimmer's activity-oriented policies. The young man would now have a chance to test his own theories of monastic life.

Oswald William Moosmueller, a Bavarian native, had an even more impressive history than Zilliox. He was a proven administrator with a distinguished history of successes in Kentucky, Kansas, Canada, New Jersey, Georgia and Rome. He had been Wimmer's choice for the abbacy in Kansas in 1876, but had demurred and actually conspired against his election.[75] Father Oswald, like Zilliox, held that monastic life required a more cloistered and contemplative flavor than Wimmer seemed to provide.[76]

For the remainder of the afternoon, Archabbot Boniface enjoyed the pleasure of his accomplishments. Both of his new abbeys had secured respected, capable, vigorous abbots. In both cases the capitulars had chosen more contemplative souls than Wimmer, presumably selecting that character as their abbeys' future.[77] Nevertheless, the saintly Zilliox and the scholarly Moosmueller represented sound futures for the communities they would head.

At half past seven that evening, [78] as the archabbot was on his way to Compline,[79] he was met by the abbey's telegrapher who handed the patriarch a folded piece of paper. Wimmer read it, "became very angry,"[80] grew sick with "terrible catarrh with a sore neck and coughing," and found he was unable to continue on his way to choir.[81] Knowing the contents of the message he had received and delivered, the telegrapher presumably beat a hasty retreat.

The telegram was from Oswald Moosmueller. It read, "I thank you for the honor, but I cannot accept. Letter will follow."[82]

Later, when Wimmer had recovered somewhat, he wired vigorous disapproval of Father Oswald's decision to refuse election. But Moosmueller was adamant, and continued to decline the office "against every encouragement."[83] For more than a month the two Bavarians argued, but in the end the younger man's refusal of the abbacy proved insurmountable.

Moosmueller had created problems for Saint Mary as well as for Maryhelp, since Wimmer was reluctant to petition for confirmation of Zilliox's election without also submitting a candidate for Carolina. It was possible that in the wake of the unsuccessful election, Maryhelp's independence might be suppressed, or the monastery might lose the right of election in the midst of the scandal.[84] Furthermore, summoning the one hundred fifteen capitulars back for another election was rendered impossible by both the finances and the responsibilities of the missionaries.[85] Wimmer was further stymied by the fact that canonically, Moosmueller had up to two months in which to make his decision, forcing Abbot Boniface to discern whether to wait the full term (hoping Father Oswald would submit to the election) or risk proceeding with the confirmation of Zilliox alone.[86] Wimmer also had to face the reality that the Holy See itself might choose to solve the election dilema.[87] Of Moosmueller's recalcitrance Wimmer concluded, "Such a trick is rather much like him."[88]

Despite the ire he had provoked, Father Oswald, isolated safely in southernmost Georgia, made every effort to appear imperturbed. He could not, after all, be required to accept, so Wimmer's weapons were severely limited. The tone assumed by Moosmueller was typified in a letter he addressed to Father Julius Pohl at Maryhelp. Pohl, who had planned to become a member of the newly independent house at Garibaldi, had written the abbot-elect a message of felicitations immediately after the election. Father Oswald's brief though pointed response specified that he had "telegraphed immediately" to Wimmer on Wednesday, 11 February. He added quite innocently then, "I am rather surprised that you should not be aware of this fact."[89]

Eventually the archabbot despaired of securing Father Oswald for the abbatial throne, and turned his attention to the confirmation of Zilliox by Rome. The request for ratification was dated 14 March 1885, more than a month after the election.

A second petition accompanied the Zilliox document. This was a carefully prepared request—that Wimmer said "took all my thoughts, my fingers, and pen"[90]—for a second election on behalf of Maryhelp. For the new conclave, Archabbot Boniface proposed that a cadre of ten monks committed to transferring stability to Carolina serve as the sole electors. This would save the expense of again summoning all the capitulars to Pennsylvania, and would provide a more appropriate constituency for the decision at issue. As he had done regarding the erection of Maryhelp the previous year, he also enlisted the aid of various prelates on behalf of this latest petition.

There was no expectation that Rome would authorize the second election promptly; nevertheless, Wimmer immediately began preparations for the election. He wanted to be ready to execute the Apostolic Brief, without hindrance, when the time did come. And this meant that two matters should be arranged: ten monks should be persuaded to commit themselves to Maryhelp; and a suitable candidate for abbot should be found and quietly (since campaigning and politicking were forbidden) promoted among the ten capitulars. Neither of these tasks promised to be easy.

Maryhelp had little to recommend it, and virtually everyone who had served there—both priests and brothers—had asked to be transferred elsewhere. Only one monk in Carolina was determined to stay, Julius Pohl. Also one monk each from the parishes in Richmond and Savannah had volunteered, Willibald Baumgartner and Melchior Reichert, respectively. The archabbot believed Father Placidus Pilz, who had been prior in Garibaldi, and Father Oswald could be persuaded to stay in the South, as well. But by 18 April, Pilz and Moosmueller had both declined to join Maryhelp, and Wimmer turned elsewhere.[91]

By appealing to the idealism of his monks—especially the young ones—a cleric, two priests, and one theology student were won for Carolina.[92] But the numbers were not stable. In a letter to Abbot Bernard Smith there were four monks who were already in the South and six from the motherhouse who had declared for Maryhelp;[93] while in a later note addressed to that same abbot the total had fallen to eight, three of whom were already working in the South.[94]

When permission for the second election was received at Saint Vincent on 10 June, Wimmer had already outlined his course of action. Four of the men who had agreed to go to Maryhelp were fraters. But as non-ordained monks, they could cast no ballot in the election Chapter. The vote had no immediate deadline since Propaganda had thoughtfully included the provision, *"Tempore quo opportunius videbitur."* But in order to have an abbot and community before the new school term,[95] and before anyone suffered a change of mind, Wimmer needed to act quickly. That required having the four clerics (Felix Hintemeyer, George Lester, Patrick Donlon, Walter Leahy) ordained subdeacons so they could enjoy the franchise.

But the road for Maryhelp, it seemed, was never to be smooth. A bishop who might perform the ordination was not easily found in Pennsylvania during the summer of 1885. Wimmer's own Ordinary was ill, and declined to officiate. The new coadjutor of the diocese had not yet been consecrated; so he could not ordain the monks. The next closest bishop, the Ordinary of Erie, was in Rome. As late as 20 June, three weeks before the planned election, there was still no bishop who was both willing and available to raise the four potential electors to the subdeaconate.[96]

Finally the "good Bishop" Jeremiah Shanahan, Ordinary of Harrisburg, "came yet in due time," for ordinations on Saturday, 4 July. And Wimmer wrote Pohl—not without a sense of triumph—"Now we are ready to proceed to the election any day we like."[97]

The other matter that claimed Boniface Wimmer's attention between February and July of 1885 was the promotion of a suitable candidate for the North Carolina abbacy. Various factors surfaced in this decision.

> 1. The candidate needed to be non-controversial enough to win the votes of whomever Wimmer finally persuaded to join Maryhelp.

> 2. In particular, the nominee should appeal to the young, who with at least four of the ten votes were the largest block among the capitulars.

> 3. The candidate would be more appealing if he contrasted with Moosmueller, giving the impression that the previous 'mistake' was being rectified.[98]

> 4. Given the tenor and Protestantism of the South, he should be native-born[99] and a good English speaker.[100]

> 5. And since Maryhelp's future was tied to its school, he should be a scholar and a school monk.[101]

It was with this reasoning that Wimmer decided on Haid for North Carolina, and started pushing his candidacy. Father Leo himself, of course, could in no way evince complicity with this movement, nor did he even choose to show he was aware of it. His greatest weakness, according to these five standards, was a possibility of controversy because of his advocacy of Wimmer's view of monasticism. But the fact that the archabbot had shown him no special favor in return tended to outweigh this. And Haid's tremendous popularity among the young, most of whom had been his students, further promoted his candidacy. Leo Haid was "still young, of fine complexion, devout, eloquent, a real pedagogue,"[102] wrote the archabbot. "A man like Pater Leo belongs over [Maryhelp]....We need good people, a good spirit among them, a zeal for science and souls and people true to the Order."[103]

On 27 June, Wimmer issued the notices of a second election for the first abbot of Maryhelp. They were posted to Fathers Melchior Reichert in Savannah, Willibald Baumgartner in Richmond, Anastasius Mayer at Saint Vincent, Julius Pohl at Garibaldi,[104] and to

Fraters Felix Hintemeyer, George Lester, Patrick Donlon, and Walter Leahy in Pennsylvania. Only Father Melchior determined not to attend the election in person, designating Father Anastasius as his procurator.[105] The man elected abbot would give Maryhelp its ninth monk; then only one more would be needed, hopefully lured by the abbot-elect.[106]

On the evening of 13 July, the electors met to scrutinize the potential candidates. The next morning the Mass of the Holy Ghost was celebrated, the oaths taken, the *Veni Creator Spiritus* recited, and the three senior monks present, Fathers Willibald, Anastasius, and Julius, were elected tellars.[107] Then the vote was taken for the abbacy in Carolina.

Father Julius, who kept a calendar of the election and the weeks that followed, recorded that the votes were counted in absolute silence.[108] The archabbot himself announced the results when the ballots had been totaled, his voice expressing the gravity the past six months seemed to dictate: Leo Haid, one day short of his thirty-sixth birthday, had been elected first abbot of Maryhelp. The vote was unanimous.[109]

The standard session of applause was inappropriate, however. As Pohl expressed it, "Joy filled the hearts of the young community. Yet a gloomy thought haunted them all: Will he accept?" Hintemeyer suggested that the abbot-elect be asked to give his response at once, and the archabbot dispatched the three tellers to summon Haid to appear before the capitulars.[110]

The three men hastened to Father Leo's cell, only to find it empty;[111] his office was tried without success.[112] The good fortune of Maryhelp seemed to be holding true to form. Nevertheless, the tellars waited, and when Haid returned from his constitutional he agreed to accompany the embassy to the Chapter Hall.[113]

Standing before the archabbot, his secretary, and the electors, Haid listened to the record of the day's proceedings. Father Leo had not volunteered to go to North Carolina; nor had he even seen the abbey he had just been elected to lead. Under these circumstances, enthusiasm escaped him. To the dismay of all assembled, Haid found himself unable to accept the office, and begged permission to speak privately with Wimmer before giving his official response.[114]

Father Julius, in a brimming indulgence of litotes, said, "Gloomy thoughts again forced themselves on our minds."The abbot-elect and his mentor left the room. They returned a few minutes later— expressionless.[115]

Haid then addressed the monks. He proclaimed his warm appreciation for the confidence they had presumed to express in him, and he assured them that his reluctance to accept the office was rooted in his own "upright intentions," rather than in any fault of theirs or their abbey's. He then submitted to the election—to the relief of all present—and received the obeisance of the capitulars.[116]

According to Felix Fellner, long-time historian and archivist at Saint Vincent, "great joy became evident in the whole house," because they recognized Haid as "the best man for the place."[117] The *Te Deum* was sung in the church, after which the monks and abbot-elect of Maryhelp visited Wimmer, at Haid's recommendation, to express their gratitude for the archabbot's kindness and indulgence.[118] That evening the monks of Maryhelp gathered together with their new superior in the garden, and "did justice to good Saint Vincent's Beer"—though "everything went on with proper decorum."[119]

The following evening, Haid's birthday, the abbot-elect gave a dinner in honor of his electors.[120] Wimmer did not attend, however; he was already working on the documents from the election. On 17 July the materials were finished and posted to Rome imploring confirmation of the election of Leo Michael Haid as first abbot of the Abbey of Maryhelp, Garibaldi, North Carolina.

To insure that Haid would not sit around Saint Vincent, idly awaiting confirmation and possibly rethinking his acceptance of the office, Archabbot Boniface posted a small notice for the monks. Acting in his capacity as *praeses* of the American Cassinese Congregation of the Order of Saint Benedict, Wimmer announced that, pending confirmation of the abbatial election by the Holy See, an interim administrator had been appointed for Maryhelp Abbey: Pater Leo Haid.[121]

Chapter II:

a Dream of Slight Promise

In July of 1885, Leo Haid was about to enter a world completely unknown to him. He had never been to North Carolina, never seen his new abbey. Maryhelp had long been regarded as a pariah at Saint Vincent, and now Father Leo, as abbot-elect and administrator, found himself the head of this unknown, unpopular foundation in the South. With no administrative experience, no desire for the office he held, no missionary zeal or Southern sympathies to support him, Haid's confidence had been quickly shattered. He was suddenly independent of the man who had guided the course of his adult life, and he was committed for life to a monastery for which he had not even cared enough to volunteer. The one common theme of his early abbatial correspondence was the reiteration of the fact that Providence alone possessed the power to impose on him the Carolina abbacy.

Of course the new abbot had witnessed monastic pioneers at work before. He had lived close enough to observe those early, struggling days when Saint Vincent was still young. But there were differences, important differences, not the least of which was the presence of a local Catholic populace to help support the Pennsylvania Benedictines. No such comfort would be available in the Protestant South.

Among the first congratulatory mesages Haid received was a letter from the Reverend Dr. Jeremiah Joseph O'Connell. This sixty-three year old priest considered himself the founder of Maryhelp, and served as the self-appointed host to the monks, although the arrangement was actually the reverse. Nevertheless, Father O'Connell wrote Wimmer of the welcome advent of Haid.

> Yesterday we heard the glad news that Father Leo was elected Abbot of this monastery and accepted. All the community rejoices and what a marvelous event in the history of the Order and the Church in America....
> I unite to offer you and our young abbot my congratulations, and beg you to present them to him and say, how glad we all are to see and receive him.[1]

The letter, though cordial and presumably genuine in its sentiment, was also presumptuous. O'Connell was not the person to offer Maryhelp's corporate felicitations: he did not head the community; indeed his ties rested only on an oblation, not on vows. The Irishman was not attached to the North Carolina Vicariate, either. He was simply not the man to tender the official welcome. The "old priest," as Wimmer called him,[2] was the donor of the property, and in making that gift—generous as it was—he had indentured the monks for his lodging, board, and transportation during life and Masses for his soul in perpetuity.[3] Having spent most of his priestly life without companions, O'Connell was ill suited for the community life he had invited upon his last years. And his gentle disposition, his generosity and good intentions did not prepare him for subordination to a prelate who was twenty-eight years his junior and inferiorly experienced in missionary life. Nevertheless, despite his rather forward and indelicate introduction to the abbot-elect, the "old priest" came with the property, and his various physical complaints not withstanding, he seemed destined for a long life.[4]

Jeremiah O'Connell was a priest of the Diocese of Charleston, whose bishop was also acting as Vicar Apostolic of North Carolina. Born 21 November 1821, in County Cork, Ireland, O'Connell came to America at age nineteen. Officially, he was the chaperone and companion for his sister Julia, who was immigrating as a candidate for the Sisters of Mercy. But Jeremiah promptly entered the seminary himself, and was ordained a priest on 24 May 1844, the Solemnity of Pentecost that year, and coincidentally the feast of Maryhelp.[5] He then entered on the life of a missionary priest, often working in concert with his brother, Lawrence Patrick, also a Charleston priest.

Believing that "as all light is gathered into the sun, so is all truth into the Church,"[6] Jeremiah promoted the Catholic Church as a source of education. Catholic schools, he believed, would serve both the perseverance of Catholics and the conversion of Protestants. His dreams first bore fruit when, in 1857, he opened Saint Mary's College, a school for both boarding and day pupils, in Columbia, South Carolina. Jeremiah was president of the institution, and his brother was vice president.[7]

The school lasted barely more than a half dozen years. According to its reverend president, "South Carolina grew jealous of the Catholic College." Bigotry, sectarianism, rage, "threats of incendiarism, midnight assault, and violence" followed.[8] The college failed, he said, yet she was

> A faithful type of the Confederacy, her youth was fair and promising, her life short and bitter, and she perished in disaster and ruin, the same hand leveling both at one stroke.[9]

Lawrence had left the school before its demise. He entered the Confederate army, in which he eventually became a major, and served as a post chaplain. In 1865, as the more active hostilities subsided, he returned to Carolina, this time centering his missionary circuit around Mecklenburg and the other western counties of North Carolina.[10] Then in 1868, when the Vicariate Apostolic of North Carolina was erected, and the new bishop, James Gibbons, made his first tour of the state, Lawrence O'Connell was named Vicar General of the territory,[11] a rank second only to that of the Ordinary himself.

The brothers were henceforth incardinated into different jurisdictions, Lawrence in North Carolina and Jeremiah in South Carolina, but they maintained regular contact. Three years later, in 1871, when Jeremiah's health seemed to be failing, the fifty year old missionary attached himself to Lawrence's work at Saint Peter Church in Charlotte, and assisted as well as he could with the needs of North Carolina's few scattered Catholics.[12]

In his semi-retirement, his thoughts turned again toward providing the central South with a Catholic college. But this time the vision was different. Unable to administer such an effort himself, he planned to lure a religious order to the work. This would need to be an order of men, he concluded, since its priests could also help with the missions. Moreover, O'Connell was determined that his new Saint Mary's would have a rural location, away from the mobs and prejudices of the city.

North Carolina's economy at this time had not recovered from the impact of the Civil War, and in places inconveniently distant from railroads, farm land could be purchased for as little as forty cents an acre.[13] Accordingly, O'Connell began looking for land sales in the area west of Charlotte—Gaston County (where the railroad had gone only as far as Stanley in the 1860's),[14] Lincoln County on Gaston's north border, and Cleveland County to its west. This area was convenient to Saint Peter in Charlotte, and with the railroad pushing slowly westward, land values would soon be rising. Quick action, O'Connell recognized, would insure a financial profit even if the college idea failed.

His opportunity came almost immediately, when a notice was posted at the courthouse in Dallas, Gaston County, announcing that the estate of Samuel Caldwell would be sold at public auction. "Land poor" after the war, the Caldwells had even tried running a traveler's inn to raise money and save the family home. But the debts mounted, and when Caldwell died, the loss of the estate was inevitable.

The Caldwells had acquired the farm almost a century before. The first Samuel Caldwell had, at age eighteen,[15] fought with distinction in the American Revolution before establishing and raising his family on this five hundred acre plot west of Charlotte. By the time of his death, Captain Caldwell was numbered among the local gentry; his progeny would carve distinguished careers in government and in later wars. In 1847, just after the creation of Gaston County, another Samuel Caldwell surfaced from that farm and was elected a solicitor.[16] Samuel S. Caldwell, who had inherited the estate, achieved the rank of captain in the Confederate army, but unlike the previous Captain Caldwell, Samuel S. Caldwell did not retire to the family farm with his prestige or his finances intact. The debts were insurmountable. And when at his death he passed on the property to yet another Samuel Caldwell, the Superior Court of Gaston County was petitioned, and a decree issued mandating the sale.[17]

But by the time of Samuel P. Caldwell's public auction of the family lands, on 3 June 1871, O'Connell had not been able to raise sufficient funds. The bidding concluded with the Catholic priest defeated, and John F. Wooten was confirmed by the Court as the new owner of the Caldwell farm. Undaunted by this setback, however, O'Connell continued seeking money, intending to be ready the next time. The opportunity came a mere six months later, when word began circulating that Wooten did not have the money with which to meet his bid. By this time, however, O'Connell did have the necessary resources, and for ten dollars, paid in cash, he purchased Wooten's bid. On 18 December they signed the bid transfer for the five hundred six acres of the late Samuel S. Caldwell, Esquire. Samuel P. Caldwell witnessed the document.[18] O'Connell immediately paid his debt and became Garibaldi, North Carolina's newest citizen, and its first resident priest.[19]

Unsuited by either training or experience for agricultural work, O'Connell took tenant farmers, mostly blacks, onto the property. Getting the Caldwell Place in shape, he said, was an act of "restoration,...for it lay a long time in a ruinous and neglected condition."[20] This was necessary work, as O'Connell quickly realized, for even a gift of five hundred acres might not be enough to entice Catholic Religious into Gaston County.

The closest town, Garibaldi, was an unincorporated village with a country store, run by Abram Stowe, who was also the postmaster and depot agent. The town was named for an earlier station master, John Garibaldi. Though small at the time, Garibaldi, North Carolina, showed promise, and soon there was a second store and even a tavern.[21] O'Connell found a county of Baptists, Methodists, Presbyterians, and Lutherans, but few Catholics.[22] There were almost thirteen thousand people in Gaston, one third of whom were black,[23] only a handful of whom were Catholics.

The topography was striking and beautiful, however, and the land rich in minerals.[24] The setting was ideal even if the residents were not warming to the priest's presence. The forestry was superb, with hardwoods particularly in evidence. Being in the foothills of the mountains, there were gentle, rolling land and picturesque vistas. Water was bountiful and pure.[25]

But the railroads were the big news in the early 1870's; that was apparently why the stationmaster's name had been accepted for the village, and abbreviated familarly and affectionately as "Baldi."[26] The proximity of ready, inexpensive transportation augured favorably for a promising future. O'Connell could also see the anticipation surrounding the first cotton being raised successfully in the county, though corn, wheat, and oats remained the largest crops. There was also the profitable post-war influx of sheep,[27] seen by some as a waste of good land in an area where the growing season lasted as long as two hundred twenty-eight days.[28] The priest's confidence would seem well justified.

Unfortunately, in emphasizing the value of the land in Gaston County, O'Connell had looked only at the external elements, and had not checked history. Gaston County, despite its rural character, had never been prime farm land.[29] Yields were normally small.[30] The Catawba Indians, who had lived in the region long before their seventeenth century discovery by adventurous whites,[31] had not been attracted by the soil, but by the woods and waters. Even in the eighteenth century, when the first slaves were imported, their work was usually domestic in nature, and did not require cultivation of the land.[32]

The Caldwell estate itself should have warned O'Connell about the relative unimportance of agriculture in Gaston. Only about two hundred acres of the farm had been cleared, most of the rest being given to timber, primarily oak, pine, and hickory.[33] Despite this, however, Jeremiah O'Connell had correctly identified a fine setting for a school. The air was clear and healthful at an altitude of about six hundred eighty-five feet;[34] good water was convenient.[35] Transportation was good and inexpensive, and there were some buildings on the property with which to start. The only missing elements seemed to be Catholics, a religious Order, and students. For these Father O'Connell planned to supply with force of will and hard work. And not until the summer of 1875, was the "Caldwell Plantation," as the farm was now being called, ready for inspection by Catholic Religious.

The first step in securing the Order was to impress the territory's bishop, in this case James Gibbons, the future Cardinal. North Carolina had no diocese at that time; its territory comprised a Vicariate Apostolic, a level of ecclesiastical jurisdiction ordinarily preparatory to diocesan status. Having too few Catholics to support its clergy and bishop, Gibbons, the first Vicar Apostolic of North Carolina, had been promoted in 1872 to an additional See, Richmond, which he then ruled in tandem with North Carolina. Gibbons had been named Vicar Apostolic in 1868 over two other nominees: Matthew O'Keefe, a priest in Virginia, and Jeremiah O'Connell himself.[36] No thought was given in 1872, however, to again nominating O'Connell,[37] and Gibbons reigned simultaneously over both territories.

With crops planted, livestock on the premises, the house furnished, Gibbons was approached by O'Connell. The bishop was in the midst of his regular visitation of the Carolina missions, a trip that included Confirmations, Masses, inspections, and simple contact with priests, penitents, and the faithful. "Nowhere on the continent," O'Connell said, "could be found another place better suited for a religious and literary institution than this."[38] According to Gibbons' account, O'Connell offered "one of the best farms in one of the most fertile counties of the state." The offer included five hundred acres, stock, and a gold mine, all of which was valued by Father O'Connell at six thousand five hundred dollars. Gibbons was impressed with the offer, agreed to find an order of "Regular Priests who would cultivate the land and evangelize the missions,"[39] and to enhance the offer, rounded off the value to ten thousand dollars.[40]

Hoping to find Religious who would accept the Garibaldi land, Gibbons claimed that, "As soon as the offer was made to me, my eyes turned to [Wimmer]."[41] That may be true. Wimmer's men were near Gibbons, working at Saint Mary parish in Richmond. But though his eyes turned first to Wimmer, his pen turned first to the Redemptorists. On 26 June 1875, the day he returned from his Carolina visitation, he recorded in his diary, "I have written to the V[ery] Rev[erend] Superior of the Redemptorists tendering him the farm which is in Gaston Co[unty]."[42]

Four of the Redemptorists had just given "a course of missions" through Gibbons' two territories,[43] and the bishop took the opportunity, while the obvious need of priests would be fresh in the Redemptorists' minds, to offer them a southern foundation. They rejected the offer without delay.[44]

As it happened, the Redemptorists were not the first Order to decline land in Gaston County. The Jesuits, who had inherited the estate of John O'Brien near the county seat of Dallas, had been so reluctant to claim that largesse that squatters had time to take possession of the whole property.[45]

On 1 August 1875, Gibbons turned to an Order noted for farms, education, and—at least since the appearance of Boniface Wimmer—a spirit of adventure: the Benedictines. His petition to the patriarch of Saint Vincent appealed to both the abbot's sensitivities and his appetites:

> I write to you on a subject of importance to religion and I hope you will give the matter your careful and favorable consideration.
>
> During my recent visit to the missions of North Carolina, I received from Rev[erend] Dr. J.J. O'Connell, the offer of his fine farm as a gift, on the sole condition that I would present it to a religious community who would cultivate it, and who with God's blessing would make it a religious center around which Catholicity would grow.
>
> The farm contains five hundred acres, two hundred of which are producing this year, wheat, corn, cotton, etc. The rest is composed of timber land. It is represented as one of the best farms in one of the healthy and fertile counties in North Carolina, and is valued at ten thousand dollars.
>
> Dr. O'Connell offers also the rolling stock, horses, cows, etc., valued at two thousand dollars and is prepared to deposit with the Fathers the sum of two thousand dollars, the interest of which he would draw, but I think, he would never demand the capital.
>
> The farm is only ten miles south from Charlotte, situated on the Richmond and Atlanta Air Line Railroad, the main line going south. The farm is a half mile from the depot....A letter will reach him addressed to Reverend Dr. J.J. O'Connell, Garibaldi Post Office, Gaston County, North Carolina.
>
> As soon as the offer was made to me, my eyes turned toward your Right Reverence, whose brothers, I trust, are destined to cultivate souls and land in North Carolina as they have done in Europe. In view of the spoilations of your property in Europe, I consider this offer as coming from the hand of Providence.
>
> The only condition which Dr. O'Connell gives, is that he may be

permitted to occupy a room on the premises during his life, which in the course of nature, is not destined to be too long, as he is old and feeble.

There are scarcely any Catholics in the immediate vicinity, but there is a small church and congregation about four miles off.

Hoping for a reply at your earliest convenience, I remain Right Reverend Father, your friend and servant in Christ,

[signed] + James Gibbons
Bishop of Richmond

[Postscript:] This place would answer well for a college, as we have no college betweeen Washington and Mobile, except one in Georgia. There is a good farm house and another residence on the premises.[46]

The letter is a persuasive and deceptive document. The value of the land has been enlarged. The gold mine—inactive for a quarter century,[47] and never very productive—is valued as an asset.[48] Neither the Jesuits nor the Redemptorists are mentioned. There is the misleading segment that says O'Connell's residency is the only condition; whereas, Father O'Connell considered the stipulations regarding the use of the property to be conditions, as well, and he would add other clauses before the documents were signed. There is no proof that Gibbons was fully aware of the inaccuracy of his missive, but he may at least be recognized as granting a character to his presentation that was rather misleading.

This offer, as phrased, did however meet many of Wimmer's criteria for new missionary monasteries. There were land, a rural setting, a farm, prospects for a school, genuine need. But this was not Wimmer's only offer in 1875, the best prospect, nor even his first invitation to the Carolinas.[49] It had, however, a special appeal for the abbot. As Gibbons remembered it, Boniface Wimmer liked the O'Connell offer for "the peculiar reason[s] that North Carolina had less Catholics than any state in the Union, at that time, and that it was the most poverty stricken of all the Dioceses in the United States."[50]

There was a General Chapter for the Benedictines in 1875, but Wimmer found there little interest in this latest scheme for expansion of the Order. Yet Abbot Boniface was not prepared to reject Gibbons' offer. He merely recognized that he could not accept it just then, and that it might be good to see the place first.[51] Gibbons sensed Wimmer's interest, knew the abbot's reputation for venting his will, and decided to delay offering the farm to a third Order.

Exactly what course Wimmer took to promote his Chapter's acceptance of the Garibaldi property went unrecorded. But after Christmas he thought there were enough votes, and a meeting and ballot by the capitulars at Saint Vincent were scheduled for 19 January 1876.

In the meantime, Gibbons had been calling "frequently" on Wimmer's two monks stationed in Richmond at Saint Mary Church. Father Benno Hegele, O.S.B., the pastor, and Father Herman Wolfe, O.S.B., the assistant, watched the bishop grow increasingly impatient, until he finally instructed Father Benno to request "a decisive answer immediately." Hegele did so—diplomatically timing his letter to arrive after the abbot had himself initiated action—and advised Saint Vincent that Gibbons had "the deed for the farm in hand and is willing to make it over at once to the Order."[52]

The capitulars in Pennsylvania voted their approval of Wimmer's Carolina adventure,[53] accepting that farm over an opportunity in Nebraska that later evolved under Jesuit control into Creighton University. Father Benno was promptly informed of the Chapter's decision, and was delegated by the abbot to carry the news to James Gibbons.[54] Hegele did so on 26 January.[55] With characteristic post-factum humility, the abbot of Saint Vincent later wrote to Dr. Joseph Amberger explaining the motivation for entering Carolina: "I have taken the place for pity sake—in favor of Faith— in order to give the few—all dispersed—Catholics a harbor of some stability."[56]

The letter to Hegele also named the first superior for Carolina. It was to be the Richmond assistant, Father Herman. Wolfe was a convert from Lutheranism. A coarse, unmannered man, he was remembered, nevertheless, as cheerful, tall, grey, angular, and a good pianist. A German native, he was born in Krummendiek, Holstein, where he became a physician. At age thirty-two, Wolfe journeyed to America, eventually settling in Saint Louis. In 1861, he enlisted as a medical officer in the Confederate army, remaining until 1865. Two years later he was ordained a priest by Bishop Domenec of Pittsburgh. The next day he entered the novitiate at Saint Vincent, where he remained until his solemn vows in 1872. Since then he had been stationed in Richmond.[57]

The abbot's logic in sending the Confederate veteran to run the North Carolina mission was transparent to everyone except Father Herman. "Had I been at Saint Vincent," he wrote, "I would have voted in favor of accepting the place but certainly would not have chosen the man who is to go there to start it." Wolfe hoped, to no avail, that Gibbons would object to the choice of superior. The prior-elect then begged exemption because of age, before finally submitting. Reluctantly he accepted his appointment and begged the Saint Vincent community to "assist me with its prayers."[58]

In this same letter, Wolfe advised his abbot of the first of the conditions that were to be added to the deed. Gibbons, it seemed, had decided to reserve "the right to reclaim the farm, in case the

Benedictines withdraw from the place."[59] The bishop later decided to omit this clause from the document, calling this aspect a "private contract;" nevertheless, he carefully recorded its terms for posterity: Wimmer agreed, according to Gibbons, "to surrender the property to the Bishop of North Carolina should it be ever diverted from its legitimate purposes, *viz.* the establishment of an agricultural farm and a Catholic college."[60] For his part Wimmer admitted the bishop had made the demand, but never mentioned such terms having been accepted.

Since no Benedictine had yet seen the Caldwell farm, Father Herman decided to travel there as soon as possible. He planned to go on Tuesday, 1 February, for a visit of one week.[61] O'Connell's recollection says the first visit was not until spring. But regardless of the date, Wolfe "made a thorough examination" of the donation, "accepted the gift and acquiesced to the conditions."[62] He then returned to Richmond, leaving the farm in O'Connell's hands, and began arranging for the legal transfer of title. Wolfe also began his long wait for enough brothers to operate the priory's farm.[63]

The troubled history of Carolina monasticism had barely begun. Wolfe learned, for example, that since the Benedictines had no charter in the state of North Carolina, the monks could not own property there.[64] This problem was solved by deciding to make the deed over to Father Herman personally,[65] who then wrote a will in which he left the farm to the Benedictine Society in Pennsylvania.[66]

But the affairs of the Garibaldi Benedictines were seldom simple. And the transfer of the land was a classic foretaste of what the future held.[67] This is the sequence:

1. On 11 October 1875, O'Connell deeded the farm to Gibbons with a stated price of ten thousand dollars. They did not, however, register the deed.[68]

2. That same day, a contract was drawn up by O'Connell that apparently *later* was specified as engaging Wolfe on behalf of the Benedictine Society in Pennsylvania, "to support [O'Connell] in a comfortable and genteel manner for and during [his] natural life." Gibbons signed this, but not until nine months later.[69]

3. On 13 March 1876, after Wolfe had seen the farm and realized the difficulties of corporate ownership under North Carolina law, Gibbons deeded the land to Father Herman for one dollar, and in consideration "of the conditions and trust hereafter set forth." These included "conduct and maintenance of a boys' school and farm under the control, direction, care and management of the said Herman Wolfe and...[the] Benedictine Society."[70]

4. On 29 March 1876, Wolfe executed a will that specified, "It is my especial desire in this device to provide for the continuance of management of a certain real estate in Gaston County, North Carolina, which was bargained, sold, and conveyed to me by Right Reverend James Gibbons, Bishop of Richmond...to the intent that the purposes set forth in said deed be faithfully carried out."[71]

5. On 2 April 1876, the deed of 11 October 1875 was finally registered, but in the adjoining county of Mecklenburg instead of Gaston County.[72] [cf., no. 1, *supra]*

6. On 5 July 1876, Gibbons finally signed the contract of the previous October.[73] [cf., no. 2, *supra*]

7. On 17 July 1876, it all started again. This time a deed was executed from O'Connell to Wolfe "in behalf of the Benedictine Society of Westmoreland County, Pennsylvania." This document was specified as superseding the deed of 11 October 1875 [no. 1, *supra*], and that of 13 March 1876 [no. 3, *supra*]. In this deed, for one dollar (and, of course, the "considerations") the property was transferred

together with all the improvements thereon, and with the stock consisting in mules, cattle, hogs and sheep, with all provisions and provender on hand, with all farming...tools and household furniture, and the crop now growing, valued at twelve thousand dollars, it being expressly understood, that all mines of gold, or any other mineral on said premises heretofore opened and worked, or not opened and worked yet, being not included in the above valuation, but valued by themselves at fifty thousand dollars are included in this grant and conveyance—to have and to hold under these conditions: The said Jeremiah Joseph O'Connell...shall have

1. his support, including clothing, during the term of his natural life, and in case either party should wish and prefer, a separate dwelling in a convenient location on the premises.

2. the use of a horse (or mule) and buggy, whenever he requires the same.

3. the exclusive use of his *vasa sacrainitis* [sic] and *paramenta sacerdotalia* [chalice and other priestly paraphernalia].

4. a weekly Mass *ab initio* and *in perpetuum* according to his intention and the said [Herman Wolfe] shall establish or cause to be established on the premises aforesaid within a reasonable time a religious community and literary institution.[74]

8. On 26 August 1876, Father Herman made yet another will. The purpose was the same as the one of March, but this time the deed of reference was the 17 July document. Wimmer was named executor.[75]

9. On 15 November 1877, another new deed was signed. This one was the same as the previous year's edition, except that it corrected the error in the legal name of the Benedictine Society.[76]

10. On 3 December 1877, however, Wimmer—still not satisfied,

and other legal impediments finally behind him—had O'Connell and Wolfe together execute another new deed to supersede its predecessors, this time expressly giving the property to Wimmer. If nothing else, this deed did save Father Herman from designing a third will.[77]

In a fitting postscript to these machinations, Leo Haid, almost nine years later, received a letter from Wimmer expressing the archabbot's dislike for and dissatisfaction with even that last contract.[78]

the haRBOR of Some Stability

In April of 1876, Father Herman finally left Richmond to start his new monastery. He was accompanied by two Richmond boys, Henry Plageman and Anthony Lauman, who were to be the new school's first pupils and the farm's first laborers. Garibaldi was reached on the twenty-first, and since Father Herman immediately established residency, the "priory" came into existence on that day. There were just two priests and two boys; only one of the four was a monk, but such are the beginnings of missionary monasteries.

Father Herman decided to name his new priory "Mariastein," in honor of the Blessed Virgin Mary and a large granite boulder that dominated the property. This stone was supposed to have been a Catawba altar. Subsequently, the Caldwells had used it as the slave block. Wolfe planned no use for the rock, but the name at least acknowledged its rather conspicuous presence.[79]

Wimmer, with uncharacteristic generosity, sent three brothers before the end of the month. Michael Irwin, an early student remembered them as "gnarled, knotty, and brown."[80] The description is indicative of the effects of the brothers' strenuous life of labor and monastic austerity. Brother Bartholomew Freundl was a farm laborer, a silver jubilarian of monastic profession, and a Bavarian. He was the senior brother. Brother Ulric Barth, a native of Belgium, had been drafted into the Federal army during the Civil War, but he returned to the monastery at Saint Vincent afterwards. He was skilled as a mechanic. The junior of the original brothers was a Prussian, Placidus Draude, a gardener. He later left the monastery and married.[81] They supervised the failure of the supposedly valuable crops that first year, until by August even Wimmer admitted that Mariastein would not be noted for its farm.[82]

As the primary step in establishing a monastery at the Caldwell Place, Father Herman designated a corner room in the small, frame house, as a chapel. He blessed it, "and from the first morning Holy

Mass was offered every day. May God assist us," he prayed, "that this Sacrifice will never be interrupted here."[83]

There were other buildings to be prepared, too. Brother Ulric began a two storey, frame, college building,[84] about twenty-two feet by thirty-nine. This structure would be moved several times in the next two decades until the more permanent, brick buildings were available. Perhaps the construction work those first few months was providential, since school enrollment doubled in the fall of 1876: there were four students, two Charlotte boys, Frederick and Samuel Gross, having been added.

To cover the teaching load—school work seemed to show more promise than agriculture—Wimmer took the unusual step of sending a teaching brother. Philip George Cassidy, who like O'Connell was a native of Ireland, had recently professed his final vows as a Benedictine. Prior to entering Saint Vincent, he had been a Christian Brother at Saint Francis in Loretto. He was dispensed on 28 September 1871, at age fifty-one, then entered the Order of Saint Benedict. Garibaldi was his first mission as a monk.[85] He was a "grave, middle-aged man"[86] by this time, but his service was undeniable. Not only did he help with the teaching, this Irish brother was also available as a buffer between the German superior, Wolfe, and the Irish donor, O'Connell, each of whom was set in his ordinary and not necessarily compatible patterns.[87]

Wolfe greeted Cassidy at the station. Brother Philip was surprised to find his new prior accompanied on that occasion by "a boy, a nigger, four mules and a wagon,"[88] but he quickly accomodated himself to the primitive and informal conditions of Mariastein. Cassidy was to teach English, arithmetic, penmanship, and geography—half the school's courses—while also serving as the students' prefect. Father Herman taught catechism, classical languages, German, geometry, and algebra.[89] He then doubled as a missionary, sometimes leaving Father O'Connell to say the conventual Mass for the non-ordained monks.[90]

Missionary responsibilities distracted the prior from the monastery, school, and farm, from the beginning. In the first year, Cabarrus County, twenty miles away, became the monks' responsibility.[91] He also went to Dallas and elsewhere so that on Sundays, when he travelled by rail, he had to leave at half past four in the morning, and could not be back before half past ten o'clock at night.[92]

To help ease the prior's burden, Father Joseph Keller, O.S.B., was sent to Mariastein as a missionary. Keller had been Wolfe's replacement in Richmond, but the needs in Carolina were greater. Father Joseph was Bavarian born, but able to preach well in

English,[93] so his services were in great demand. At the monastery it was he who started the first chapel building. This was a frame structure, whitewashed, about eighteen feet by thirty, with a maximum capacity of one hundred worshipers. On 8 September 1877, Keller offered the first Mass in the chapel.

But it was for another and more significant effort that Father Joseph would be remembered in the monastery's history. Keller was the first of the many Garibaldi missionaries to beg release from the Carolina wilderness. Claiming there was no real need for his presence, he unsuccessfully petitioned for transfer in March of 1877.[94] One month later, the brothers appealed *en masse* to Wimmer, imploring reassignment away from Mariastein.[95] They too were unsuccessful, but the obvious trouble brewing in Gaston County finally brought Wimmer to Mariastein.[96]

The sight that greeted the founder of American Benedictine monasticism in June of 1877 was pitiful. There was a rough board house, a delicate frame structure for the school, and the waste of the badly managed farm. The personnel too, decidedly unenthusiastic about the prospects for success, were less than edifying. Only O'Connell seemed to be pleased; he thought the first year such a success, that he announced his intention to become a Benedictine Oblate.[97] The monks, however, projected a more subdued character than the donor. There were two German-born priests, and now five brothers—an Irishman, one from Belgium, a Prussian, and two Bavarians—all stranded outside a three house hamlet in a Protestant state. This was not the substance from which permanent American monasteries were formed. Wimmer commenced his efforts by renaming the monastery, providing what seemed a more reasonable label. "Mariastein" would be used no more; the school would be called, as O'Connell had requested, "Saint Mary's College;" and the whole complex was placed under the patronage of Blessed Mary, according to her title "help of Christians." The monks were henceforth part of the "Benedictine Priory of Maryhelp," and they trusted the help would come posthaste.

Wimmer's visit was intended to engender spirit. He told Keller to build the chapel of Maryhelp, and promised to send an organ. To ease tensions, O'Connell was given a small and separate cottage on the grounds. The monks were told to cease murmuring and start working. And with typical optimism, he noted that conditions were not really as dismal as they seemed. With three priests, five brothers, and four students, Maryhelp was "already the principal Catholic center in the State."[98]

This was the first of several such visits from Wimmer.

maryhelp

The priory developed so slowly that the abbot did not institute a regular monastic horarium until his visitation in the spring of 1882. The painfully slow progress of the Carolina monks stemmed in part from a pervading bitterness of spirit. The move by Keller and the brothers to abandon the project in 1877, was merely the beginning of the disquiet that continually attacked and undercut the monastic values and standards that needed to be established if the foundation were to succeed. In 1878, Wimmer had to write a letter complaining that no one at Maryhelp would tell him how few students there were.[99] In 1879, there was widespread discontent regarding the poor monastic observance.[100] That same year Wimmer wrote reprovingly that the farm had to be improved lest the whole operation suffer.[101] Yet the school was equally bad, and they could not even afford paint for the buildings.[102]

But it was in 1883 that problems in Carolina reached their worst level. Wimmer sent Fathers Pauline and Benno to Garibaldi merely to visit, in the hope that they might be impressed and argue against the "bad will, indiscretion or misunderstanding that have so decried [Maryhelp] that no one wants to go there."[103] That summer, the monks decided to try cutting tuition in order to win more students.[104] They advertised, too, in Chattanooga, Atlanta, Savannah, Augusta, Columbia, Charleston, Wilmington, Raleigh, Norfolk, Portsmouth, Lynchburg, and Richmond. One monk stayed a month in the Virginia capital for recruiting new boys; another spent five weeks touring southern cities in search of students. The result was ten students at the start of the year—this jumped finally to twenty-one—no one from Richmond or Charleston even applied; there was only one from Columbia, and the whole state of North Carolina yielded one application, a boy who subsequently decided not to attend.[105] The farm too was at its worst that year, with oats yielding only nine bushels per acre, and corn only ten; there were no peaches; potatoes were poor. There might not be enough provender to feed the stock, Father Edwin lamented. "About our farm," he wrote, "there is not much to be said."[106]

Oswald Moosmueller, on the pretense of escorting Brother Altman Alt to his new assignment in Carolina, had inspected Maryhelp for Wimmer in 1877. He found the place overly crowded and dingy. The brightest light, he said, was Father O'Connell, who wisely recognized what poor farmers the monks were and gathered around him families of black sharecroppers and tenant farmers.[107]

Finally in 1878, the abbot tried a new approach. He sent an emissary to assume residency at Maryhelp and report regularly regarding the tenor and state of the monastery and its works. For this unusual assignment Abbot Boniface appointed Julius Pohl, a talpid-faced cleric at Saint Vincent, and a personal favorite of Wimmer's. Frater Julius had recently had some minor health problems and was in need of a more healthful climate than Pennsylvania winters provided. So he volunteered for Garibaldi—that alone was enough to distinguish him—where he would continue his studies for priesthood under Father O'Connell. Pohl was the priory's first American-born monk, an Ohio native, and the perfect man for this delicate mission. There was no way for Pohl's assignment to be held *sub secreto*, since the abbot insisted on communicating through him, even in giving instructions to the prior. But Frater Julius was capable of inspiring a true and generous affection in the people who knew him, and there is—surprisingly—no extant evidence of his being resented in his unusual position at Maryhelp. From the beginning, young Pohl sought to engender a wholesome new spirit in Carolina. He was scholarly, good humored, a skilled violinist. Frater Julius was also willing to give himself as generously to the school as to the missions, immediately separating himself from the factions in the priory. Totally dedicated to the upbuilding of Maryhelp, even taking the care to record early events of historical interest for later generations, Julius Pohl came to represent the promise than even Maryhelp Priory might prove to have. Even in the boys of the college, Pohl could elicit an amazing affection, respect, and loyalty.[108] But at no time did his personal interests keep Frater Julius from his primary task, and the reports to Wimmer were frequent and detailed.

A second, exceptionally gifted, American-born, Benedictine was sent to Maryhelp in these early years, too. But he was sent for a different reason. Stephen Lyons was a charismatic figure to parishoners and students; he was a gifted teacher and a tremendous asset to the pastoral work of the house. Unfortunately, the monks found Lyons to be a chronic malcontent.[109] His attitude in the monastery was unpleasant, but since he had been sent to Carolina primarily to establish the reputation of the missions, and to a lesser extent the school, he was tolerated. And like Pohl, he executed his special assignment well.

Despite his gentleness and good intentions, however, Herman Wolfe was quickly spotted by both Pohl and Lyons as a negative force in the development of Maryhelp. Lyons, both because of the more personal nature of his complaints and the fact that he was making a rather blatant effort toward taking over Wolfe's missionary circuit, never succeeded in winning Abbot Boniface's confidence, however.

Pohl did enjoy the abbatial favor. His letters from Wimmer are peppered with terms of endearment. But the story that Pohl had to expose was far from pleasant; so he wrote it first to the prior of Saint Vincent, James Zilliox, and from there changes started happening.

The charges suggested an overall failure of the Wolfe administration. Father Herman seemed to "take to drink;" the food he served was bad ["meat we get—none—and if we do—*rotten* meat"] his "inventiveness" involved serving the potato greens rather than the vegetable's meat; the boys were not returning to school because of Father Herman's practices; parishoners in Concord stopped attending church rather than face another Sunday morning with Wolfe.[110]

Wimmer's response to the charges had elements of politics, diplomacy, and prudent administration. Pohl—"in whose mouth such a petition sounded particularly wrong"—was scolded. Father Stephen was warned.[111] And the next year, much to Father Herman's relief,[112] the aging prior was transferred to a parish in Alabama. Father Julius was saved from the taint of villainy; Father Stephen was finally given his overdue correction; and Father Herman was spared the embarrassment that might have accompanied his failure. The departing prior left behind eight hundred ninety-two dollars and twenty-one cents in debts, and a poor excuse for a monastery.[113] Pastoral work occupied his energies until his death in 1884.

Father Prior Herman was succeeded at Garibaldi by Placidus Pilz, a Bavarian-born Benedictine whose special talent for erecting buildings made him an obvious candidate for fledgling monasteries. Before the advent of Father Placidus, construction projects at Maryhelp had been small, inexpensive, and often temporary in intention. The chapel had cost a mere four hundred fifty-two dollars.[114] The two-storey, frame college building had cost one thousand one hundred fourteen dollars and fifty cents.[115] But Pilz had been told to construct a three storey brick structure, the core of the permanent buildings for Maryhelp. The cost was estimated at two thousand five hundred dollars, with a seventy-five by thirty-five foot floorplan.[116]

Brickmaking had already started on 1 April,[117] with blacks being hired to assist Brother Ulric and the other brothers.[118] So Father Placidus had only to stake out the rectangular frame, assign jobs, sketch a rough design, and anticipate and provide for needs. At the last minute, Wimmer decided to splurge, telling Pilz—through Pohl—to include a full basement in his plans.[119] On 10 November, the cornerstone was blessed, ground broken, and work begun.[120]

Construction stretched over nine months, and finished fifty-five dollars and seventy-eight cents under budget.[121]

Though this narrow building, fashioned of irregular bricks, was a solitary standard of ambition, it was at least visible evidence that the Benedictines had given some thought to permanent residency on the Caldwell farm. All college functions were to be held in this new building—except that, it was thought, the anticipated quantity of students might require the placement of some boys in the old dormitories as well. It was a problem that did not materialize, however. The Catholic school, in the Protestant South, run by German-born Yankees, was slow in achieving local popularity.

Personnel changed regularly in the early years of the College, according to variations in both monastic temperaments and school enrollment.[122] In moving from four students in 1876, to six in 1877, there seemed little progress. But 1878 had twelve boys, and the next year there was a respectable enrollment of thirty-eight. The release of Father Herman saved the next year's total, and as the College Building was started there were forty-three scholars, living in "a plain wooden shed...unsealed within—rather frigid as to the temperature."[123] But that was the peak: 1881 had twenty-five boys; there were two fewer the next year; another two fewer in the 1883 term. In 1884, when the monastery became an abbey, the school had improved, but only to twenty-seven pupils. This low enrollment continued despite considerable interest and promotion of the school. Bishop Northrop, who headed the Vicariate at this time, showed great support for Saint Mary's College,[124] even sponsoring some students,[125] and sending his own nephew to Garibaldi.[126] Father Stephen in particular was admired by the laity, and Father Lawrence O'Connell encouraged the bishop and priests to assist the struggling institution.[127] A brochure was printed in 1877 to promote the College.[128] But it was all to no avail.

Exasperated, Wimmer finally wrote Pohl, "You have every year good *prospects* for a crowded school, but it seems you are a little visionary, for after all, the boys seen do not come."[129] It was Pohl, then, who took matters in hand and set about improving the school and its image. At times, however, he stretched reality to suit his purposes. For example, in the school catalogue published just before the brick College Building opened—while students were still lodging in the board shack described as "frigid"[130]—he wrote this interpretation of the effects of Maryhelp's primitive conditions: "The improved physique of the students on their return home is a subject pleasing to parents; and boys of delicate constitution are sent here in recognition of this fact."[131]

Despite his rather creative promotional literature, however, Pohl was able to communicate to the college the same sense of purpose, the same tenor and enthusiasm that he had tried to impart in the cloister. Through this effort, Father Julius became the primary force in upbuilding the school, and when he became rector in 1884, Saint Mary's College actually seemed to have promise. By this time Pohl was also, though young in years, the institution's only voice of continuity. In the school's brief history, there had been five rectors: Herman Wolfe (appointed in 1876), Stephen Lyons (1878), Father Alban Rudroff (1881) from Kansas, Father Edwin Pierron (1882), whom Wimmer thought might help the farm as well as the school, and finally Pohl (1884). These personnel problems gave Maryhelp an image of instability from the beginning. Lyons petitioned regularly for reassignment, finally lamenting in July of 1881, that he was "dishearten[ed]...to think that my prospects of being released this summer, look so poor."[132] And Cyprian Creagh, who had tried his vocation in Ireland first as a Redemptorist,[133] but at age forty-three applied to the Benedictines as the first priesthood candidate specifically intended for North Carolina,[134] was begging for a transfer to Savannah a mere two years after ordination.[135] When the move was denied, he asked simply to go anywhere else.[136] Only Pohl liked North Carolina and never requested or expressed a desire for reassignment.

In the context of these conditions—unwilling personnel, poor farm, low enrollment in the school, little income, and even that useless gold mine—it was little wonder that Wimmer fought so anxiously in 1884 to divest himself of responsibility for Maryhelp Priory. Through its two dependencies there was at least some promise of solvency, but Garibaldi itself was a dream of slight promise.

advent of haid

Nevertheless, in July of 1885, Leo Haid, as administrator and abbot-elect, was lord of this minor disaster near the southern border of North Carolina. And he decided to go south for his first view of his domain as soon as possible.

Before leaving Saint Vincent, Father Leo's popularity in the schools earned Maryhelp some unexpected additions. Two of the motherhouse's clerics, both students of Haid's, announced for Carolina. They were Roman Kirchner, a twenty-five year old Pennsylvania native, and Charles Mohr, age twenty-two, from Ohio. They joined Haid on 15 July.[137]

That same day, Father Leo sent Father Willibald back to his assignment in Richmond at Saint Mary Church, and Pohl to his rectorship of the college in Carolina.[138] Three more of Haid's students, all members of that year's graduating class, announced their intention to enter the novitiate for Maryhelp. They—Bernard Haas, Benedict Roth, and Francis Meyer—remained at Saint Vincent's novitiate, then made their professions for Maryhelp the following summer.

On 20 July, the abbot-elect in the company of the archabbot left Saint Vincent for New Jersey, where they were to attend the solemn abbatial blessing of James Zilliox on the twenty-second. Four fraters—George, Patrick, Walter, and Charles—took the train to Richmond where they would await the abbot-elect.[139] Hintemeyer, as the premier intellect of the group, stayed at the motherhouse for further studies.[140]

After the festivities in honor of Zilliox, Haid proceeded to Richmond where he investigated his dependency, preached at Saint Mary's on the twenty-sixth, and "was introduced to the leading members" of the parish.[141]

Then on 27 July, the five monks[142] boarded the southbound train for Garibaldi station, North Carolina. Of the group only Leahy and Donlon had ever seen their new home.[143] Yet the whole group must have been encouraged by the vision of the future. This one month had seen a promising abbot elected; thus eight monks had become nine. Two additional volunteers followed Haid; then three novices enlisted, so that in two weeks, Maryhelp had gone from eight to fourteen monks, not counting the brothers.

Arriving on 28 July 1885,[144] the monks of Maryhelp were met at the depot on this hot summer day by Father O'Connell. The donor of Maryhelp had brought with him a farm wagon, administered by the college's factotum, Alexander Nevins, and powered by an aging mule. Haid surveyed the "abbatial carriage" and concluded that prudence demanded that they walk to the abbey. Accordingly, O'Connell and Nevins rode, and the monks followed on foot.[145]

Twenty-five years later, the abbot recalled his first sight of Maryhelp. "A straggling, rut-ribbed road led...through the undergrowth to the spot" where they were to make their home. It was a plot of land as primitive as the road and as rickety as the wagon had been. The abbot-elect's heart sank at the miserable sight. Even with his greatest charity, Leo Haid could describe Maryhelp with no more generosity than to say that, "In spite of its forlorn appearances, nature had favored that spot." As he surveyed his domain Haid concluded that "the sturdy old Benedictine spirit of labor, sacrifice and prayer would [have to] do the rest."[146] By Pohl's recollection, the new monks of Maryhelp were "agreeably surprised" by their first sight of the Abbey.[147] But Haid's version is more readily substantiated. These monks, who were accustomed to the imposing grandeur of the Pennsylvania archabbey, suddenly found themselves in Carolina where there was a single brick building, strangely proportioned and singularly unimpressive. Maryhelp's church was smaller than the refectory at Saint Vincent. There was the rough, two-storey, frame "monastery" beside the "College Building," and at least two smaller temporary frame buildings, randomly scattered before the brick structure. There was an unproductive farm, improved but still poor—and of course there was the deserted gold mine. Finally there was the cottage of their boarder, Father O'Connell. Haid's first vision of his domain was of an underdeveloped farm, well placed, brimming with potential, but woefully untapped, thoroughly disorganized, and in a state of critical disrepair.

The moment was too important to pass in silence or murmuring, and without delay the abbot-elect took control. For Haid, as for Wolfe nine years earlier, there was one sign of permanence and stability that met the eye. And upon arriving at the farm, Father Leo headed first for the large granite block—situated now in the shadow of the new, brick College Building. The abbot-elect mounted "Mariastein," where the Catawbas had worshiped, and slaves had been sold, and he addressed the small band of pioneer monks and their host, announcing "the glad tidings of the new monastic foundation."[148]

With this act, Leo Haid embraced the future of Maryhelp Abbey.

Chapter III:

A Mitred Abbot

Inhabited for nine years by disgruntled monks, Maryhelp's buildings—pitiful in their own right—had been allowed to deteriorate. Even Haid, who was determined to promote a spirit of adventure and enthusiasm, admitted the atmosphere of his new home was depressing. Wimmer openly described the abbey as "just a farmhouse."[1] Father Placidus, who continued as prior until the administrator reached Maryhelp, was so elated to be relieved of residency in Carolina, that he allowed himself only one full day for introducing the new superior to his charge. On the morning of 30 July, Pilz flagged down the first train, boarded it, and happily and finally departed Garibaldi. Father Leo soon came to the realization that prompt action was necessary in order to fight such attitudes and to involve the monks in the needs of Maryhelp Abbey.

Haid's methodology was taken directly from Benedict's *Regula:* he decided to keep the monks busy. The monastery was a "school of the Lord's service,"[2] according to Benedict, a training ground for a life focused on God. And nothing, he believed, was more likely to distract from God and promote a poor spirit than idleness. In the *Regula*, indeed, it was provided that labor might be assigned even on Sunday, if that were necessary for fighting a monk's lack of industry.[3] Haid subscribed to this theory wholeheartedly, and set the monks to work without delay.

The college not being in session, all the monks—priests and brothers—did manual labor. Their first project involved the library. The capitulars of Maryhelp had prudently brought from Saint Vincent various items necessary for the work of the new abbey, and books were a prominent part of their imports. These were unpacked while Father Leo walked through the buildings and instituted appropriate rearrangements for the good of the school and monastery. Finally the administrator decided that the library should be moved from the second to the first floor. On 31 July the entire book collection and its shelving were dismantled and reconstructed according to Haid's design.[4] Then the abbot-elect ordered that the volumes be recatalogued to more properly incorporate the new and greater quantity of books.

On the morning of 6 August, Father Anastasius, who decided to enter the new life of a new abbey with a new name, and thus became "Father William," reached Garibaldi. With him was Frater Roman. What they discovered was a flurry of activity with monks and abbot alike cleaning, painting, and ornamenting the ramshackle structures, hoping to lend "a more cheerful look."[5] Mr. Nevins was painting in the College; the brothers were working on the farm. The abbot-elect, his priests and clerics were being true to Benedict with no idleness in evidence.[6] Haid himself had already scrubbed the church. The monastery was painted on the outside and cleaned within. Whitewash was applied to the exterior of the chapel, and interior of the college. And Haid cheerfully reported, "We are not idle....The work keeps us in good humor!"[7]

Father Leo was determined that those first days would be busy and create immediate and obvious results. From the list of improvements,[8] it would seem he achieved his end. In addition to the monks and Alexander Nevins, William Steward, a student, also came to help. Finally Pohl reported that "everything seemed to have donned a holiday dress."[9]

The work and its results generated a good atmosphere and a pervading aura of achievement at Maryhelp. But at least one person's spirits did not improve: the administrator and abbot-elect, Haid, did not profit from his new regimen and responsibility. The new superior was keenly aware, it seems, of how ill-prepared he was for the abbacy. He was young, inexperienced; his background was provincial and undistinguished. In monasteries, ambition for personal advancement is not a virtue, and Haid, who had been so happy with his balanced life of monastic routine and school duties, had not anticipated his acquisition of the mitre. He found nothing in his background or experience to explain or justify his promotion. And he, like every other monk both at Maryhelp and Saint Vincent, was fully conscious that he was no one's first choice for the office. His name had only been advanced as a replacement and a compromise candidate who was inoffensive and perhaps undistinguished enough to draw little dissent, and thus to expedite the election.

This was not the best foundation for confident leadership. For example, Haid immediately began writing sad letters to Wimmer, begging help and imploring extra men and supplies. Nevertheless, despite his depression and this consciousness of his inadequacies, Father Leo was determined to impart to his new charge some stamp of his own—or at least of his ambitions. Even in this disconsolation there surfaced the first gestures of independence, the first signs of a tentative departure from Wimmer's shadow. But it was a movement which Haid was reluctant to admit, and which he refused to flaunt. He secured his role and his abbatial identity in the only manner he knew: he tried to involve himself in every job, every duty the monks would have to fill. There was farm work, and painting and cleaning. On the first Sunday, 2 August, he took the public Mass himself, and preached.[10] The next day, rather than have his monks leave the monastery grounds, he personally undertook the buying trip, traveling all the way to Charlotte, and returning "abundantly supplied with everything in the line of culinary usefulness. It was, for the good brother cook, a gala day."[11]

In establishing new monasteries, Wimmer's ordinary practice had been to delay instituting the full monastic horarium until the foundation was well established. He maintained that in missionary monasteries the observance of the monks had to be adapted on occasion or in general according to circumstances. On Sundays in particular, when priestly obligations could be extensive, the daily schedule would be adjusted. But Leo Haid, in his first significant departure from the example of the archabbot of Saint Vincent, instituted the full monastic horarium on 8 August, less than two weeks after his arrival in North Carolina. And the decision was more than merely the first zeal of his new office. From being the staunch defender of Boniface Wimmer, with all the activity that implied, all the distraction that required, Leo Haid emerged with his new abbatial dignity as a determined champion of more traditional monastic values. There was nothing particularly extraordinary about the regimen Father Leo instituted except that it had come from him, and had come so early. He was determined to fight his inadequacies with serious effort, and so relied more heavily on the monastic theory he had learned in the *Regula* and during the novitiate, than on the very practical example of observance Wimmer had required in the earliest days of the various daughterhouses.

The horarium of 8 August[12] mandated above all else the choral recitation of the *Opus Dei*. For these common hours of prayer, the monks assembled in the house chapel or church and recited the psalmody antiphonally; the superior presided, and one of the monks, the hebdomadary, officiated. Meals were taken in silence or with reading; from Compline until after breakfast no talking was permitted.

The monks arose at fifteen minutes before four o'clock each morning, and appeared in choir for Matins and Lauds on the hour. These offices were the morning prayers, and consisted primarily of psalmody, hymns, and the day's most substantial Scriptural and patristic readings. Fifty minutes later there began a period of silence for meditation, followed by Mass at fifteen minutes past five o'clock. Each monk attended at least two Masses a day, since in addition to the public Mass at a quarter past five, each priest said Mass *sine populo*[13] assisted by a brother or another cleric.

At forty-five minutes past five o'clock there were brief offices, Prime and the "Little Hours," followed by breakfast at six o'clock. Lecture preparations, classes and work followed until fifteen minutes before noon, when the monks gathered for the Particular Examen, wherein they considered their weaknesses and sins, and were to resolve correction and amendment. Luncheon followed at noon, then Vespers at half past twelve.

Following the afternoon's labors, the monks did *lectio divina* at half past five. The evening meal was at six o'clock. At half past seven the last common exercises were held, Compline (night prayer) and devotions.

The horarium, instituted in all its rigors, was Haid's message of commitment. Though he did allow it to be interrupted briefly while the chapel was being painted and carpeted,[14] the schedule was intended to be essentially inviolable, concretizing the monastic emphasis Abbot Leo wished to promulgate and promote. He further buttressed his values by declaring that missionary work, Wimmer's special sphere of achievement, was to be the duty only of excess personnel, and not a primary apostolate. These were sound monastic values that the abbot-elect was sponsoring; they were ordinary and expected in established houses. But for a monastery that had acquired its personnel less than a month before, whose abbot was not yet blessed nor even confirmed by Rome, for a house in the middle of the nation's most non-Catholic state, and a monastery founded by Boniface Wimmer, these values were extraordinary, perhaps even premature. Leo Haid was aware, of course, that his neighbors in

Gaston County were primarily curious about black robes, mysterious hooded figures, bells at odd hours, and similar externals.[15] But the young abbot-elect wanted his monks characterized, in their own minds at least, primarily by the exigencies of monasticism, and he wasted no time before mandating a clearly monastic organization of daily life. It was the first evidence of the seriousness with which he intended to give his monastic duties and abbatial paternity precedence over all else.

The superior's early commitment was genuine, and the ever consonant Pohl was, of course, thrilled: the new horarium marked for him a "red letter day,"[16] and he prayed fervently, "God grant that we may punctually observe the various points to which our superior alluded."[17] Nevertheless, perhaps through his inexperience as an administrator, even in these earliest days Father Leo exhibited a quality that would repeatedly hurt his objectives throughout the years of his administration: over-diversification. While trying to clearly focus his monks' lives on their monastery, he fragmented their efforts and disoriented their labors. The monks were farming, painting, cleaning, building, preparing for a new school year, making contacts, receiving guests.[18] Haid had Brother Philip teach all the monks how to make wine.[19] And on the day he announced the school assignments for the year, the abbot-elect also began his first construction project, the east veranda—a concession to Southern living.[20]

The reverend administrator also made his first foray into the entanglements of the secular world during these early days in Garibaldi. This was an arena in which ecclesiastical muscle could not necessarily be depended upon. But Wimmer had been a master at earning his way—regardless of the forum—and Haid may have presumed such powers of persuasion came with the title. Father Leo, however, was not yet a master of the political skills that marked the archabbot's successes.

His first rebuke came from the Richmond and Danville Railway Company. Haid had petitioned the firm on 31 July to schedule a regular stop for trains number fifty-two and fifty-three at the Garibaldi station. This was primarily for the convenience of students. The petition was ignored. He requested this service again on 28 August. This time he got an immediate but negative response. A.L. Rives, a Vice President and General Manager, did however agree that the trains might stop if 1) Haid notified the Atlanta office in advance, and 2) the superintendent in Georgia thought the abbot-elect had "a sufficient number of passengers to justify" the stop.[21] In October he was even denied a clergy-pass for himself, though the company did at least express pleasure in "welcoming [Haid] to the sunny South."[22]

Father Leo's second pursuit of accommodation by secular authorities was somewhat more successful. The road from Garibaldi to the abbey was a narrow, muddy avenue that came within a few yards of the College Building—close enough for people to peer through the window as they passed—before taking a sharp turn west, then another northward to bypass the monastery. Haid considered the road both a nuisance and a danger. On one occasion he reported, "Last Saturday the Negroes had a PicNick [sic]. That night they made such a noise before the College that we were badly scared. One was shot a little down the road and one nearly stabbed to death. Five others were hurt. You see we must remove the road."[23]

This time Haid did get the results he wanted: the road was moved. It was only a partial victory, however, since the monastery had to assume responsibility for the weight of the work and expense.[24] The road remained a mere dirt surface—macadamized roads did not appear in Gaston County until 1906, when convict labor made such work feasible[25]—but it was at least moved. Still, Father Leo had not proven the man of influence he had expected to be, and as the beginning of the school term approached, he restricted the scope of his vision to the more immediate problems of the college.

Haid's first address to the professors of Saint Mary's College—seven of his monks[26]—was in keeping with his monastic emphasis for the fathers' varied labors. He reminded them of their religious duties primarily, and secondarily of the importance of their position as founders of Maryhelp and Saint Mary's College. They must pave the road to virtue, he warned, so that each succeeding generation could be confident in the wisdom of imitating their example.[27]

Educational theory fascinated Haid, and he had the highest regard for the type of instructors who were both edifying and erudite, and who thus imparted values as well as learning. Primarily because of these criteria, Pohl was retained as director of the college. He, more than any of the other six professors, was proven in the educational approach the abbot-elect wanted. Indeed, Pohl was the only administrative subordinate appointed at Maryhelp that year. There was no procurator, prior, subprior, master of novices or clerics. Only Father Julius shared the burden of leadership.

The institution that Haid envisioned promised above all else to give moral and religious training. In academic matters the instructors intended to "stimulate, test, and develop natural talents" while seeing that the training and scope of education were thorough.[28] "If learning, experience, and devotion to duty," Haid resolved, can contribute to the education of boys, then Saint Mary's College should be exemplary. "Nothing which will add to the spiritual or temporal well-being of [the] children will be wanting."[29]

The abbot-elect's enthusiasm for creating the proper environment for education occupied much of his time. He wrote the text for the school's charter himself,[30] fostering it so that when approved the following year, degrees could be granted in "various branches of science, literature, and the arts."[31] His interest in dramatics resurfaced, and he wrote longingly of the need for a campus theatre.[32] The students even produced *Saint Hermenegild of Spain.* He had Father Roman form a brass band.[33] And Father Leo established the debating society himself[34] and ordered leather bound volumes for recording its activities.[35]

abbot leo

Though his appointment as administrator imparted all necessary executive power over the monastery and school, Leo Haid could not assume abbatial authority—legitimate paternity over the monks—until the Holy See confirmed his election. The ordinary expectation was that no actions were taken in Rome during the stifling months of summer. Accordingly, a substantial delay was anticipated before Haid would be properly styled an abbot. Wimmer and his Roman allies pressed, however, and the confirmation was granted without problem on 30 August.

The American Cassinese's Procurator in Rome advised Wimmer of the decision at once, but his cable was considered an unofficial notice. The documents of confirmation, yet to be issued, constituted the legal notifcation of Rome's judgment. Once the decision had been made, an official text had to be composed, then executed by hand on vellum in duplicate, and weighted finally with the official seals. One copy would be dispatched then to the *praeses*, in this case Wimmer. Finally the archabbot would forward the document to Haid, whereupon protocol demanded that the local bishop—Henry Pinkney Northrop in Charleston, as head of the Vicariate Apostolic of North Carolina—be informed of the Confirmation before the news was released.

That sequence was followed only through the part where Wimmer received the documents. Then the procedure loosened somewhat, and affectionate but alien hands interceded. Before Archabbot Boniface could inform Haid that the papers had been posted, Father

Jerome Schmitt, O.S.B., of the archabbey, had already written Carolina.[36] The materials finally reached Wimmer on 21 October;[37] in the meantime, however, Haid had already told his monks of the confirmation, and Pohl had decided to plan a celebration for the day the documents reached Garibaldi. The papers were moving more quickly than the party arrangements, however, so Father Julius presumed to ask Wimmer to delay forwarding the documents to Abbot Leo. The archabbot no doubt registered some dismay at this request, but Pohl assured him that if "perhaps I am taking undue liberty," it was not from any "unworthy motive."[38]

Unbeknownst to Father Julius, Haid had already been in contact with Northrop—despite the absence of the documents. It was the bishop who would bestow the solemn abbatial blessing, and an impatient Father Leo had already made initial inquiries in September about the ceremony. Northrop decreed that the Blessing would take place in Charleston[39]—not Wilmington[40] or Garibaldi—but no date should be scheduled until the documents were actually issued and received. Again in the fall—still without seeing the authorization—Haid had requested Thursday, 26 November, Thanksgiving Day, for the blessing. He did not know that the Roman documents were then being delayed for the sake of party preparations.[41]

This time, aware that the papers were yet to appear, Northrop did not answer Haid's letter. Instead he had William Wright, one of his Charleston priests, inform Father Leo that the proposed date of the blessing was acceptable. This notification was, of course, unofficial. Nevertheless, on 1 November, Haid mailed both the invitations to the blessing and—to Archabbot Boniface—notice that at last the decree and letters were in his possession.[42]

Father Julius' party had inspired "great rejoicing" at Saint Mary's College. But for Leo Haid it also aroused a painful melancholy. "I think I am the only one who did not feel glad," he wrote Wimmer. The conflict of the monk, the son of Wimmer, caught now irreversibly in the active web of a new abbey, its college, and its missions, weighed heavily on the freshly confirmed abbot. He might want to keep his monks at their abbey, but he was also responsible for dependent monastic foundations in Savannah and Richmond. They were his to guide; they were his to staff. What overwhelmed Abbot Leo at this point, was the thought that he could not face these responsibilities without Wimmer. He wrote the archabbot

I hope, dear Father, you will not consider it a formality when I earnestly beg you to be with me on that day [of the abbatial blessing]. Indeed, I am only expressing the sincerest wish of my heart. Without you, the day would be a sorry one for me.[43]

It was a journey Wimmer dreaded. He was nearing his seventy-seventh birthday by this time, and his stamina was failing. But "I have to attend the solemnity," he complained to Joseph Amberger, "which means a long trip for me, during the winter—and it might mean being absent three or four weeks in all."[44] To Haid, however, the old man merely sent a promise of attendance. Wrote the abbot in return, "Oh, I wish everything was over!"[45] Wimmer, one assumes, concurred.

Haid drafted the invitations himself, giving them the cordial informality of an epistolary format:[46]

> Abbey of Saint Mary of Perpetual Help
> Garabaldi P.O., Gaston Co., N.C.
> October 1885
>
> You are cordially invited to be present at my Benediction which will take place in the Cathedral Chapel,[47] of Saint John the Baptist, Charleston, South Carolina, Thursday, 26 November at 9:30 a.m.
>
> Most fraternally,
> P. Leo Haid, O.S.B.
> Abbot

The text is striking in its humility. The rather egalitarian "most fraternally," replaced the first draft's more formal "very sincerely." The signature "P. Leo Haid" was the same as an ordinary priest would use. And the tone of the invitation seems clearly distanced from the aristocratic overtones that would appear later in his reign.

Haid's text for the invitation also included two errors.[48] He used the wrong title in reference to the titular and patroness of the abbey—"Perpetual Help" rather than "Help of Christians"—and the variant spelling of Garibaldi is substituted. The latter error may have been an effort to allay any suggestion that the town had some connection with the Italian politico of that name; the monks had also placed the alternative rendering on the stamp for the college library, for example, though they used the correct spelling for mailing purposes and the official catalogue of the school. There is no extant rationale, however, for either of the two inaccuracies in the invitation.

Gibbons, by this time archbishop of Baltimore, was invited to preach[49] at the first abbatial blessing for the monastery he helped establish. He neither preached, nor even attended, however, citing conflicts—he planned to be in Rome. The Bishop of Nashville,

Joseph Rademacher, who had studied at Saint Vincent, preached in his stead. Abbot Leo invited the bishops from Galveston, Mobile, Richmond, San Antonio, and Saint Augustine, too, as well as the three Benedictines who were bishops, from the Sees of Leavenworth, Yankton, and Saint Cloud. The abbots of Saint Vincent, Saint John (Minnesota), Saint Benedict (Kansas), Saint Mary (New Jersey), Saint Meinrad (Indiana), and Conception (Missouri) were invited, as was Isidor Robot from Sacred Heart in the Indian Territory.[50] Attendance, however, was rather disappointing. Haid, who was determined that everything "be made to accomodate our dear friends,"[51] found only a fraction of the invited dignitaries available. Wimmer, more experienced in the political overtones such occasions tended to acquire, gave the new abbot no sympathy. Bishop Keane of Richmond, Wimmer noted for example, should hardly have been expected since "with him the Benedictines rate only as brewers and drinkers of beer"[52]— a comforting observation, no doubt, for a new prelate who had to operate a mission in Keane's territory.

The solemn abbatial blessing of Leo Haid[53] was an unpretentious ceremony; yet because it was the first in the South it attracted considerable attention. Of Haid's monks, only Fathers Willibald, Melchior, and Julius—one from each of the monasteries—were present. Melchior was crucifer; Willibald was *ceremoniarius*, and Julius assisted. Of the bishops, only Northrop, who officiated, and Rademacher, who preached, attended. All of the Cassinese abbots were there, however: Wimmer (Saint Vincent), Edelbrock (Saint John), Wolf (Saint Benedict), and Zilliox (Saint Mary). The latter two served as the new abbot's pontifical chaplains in the ceremony.

The blessing, though small in scale, was not without solemnity. The official party processed into the chapel where Northrop, standing to the right of the altar, received the vestments of the Mass. Haid went to the side altar and donned the stole and cope. The abbot-elect read the profession of faith, after which the notary read the Apostolic Brief confirming the abbatial election. Northrop responded with *"Deo gratia."* Haid knelt before the episcopal Ordinary and took the oath of fidelity; he then underwent the examination. The Mass and the intricate ritual of the blessing—punctuated with excerpts from Haydn's *Creation*—proceeded, taking three hours and forty minutes. He received the *Regula* of Benedict, which it was now his solemn duty to preserve and to actualize with his monks, then a gold and amethyst ring—a gift from his mother[54]—which symbolized the obligation of constancy and fidelity; the abbatial mitre was placed on his head; the crozier, indicative of his stewardship over the monks of Maryhelp, was placed in his left hand. Abbot Leo Haid received the obeisance—a kiss of the ring—of Fathers Melchior, Willibald, and Julius representing the monks of Savannah, Richmond, and Garibaldi, respectively. The abbot passed through the church blessing the people, with Pohl at his side. Not until ten minutes past one o'clock that afternoon did Abbot Leo, dressed in the prelatial livery of his office, step outside the Chapel of the Baptist.

That afternoon, Northrop entertained the visiting and local clergy at the episcopal residence in Charleston, and Captain Young gave the guests a tour of the city's harbor aboard the tug *Monarch.* But the true finale was to be an address by the new abbot, presented that evening in the Cathedral Chapel. The bishop had requested the speech, and had scheduled it for that same, and already busy, day in order to capitalize on popular interest while memories of the morning's pageantry were fresh. The topic assigned to the speaker was monasticism.[55]

The address was Haid's first opportunity to expose both his erudition and his concept of monasticism to people outside the cloister. Dressed in his monastic habit, with the pectoral cross, zuchetto, and ring, the regalia of his abbatial character, Leo Haid recited a full hour of monastic history, with a pointed emphasis on the centuries of misunderstanding suffered by Benedictines. The response was not favorable. The audience found him too glib; the Pittsburgh *Dispatch* called the abbot "sarcastic."[56] Haid had overplayed the occasion. His images of people who had seen the first blessings of abbots—these "savage bands gazed in awe," he said, they were "fierce barbarians, [who] like pent-up wolves broke from their forest homes and spread ruin and desolation over civilized Europe"—overshadowed his explanations of monks and their purpose. The bombast outweighed the eloquence. That was especially unfortunate since the hour was not without moments of valuable revelation regarding the abbot's concept of the monastic ethos. But warring hoards of barbarians tended to seize the mind more readily than the "yearning in every human heart after solitude and quiet."[57] The speech was an embarrassing failure, and not the successful debut he had anticipated.

The five abbots—Wimmer, Edelbrock, Wolf, Zilliox, and Haid—left early Friday morning by train for Garibaldi. The excursion was Wimmer's idea. It not only got Abbot Leo out of town after his anticlimactic address of the previous evening, it also allowed the visiting abbots to "see for themselves the condition and prospect" of Maryhelp. The prelates spent two full days studying the foundation in Carolina, meeting students, and considering the future of the isolated abbey and its inexperienced leader. They left Monday morning admitting, according to Wimmer, "that the small monastery offers all that would be required for a speedy and prosperous development."[58] It is no longer possible to document whether the archabbot correctly surmised his colleagues' impressions, but there was at least one auspicious result of this journey: Abbot Alexius Edelbrock of Saint John Abbey and Abbot Leo developed what was to prove a lasting friendship that would bring considerable comfort to each prelate during the ensuing imbroglios for which their reigns would be noted. Leo Haid counted very few people as true friends, so the discovery of Edelbrock was of particular importance to him.

While the abbots of Saint John, Saint Benedict, and Saint Mary travelled northward on Monday, 30 November, those of Saint Vincent and Maryhelp went south to Savannah. The Georgia house was to be the most successful of Haid's dependencies eventually, and already showed great promise. It was older than Maryhelp; its land mass was greater; the local Catholics were supportive. All it seemed to lack was abbatial rank. And were the project not situated so far south, Savannah rather than Garibaldi would surely have been the abbey erected in 1884.

Dom Garbriel Bergier, O.S.B., a monk of Subiaco, and Dom Raphael Wissel, O.S.B., from Pierre-qui-Vire, had established the Savannah monastery in 1874, centering their work at property on the Isle of Hope. In 1878, a large block of land on Skidaway Island was added to their holdings. But the yellow fever epidemic in Savannah left the Benedictines with little future there, and too much loss to recoup. So the remnant was removed to the more promising territory of Oklahoma, and Boniface Wimmer agreed to staff the abandoned Savannah monastery. Oswald Moosmueller was appointed the first superior, arriving in Savannah on 1 March 1877, and he had been there since then, working primarily with the blacks through parochial ministry and a small industrial school. The foundation was ceded to the Carolina monastery when the latter achieved the abbatial rank.

Wimmer had given the Savannah mission to Maryhelp, however, without deigning to remove his own personnel. And in the four days Haid and the archabbot spent together in Savannah no action was taken to correct the situation. So when the two abbots left—both men going to Atlanta, and from there Wimmer toward Chattanooga and Haid back to Garibaldi—Oswald Moosmueller of Saint Vincent was still in charge, with Melchior Reichert of Maryhelp under him. Relations were quickly and severely strained.

The problem was that Moosmueller, who was primarily responsible for the success of the Savannah mission, had no desire to leave his work there, or to subordinate it to the monks of the new abbey. Had Father Oswald followed Wimmer's suggestion and joined Maryhelp's founding monks, the new abbot could have kept the same staff in Savannah, leaving Moosmueller's ministry intact. But since the older priest had refused to transfer stability, and had shown hostility toward the young foundation, Haid was obliged, as the major superior, to insure that his own abbey assumed true responsibility for Benedictine life in Savannah.

Initially, however, Haid had been open to the prospect of Moosmueller remaining temporarily in Savannah. Father Oswald was a popular, well established Benedictine representative, and the longer his attachment to Savannah was allowed to endure, it seemed reasonable to presume, the more the prospects of his affiliating with Maryhelp increased. Moreover, because Abbot Leo was short of personnel, and one of his monks, Father Melchior, was already assigned to Georgia, Garibaldi had no other priests to contribute conveniently to the Savannah work. Accordingly, when in 1885 word circulated that Moosmueller would leave his work with the blacks, Haid had to appeal to Wimmer for the replacement. The congregation under Father Oswald was very promising and required experienced hands, he said; the archabbot would have to supply someone.[59] Accordingly, Wimmer left Moosmueller in Georgia, and retained control *de facto* if not *de jure.* Haid was in no position, and had no inclination, to fight the Pennsylvania abbot, and assured his mentor, "Whatever you may do there I certainly will be grateful for."[60] While on that first visit to Georgia, however, Abbot Leo did take the precaution of having the corporate structure transferred to the jurisdiction of Maryhelp,[61] and Wimmer was pleased at his largess in having "turned it over to him."[62]

The Ordinary of Savannah in 1885 was William Gross, C.SS.R. Bishop Gross' brother, Mark, was a priest of the Vicariate Apostolic of North Carolina, stationed at this time at Saint Peter in Charlotte. Mark Gross was in a good position to study the new abbot at Maryhelp and advise his brother, the bishop of Savannah. As a result, both the Gross brothers thought highly of Haid, and made every effort to promote his work. Unfortunately for good diocesan relations in Savannah, however, Bishop Gross was promoted in 1886 to the archiepiscopal See of Oregon City.

During the substantial interregnum that followed for the Church in Savannah, Father Edward Cafferty served as administrator of the diocese. This priest, a confidant of Father Oswald's, bore no particular affection for Haid or his activities in the Diocese of Savannah. Within a month, Cafferty was ready to issue a formal complaint against the Carolina Benedictines. Claiming to have been informed—apparently by Moosmueller—that Haid was "corresponding with Reverend Father Melchior with the view of giving up, or moving the industrial School for colored boys on Skidaway Island," the diocesan administrator wrote a rather caustic reprimand to Wimmer.[63] This was brash on several counts: 1) neither Wimmer nor Haid was first *asked* about the situation on Skidaway; thus they were accused without contrary evidence being requested; 2) the legitimate superior in Georgia, Haid, was snubbed on the pretext of the original invitation into the diocese having been extended not to Abbot Leo, but to Boniface Wimmer;[64] 3) the archabbot was being rebuked for a situation not technically under his jurisdiction: and 4) the letter carried a particularly insulting reference for an autonomous Benedictine abbot, in this case Haid, wherein the head of the Garibaldi abbey was described as a "subordinate" of Wimmer's.[65] Both abbots were incensed.

The roots of the rumor lay in Haid's desire for an economical and efficient arrangement of Benedictine personnel in Georgia. Because the monks' labors were so dispersed in Savannah, with parish work in the city, a chapel on Isle of Hope, and the monastery, industrial school and farm at Skidaway, more monks were required than the labor justified. Time and efficiency were destroyed by the fragmentation of efforts. Moosmueller, whose work centered on the parish, wanted to insure the retention of that apostolate even though it offered less land and security for the monastery than did the rest of the Georgia project. Cafferty, as administrator *sede vacante*, was required to hand over the diocese intact when the new bishop took office. Moreover, decree 407 of the Second Plenary Council of Baltimore, he charged, required a six months notice before an Order could abandon such an apostolate. It was Cafferty's intention not only to secure what church law required, and to delay or block a reduced Benedictine presence in Savannah, but to insure that Moosmueller's apostolate would be saved as well. "It is obvious that the house on Skidaway needs the house in the City," he wrote Wimmer, "both must be kept and work together and must not be separated."[66]

The affair was settled easily, since Haid had not seriously entertained closing Skidaway anyway. But the necessity of staffing Savannah with his own men became even more obvious, and Abbot Leo began considering the necessary shifts in personnel that would facilitate the departure of Oswald Moosmueller.

But by summer, there appeared to be yet another problem in Savannah, this one more pressing than the first. This time Moosmueller reported to Haid that Father Melchior, who usually lived on Skidaway, apart from any other priests, was taking to drink. Haid immediately recalled Reichert to Maryhelp, hoping to prevent scandal, and Wimmer was persuaded to send Cyprian Creagh to assist in the Savannah work. At the abbey, Father Melchior was found to be suffering from exhaustion rather than effects of alcohol.[67]

In Father Melchior's absence, Oswald Moosmueller moved to acquire for himself the new parish of Saint Benedict the Moor in Savannah.[68] Wimmer acquiesced, on the condition that it be turned over to the Carolina abbey. This was not, however, what Moosmueller had in mind. Agreeing in principle, Father Oswald suggested to Wimmer that Abbot Leo should only take possession of the Savannah missions one place at a time. And until Haid was able to staff this new parish, Father Oswald should plan to live in town, while Maryhelp's men resided at Skidaway. And if one of Haid's priests "likes to come in town for a certain Sunday to preach in my Church, I will pay them for it."[69]

Not necessarily by coincidence, Abbot Leo suddenly decided he had two priests too many assigned to the college in Garibaldi. And since it was imperative by this time that from Haid's men "someone becomes acquainted with the Savannah Parish,"[70] Father Patrick Donlon was sent to Georgia to replace Father Cyprian, at least for the present. Moosmueller understood what was happening, and finally concluded, "I supposed the best will be that I make myself also ready to leave the diocese."[71] Wimmer concurred, and at his instruction Father Oswald agreed to write Abbot Leo tendering all the Savannah missions "into his care."[72]

Of course, all of these machinations were being undertaken without consulting Haid. Boniface Wimmer, a patriarch to the end, was still supervising the Savannah missions he had theoretically abandoned more than a year before. And since the archabbot had already announced Saint Vincent's intention to remain in Savannah for yet another year, Oswald Moosmueller's letter of resignation, addressed to Haid, who was not even the man's superior, posed a substantial shock. Abbot Leo was in the difficult position of wanting control of his missions, being uncertain of his resources for staffing them, contemplating the potential damage from Moosmueller's diatribes if that priest were forced out of his Savannah work, and above all of not wanting to offend Boniface Wimmer. "In a former letter you said you wished to keep Savannah, etc. for another year," he lamented to the archabbot.

> I do not wish to do anything in this matter except I have definite informa-
> tion from you; if you wish to keep the places for one year more, I am

satisfied; but if you think it better that I should take them now very well, I will, but write *immediately*. I then will write to Father Oswald and *appoint some older Priest* to take his place. From his letter it would seem he wishes to go.[73]

Finally, it was again decided that Moosmueller would remain in Savannah. George Lester, a priest of Maryhelp, was sent to help Father Melchior during the week and Father Oswald on Sundays.[74] And the contretemps was clearly resolved in favor of all of Oswald Moosmueller's desires. He even acquired to the bonus of a non-resident assistant, Father Lester.

When Bishop Thomas Becker of Wilmington, Delaware, was transferred to the See of Savannah, Moosmueller wasted no time in ingratiating himself with the prelate. The result this time was a reported episcopal recommendation that the Savannah Benedictines be constituted a central mission station, with their own novitiate. And as Father Oswald cunningly wrote Wimmer, the new bishop "understands very well, that Abbot Leo is not able to do what he wants and expects that the Benedictines should do for this Mission."[75]

With this scheme Moosmueller's days in Savannah finally earned a deadline. Haid refused to entertain any motions for Saint Vincent acquiring yet another year in Georgia. By summer, Abbot Leo was totally enraged with Moosmueller, his murmurings against the Maryhelp Benedictines, and his efforts to sabotage relations with Becker. He wrote to Wimmer,

> Our Fathers with good reasons do not wish to live under Father Oswald, and I cannot expect it. Father Oswald first wanted to take Savannah from us and make it independent. Then he wished to unite it to Florida–then to Newark. This certainly does not look as if he cared for us. He would have been welcome had he desired to join us–but this he will not do. If he remains in Savannah, our Fathers can beg–for all money will go to him. He has the confidence of the Bishop too, and in every way it would be better for us if you could appoint him to another field. I appreciate his labors–at least his good intentions–but that is no reason why we should bear the burden. I labored for fifteen years in the College and had to be satisfied to go into a new place too. Personally I have nothing against Father Oswald; but it will never do any good as long as two monasteries are working in the same place–as the affair stands in Savannah. I only make these suggestions; you are still at liberty to do as you please.[76]

It was a surprisingly strong declaration of autonomy for Haid to issue, and it brought the Savannah conflict into the open definitively. This time the abbot of Maryhelp was determined to outflank Oswald Moosmueller.

Father Melchior, presumed innocent of Moosmueller's charges of intoxication, had returned to Savannah, but the Saint Vincent

Benedictine wasted no time in raising the charges anew.[77] Accordingly, the following summer, Reichert was again recalled to the abbey, where he lived "more like a Saint than a bad man as he was described."[78] And by July Haid had resolved to end Moosmueller's interference in the work of Maryhelp.

Becker scheduled an interview with Haid that same month. Melchior Reichert, they agreed, was guilty of no offenses, and should be reassigned to Savannah. It was further arranged that Maryhelp would station three priests at the Skidaway monastery, from which they could cover Sacred Heart parish, Skidaway, and Saint Benedict the Moor; they would also be willing, the abbot suggested, to receive male negro orphans at Skidaway. The new arrangements increased the efficiency of the Benedictines' apostolic activity in Georgia, and by having the monks live in community, Haid would "not expose anyone to the dangers of living alone; at the same time they can encourage and help each other."[79] There was no more need for Oswald Moosmueller in Savannah. Haid wrote Wimmer, "You can call Father Oswald away in eight or ten days." Father William became prior of the monastery; Melchior Reichert took over Moosmueller's charge; and George Lester administered Skidaway. The deeds and official papers were transferred from Father Oswald to Abbot Leo in the presence of Bishop Becker, and the troublesome "divided jurisdiction," as Becker called it, was officially at an end.[80]

Life in Carolina

The turmoil in Savannah was not the only problem of Leo Haid's early years in Garibaldi. Even nature seemed to conspire against him. He found poisonous copperheads on the grounds;[81] the trees were endangered by the county-wide blight;[82] the winter of 1885-1886 was one of the coldest ever, with temperatures as low as thirteen degrees below zero, and ice six inches deep on ponds.[83] The most dramatic of the first year's calamities was the Charleston earthquake. It occured at the end of August 1886, with after-shocks continuing for months.[84] The quake was strong enough to shake Gaston County residents from their beds,[85] although at Maryhelp the only real damage consisted of some cracked arches in the College Building.[86]

A more constant problem for Haid was his chief boarder, Father O'Connell. There is no reason to doubt the old priest's good intentions or his faith in Maryhelp. Through these Benedictines, he believed, "the sacred influence of religion will be spread around until the wilderness will blossom like the rose, and the praises of God day and night fill the air, breathe in the valleys, and mingle with the voice of the waters."[87] And Haid responded to the man with genuine warmth and solicitude. He praised his boarder's kindness,[88] and worried about his illnesses;[89] Abbot Leo even gave O'Connell a Benedictine habit and cuculla, which reportedly made the old man as happy as "a boy who wears his first boots."[90]

But Jeremiah O'Connell also displayed what the abbot charitably described as "a great interest in everything."[91] And various frictions developed. The clerics objected to studying theology, as Pohl had done, under their secular counterpart. This left the abbot to handle the duties of Master in the theologate.[92] O'Connell expressed constant displeasure about Brother Cornelius, who had served as the old priest's manservant since before Haid had even seen North Carolina. Brother's rheumatism, it seemed, interfered with waiting upon the clergyman.[93] So Haid was pressured into making his first shift within his limited personnel in Carolina, replacing the rheumatic servant with Brother Bruno.[94]

Father O'Connell also quarreled with another brother during Haid's first months in the South. In an effort to lure him into a permanent affiliation with Maryhelp, Philip Cassidy was invited to North Carolina at the end of August 1885. Remembering O'Connell's past friendship with the Irish brother, the two men were lodged together in the priest's cottage. But without Herman Wolfe to amuse them, the two Irishmen turned on one another. They quarreled. O'Connell petitioned Haid to remove Brother Philip from the premises, and in the interest of domestic peace, Cassidy was permanently lost to Maryhelp.[95]

With O'Connell at the center of so much contention, at least Abbot Leo had the comfort of the priest's enjoying separate living arrangements. In this way, the monks and the old missionary could achieve a comfortable distance when conditions demanded. It was, then, a double shock when the monks were awakened at three o'clock, on the morning of 9 January 1886, by the flames of Father O'Connell's cottage, just a few feet from the monastery.

The priest's house was a frame structure, and once the fire started it spread readily. Some furniture was saved, but few of the old man's mementos and possessions were spared. And there was no insurance on the cottage.[96]

In the cellar beneath O'Connell's residence the "New Catawba Mass Wine," made by the monks, was stored.[97] All twenty-eight gallons of that were lost when the brothers mistakenly saved a cask of vinegar instead of the altar wine.[98] Two hundred empty bottles were sacrificed, as well,[99] along with the seeds for the spring crops.[100] It was a costly fire for both the monks and for Jeremiah O'Connell. Nevertheless, Haid was thankful for the warning the fire granted, "for had the wind turned only a little, nothing could have saved our frame [monastery]."[101] Never again, the abbot resolved, would wooden structures be placed in such close proximity to one another.[102]

While awaiting construction of a new dwelling, Father O'Connell moved into the monastery, where he complained of discomfort and missing possessions.[103] "He does not wish to remain [in the monastery]," wrote Haid, "nor do I want him."[104] This mutual displeasure did not, however, speed agreement regarding the type of dwelling to be constructed for the old gentleman. Abbot Leo wanted to erect a brick house of some size, one that could later serve as a guest lodge, and immediately double as a residence for visiting priests. O'Connell objected, out of fear that he would be impeded from his desire to live alone, and he finally won because he refused to contribute more than two hundred dollars toward the cost of a new building, whatever size it was. So a small, four room, frame cottage was designed and carefully erected by the brothers.[105] Haid had it positioned a safe twenty-five yards south of the center of his campus.[106] The abbot's cost totalled about one hundred dollars, plus a month of labor by the brothers.[107]

While dealing with O'Connell was initiating the young abbot in techniques of diplomacy and domestic bargaining, other skills— equally necessary—were being sought by Haid. Agricultural exper- tise was the most pressing of these. Wimmer, of course, had loved far- ming, and proposed it as a positive virtue. Benedict too provided for this work. Yet although Abbot Leo acquired a reputation as "a reasonable and zealous farmer...almost as proud of his cows and his farm and fields as of Church and Cloister,"[108] he detested the work, and accepted it only as an obligation.[109] His one determination was that the abbey farm be a paying proposition.[110] Accordingly, the more experienced Brother Stephen was made the farm's immediate supervisor, and winter grains and summer staples kept the land in constant use.[111] The abbot ordered an additional one hundred sixty acres cleared for his crops; a peach orchard was planted; the vineyard expanded; a vegetable garden for house supplies supplemented the larger crops. Haid had seven dairy cows, and he did the milking himself, alongside "my faithful darkey."[112] He found wild strawberries on the grounds, too, and had them harvested.[113] By the spring of 1886, he could already boast confidently, "Farming will pay this year."[114]

In his first months in North Carolina, Haid farmed, ruled his monks, followed the monastic horarium, gave missions, taught in the college, taught the theologians twice daily, learned wine making, juggled personnel and finances. At the end of only nine weeks in the South he reported a loss of seventeen pounds[115] from his already slight frame. But he refused either to slow his pace or appoint other officials. Monks were in short supply, and he accepted a plethora of duties that should have been shared, covered by as many as five men. "I am just driven to work by circumstances," he reported to Zilliox, "in fact my poor conscience squeezes me awfully for idleness at times."[116]

Both the personnel problem and the burden of Haid's conscience and personal work load were rooted in the stricter level of monastic observance he expected of his monks. Wimmer, for all his failings, his gruffness, his self will and determination, was a deeply pastoral man. He enjoyed the paternalistic duties that followed on priestly solicitude. Benedictine moderation was a sacred trust, in the archabbot's view, a peculiarly astute psychological insight into the guidance of men toward God. But Haid had no parish experience, and the only souls he had guided were those of carefully supervised young men in the seminary in Pennsylvania. He had not yet learned the balance required in spiritual paternity any more than he had a concept of the diplomacy needed for handling an old man like O'Connell. Lacking the skilled use of such tools as subtlety, he resorted to work as an answer, personal hard labor. He depended on energy and effort to supply for the talents he neither understood nor believed to be at his command or within his potential.

Theologically, Abbot Leo's principles of monastic life centered on the proposition, "God is a necessity in life." In the secular world, men were distracted from the Deity by the pressing demands of their possessions, he suggested. For this reason, goods were—ideally, at least—put aside so the monk could focus on the one true necessity, God. Then, because the Divinity was not indifferent regarding His service by man, He offered the monastic vocation; He called some men to this particular focus on the Lord. The monk abandoned possessions, turned his life, work, and thoughts to God, and thusly recognized the Godhead as the "all sufficient possession," one that was able to lend peace to the soul and to satisfy its longing. On a more external level, the monk served the two-fold purpose of being a holy offering—a sacrifice—to God, and of edifying, being an example to other men.[117] But the monks' abandonment of things "of the world" was a basic and essential element of their lives. It was also the reason they were willing to exert the extraordinary effort their abbot asked of them, and to give themselves totally to the values and conditions of monasticism.

Haid reasoned that his monks should recognize an obligation in their monastic lives to strive after perfection, to be a saint, to be "in miniature a picture of God." That in turn should support both their vocations to holiness, and to sacrifice and edification, and thus prove a support for their spirituality and their work. In this intricate admixture of God and man, personal needs and charitable efforts, Leo Haid found the font for "the holy enthusiasm which animated the children of Saint Benedict." It was an exciting and real element of theology, of the presence of Divinity in his life. For him, "it makes monastic life sweet, lightens every cross, and seasons every deed."[118] As abbot, he considered it his duty to communicate these principles to the monks of Maryhelp. Each was to exhibit the focus on God through sacrifice and edification.

To aid the monks in considering the integrity of their monastic lives, Abbot Leo drew up a spiritual inventory of twenty questions. The list was generally undistinguished, drawing on the basic elements ordinarily represented in such documents and in the monstic *Rituale*. What was of special note was the question he wrote at the head of the list, underscoring its emphasis: "Do I really *long* to become a Perfect Religious?"[119] This was the crux for the abbot of Maryhelp, and there was little he would not do for willing spirits who did manifest this longing. It even prompted him to offer periods of trial at Maryhelp to at least twenty monks who had proven unsuitable at their original monasteries. He intended to be

> kind to them all. I look upon each [monk] as called by God, and treat them accordingly. Yet, I must see to it that the *Rule* is kept. But I never correct one harshly. I preach to them every Sunday, and find no difficulty in keeping them to their duties. As they are the first, I must see to it that those who follow will have a good example to imitate.[120]

Nevertheless, at the same time, there was nothing Haid proved less capable of understanding throughout the years of his monastic tenure, than an unwilling spirit. Recalcitrance, ill will, deception, these mystified him, and he was never able to deal effectively with the weaker spirits who came to his monastery. His one answer was activity. "I must have work for my priests,"[121] he would lament; indeed, he intended never to have more men at his disposal than there was work to keep them occupied.[122]

The great variable in the scheduling of the duties of Maryhelp's monk-priests was pastoral work. In his first two years, when men were in short supply, the abbot gradually relinquished some of the parochial commitments in North Carolina. Lincolnton was retained, as was Saint Mary and Saint Joseph, about four miles from the abbey. But Dallas was discontinued permanently; the monks withdrew from frequent visitations of Salisbury, Greensboro, Statesville, and Winston; Saint James in Concord became irregular. The only mission added was Saint Benedict, a chapel Haid had constructed on the abbey's grounds for the blacks—who he believed were uncomfortable in the company of southern whites.[123]

Regarding priests, however, the monastery was growing at a very respectable rate. So the initial reduction of pastoral commitments may not have been as permanent in intention as it first seemed. In December of 1885, Bishop Northrop went to the abbey to preside at its first ordinations. On Thursday, 17 December, Roman Kirchner and Charles Mohr were ordained subdeacons; on Friday, Kirchner and Mohr, plus Patrick Donlon, Walter Leahy, and George Lester were raised to the deaconate. And on Saturday, Lester, Donlon, and Leahy were admitted to the presbyterate. The abbot concluded, "God's blessing rests on the labors of the new Benedictine Community."[124]

In March of 1886, Hintemeyer was ordained a priest and finally journeyed to his new abbey. Haid's first three novices, Benedict Roth, Bernard Haas, and Francis Meyer were summoned to Maryhelp from the Congregation's novitiate at Saint Vincent, arriving on the twelfth. On 22 June, Mohr and Kirchner were ordained priests. Frederick Mueller became the first student in the school to enter the Benedictine novitiate for Maryhelp; he was received on 10 July. The next day the older three novices pronounced their vows, after which Haid administered the Minor Orders for the first time. "I am so glad these young people are so good,"[125] he wrote Abbot Alexius in Minnesota. Mueller, who took the name "Joseph" in religion, was sent to Saint Vincent for his novitiate training. He "has shown a good will," Haid told Wimmer, "and I hope, as he has talents, he will do well"[126]

Indeed, there was a great deal of talent being manifested in Haid's cadre of clerical monks. Father Roman showed signs of gifts for managerial and pastoral work. Leahy was turning into a forceful young man, a leader possessed of strong convictions. Father Charles showed academic promise. And Abbot Leo was determined that all these skills and interests should be developed and wisely employed. But one man surfaced who was not only gifted and intelligent, but who was also destined to become as close to a personal friend as Haid would ever know at Maryhelp during his years as abbot. There would be various warm professional friendships—such as the one with Edelbrock—but few instances of genuine friendship with those whom the abbot encountered daily. And surprisingly, it was not Julius Pohl with whom these ties developed. Father Julius, although idolized by the boys, was never at ease with the younger monks who entered Maryhelp. He became moody and even had to be coaxed from his cell,[127] until finally Abbot Leo sent the priest to other work.

The man who became Haid's closest advisor and friend was young Felix Hintemeyer, the intellectual cleric who had remained at Saint Vincent in 1885 for advanced studies. Hintemeyer was that rare combination of gentleness, leadership, and devotion that Haid considered ideal in his monks. Father Felix was a bespectacled man of almost twenty-five when he reached Maryhelp in 1886. A bit of baby fat made him appear even younger, while his wavy hair was reminiscent of his abbot's at that age. Hintemeyer was tender-hearted, too. He loved the sisters when they moved near the abbey, and he had a special fondness for children. He even chose to celebrate his silver jubilee by having a grand first communion Mass for twenty-five children.[128]

Hintemeyer was a remarkably humble man who dedicated his actute intellect as well as the full breadth of his spirit to the needs of his monastery, and more particularly to his abbot. Father Felix had the personal confidence and clarity of vision, balanced by genuine selflessness and ready chairty, that made him Leo Haid's ideal complement. He shared with the abbot intellectual interests, pedagogical skills, a common piety, and thorough devotion to the Order, the abbey, and their work. He surpassed the abbot in the ability to deal with subordinates. But the true distinction of Felix Hintemeyer's service was the ability and desire to focus that intellect, will, and talent on a single person or cause. In this case the person was Leo Haid; the cause was the "glorification of God" through Maryhelp Abbey. His selflessness and imposing capabilities were channeled into the manifestation of a loyalty he never compromised. Through that virtue, Hintemeyer gave the abbot a support that existed in no other forum of his jurisdiction.

Felix Hintemeyer had originally committed himself to Maryhelp with reluctance and reservations. The young man "dread[ed] the unknown evils [down] in poor North Carolina—which...even Saint Benedict could not find."[129] As abbot-elect, Haid encouraged Hintemeyer, however, thinking this intelligent young man a potential professor for the planned seminary.[130] Then as the two men grew closer, Father Felix was gradually invested with virtually every position of trust and major importance that required proximity to the abbot. The first of these assignments was *ceremoniarius*, which he assumed immediately upon his arrival in North Carolina. The rest of his life was given to the interests of Abbot Leo Haid.

But just as Maryhelp's clerical monks were full of promise, its brothers were full of trouble. Brother Cornelius had a violent temper and terrorized the others.[131] It seemed Brother Adalbert, the baker, could not cook,[132] so Haid sought to send the man back to Saint Vincent. It was later discovered that Brother Adalbert was a fine baker, but his flour had been sabotaged, apparently by one of the other brothers.[133] Brother Altman was sickly, and Brother Bartholomew had rheumatism and wanted to go back to Pennsylvania.[134] Brother Amandus was more interested in being a boss than a gardener and stonemason.[135] Brother Bruno was bitter, and returned to Wimmer.[136] Then Haid received a negro candidate, Brother John, for the monastery. Brother Cornelius tried to lead a small revolt, claiming the abbot "preferred Niggers to Brothers."[137] Finally Cornelius settled for an animated quarrel with Brother John, after which the black left for the sake of peace.[138] Cornelius was finally shipped back to the archabbey in Pennsylvania.[139]

Boniface Wimmer grew increasingly impatient with his protege in Carolina as the stream of requests to exchange brothers continued.[140] Haid too was exasperated, but he could see no alternative to the appeals to the archabbot. The Carolina brothers were largely German-speaking men of humble origins, who resented English-speaking personnel. When a potential native vocation appeared, his perseverance became little more than an endurance test—one which the American invariably failed. Also, since few brothers wished to be stranded in North Carolina, there was no affinity for the monastery,[141] and thus no stability.

Finally the abbot resolved "not to receive anyone here who does not wish to make [Maryhelp] his home."[142] And he asked Wimmer to supply him with enough manpower for a permanent staff.

> *Please help me immediately....*I want *all* German Brothers, *Green* Germans if you like. They agree better than when nationalities are mixed. I need three men for the farm and such labor. These I have. I need four in the kitchen; one in the refectory, one in the College. I have enough if you send me three for the two I will send you. Please *don't send anyone who does not wish to make this his home.*[143]

In another letter of specifications, Abbot Leo said no "growlers" were to be sent south.[144] He also suggested that Wimmer should cover the cost of transporting all these men between Pennsylvania and Carolina.[145] And finally he asked if the archabbot could send two middle-aged, German Catholic, male seculars who had no taste for beer, and who could work with both food and cows.[146] Boniface Wimmer was not pleased.

Break With Wimmer

Abbot Leo was generally oblivious of Wimmer's annoyance. Even when the archabbot began picking petty quarrels, the abbot of Maryhelp insisted on taking invective as if it were paternal advice.

An argument typical of their disagreements occured over Haid's sale of a thirty year old mule in order to acquire a horse for the missions, plowing, and O'Connell's buggy. Wimmer railed against Haid's imprudence. And in response Abbot Leo comforted the archabbot with the news that the horse was too lame to be fast, and thus was perfectly safe.[147]

Wimmer tired quickly from trying to please the abbot in the South. He even kept North Carolina's deeds in Pennsylvania, apparently as part of his pique. Haid pleaded for them to be sent, since without them he could not get insurance.[148] But the transferral of land from Saint Vincent to Maryhelp was not finalized until the summer of 1886.[149]

Next Haid annoyed Wimmer by summoning Maryhelp's novices south before the completion of their novitiate. The response of Haid to this explosion by Abbot Boniface presented the same innocent appearance Abbot Leo had used in the mule controversy: Haid asked Zilliox to help him petition Rome for a separate novitiate, lest "the good Archabbot [who] does not like my doings" should be taxed again.[150] This time Abbot Boniface was even more infuriated than before.

What Wimmer, a natural leader who enjoyed power from the beginning, seems never to have realized was that Leo Haid was unhappy and lonesome; he had only accepted North Carolina out of duty; and he dreaded the responsibility of the abbacy. "I have always had a dread of official life," he wrote to Father Prior Michael at Saint Vincent, "even though my Priests give me every reason to be grateful."[151] When a man is elected abbot, he later explained, "you just accept. The community has called you, and you must respond."[152] For that reason, he had accepted the burden of the abbatial office, but the loss of Wimmer's favor was a weight he had not expected and was not prepared to bear. "I feel lonesome,"[153] he finally admitted after his first Christmas in Carolina. He begged Wimmer to pray for the Carolina monks and at least "think we are trying to do well."[154] But there were no words of encouragement or support in response. What was manifested as confusion and a lack of ease in the first days of Haid's reign finally developed into a seriously depressed state.

In the spring of that already painful year, Haid went to Pittsburgh, gave his mother Viaticum, and watched her die. The death of his step-father came one week later. The young abbot's depression continued to grow. He wrote frequent letters and expressions of devotion to his old mentor during this period, but none elicited the desired response from Wimmer. Gradually, Abbot Leo modified his tone. From "rejoicing in the hope of seeing you soon," "with sincere affection," and "your son," the closings of his letters turned to sundry variations of "sincerely" and a more formal hue overall.[155]

Haid even toyed with the idea of resigning from office. And when Zilliox was relieved of the mitre, Abbot Leo admitted he wanted to congratulate the New Jersey prelate. "The idea of 'Liberty' must be most grateful to you,"[156] he wrote.

The abbot was finally roused from his depression, and forced to resign himself to the status of the Wimmer situation, by pressing matters in North Carolina. Maryhelp was growing. Students were enrolling; new monks were joining. More space was needed immediately. O'Connell had resisted Abbot Leo's first plans for brick buildings, but this time the old priest could not countermand the abbot's ambitions. A brick college was necessary and would be erected. And the building was to symbolize Leo Haid's slowly emerging confidence and ambition. Construction work was the activity he chose for raising his own spirits and commitment to Maryhelp.

CRESCAT

In his first month at the abbey, Haid happened upon a brother about to fell a cedar near the front entrance of the chapel.[157] The abbot stopped the effort with the Latin command, "*crescat*," which means, "let it grow." The "*crescat* tree," as it came to be known, then stood until 1960 when lightning finished what the brother had started.

The image of the tree was impaled in 1885 on the abbot's and the abbey's first escutcheon, and "*crescat*" was designated Maryhelp's motto. Although Abbot Leo was inconsistent in his heraldic devices, their use and application, he took the *crescat* theme as a serious obligation, and became rather impassioned during his first fifteen years in the South about the necessity of having growth—witnessed in construction projects—in progress.

Archabbot Boniface had ordered Abbot Leo to undertake no new buildings during his acclimation to abbatial life, and the younger man had informed Wimmer of his acquiescence in the directive.[158] In his first five months in Carolina, the new abbot spent merely six hundred fifty dollars on necessary minor improvements, and in January of 1886, he proudly reported a balance of eleven hundred dollars in his favor. Finances looked good, he said, but there was something for which Maryhelp needed to use those surplus funds. And—presumably with some caution—he finally said it: "Room is what we must have and soon."[159]

Building O'Connell's cottage had whetted an appetite that would never be fully sated. Visions of rising buildings, invariably of brick with auburn coloring, ignited Leo Haid's sensibilities more than anything else outside of religion. And his first rationale for a building project was a masterful piece of evocative writing. It was intended to convince Wimmer that a new brick College Building should be erected, so the poor monks—shivering at that very moment in their pitiful frame "monastery"—could move into the current brick college. He wrote,

> The weather has been terribly cold for four or five days; I never experienced so much discomfort. The house is very good for summer—plenty of air, but for winter it is a total failure. We said our Matins in the refectory; the prime and hours in my room *with overcoats*—some wore gloves. All are pressing to build enough, so that we can use part at least of the old College for a monastery. I feel I must do something for them...[160]

Wimmer responded with a promise to send Brother Wolfgang Traxler, O.S.B., who was skilled in both architecture and construction supervision. But, the archabbot cautioned, no more should be built than Maryhelp could afford.

Unfortunately, that idea was unappealing to Haid. "Your proposal to build as we have the money," he reasoned, "would keep us from getting money for want of room to take students." Accordingly, Abbot Leo proposed not only to borrow the money, but to have Wimmer arrange for the loan, secure the lowest possible interest rate, and put up the security. He was sure Maryhelp could at least meet the interest payments on a three year loan. And besides, "a little debt will also give me help in enforcing Poverty in my community."[161]

The Bohemian-born Traxler reached Carolina on 24 February. Brother Wolfgang was a vigorous man of thirty-one in 1886, twelve years professed, and more skilled than Pilz as a builder. Unlike Father Placidus' brick-based wing, Traxler's was to have a firm granite foundation. Within two days of the young man's arrival, Haid wrote Wimmer that lumber had been selected, windows, sashes, and plastering priced. They had decided to construct a building seventy-five feet in length.[162]

At the same time, Traxler laid out the full schema for all the central buildings at Maryhelp, even though only the one small section was to be erected at present.[163] The plan called for a squared, U-shaped building, at the center of which the church would eventually be placed, independently situated, and flanked symmetrically, though at some distance, by the north and south wings of the monastery-college building. The three angles of the monastery-college were each to be of a different interior design, though they would approximate one another in exterior appearance. The north wing (whose length would extend east-west, and front on the south) was to have no center corridors so that some rooms could have windows on both sides. This building would have only two stories, but would be situated on higher ground so that it might join the three-storey buildings, via a wing running north to south,[164] without compromising symmetry.

The east wing, which would be built south to north and would face west, was to be used exclusively as the monastery after the initial years. Its southern-most end would be the Pilz construction of 1880. The monastery would have three stories, plus a full attic level and basement. The single-loaded corridors of the Pilz design were to be continued through the planned three extensions of this building.

From the beginning, the southern wing—which would be built in three stages, progressing east to west, and facing south toward Garibaldi—was to be the principal and most substantial part of the college's buildings. It was the only double-loaded structure in the original schema, and was designed to fill all the college's initial needs from the feeding of youth, to educating them, to bedding them at night.

Though he briefly considered building one hundred twenty rather than seventy-five feet of the College Building, the abbot had to settle in this first effort for the smaller size. It was all they could hope to accomplish before the fall term of the college opened, and the space would be a necessity by then. A craftsman who promised to produce one hundred thousand bricks per month was brought onto the property to supervise the brothers' work. Haid estimated the cost of the one wing at five thousand dollars.[165] He wanted it to be ready for use in September. [166]

The laying of the cornerstone on 4 May, was the largest quasi-liturgical ceremony at which Abbot Leo had ever officiated. Wimmer, in Pennsylvania fuming over the cost and debt, would not attend, but Haid organized an impressive affair nonetheless. The McAdenville *Times* covered the event on page one under the headline, "Another Mark of Southern Progress."[167]

The cornerstone ceremony was a showcase for Abbot Leo as a public speaker. Taking for his theme "Unless the Lord build the house, in vain do its builders labor,"[168] the abbot made none of the mistakes of his Charleston speech. Here Leo Haid was at his best, addressing his audience with conviction and in the slowly growing security of his prelacy. The focus of his remarks was the abbot's paedeutics, which he saw represented in this new building and manifested in the daily work of his college. He spoke of looking at the faces of his monks, and knowing this would "be God's house...an asylum for the true religion of the All Holy God."

He saw his students, and he recognized that this must be a house of education, where boys "will come in order to develop their minds as well as their body," where they would be "fitted for the world, and still more for the world to come."

> This is to be, God willing, a house of education. To educate young men and to expand the powers of their youthful soul, and to make that soul more like its God, and to make it more resemble the perfect type of its Creator, more and more by polishing it and by instilling in it on all occasions true Christian principle: This, then, is to be the work to which the house of which the cornerstone has just been laid, is to be dedicated.

The monks themselves were to be a type of cornerstone, because "God shall find here, at least, a devoted body of men, who have dedicated themselves, soul and body, to that Great Father's service." And their prayers "shall spread God's blessing over this beautiful country in years to come, when perhaps few of you who are listening to me now shall be among the living."

Finally the abbot prayed

> I give this building to God. It belongs to him. Take it then, O Heavenly Father, and protect it. And next to God I give this building to the Blessed Virgin Mary, the protectress of the Institution. Oh may she make it worthy of her glorious name. And then not to forget the holy Founder of our Order, I place it under the protection of the great Saint Benedict. Be this then our dedication: First to God above all, then to the Blessed Virgin His mother, and then to Saint Benedict our Holy Father. Amen.

The reign of Leo Haid, after a weak beginning, had commenced in earnest. Its tone and ambition were finally discovered and pronounced. From this brick building, the first image of stability he had imposed on Maryhelp, the abbot began to draw the substance of his own confidence in the work that was now his for life.

Work began that same day, as the brothers buried all but the top of the old slave stone, lest it detract from the new building. Brickmaking was in progress that afternoon, east of the construction site, and the sawmill was functioning northwest of the monastery and across the road. There was activity everywhere. The boys, who had been given a free-day in honor of the blessing, cancelled their planned baseball game in favor of carrying lumber, laying out the bricks to dry, and digging up the ground for the foundation. The abbot envisioned blessing the building precisely four months from that day.

Before the end of May, however, the rains started, continuous rains. When new storm clouds appeared, monks would be awakened in the night to cover bricks that were drying.[169] The dampness was so severe that only one kiln stayed in operation.[170] In July the completion date was moved back to mid-September; nevertheless, spirits remained high.[171] In August the rains continued, and brick costs were rising at an alarming rate.[172] September was the same, and October, and November. In December, Haid wrote Zilliox that the building could not be finished for perhaps as long as six more weeks. Some rooms were completed, but a staff of as many as eighteen men, plastering for over seven weeks, had been unable to finish. The one spark for optimism was the addition, twenty-seven feet in length, appended to the frame chapel that year; it was ready in time for Christmas.[173]

Finally on the night of 5 January, the boys occupied the third floor dormitory of the new College Building for the first time. The temperature that night was sixteen degrees, and the students "did not like it over much," but at least they were there. The trunk room was also ready, as were the lavatories, the shoe room, and two classrooms. For the Study Halls, there was still a week to wait.[174]

The new brick building was a dramatic change from that first student dormitory that had been noted for its irregular roof through which students could see the stars at night. It had been a letter from a Richmond student to his parents, saying he lived in a "house that hasn't any roof, and if it comes a big rain we will all get to go swimming,"[175] that got that dwelling fixed. But here the boys had a dormitory of seventy-five feet, well ventilated, and—despite the temperature—relatively comfortable. Haid was greatly relieved.

The old college was converted into a monastery, though the monks did not move into it until 23 February of the next year. But more reasonable facilities were at least beyond the stage of fantasy.

Despite the building being finished more than four months behind schedule—taking twice the anticipated time—Abbot Leo immediately began planning his next construction project. He had already completed the chapel expansion with a fifty percent increase in seating capacity and a larger sanctuary. A new belfry also appeared. The building was painted white with a brown border; it acquired green shutters and a red roof. Haid added a communion railing of black walnut, a blue ceiling with rosettes, and a new altar.[176]

The abbot was exhilarated by the construction efforts, and even though the College Building wing was completed, the bricks continued to be amassed. By September there were one hundred forty thousand on hand, and three hundred twenty-six thousand by mid-October. Haid asked if Brother Wolfgang could come again in January 1888 to build the center section of the monastery.[177] But soon the abbot was impatient and wanted Traxler as soon as possible. In Pennsylvania Brother Wolfgang was wasted, Haid reasoned, while in North Carolina with its more moderate climate the man could build even in winter.[178]

The brother was sent, but a major quarrel ensued between the two abbots as Haid's schedule stretched on seemingly without end. Finally, in January of 1887, Wimmer demanded Traxler's return, and to achieve this end he wrote directly to Brother Wolfgang, without further consultation with Haid. The Garibaldi prelate did not think he could let the craftsman go—a water closet was in progress—but Haid promised to send Brother Wolfgang by 6 February, and told Wimmer to wire if that was not acceptable.[179] The archabbot wired immediately, and received in reply another report of delays. Traxler was not sent, and Haid even said he would require the brother's services again in the spring of 1888.[180] Wimmer fired off another order for the brother's return; this time Haid cheerfully reported he would accompany Brother Wolfgang himself—in mid-February—when traveling northward for the blessing of the new abbot of Saint Mary in New Jersey.[181]

The rest of the construction during this period was for the farm. The Christmas holidays of 1885 were used for the creation of a new hog pen of thirty by twenty-five feet, at a cost of only forty-eight dollars.[182] But the main project was the erection of a large barn. The brothers had been pressing for one since 1885,[183] but the structure did not appear until 1887. There were new stables, too, with a blue granite foundation. The stables measured fifty-five by ninety-five feet[184]; the barn was eighty-five by fifty;[185] and the new wagon shed stood at sixty by twenty-two feet.[186] By Haid's report, Maryhelp had the largest farm facility in the county. As a special bonus for the abbot, the farm produced well in 1887—three crops of hay from each field, and a corn yield of four to five hundred bushels—so all the expenditures seemed worthwhile.[187]

Belmont township

In the spring of 1886, Haid tried his diplomacy again. This time it was with the town fathers in Garibaldi. Abbot Leo wanted the name of the village changed, and since the place had not been incorporated, this was more a question of achieving a consensus than securing a legislative mandate.[188]

The abbot found the name "Garibaldi" objectionable because it conjured images of Giuseppe Garibaldi, who had not been noted for his cordial relations with the Holy See. Actually the town's name, referring to the former stationmaster, had nothing to do with the Italian nationalist. Indeed, there was some disagreement regarding whether the name was properly rendered "Garibaldi" or "Garabaldi"; the Benedictines were partial to the latter version, but were clearly in the minority. "Garibaldi" was never a popular name, however. The New York *Sun,* in a feature on the abbey, suggested that the name was "as unattractive as any other name found in the nomenclature of our frontier classics."[189]

The town's name was finally changed after Haid presumed to call a meeting of the business leaders of Garibaldi in the spring of 1886. He delivered on that occasion an impassioned speech regarding the need of a city to have a name of dignity and distinction.[190] Perhaps gambling a bit, or maybe offering a ludicrous demand so that his second—and real—effort would be thought a compromise, the abbot recommended that the town be renamed "Saint Mary's."[191] None of the Protestant denizens seemed particularly enthusiastic about that suggestion. So Haid, reasoning from the village's pride in its picturesque location in the foothills of the mountains, suggested "Belmont." He explained the Latin derivation and meaning; the town fathers voiced their approval; and "Garibaldi" became "Belmont." Nine years later, in 1895, the change was codified when the village was incorporated.

There was nothing extraordinary in the change of name. And "Belmont" itself was pleasant enough, if perhaps undistinguished. Certainly neither Haid nor the town fathers anticipated the interest that surfaced twenty-six years later regarding the change of name. Abbot Leo was at least partly responsible for the misunderstandings of 1912, and his reluctance to clarify the misconceptions permitted them to continue into the decades that followed, even to the point of official recognition.

Of the several supposed rationales that later surfaced regarding Belmont's new name, the one that arose last chronologically is the easiest to refute. This theory suggested that the town's name honored

Belmont Abbey in England.[192] This version has no foundation in fact or motivation, since in 1886 the Benedictine monastery of Saint Michael at Belmont in England did not enjoy the rank of an abbey. And Leo Haid was hardly likely to name his home for an institution of inferior rank. There is also the attendant fact that Abbot Leo was no Anglophile, and bore no particular love for anything related to the country he considered a mere pause on the way to the continent.

The two principal fables regarding "Belmont" are more complex, however. In these editions, the town was named for either August or Perry Belmont. These are the stories, particularly the latter, that aroused the interest of the press and the Belmont family in 1912.

The August Belmont (1816-1890) in question was the Rothschild-trained financier who made his personal fortune after coming to America. The story does not refer, as has occasionally been suggested, to his son August (1842-1924). Belmont, supposedly of Jewish origins, was an Episcopalian of enormous wealth. He was also chairman of the Democratic Party (1861-1872), and did diplomatic service.

Perry Belmont (1851-1947), August's eldest son, was also a staunch, wealthy Democrat, and a member of the diplomatic corps. He spent eight years in the lower house of Congress, as the Representative from New York's first Congressional district. His brief period of service in Washington included 1886, when "Belmont" was taken as the North Carolina town's prenomen.

The state of North Carolina recognizes August as the inspiration for the town's name. The elder Belmont supposedly was a benefactor of the abbey's.[193] But there is no evidence to suggest either that he ever assisted the monks financially or even knew of the monastery's existence. Furthermore, Gaston County, North Carolina, had not by the 1880's forgotten August Belmont's vocal role in defending the Union against the South, nor his work in 1860 on behalf of the Baltimore Convention over the Charleston Democratic meeting. It cannot be presumed that Garibaldi's citizenry would have embraced this Belmont quite so readily.

In 1886, Perry, though still young, had already made a name for himself in Democratic politics. And Haid, like Wimmer, was very proud of his allegiance with the Democratic Party. The junior Belmont had risen quickly during his brief time in Congress to the chairmanship of the House Foreign Affairs Committee. And he had earned fame and repute through his interest in the government's South American policy, and in particular through his name-calling exchange with the Secretary of State, Mr. Blaine, on 4 May 1882, during a committee hearing. At the time of the name change in North

Carolina, Belmont's press coverage was featuring his opinions regarding the Congo Conference.

There is, however, no evidence that Haid was particularly interested in either South America or the Congo. Furthermore, neither August's nor Perry's name surfaces in Haid's papers until 1912, more than a quarter century after the change. Perhaps memories of August's prominence or newspaper coverage of Perry brought "Belmont" to mind as a possible name. But there appears to be no reference from the 1880's to even infer that honoring either of these gentlemen was considered when the abbot suggested "Belmont" for the town's new name.

The confusion seems to stem, at least in part, from Haid's always casual use of two key words. One is *namesake*. Haid used the word commonly, and discussion of any two persons, places, or things with remotely similar nomenclature was likely to have the younger party labeled a "namesake." He liked the word, and used it frequently and imprecisely. The other word is *founder*. Firstly it is as ridiculous to call either Belmont the "founder," as it is to suggest that Leo Haid would name a town, a monastery, or a college after a Protestant—especially one who was not a donor. Haid had no inclination toward ecumenism whatsoever. And as for "founders" of Maryhelp, Haid—according to convenience and circumstance—called Wimmer, Gibbons, O'Connell, and Saint Benedict by that title. Actually, however, he considered only himself to be the founder, and in substantiation of that concept he had the silver jubilee of the institution commemorated with reference to his own advent—as if 1876 through 1884 had never transpired.

The confusion with Perry Belmont got out of control—and Haid encouraged the situation—when Bird S. Coler, comptroller of the City of New York, and a friend of the abbot's, was seated next to the Honorable Mr. Belmont at a dinner at the Sulzers' residence, on Saturday, 21 December 1912. During the meal, Mr. Coler—who had previously discussed with Abbot Leo the interesting happenstance of the name—introduced the former Congressman to the existence in North Carolina of Belmont Abbey/college/township. The Comptroller subsequently asked the abbot to write Belmont, who it was thought might be open to a publicity-motivated visit to his supposed namesake.[194]

Haid then wrote Coler a carefully worded letter that was designed to be shared with Belmont.

> I am glad you saw Mr. Perry Belmont, and spoke to him of his namesake in North Carolina...When we came in July, 1885, Belmont station, a poor

little place with some forty-five inhabitants, was dubbed "Garibaldi." I did not like that name and after some trouble, succeeded in changing it to "Belmont." I was a good Democrat...[195]

To anyone familiar with the Haid style, it is obvious that the abbot carefully refrains from stating that the place was named for the Congressman. But that is, of course, precisely the inference Belmont drew, and so much publicity attended the mistaken conclusion, that the story slowly began to acquire credence.

By the time of Perry Belmont's memoirs,[196] it was the abbey itself that was supposedly named for the Protestant Congressman. An illustration representing the monastery was one of only twenty-eight pieces he chose to include in the seven hundred page opus, and the abbot of Belmont was given an autographed first edition after publication. Belmont Abbey/college/township was, the distinguished gentleman said, "the greatest honor that has ever come to me."[197] He was even flattered that he was not told in 1886 about the village's new name.

In 1928, Mr. Belmont went a step further and announced to the press that he intended to leave his library to the abbey, in honor of the college's golden jubilee.[198] Vincent Taylor, Haid's successor as abbot, had invited Perry Belmont to attend the anniversary festivities. He tried to entice the former Congressman with further revelations about "Belmont," saying, "I have often heard my predecessor...say that he named the place and the school after you."[199] Neither man apparently remembered that the school did not become "Belmont Abbey College" until 1913.

Mr. Belmont sent Taylor his regrets, then announced the proposed donation of the library. That announcement caught the eye of Agnes G. Regan of the National Council of Catholic Women, who placed discreet inquiries into the veracity of this unlikely tale regarding a Catholic college and monastery named for a Protestant politician in 1886.[200] Taylor proved unavailable for comment, but he delegated the abbey's historian, Father Thomas Oestreich, O.S.B., to respond in his name. This was written just one month after Taylor's letter to Belmont:

Abbot Taylor regrets that he has no information to give you concerning the naming of the town of Belmont, North Carolina. The town had received its name long before he came here as a student, and since his ordination he has been away for more than twenty years. He has heard of course the report current that the town was named after Mr. Perry Belmont, and has from time to time seen press reports to that effect, but he has never heard the subject discussed by Bishop Haid. The patron of the Abbey (called commonly Belmont Abbey for its location at Belmont) is the Blessed

Mother of Perpetual Help; its official title: *Abbatia Nullius Sanctae Mariae Auxiliatricis.*[201]

Regard for Haid

After two years of abbatial reign, Leo Haid was showing signs of potential for mature leadership and an unexpected gift for personal popularity. Father Mark Gross, the Vicariate priest whose brother had been bishop of Savannah, found the abbot "a very gifted man, so sensible and solidly good."[202] Gross closely followed Abbot Leo's speaking engagements, his missions and retreats, and reported them favorably to his friends in the American hierarchy. "The more I see of Father Abbot," he wrote Gibbons, "the better I like him and [the] Community." Gross even requested and received permission from the Holy See to apply for admission to the Benedictine Order,[203] though Haid never received the priest.

The growing respect for Abbot Leo opened a variety of new projects to the Benedictines. They accepted charge of Saint Vincent's parish commitment in Florida. Haid agreed in principle to Gross' never-to-be-actualized proposal for a grand "Apostolic College" and seminary at Belmont, where young men could be "safely down in the country and be removed from the intercourse of those who [would be disedifying]."[204] In July of 1886, Pio Nono College, a work of the secular clergy in Macon, Georgia, was offered but declined.[205]

There was also a growing reputation on behalf of the abbot regarding sacred oratory. The New York *Sun* described Haid as

> deservedly esteemed one of the foremost pulpit orators in America. Unconscious of self, his every sermon is an entire tract—embracing all the important truths bearing on the subject. Its leading features are distinctively traced in a rich, sonorous voice, and relieved by appropriate ornament. None tires of listening to him.[206]

Indeed, there was so much publicity for Maryhelp and its abbot, that Haid had to write Zilliox in New Jersey, assuring him "it is not my fault that our little Abbey appears in print—so much."[207]

Actually, most of the early criticisms of Abbot Leo, at least the ones of which there is still a record, came from the Benedictines themselves, especially from some monks at Saint Vincent. In particular, Carolina's frequent changes of personnel were seen as evidence of trouble. Wimmer and others who would "cruelly pick at my little Monastery" caused the young abbot much pain, and added to his early insecurity. At one point, Abbot Leo even cancelled a planned journey to the archabbey. "I was going North," he explained to Father Chrysostom at Saint Vincent, "but now I find no necessity for such a long trip—one, too, which would mingle pain with pleasure. I am a little-well pained at some things which were said and done. Still," he concluded, "they are of the past—and there let them rest."[208]

There was, however, some consolation for the young abbot—his monks. The priests and clerics were a special comfort for him, even while his mentor, Wimmer, seemed to be abandoning the southern prelate. In March of 1886, Haid could still proudly report, "Up to date *not one* has missed choir here. All are used to getting up;...no one wishes to be excused or [to] shove the burden on others."[209]

Consolations like that were the reason that even in the midst of so many problems, Haid could meet his responsibilities, build his abbey and college, and edify onlookers with the progress he sponsored. These were years when Leo Haid could be at his best. He could stay at his monastery, set an example; he could enkindle spirit and enthusiasm, and develop the special gifts that made him an effective monastic leader. He grew more confident; he was more respected; he was happier. He wrote Edelbrock, "indeed, I am most fortunate."[210] Still, the abbot of Belmont never did understand the movements around him. When soon afterwards, his duties began keeping him away from the monastery, when increasing numbers of his men were assigned outside the cloister, he was never able to grasp why that changed the spirit of Belmont. If a monk were disobedient, it was mystifying to him, as incomprehensible as when he had fallen from Wimmer's favor. Leo Haid never realized the personal loyalty he inspired—or perhaps more importantly, that the loyalty he inspired was personal. Even when the monastery's membership had increased by two-thirds in 1885, solely on the strength of his election as abbot, his appeal had not registered in his own mind. And Abbot Leo had no way of knowing in 1887, that this was the last year of his life in which he could be at peace in his North Carolina monastery, teaching through his ever-present example.

Chapter IV:

a Second Jurisdiction

Catholic development in the Carolinas had not been marked by success during the previous two thirds of a century. In Haid's time no state had a smaller percentage of Catholics than North Carolina. Conditions were still so primitive that no diocese had been erected. From 1820 until 1868 the North State had been part of the Charleston diocese. But on 3 March 1868, Pius IX separated the forty-nine thousand four hundred twelve square miles of North Carolina from Charleston, forming a separate and independent jurisdiction of subdiocesan rank. James Gibbons, then a priest of Baltimore, was consecrated bishop that August, and assigned to Wilmington, North Carolina—then the largest city in the state, and the See of the recently created territory. Gibbons was installed in the Pro-Cathedral of Saint Thomas on 1 November 1868.

Finding only approximately seven hundred Catholics scattered throughout the state, and with no more than a half dozen priests, Rome had declined to erect a North Carolina diocese, creating instead a Vicariate Apostolic. This was a level of governance preparatory to diocesan status. An ordained bishop was its head, or "Ordinary", with the title Vicar Apostolic. Once the church was sufficiently developed in the territory, a diocese could be established.

After only four years, Gibbons was Ordinary to eight priests and fourteen hundred Catholics. There was a need for more priests, more churches. But there were no funds to support even what already existed. The bishop had insufficient income to cover his own expenses, and no hope whatsoever for educating and luring new priests. Accordingly, the Holy See decided to again unite North Carolina with another jurisdiction. This time, in 1872, Gibbons was promoted to the Diocese of Richmond. The vicariate continued to exist, but Gibbons ruled it from the Cathedral in Virginia—a wealthier and more secure sphere of authority.[1] Lawrence O'Connell, Jeremiah's brother, served as Gibbons' Carolina Vicar General.

When in 1877, James Gibbons was promoted to the archiepiscopal See of Baltimore, John J. Keane succeeded him in Richmond; his appointment as Vicar Apostolic came on 25 August 1878. Three years later Rome again sought to separate the vicariate from its diocesan companion,[2] but finding a new vicar proved an unanticipated hardship.

The *terna*—the list of nominees for bishoprics that Church provinces submitted for their vacancies—as originally drafted in 1878 after Keane's episcopal consecration, nominated, in order of preference, Mark Stanislaus Gross, Henry Pinkney Northrop, and Francis Janssens.[3] Gross had experience in the vicariate, the respect of both the clergy and laity, proven administrative ability, and even a reputation for sanctity. Then too, he was not hurt by his warm friendship with Gibbons or the status of his brother, William, who was already a member of the hierarchy. He was clearly the most appropriate of the candidates, and the Holy See responded with his appointment as Vicar Apostolic in September of 1879. Gross humbly accepted the office as a recognition of Gibbons' affection, rather than of his own worthiness.[4] The 1880 Catholic *Directory* went to press listing Gross as Vicar Apostolic, hypothesizing his consecration date as merely "1879" and leaving a blank for the name of his titular See.[5] But Mark Gross was never ordained a bishop. He returned the letter of nomination;[6] Cardinal Simeoni in Rome reluctantly permitted the renunciation,[7] and Bishop Keane found himself still holding the unwelcome reins of the Vicariate Apostolic.[8]

The office finally went to Father Henry Northrop. On 8 January 1882, he was consecrated Titular Bishop of Rosalia and Vicar Apostolic of North Carolina. Northrop, like his predecessors, was reluctant to accept the post, and abandoned his objections in a mood fraught with "doubt and anxiety."[9] Bishop Northrop tried, but he never found even the minimal support a North Carolina bishop required; there was no way to cover his expenses, transportation, or to solidify Catholic observance in the state with the resources at hand. Accordingly, just one year later, on 27 January 1883, Northrop was promoted to the bishopric of Charleston, while retaining the vicariate. Once again North Carolina had no resident bishop and little prospect for Catholic growth.

Northrop was a gentle man of cultivated tastes, who was never at ease among the rough conditions of missionary labor in the North State. Nevertheless, he did succeed in luring more clergy into North Carolina, and he more than doubled those figures when he saw Maryhelp erected as an abbey, and thus as a permanent settlement. By 1887, the Vicariate Apostolic had approximately fourteen priests and about twenty-six hundred Roman Catholics. But the vicar wanted out; he longed to concentrate on the more prestigious See of Charleston. And Northrop, Gibbons, and the Gross brothers each suggested Leo Haid for the office of Vicar Apostolic of North Carolina.

Actually the rumors of the abbot's promotion to the episcopate pre-dated Northrop's decision to endorse a replacement. The first recorded mention of Haid as a future Vicar Apostolic is in a letter from Edwin Pierron dated 16 July 1885, just two days after the abbatial election.[10] And it was not pure speculation either, even then. There were strong arguments in support of his nomination at that time, and even more by 1887.

These were the most significant and persuasive points:

1. A Benedictine bishop could more readily summon the monks into missionary work.

2. The abbot's apppointment should terminate the movement toward a reduced Benedictine involvement in parochial ministry.

3. The monastery could be expected to provide lodging and reasonable support for the vicar.

4. Haid was young, vigorous, a proven administrator and builder, the leader of Catholic education in the state, a good speaker, zealous.

5. Because of his ties to both monastery and vicariate, he was less likely to try to abandon the post, as had each of the previous vicars.

6. His wide contacts both through the several monasteries and in particular through his seminary work at Saint Vincent could help secure vocations.

7. Saint Mary's College could provide seminary training for vicariate clerics.

Haid seemed to offer exactly what North Carolina needed: stable, promising, vigorous leadership with no problem regarding the bishop's income. Accordingly, Archbishop Gibbons, as Metropolitan of the ecclesiastical province that included North Carolina, wasted no time in summoning his suffragans to Baltimore to prepare a *terna* for North Carolina. On 11 May 1886, they determined to submit a petition in which they unanimously endorsed Leo Haid for the vicariate.[11] His appointment seemed both logical and assured.

In theory at least, the *terna* was not a public document. Nominations for the episcopate were considered confidentially submitted and were not openly discussed. Father Gross, however, learned of the provincial petition and immediately began devising a scheme for Haid's evangelization of North Carolina. It was an elaborate plan, created without consulting Abbot Leo. Though soundly rooted in Benedictine missionary procedure, it sadly presupposed an abundance of monastic and priestly vocations that never appeared. Father Gross wrote Gibbons,

> Our Abbey can be made the nursery of numerous Priories put down in the most unsettled and uncatholic precincts. At once the Priory is independent with its farm and brotherhood, and the Fathers require little to support them. In such priories everything is found, a permanent centre of religion, the home of religious intercessors for the missioner and the school for the children. Every Priory becomes an ever widening centre of religion and enlightenment. It is a fixture. Imagine several of such Priories—of two or three priests—located over the vast territory of North Carolina and the good resulting from them....You can become a second Gregory in some sense, in the Province.[12]

These grandiose dreams, flattering as they were both to himself and the Order, did not impress Haid, and he tried to ignore the rumors of his nomination, even withholding the news from Wimmer. He also ignored the rumor that he had been nominated as Gross' replacement in Savannah.

Rome too declined to entertain Haid's episcopal nomination seriously. The Propaganda promptly returned the province's petition, and reminded Gibbons that a *terna*, by definition, consisted of three nominations. One name was insufficient.[13] So James Gibbons, who by this time was a Cardinal-elect, consulted his suffragans again, and submitted two additional names, Fathers John Murray and Peter Moore.[14] The list complete, Gibbons settled down to await action by the Holy See.

Leo Haid, however, did not wait peacefully. Assaulted by conscience and afraid that the episcopacy would undermine his monastic vision and responsibility, the abbot made some vocational decisions of his own. Unable to act directly, however, since he did not know officially that his name had been submitted, Abbot Leo began quietly to spread the word that he was unwilling to abandon his monastery.

To Zilliox he wrote,

> As to becoming Vicar Apostolic—I came South as an Abbot, and such I will remain, God willing. Others have been Vicars Apostolic before me, and were glad to get away—because they could not live as bishops. Why should I desert my host, leave those who chose me and the life of a Monk, to take a post which abler and better men were glad to forsake? One thing is certain: unless I am obliged, I will not resign my Abbey—even to become Bishop of *Savannah*. You may tell Bishop Becker the last testament, if he wishes to be set right. Excuse my plain talk; I am speaking to *you*.[15]

If Haid was intent on retaining his abbacy, there were only two options. Either his episcopal nomination had to be withdrawn—in order to prevent another embarrassing refusal like Gross'—or Rome would have to be petitioned to allow simultaneous jurisdiction over both the monastery and vicariate. This last proposal was not easily arranged. The pressure a double mitre would place on the abbot, however, to send his monks to the missions and thus provide North Carolina with a stable clergy seemed to justify the effort. And Gibbons, convinced that Leo Haid was the man to secure Catholicism in North Carolina, began to arrange the permission the abbot required. It may also have occurred to both Rome and the archbishop, that once he perceived how impractical it was to govern both entities at once, Leo Haid would choose the greater office, and resign his monastery.

In January 1887, the Propaganda began inquiring into the abbot's worthiness for the episcopal dignity. The long delay was due in part to the desire to first consider other assignments in the province. Wilmington, Delaware, and Savannah, Georgia both had new Ordinaries named late in 1886. Bishop Keane of Richmond was awaiting his transfer to the rector's office at the new Catholic University of America. The jurisdiction of North Carolina was to be separated from Charleston's Ordinary. With so many changes in the offing, Haid's nomination—especially since it came, as had his abbatial election, only after the first choice had demurred—was not a high priority.[16]

One of those consulted about Abbot Leo's proposed episcopate was Archabbot Boniface. The two abbots were not on the best of terms at this time, and Wimmer was caught between conflicting desires, wanting for the Order the honor of an additional Benedictine bishop, and yet finding himself ambivalent about the monk who was nominated. The archabbot was also incensed that he had to hear of Abbot Leo's proposed elevation from Rome instead of from the nominee. Wimmer, however, blaming Cardinal Gibbons for the whole affair, fired off his response without delay. The evaluation of

Haid was favorable, but the patriarch of Saint Vincent made clear his belief that the man should not hold both jurisdictions, monastery and vicariate, at once.[17] Imprudently, but in character, the archabbot allowed his reservations about Haid's episcopacy to become general knowledge.

Abbot Leo wrote Wimmer immediately after hearing of the archabbatial displeasure. The Belmont abbot tried to explain why he had not told Wimmer of the rumors and of his reluctance to take the office anyway. "One mitre has thorns enough," he wrote, "two would be too much."

> I told Bishop Keane I would *never* leave my monastery to become Bishop—also that I thought it better if I could remain where I am and what I am—For this reason I never thought it worthwhile to write to you about the matter. It was known here for some time, but I believe the Fathers would not like their Abbot to become Bishop, for then I would be obliged to be away a great deal; I have to teach daily and so many other things demand my care. I am afraid I could not do one half what the Bishops expect. There are but few Priests (secular) almost no Catholic Schools, and only a few Catholics. Our students increase in number faster than Professions and lay brothers—Well, if you had given me a [poor recommendation] it might have saved me much trouble.[18]

Mark Gross, whose acceptance of the episcopate in 1879 could have averted this whole problem, heard of the archabbot's reluctance to endorse Haid's elevation, and wrote Wimmer a lengthy letter. The dual jurisdiction would "give greater dignity, channels, and stability" to the abbey, he reasoned. Also, the double dignity of having an abbot-bishop as the college's president would enhance the school's future. On a more immediate level, the priest cautioned Abbot Boniface against writing "to Rome to discourage [Haid's] appointment and to run counter thus to the wishes and ardent desire of his Eminence and many of the bishops...I know you will leave his appointment to the wisdom of his Eminence, the Cardinal, and the Council of the Province."[19]

While so many others were debating his future, Leo Haid remained quiet. Although he seems not to have feared the episcopacy as much as he had the abbacy two years earlier, he would do nothing to promote his nomination. Yet since Wimmer had decided not to fight the appointment, and Gibbons had enthusiastically endorsed the proposal of the double mitre, the promotion began to appear inevitable. Abbot Leo's only glimmer of hope was found in the extended time between his nomination by the American bishops and its endorsement by Rome. The silence held promise; "yet I do not know that the 'idea' is dead," he lamented. In May he survived the false rumor that Gibbons had received the decrees for the abbot's elevation.[20] In October he was happy to hear the rumor, also false, that Abbot Alexius would be made a bishop[21]—two American Benedictines would not be promoted at once, it seemed safe to reason.

But the inevitable finally happened on 7 December, when the Holy Father confirmed the appointment of Leo Michael Haid as Vicar Apostolic of North Carolina. The news was cabled to the abbot in Carolina, announcing his episcopal appointment and the retention of his abbacy. Not wishing to offend the archabbot again, Abbot Leo wrote Wimmer without delay. But the missive crossed with a black-bordered telegram on its way from Saint Vincent. Boniface Wimmer, patriarch of American Benedictine monasticism, had died at ten o'clock, on the morning of 8 December, unaware that another of his sons had been promoted to the episcopal dignity.[22]

The potential for conflict in the reign of a single man as both abbot and bishop was quick in revealing itself. The bishop-elect received in early April his Papal Briefs naming him Vicar Apostolic, and mandating his episcopal consecration for the titular See of Messene in Greece. Church law required that Abbot Leo be ordained a bishop within three months, so the ceremony was scheduled for 8 July 1888.[23] The date was announced, then Abbot Alexius reminded Haid that as an abbot he would need to be in Pennsylvania for the General Chapter on 8 July. Furthermore, it was especially important that the bishop-elect be present since Andrew Hintenach, who had been elected the new abbot of Saint Vincent, was to receive the abbatial blessing at that time. Abbot Leo begged Edelbrock to shift the Chapter and Blessing dates to precede the eighth, so that all the abbots would then be free to go to Baltimore after the Chapter to attend the consecration. Gibbons did not want to change Haid's date, since both it and a dual installation—one in the East at the Pro-Cathedral in Wilmington, then at the Abbey in the West—were already scheduled.[24]

Haid and Gibbons then belatedly realized that the eighth was too late for the consecration anyway, falling just outside the three month time limit. So they changed their ceremony to 1 July, leaving the installations as originally scheduled. This left Haid free to attend the Benedictine ceremonies between his two episcopal services.[25] The bishop-elect promptly wrote Abbot Alexius of the change, claiming as its motivation a fear of crowding the Benedictine celebration.[26]

Edelbrock, however, had already rescheduled the monks' activities to accommodate Abbot Leo's 8 July consecration. Gibbons declined to change his schedule again, so Leo Haid wrote Abbot Alexius that the abbot of Belmont would be unable to attend the General Chapter.[27] Assured that the Cardinal would not again change dates, Edelbrock and Hintenach conferred, and finally arranged a schedule that satisfied all the concerned parties.[28] Just scheduling the new abbot-bishop's elevation to the episcopacy had caused the Benedictines five weeks of problems and delays. It did not augur well for the future.

Once again Haid chose an epistolary format for his invitations. But this time, with Archabbot Boniface deceased, the special letter went to Alexius Edelbrock in Minnesota.[29] The tone of the official invitation was somewhat more formal this time, but the sense of the personal was not totally lost.[30] To heighten Benedictine involvement, Father Edward Hipelius, O.S.B., Saint Vincent's first monk to earn a Roman doctorate in theology, was invited to be the prefect of ceremonies;[31] he consented, but later reneged on the commitment.[32] The Benedictines did arrange to function as the choir, however.

The bishop-elect made his pre-consecration retreat at his abbey, not going to Baltimore until Friday, 29 June.[33] Father Willibald joined him on the train in Richmond and served as his chaplain. Mark Gross also went to Baltimore; he was the official representative of the secular clergy of the vicariate. Bishops Becker and Northrop were to assist the Cardinal; acting as co-consecrators, but the bishop of Charleston had to withdraw from the ceremony, and Bishop John Joseph Kain of Wheeling took his place. Archabbot-elect Andrew Hintenach attended, as did Abbots Alexius (Saint John), Hilary (Saint Mary), Fintan (Saint Meinrad), and Frowin (Conception). Bishop Rupert Seidenbusch, O.S.B., was there, accompanied by Bishops Rademacher (Nashville), Moore (Saint Augustine), and Curtis (Wilmington). Bishop Keane was the homilist.

The ceremony began on Sunday morning, 1 July at half past ten o'clock forenoon.[34] Thurifer, crucifer, and an army of forty altar boys in scarlet cassocks led the procession. They entered the church—filled with people, many of whom stood through the entire Mass—followed by monks, clergy, bishops, and finally the Cardinal, with his train held aloft by acolytes. The ceremony went smoothly and without complication, and the principals recessed out of the Cathedral of the Assumption a mere four hours later.

The Baltimore *Sun* described the bishop-elect as a "slender man of good figure and decided brunette type, having dark hair, full beard and dark complexion."[35] Actually the new bishop was not ordinarily particularly dark, but his work in the fields had left him tanned. The manual labor had also lent a certain confidence to his intention to be an abbot-bishop and not a bishop-abbot. And he was determined that his commitment to avoid an imbalance between the priorities of his jurisdictions would be achieved.

On 5 July, Archabbot Andrew was blessed at Saint Vincent, with Bishop Haid proudly present; then the General Chapter met from the sixth through the eighth. Abbot Leo attended all of these functions, but left immediately after their conclusion to join the Cardinal and Bishop-elect Foley of Detroit for the trip to Carolina, where the Vicar Apostolic was to be installed in his Pro-Cathedral on Sunday, 15 July, his thirty-ninth birthday.

Arriving in Wilmington on the evening of 12 July, the prelates were met by a large crowd organized by the Young Catholic Friends Society. Carriages awaited the bishops, and carried them to the home of Colonel F.W. Kerchner where a reception was planned. The Cornet Concert Club led the procession and entertained at the reception. The next two days were given to recreation, including a trip to Wrightsville Sound. On Sunday, the installation took place in the Pro-Cathedral of Saint Thomas at half past nine o'clock. On the sixteenth, Gibbons took his entourage to Carolina Beach for more relaxation. They then journeyed to the abbey. From Belmont, Gibbons went to Charlotte for a day, then to Asheville. Haid's installation—which incidentally marked the first visit by Gibbons to North Carolina since being created a Cardinal—occasioned "the largest number of Catholic clergymen ever assembled in North Carolina."[36] It was also the busiest month of Leo Haid's life, a portent of the character that would attend him henceforth.

Episcopal Residence

At home in Belmont, the new Vicar Apostolic was in need of rest. He found instead a minor revolt in the making. The tumult had begun stirring when the episcopal appointment was first announced, but not until the bishop returned home did the conflict and its conspirators break fully into the open.

At the core of the discontent was the suspicion that the monks had been abandoned by their superior. Abbot Leo had turned the full weight of his eloquence during the previous three years on the precedence of monastic duties over missionary commitments. Now that same abbot had accepted charge of a tremendous missionary territory, knowing that the only concentrated supply of priests at his disposal was the Benedictines. The monks had adjusted their thinking from the Wimmer mode; they had trusted and followed their abbot, only to be committed, it seemed, to parish work after all. The imbalance between monastic vows and clerical demands, the plague of American Benedictinism since 1846, raised its head anew. And to the idealistic younger fathers at Belmont, what seemed most obvious was that the abbot had a conflict of interest, in which his monks would be the ones to suffer.

The leader of this monastic unrest was Father Walter Leahy, O.S.B., whose edifying forthrightness and determination had turned into a contentiousness that was not incapable of malevolence. Father Walter, one of Belmont's founding monks, had been a wholehearted supporter of Haid's monastic vision. He had already been somewhat disillusioned when assigned to a year in the most arduous of the monks' missionary circuits.[37] Then when the abbot accepted the office of bishop, Leahy could only imagine further disappointment, and began inciting the brethren to oppose any effort by Abbot Leo to further clericalize the monks of Belmont.

Leahy's concerns, rooted in what he perceived as the abbot's betrayal of the abbey's special theme, did not lack foundation. The expectation that an abbot-bishop would be more prone toward committing his monks to work outside the cloister than would a simple abbot was logical and soon to be substantiated. What the young priest did not seem to consider, however, was the damaging effect of such invective on the observance of the house. A monastery, by its nature, functioned as a closed community that both profited and suffered from its routine. Its sense of sameness was not easily changed, either for improvement or otherwise, without a certain rather wrenching realignment. Because of the intimate proximity of the inmates to one another, their common substructure, work, and goals, change could not occur in isolation. One factor necessarily affected a score of others, and a person who whether from motives good or bad disrupted one facet of the house, would probably also have an impact on the monastery as a whole. The format of cloistered existence had a natural influence within its own parameters that disproportionately magnified problems, while virtues or general happiness—associated as they were with the routine—enjoyed no enhanced status and thus could be handily overshadowed.

In 1888, the Belmont monastery was still small; customs were not yet clearly established; this magnified Leahy's impact. The tone of the house seemed drawn legitimately into question by the abbot's new duties, and Walter Leahy was able to arouse an incredible and provocative impulse. The moral authority of the abbot within his monastery—that is, the values he had come to represent—was being undermined. And the undeniable undercurrent of the conflict was that Father Walter, despite his hauteur and insouciant evaluations of his spiritual father, appeared in all probability to be correct in his predictions for the abbey's future. The effect was pandemic. The monks in Georgia and Virginia feared reassignment; the Florida project was called into question, and abbey discipline itself was threatened. The episcopacy was clearly to be a mixed blessing.

This interior dissension was a problem for Haid on three levels. It hurt the monastic spirit of his abbey, and in particular he believed it a threat to Father Walter's virtue. It threatened scandal. And, on a more personal level, it added weight to insecurities that had already waged an initial assault when he had first acquiesced in the appointment to the dual jurisdiction. Leahy's argument was so cogent, that even the abbot pondered its validity.

But the possibility of public scandal was the most immediate of the problems. In the early months of 1888 two occurrences had already threatened the reputation of the abbey and its relations with the locals, and a third, caused by an ideological revolt, had to be forestalled.

The first of the scandals had involved Father Bede Northman, O.S.B., a Minnesota monk who was on assignment in the South. While Abbot Leo was away, Northman slipped out and went to the neighboring town of Mount Holly. There he drank to excess and "acted very boisterously." The next day, Father Julius succeeded in locating the man and transporting him back to the abbey. Father Bede found life in Carolina too loathsome to be endured, and demanded fifty dollars in travel money so he could return to his own home. Receiving forty-five dollars, he left. Between trains in Atlanta, Father Bede again satisfied his thirst, and this time found himself arrested and jailed. The priest was allowed to pay his fine there— apparently using funds he had secreted after attending his mother's funeral the previous fall—only after, as Haid phrased it, he "gave away our poor house," claiming to be a monk, cleric, and professor at *Maryhelp*.[38] The incident did little to promote a respectable image for the abbey, and it seemed particularly expressive of an apparent lack of discipline.

The second problem in early 1888, came not from scandal as much as from a controversy that fed the fears of local Protestants regarding their Catholic neighbors. That spring, North Carolina hosted an Immigration Convention. It was convoked to consider the possibility of securing from among the ranks of recent immigrants to America, new citizens for the southern states. The skills of these people, it was suggested, would prove a positive economic factor. There were approximately two hundred delegates from the eleven states of the South. The governors of Georgia and South Carolina were there;

even the mayor of New York City attended, as did representatives of the railroads and industry. A substantial percentage of the prospective immigrants were Catholic, so Haid wholeheartedly endorsed the convention, believing it might help enlarge the Catholic population of North Carolina. He attended the meeting, too, as did the bishop of Savannah. Gibbons also appeared in Hot Springs for the convention, and addressed the delegates.

The Cardinal's presence confirmed local fears that the meeting was a Roman plot, a lunge by the Catholics for greater numbers and influence. The press spoke out against the assemblage, creating so much excitement that the governor of North Carolina decided not to attend. He did not, however, withdraw the government monies that supported this "Catholic" convention. The Protestant clergy, who were invited in greater numbers than were the Catholics, absented themselves on the whole, reportedly—or presumably—in protest.

Haid objected to the newspaper coverage that labeled the meeting as Roman and anti-American, and decided to make a public response. He chose as his forum the Gastonia *Gazette*, a paper in Gaston County that ordinarily ignored both the abbey and the supposed Catholic "menace." The abbot wrote a long letter to the newspaper in which he noted the early involvement of Catholics in the praise of God on Carolina soil, the economic benefits of having an influx of immigrants, and the equality of Catholic Americans with Protestant citizens. Unfortunately, he also made sarcastic references to the "silly twaddle" about Romanism, that "no man of sense believes," and reported he was yet to discover a Protestant who was "unwilling to take money because it came from Catholics."[39] The letter, which Haid signed with his title as president of the college, was published, but did not win the author a warm outpouring of local affection.

It did, however, earn him a public rebuke in the *Gazette*. The "distinguished writer," the editor maintained, ignored the gist of the paper's objections to "the Hot Springs scheme," namely the appropriation of public money for a "Catholic" meeting. The *Gazette* claimed to have "said nothing but what our convictions as a citizen and a Christian demanded." And as for the arguments Haid considered to be "twaddle," the editor suggested in a deliciously pithy rejoinder, "We know it was Protestants that made this country what it is; Catholics made Mexico what it is; take your choice."[40]

His "choice" was to try to stay out of print for a while.

The effect of Father Walter's activities, however, demanded a more immediate and direct approach. Correcting the monk in this regard proved especially odious to the abbot, since he was inclined to agree with at least the foundation of the priest's fears. Nevertheless,

Leahy was disrupting the whole house and had to be stopped. Haid cautioned him first, then gave a warning. But the peace of the rebuke seemed to fuel the priest. He began to "torment and [even] tease"[41] his abbot, giving "more trouble directly and indirectly than all the others together."[42] The disruption caused by Leahy fed on Abbot Leo's discomfort at having accepted a position that would regularly take him from his monastery and its needs; the problem festered; in his guilt, the abbot decided Father Walter's complaints were indeed substantial, and he determined to render the Benedictines greater service by resigning the abbacy. "I felt that I was unjustly treated by those for whom I was ready to make any sacrifice, and for whom I had labored without ever thinking of myself," he said, but he understood their complaints. His only reservation about resigning was reluctance to leave his young abbey with so many debts.[43]

Leo Haid had learned monastic obedience on its simplest level. Having been told to do something or to stop it, he believed there was only one proper course of action consistent with the monastic vows. Walter Leahy, however, did not respond within these parameters, and the abbot-bishop was helpless at dealing with this young priest's incorrigible will. Although Haid was sympathetic on a rational level to Father Walter's view of the problem, the recalcitrance was unintelligible to him. So the abbot finally decided his own duty lay in the performance of both jobs, as assigned by the Holy See. The same applied, he reasoned, to Walter Leahy who was bound by his vows to be obedient to his abbot. Accordingly, Haid did not resign his monastic office; instead he decided to confront Father Walter with the duties incumbent on the monk by virtue of his religious profession.

Leahy had been given responsibility for the new high school Belmont had established in Richmond the previous year. Joseph Heppert, of the Virginia capital, had erected a new building for the institution,[44] and Father Walter's position was considered a choice assignment, showing Bishop Haid's trust in the younger priest. Leahy had proven gifted for the work. Nevertheless, Abbot Leo decided that his only chance for securing Father Walter's soul and for re-establishing his monastery's spirit, was to isolate the priest for the present from the other monks. Accordingly, in August, Haid gave the principal in Richmond a new assignment, sending him to the recently acquired missions in Florida. "Father Walter is not over well pleased," the abbot wrote to Archabbot Andrew, "but that does not surprise me."[45]

"Not over well pleased" was a very modest version of Walter Leahy's response. The logic of responding to complaints about monks in parishes, by sending a monk to a parish hundreds of miles from his monastery, seems to have escaped Father Walter. In October he asked to transfer his stability to Saint Mary Abbey in Newark. "I never signed a paper more gladly," Abbot Leo reported, "May he find the source of all his troubles: *himself*, and having found it correct it."[46] There was no victory for either Haid or Leahy; the settlement evaded the problem and its issues. But with the young priest gone, the abbey regained some measure of peace.[47] "A new spirit seems to reign,"[48] said the abbot, and he finally turned to his newly diversified labors.

As it happened, Walter Leahy was not happy in Newark either. Eventually, he left that abbey, too, and was incardinated into the Diocese of Trenton. There he spent the rest of his life, as irony seemed to demand, as a parish priest. His parochial service was sufficiently distinguished to earn him the title of "monsignor". He also wrote a novel, *Clarence Belmont*, a thinly veiled romance of school boys at Saint Mary's College. Eventually he and Haid were reconciled, and Leahy became a friend and benefactor of the Carolina College.

Abbot-Bishop

The Leahy affair, unpleasant as it was, had the salutary effect of forcing Leo Haid in the first days of his episcopacy to consider the balance that had to exist between his mitres. He held two full-time positions, each of which reserved to him personally some particular duties that precluded delegation. Other responsibilities, especially subordinate ones, could be shared by his subalterns.

To give each of his positions its necessary tenor, the bishop considered first their points of unity, and from there he developed his distinctions. The Church—which was for local purposes personalized perhaps, but not personified, in himself—appeared to be the simplest denominator. Both the bishop and the abbot were heads of the immediate Church, each in its respective sphere. And Haid held the offices of abbot and bishop, in each case, as a matter of obedience. The positions came from a single source, the Church, and were to be held concurrently. Nevertheless, they indisputably were not coterminous, nor should they be treated as if they were.

Leo Haid began to trade, then, on the uniqueness of his new identity. The Church had named him both abbot and bishop. Thus he functioned as abbot when at the monastery, and bishop when in the parishes. But he was still the abbot-bishop, both at once, both at all times. To help in creating the image he wanted, the first tour of the missions by North Carolina's new Vicar Apostolic featured an often repeated "lecture on Monks, as the honor and glory of monastic life is really entwined about our Mother the Church." He toured the state presenting himself as a sort of epergne, holding a variety of not wholly disparate treasures, the episcopal ones enriched by the monastic. "The people," he concluded, "really feel most happy to have a monk-bishop."[49] The more internecine aspects of his responsibilities were at least obscured for the present.

Further emphasis was granted to the abbot's double dignity through his employment of the abbey as a second cathedral. Gibbons had endorsed this by enthroning him at Belmont as well as in the East. But the use was still unofficial; Wilmington was the only See of the Vicariate. Yet by maintaining his residence in Gaston County, in the western portion of the state, and so obviously giving the facilities of his home to the enhancement of the Vicariate Apostolic, he established an immediate breadth of concern, a quality of which his episcopal predecessors had proven incapable. The Catholics of western Carolina were no longer to be neglected. This was important as an indicator of his priorities, also. For although Haid was interested in spreading the faith, the more pressing concern, as he saw it, was the preservation of the few Catholics already living in Carolina; before attempting evangelization, spiritual and sacramental provisions had to be secured for those already numbered among the faithful. "It will be a long time," he wrote to Saint John Abbey, "before we can hope to breathe the air of Catholic progress."[50]

On the whole, these discernments proved wise. Bishop Haid created a character around his reign that emphasized both his difference from his predecessors—who had been only moderately successful at best—and his stability. The abbatial residence in particular served to emphasize the permanence of his positions: Leo Haid would not leave North Carolina for a more secure See as had each of the previous Vicars Apostolic. Priorities also were recognized as well arranged, with attention given to the whole state, not just the East, and with the needs of his present clientele preceding goals of growth and magnitude. As usual, Leo Haid was impeccably organized; the vicariate had goals, good prospects for means, and a fresh beginning. The abbot-bishop, anxious to capitalize on the good will of the Catholics of the state, wasted no time in showing himself as well as his program. From this there came spirit and optimism. And the people and clergy warmed to him immediately. He seized the opportunity, then, and spoke to them of Church and religion. He spoke too of monks, and emphasized their spiritual value; these monks, he would relate, were praying for all the people, upbuilding the Church as surely as the priest in the parish. He would then present himself, the bishop, the abbot, the priest, the monk, all of these in one man, come from the monastery to speak of God, to give Christ's Sacraments. Then he would move on to the next church to continue his work. Even Haid was dazzled by the effect of the first tour. "My visits through the 'diocese' give me much consolation, as [it seems] I can do something for religion and God."[51]

The tour revealed Leo Haid's facility for representing solid and idealistic standards of religion and virtue. It also used his sense of privacy and modesty to good effect, allowing him to be shrouded in just enough personal mystery to have even his enemies grant him reserve from their doubts. But the abbot-bishop was still hopelessly incompetent at dealing with people who questioned or disagreed with him. And prolonged exposure would apply this weakness to his detriment throughout his reign. His gentleness hurt his commands. Once filtered through his native sensitivity, orders appeared as hopes or aspirations perhaps, but never as requirements. In the monastery where obedience drew from the abbot's paternity and solicitude—and in Haid's case, from the impact of his presence—discipline could be maintained in this way. But in a diocesan environment, particularly in nineteenth century America, bishops were expected to be strong masters, authoritative and clear. Haid knew this; he even allowed some monks, as necessity demanded, to enter the service of a diocese in the belief that "with the strong arm of a Bishop to guide him, he will do much better than under the paternal guidance of an Abbot."[52] But the bishop of North Carolina did not possess these mighty thews and sinews. Perhaps if Leo Haid had explained his theory of obedience, the vicariate clergy would have united behind him. Through the years, however, never grasping the subtlety of his approach or its inherent respect for their potential for mature response, the secular priests would come to find Abbot Leo ineffectual, just as he—equally oblivious of the misunderstanding—would see them as disobedient ingrates.

Bishop Haid compounded his difficulties through poor communication. This problem arose from his ordinary, very practical approach. It is part of the complexity of his story that this man whose virtue was the inspiration of lofty idealism in others, was himself rooted in the strictures of practicality and the thinly traced circumference of a schoolmaster's logic. To Abbot Leo it was perfectly logical that with two jobs and a vast territory, his presence was limited, of necessity. Accordingly, he communicated largely by mail in dealing with the vicariate priests, with missives going out to his clergy regularly, regarding any number of concerns. In this way—

although it was a perfectly logical and practical approach—Leo Haid separated himself from his secular co-workers. Stylisticly his writing was as conventional and ordinary as his presence and oratory were electric. Success in building cohesive bonds with his vicariate and its personnel depended upon presence. It is true that he was not available any less than his predecessors who ran dioceses outside of North Carolina, but for what he inflamed his priests to expect, the presence of the Ordinary was necessary. He, Leo Michael Haid, bishop and abbot, was needed. But he could not grasp the mystery of charism; he did not comprehend its logic, and as a result, he tore away the foundations of his own dreams. An artificial, impersonal presence did not work for him.

The abbot-bishop tried also to deal with the involvement his monks would have in the vicariate. With Leahy gone, he found the monks surprisingly willing to assist, but he was determined to be mindful of the different vocation a monk-priest had from that of a secular priest of the vicariate. Among the differences, he assigned priority to the affiliation with the monastery itself. Missionary priests, he reasoned, expected to live alone and travel incessantly. For a Benedictine, however, such a life would be dangerous, since it "breeds a spirit of independence...not in keeping with our vows."[53] Accordingly, when Benedictines were assigned to missions, the abbot preferred that they work within a reasonable proximity of the abbey. If more than one monk were assigned, and some semblance of cenobitical existence secured, a greater distance might be indulged. Unfortunately for Haid in his role as bishop, this arrangement gave the abbey's priests a concentrated field of endeavor that kept the bishop, in residence at Belmont, surrounded primarily by monastic rather than secular clergy. Only on rare occasions or for temporary assignments would the abbot-bishop place monks and seculars in the same parish; thus when pairs of monks went to a parish, they tended to displace the seculars who had established and developed the particular church. That created friction. Furthermore, since only the larger and more secure urban parishes merited more than one priest in permanent residence simultaneously, the vicariate's men saw the monastery's priests slowly gaining possession of the best of North Carolina's parochial churches. From Bishop Haid's perspective he was making logical assignments that reflected the unique vocations of the two clerical groups at his disposal. To the secular priests the villainy seemed unmistakable: the grasping and proprietary movements of the Benedictines were unchecked.

The abbot-bishop endured an additional element of insulation from the secular clergy because of his advisors. Hintemeyer, of course, was the bishop's first and only choice for Vicar General, the second authority in the territory. And through simple availability, Haid—who really did not often convene his councilors anyway—most often let his monastic curia double as his diocesan staff.

The seculars would have been further dismayed had they known that the bishop considered their lot far easier than the monks'. Charles Mohr was sent to the parish in Greensboro, for example, in Haid's first month as Ordinary. The reason for the assignment was Father Charles' poor health; it was poor from the fatiguing routine of the monastery and classroom, and the parish and missions should, it seemed, provide the needed rest.[54] Haid even maintained that the relative comfort of life in the secular clergy was the great deterrent that kept young American men from entering the monastery.[55]

Leo Haid saw the placement of monks in parishes as a temporary arrangement. His Benedictines perceived the subject somewhat differently, however, but the abbot did not discover their difference of opinion until more than two years had passed. In the meantime he opened his seminary at the abbey to candidates for the secular clergy. At Belmont the seculars studied alongside the monastic candidates— though both sets of seminarians were largely sequestered from the college students—and they had the benefit of attending classes conducted by the Vicar General and by the bishop himself.

As the monastery and vicariate became increasingly intermingled in their interests and practical affairs, their finances became hopelessly entangled, too. Gibbons, of course, had made no secret of the financial woes he hoped to alleviate by having a single head for the abbey and the 'diocese'. Based on the Cardinal's rationale, Abbot Leo believed he had *carte blanche* leave to finance both operations without careful distinctions being maintained. For a man who taught bookkeeping for more than a decade, it was an amazingly negligent and sloppy set of ledgers that resulted. It would lead to unfortunate legal complications, too, and arouse the ire of the monks and suspicions of the seculars. But to the bishop—as usual—it was all perfectly logical. Both jurisdictions were united in the Church. The vicariate helped the monastery by establishing the Catholic Church in Carolina. That would breed both vocations and students. The monastery helped the vicariate by educating its young and its priests, praying, witnessing to eternal values. It provided a much needed balance to the active life that surrounded it, and it displayed specifically Catholic standards and values, which in turn attracted fresh interest from Protestants and encouraged new fervor among the faithful. The vicariate and abbey profited from one another in their work. But neither had even minimal security of a financial nature. The Benedictines were in debt; the vicariate had no money with which to do its work or build and grow. In a sense the genius of the new arrangement—Gibbons' in inception and Haid's in execution—was that it united the two unparticularized (and impoverished) entities, and bestowed on them a character, a unique identity. And with this individuation or distinction, money began to appear for both bodies for the first time. When Abbot Leo toured the North on begging trips, he was not just another bishop of a poor vicariate, not just some minor abbot who had more monks than cells, more bills than students' tuitions. No, this was Leo Haid, America's monk-bishop, striving to give Roman Catholicism a foothold in the Protestant South. And the abbot-bishop was a tremendous success on these excursions; he detested begging, but he did it well. When money appeared, it paid whatever bills were current—vicariate, abbey, college—and the bishop assumed that somehow it all balanced eventually. The distinctions between these bodies were obscure to the donors, and equally unclear in the spheres of daily functioning. But bills were being paid; there was progress, and neither condition was the case before the vicariate and monastery were united in Leo Haid. In the years to come, however, his disregard for documenting the association between the two bodies would haunt him and threaten to blemish his reputation.

The burdens of episcopal office were lightened somewhat by Haid's sense of organization. But the expanse of the state required extended blocks of time for travel, and frequent repetition of similar services. In May 1889, for example, the bishop administered Confirmation on six occasions, yet only thirty-two received the Sacrament. In October 1892, he gave the Sacrament in ten cities, but still with only a minimal quantity of recipients.[56] Yet these excursions kept the abbot away from his monks for substantial periods of time. In 1889 he spent the spring begging in New York state. Another year it was Pennsylvania; he tried New Jersey. He even went to Iowa. Then to these travels he added retreats for diocesan clergy, sisters, Orders of men. In all of the travels he was just "trying to do a little good for others and also help to keep up our institution, for we are poor, have a considerable debt, etc."[57] In his talks he raised funds for the "progress of religion;" in letters to benefactors he sought money for some specific projects. But he required his parish clergy, whether secular or Benedictine, to undertake their own fund raising efforts when their congregations did not respond adequately to local needs.

Long absences were already a problem for Haid when, in 1890, he found himself elected *praeses* of the American Cassinese

Congregation. With this office, the abbot incurred responsibility for visitations in the Congregation's monasteries throughout the country; he was expected to officiate at all abbatial elections, and to coordinate dealings with Rome. The six years of his service were marked by considerable growth for the Order in America. Bishop Haid assisted in the elevation of monasteries in Alabama and Illinois to the rank of "abbey," of the Florida priory to independence, and of Saint Vincent to archabbatial status *in perpetuum.* Abbots were elected or appointed in Pennsylvania, Minnesota, Alabama, and Illinois. The *praeses* also worked to have the monastery in New Hampshire erected as an abbey, with Alexius Edelbrock appointed as abbot-for-life, but that effort failed. Florida did not acquire abbatial status until 1902, but at that time Abbot Leo performed the blessing himself, the candidate being his protege, Charles Mohr.

Another matter of particular interest to the Cassinese *praeses*, permissions for novitiates in individual monasteries, consumed much of his time. Haid thought the practice of sending all the Congregation's novices to Saint Vincent was expensive, required unnecessary travel, and endangered the young men's health.[58] It was a battle never fully resolved to the abbot's satisfaction, and presumption of permissions by the *praeses* resulted in the invalidation of Belmont's formation class of 1892.[59]

The service of which *Praeses* Haid was proudest was his Roman mission of 1893, in which he was one of the leaders in the effort to limit the authority and powers of the Abbot Primate. Abbot Leo was but one of many spokesmen against the primate's acquisition of any real powers over the exempt, autonomous monasteries of the Order of Saint Benedict, but he turned the full weight of his influence and connections to the struggle, and did make his mark. Leo XIII had created the controversy with *Summum semper*, issued finally after great anticipation and exchange of ideas, on 12 July 1893. The Sacred Congregation of Bishops and Regulars had authority subsequent to the papal pronouncement to define and particularize the new position. Haid fought during the spring to lay the groundwork for his cause, and in concert with several other abbots issued a document of Benedictine history, customs, and law that was submitted to the Pope and Curia. Returning to America, a modest victory secured, he believed he had performed a service on behalf of the whole Order, not just his own Congregation. He and his party, the bishop later recalled, had managed to "clip the Primate's wings."[60]

Abbot Leo's tenure as *praeses* was a small and minor chapter in his life. It was an unhappy service, too. "Whilst I am very willing to give

99/100th of my life to the Order, there is a limit," the abbot wrote. Besides, he found that he was regularly "censured for things I cannot help,"[61] an added burden he did not need. Haid had been accused, for example, of "execrable officiousness" and of "shak[ing] the very foundation of this great Abbey," because he had executed his duty and forwarded Archabbot Andrew's resignation to Rome in 1892.[62] In 1893, considerable displeasure was expressed after he dutifully acted on the General Chapter's decision to meet next in Illinois. By the time of the General Chapter of that year, Leo Haid had enough pettiness with which to deal, without suffering the complaints of a whole federation of monasteries, and he determined not to continue in office as *praeses.*[63]

Even more than the disgust with the office itself, Abbot Leo was having to face growing dissension at Belmont regarding the quantity of his absences. Accordingly, when Maryhelp's Chapter met to elect its delegate to the 1893 Congregation Chapter, the abbot announced that he "would beg to be excused from again accepting the office [of *praeses*] if tendered."[64] But at the Congregation's conclave, the position was offered to him again, despite his objections; Haid demurred; the delegates to the General Chapter insisted; and the abbot-bishop found himself in the embarrassing position of having to return to North Carolina again as *praeses.* Not until the Congregation's Chapter of 1896 was Haid permitted to retire from the *praeses'* chair. Abbot Leo wrote the primate then, "I thank God!"[65]

Annexation

The revolt over the abbot's absences had not wholly terminated with the departure of Father Walter. And when to the bishop's travels there were added the *praeses'* many journeys, the monks of Belmont began expressing their reservations regarding the attention given to what they saw as Haid's first and primary responsibility: his abbacy. The fathers of Maryhelp also objected to their own increasing absences. Missionary work was becoming a larger part of their lives, drawing them out of their cloister, away from their confreres and students, and thus changing the character of their monastic observance. It is a mark of how successfully Abbot Leo had initiated his men into the ethos he originally created for Maryhelp, that his monks did object so strenuously to the shift—so gradual it might have proven almost imperceptible—in emphasis.

For the abbot, options were limited. The responsibilities that were his as abbot and as bishop had been assigned to him by the Holy See;

he had to tend to both simultaneously, and each was considered a life-long position. The *praeses'* job, however, was only for a specified term. It was temporary, and thus its burden was only passing. What was needed by the abbot-bishop was a manner of incorporating the monks into his vicariate work in a way that would lend the same sense of permanence, stability, and corporate unity as his titles lent him, but which would do so without offending the men's monastic values. There was no substantial problem in their intimacy with the monastery and its work, especially the college. But the monks needed, Haid reasoned, a type of involvement in the vicariate that would seem less ephemeral than did the upbuilding of scattered parishes for conveyance to the secular clergy.

From this need, the abbot decided in July of 1890 to petition Rome to entrust the counties surrounding the abbey to the perpetual care of the Order of Saint Benedict. The idea had originally occurred to Haid in 1888,[66] when documents regarding the Florida parishes were being transferred from Saint Vincent to Belmont. Bishop John Moore of Saint Augustine had given the Florida Benedictines Hernando County. While Rome was considering whether or not to approve the gift, the state government divided Hernando County, creating three political distinctions in the original territory, the new counties being called "Pasco" and "Citrus". The decree for the Benedictines was approved in the summer of 1887, naming only Hernando County. Since the monks' work, after the territorial partition by the state, no longer centered on Hernando, but on Pasco County, some adjustment was obviously necessary. And the decision reached was that the land originally specified should be respected, rather than interpreting the document according to the area's name. In this way, although the territory was still at its original size, the grant covered the more expansive sounding breadth of three counties.[67] Haid acquired a copy of the decree[68]—which Wimmer had written, Moore had signed and submitted, and Rome had approved—and began preparing his own request. He anticipated no problem that might preclude the grant since he understood that gifts of a similar nature had recently been recorded not just in Florida, but in Alabama and Colorado, too.[69] Besides, this was sure to be a case where the local "Bishop and Abbot can agree for once!"[70]

In all probability, the petition would indeed have been approved, were it not for the manner of its submission. Haid was still relatively new to the episcopate, and unsure regarding the precise manner in which he was to balance his two jurisdictions. This petition, since it affected both entities, proved particularly muddled. Reasoning that this was a gift for the Benedictines, and knowing his monastic channels to be more efficient than his episcopal contacts, Haid entered the proposal in Rome as a petition from the abbot of Maryhelp, endorsed by the Vicar Apostolic of North Carolina. Unfortunately, he had things backwards, and curial suspicions were aroused. Bishops, not abbots, entered requests regarding diocesan churches.

Rome wrote to Cardinal Gibbons in Baltimore. The vicariate lay within the archbishop's province, and he might have been expected to endorse or at least acknowledge the request before it was sent to the Holy See. Apparently for reasons of inexperience, Haid neglected to request the Cardinal's opinion, however; so the Propaganda contacted the rather surprised prelate on its own in December of 1890.[71] Bishop Haid thought nothing of the delay, attributing it to Rome's "well-known slowness,"[72] and waited patiently. He was reluctant to press for an answer lest this Benedictine petition distract from what he considered a more important request for the Order, the elevation of Saint Vincent to archabbatial status.[73]

Gibbons finally wrote his response after the beginning of the new year. Because of the circumstances of the inquiry itself, the Cardinal's report was prepared without consultation with Haid. The Benedictines were worthy of great praise, he suggested, for their generous service to religion in North Carolina. They were selflessly giving themselves to every manner of missionary labor, and they should be rewarded. This particular petition, however, seemed to His Eminence to solicit a recompense that would be imprudent, since it was sure to cause complications later between secular Ordinaries of North Carolina and the monks. Rather than give parishes in perpetuity, it was the Cardinal's counter-recommendation that the territory be given to the Order of Saint Benedict for a period of forty or fifty years.[74] In August of 1891 the monastic Chapter told Haid the compromise was acceptable, but Abbot Leo was not yet ready to concede defeat.

Gibbons, Rome, and Haid, it seems, were keenly conscious of the difficulties in the American Midwest at this time, regarding Benedictine parishes and unhappy Ordinaries. Edelbrock was assaulted throughout his reign with these problems, as were other abbots. Gibbons wanted to avoid such controversies. He recommended that Rome should be conscious of the rights of future—probably non-Benedictine—bishops in North Carolina. But Haid was equally concerned that since his monks were to share in the effort to build up the Church there anyway, "some territory [should be] set apart for this work where it can be done without danger of clashing with secular Priests." Thus despite the first discouraging report from Simeoni at the Propaganda, filled with reservations about the time frame, the abbot-bishop decided to "insist on a Perpetual Concession—the reasons [being] quite evident when we remember how frequently Religious are ousted after years of sacrifice."[75]

In deciding to fight Rome's reluctance, the abbot-bishop committed what should have proven a significant, tactical error. Opposition was not ordinarily received cordially in Rome. And while men with contacts and influence could push and maneuver, recently consecrated bishops in impoverished Vicariates Apostolic did not tend to flourish within the elite corps of ecclesiastical politicos. Yet somehow Leo Haid made the right contacts and the right impressions, and the petition started to break its restraints and trudge forward through the Church's bureaucracy. Apparently the initiatory force that worked on Cardinal Simeoni and his cohorts was Abbot Bernard Smith, O.S.B., who as Haid's Roman procurator handled the abbot-bishop's intercourse with the Holy See. This Benedictine took the North Carolina bishop's petition to every imaginable office; he pleaded for the needs and integrity of religion, and he brought to the attention of the curial offices a man and monastery known to them before only from the episcopal nomination submitted by the American Cardinal. Now, however, they heard a larger story, of an eloquent abbot-bishop striving to manage a monastery, college, and farm that were growing so fast that new buildings had been required in each year of his reign; his vicariate was building an average of more than two churches per year. After decades of dormancy, Catholicism had taken root in North Carolina, and all of this was happening under the leadership of Leo Michael Haid, abbot and bishop. It was a marvelous, vivid image of a beleagured but successful churchman in missionary America, and it would serve Leo Haid for years to come.

Abbot Leo never discovered that it was Gibbons who had first blocked the petition in Rome,[76] nor did he realize the jeopardy in which he had placed his petition when he decided to continue fighting for a perpetual concession. The abbot also never knew why the Holy See was thereafter so conspicuously at his service, so consistently indulgent of his requests. The shrewd and inspiriting service of Bernard Smith was not fully understood in Carolina. Haid was pleasantly surprised when, in Rome in 1893, the Holy Father gave him a private audience, and proved so interested in his work and success. Even when Gibbons himself fawned over the abbot and said, "If I did nothing else in North Carolina but to introduce there the Benedictines, my work was not in vain,"[77] Haid was oblivious of the charism at his command and the image being created and promulgated in Rome.

But he did know that on 4 December 1891, Joannes Cardinal Simeoni, Prefect of the Propaganda Fide, affixed his signature and thus "confirmed and ratified" a convention which ceded to the Order of Saint Benedict for fifty years the spiritual administration of the counties of Mecklenburg, Lincoln, Cleveland, Cabarrus, Rowan, Davidson, Guilford, Forsythe, and Gaston" in North Carolina.[78] Leo Haid had been granted for his monks nine full counties. From his original request nothing had been changed but the time span, and that alteration in itself was a blessing of sorts, since it left open a perpetual grant in the future, one that might even include a better territory. But even for the present, the Benedictines found themselves in possession of a clear field of exclusive missionary responsibility. "I hold Deeds as Bishop," he proudly reported to Archabbot Leander Schnerr at Saint Vincent, "but the Order has the *cura* [of souls].'"[79]

"If I had one or two good [extra] O.S.B.'s," the abbot had mused in the first year of his episcopacy, "I would certainly annex unmercifully."[80] But with the annexation of 1891 secured, the abbot-bishop shelved those plans. More than missionary territory, Abbot Leo wanted a buffer zone around his monastery in which the rivalries between secular priests and religious would not exist. The grant of fifty years, which for the most part merely recognized the current sphere of Benedictine labor, gave both the monastery and vicariate a period for intense work, for establishing and nurturing the Roman Catholic Church in North Carolina. When half a century had passed, the Benedictines could ask the reigning bishop to petition Rome for an extension; they could withdraw, or some other arrangement might be created. But for the specified time, assuming the Benedictines tended to the Catholics within their territory, no non-Benedictine bishop who might follow Haid could arbitrarily relieve the abbey of these missions.[81] The monks were placated by the gift of their own missionary field, and seem not to have noticed that the bishop subsequently manifested a rather benign attitude toward its development, caring for its Catholics but exerting little effort toward spreading the faith. The secular clergy also seemed pleased since the western part of the state might now be expected to start developing a greater Catholic population, and the Benedictines had apparently resolved to do their share of the work.

Charlotte, the sole large city in the territory, had the only significant parish not already tended by Benedictine priests. From that church came, lamentably, the worst immediate effect of the grant. Mark Gross, pastor of Saint Peter Church there, believed he had been betrayed; apparently, Gross had assumed himself to be somehow exempt from the effects of the decree. So distraught was this priest at being assigned to a parish outside the Benedictines' territory, that he finally left the state entirely, ending his years of friendship with Maryhelp and of distinguished missionary service to North Carolina. But the abbot-bishop would allow no exceptions. As he understood the situation, for any church in the nine county territory, "by Papal Decree the church is a monastic church;" they were to be staffed by Benedictines, not by seculars, and major decisions regarding them were to be submitted to the monastic Chapter.[12]

felix hintemeyer

While the growth of Haid's abbey was slow, it was unquestionably steady. Ideally, the vicariate was not allowed to distract the bishop too long from the monastery and college, and when it inevitably did, Hintemeyer stayed behind to build in the abbot's absence. The contributions of Father Felix were, on the whole, less practical than Abbot Leo's, or at least less confined to function. Yet, perhaps for that reason, they tended also to do more to enhance the image of the abbot-bishop, and to add a visionary quality to his ambitions that was otherwise lacking. Then too, because the prior was a man who did his work efficiently, expeditiously, quietly, then stepped into the background whenever the bishop appeared, the two monks constituted an astoundingly complementary pair of leaders. And as Haid was called out of the monastery with increasing frequency, Father Felix discreetly picked up the reins and the initiative, and began creating the atmosphere that came to surround the bishop, and which in turn created in America some of the same aura Bernard Smith had designed for the abbot at the Holy See. Hintemeyer, with his gentle ways, refined tastes, and unqualified devotion to Abbot Leo, started bringing to Belmont the trappings that would speak of the abbot-bishop's prominence.

Many of Father Felix's contributions were small and insignificant, but each played a part in the aura that came to surround Leo Haid. Through Hintemeyer, to the abbot's world of squared, brick buildings there came religious art, precious vessels and appointments for church use. His refinements ranged from administrative stationery ("Episcopal Residence, Saint Mary's College, Belmont, NC") and envelopes that expressed the abbot's local fame ("L.H., Belmont, NC"), to episcopal jewelry. He also tried to enhance the abbot-bishop's projects; for example, he converted one room of the college into a museum, a showcase for the abbey's mineral collection and its many gifts. No detail was too small for Father Felix's attention. It was his work, touching on every facet of life on which the abbot himself touched, that allowed Bishop Haid to hold both positions, head of monastery and vicariate, and to meet the demands of each. For while Hintemeyer did enhance the bishop's reign with these countless embellishments, his primary contribution was the coordination of administrative activities for both these bodies.

But Hintemeyer also fathered some special projects that added distinction to the Haid administration. One of the more picturesque monuments for which the bishop was often given credit was the abbey's Lourdes Grotto. In June of 1890, Father Francis Meyer, O.S.B., a young priest of the abbey, contracted typhoid fever. As the disease lingered into its second month, Haid wrote, "I am afraid he will die, [although] we have prayed and still pray for his recovery."[83] Father Felix, who had organized these prayers, appended to the pious petitions the promise that should Father Francis be cured, the monks would build a grotto in honor of the Virgin, whose apparition before Bernadette Soubirous at Lourdes in 1858, had sparked great interest and devotion throughout the Catholic world. Meyer recovered, and Father Felix set the brothers to hauling granite boulders, while he searched for donors to finance the work.[84]

The Grotto of Maria Lourdes was a tasteful, period creation in a cove just northeast and below where the monastery then extended. There was a niche for the statue of the Blessed Mother, an altar of wood, granite, and marble, with brass accessories. The area was spacious, shady, and included a spring and creek. It was also a favorite habitat of the copperheads, but when someone was bitten, the brothers would stick the afflicted limb inside the carcass of a chicken to draw out the poison.[85] No deaths were recorded.

The grotto was typical of the Hintemeyer flair. Of itself it was simple, attractive; it exuded an atmosphere of peace, piety, and prayer. But Father Felix, as usual, stepped back from the monument he had erected and allowed it to frame the gifts of Leo Haid. At his prior's suggestion, Abbot Leo agreed to bless the Lourdes Grotto as a Pilgrimage Shrine—the only one in the state. Hintemeyer then planned the festivities, arranged press coverage from as far away as Baltimore, and of course ordained that the highlight of the ceremony would be an address by the Right Reverend Bishop.

The blessing was scheduled for 7 May 1891, the Solemnity of the Ascension. Clergy and the faithful attended from across the state, eager to witness the ceremonies. Interest had been encouraged by Father Felix's announcement that the grotto was to be, above all else, "the Southern shrine of the Queen of the Clergy for Priestly Vocations."[86] And praying for more priests was always a popular cause, in missionary territory in particular. The bishop pontificated at High Mass in the Abbey Church of Maryhelp at nine o'clock on May seventh. Professor F. Mutter of Richmond composed a special Mass for the occasion,[87] and Father Bernard led the students' choir and orchestra in its performance.[88]

After Mass and a brief respite, a procession was formed outside the chapel. Led by the seventeen piece brass band, the laity, monks, clergy, and bishop descended into the cove. A hymn opened the ceremony; then came the prayer of blessing. The program of the day noted that at the unveiling of the statue, the "audience may cheer,"[89] and according to the Catholic *Mirror*, the appearance of the statue "was saluted with the joyous acclamations of the large assembly."[90] Then came the bishop's turn.

Abbot Leo spoke that day with Francis Meyer at his side, well and happy, sharing the dais. When the story was told of the promise and the cure, Haid himself was so touched that his voice cracked. "The young Priest sat at his side, and the sobs of many . . . were audible amid the almost deathlike stillness around." The Vicar Apostolic was in his best form that day, and before the "attentive throng" his voice "rang through the valley," and "frequent and enthusiastic applause" interrupted the address.[91]

Following more hymns, the pilgrims returned to the church for Benediction of the Blessed Sacrament. That evening the people returned for pyrotechnics in the grotto at half past seven.[92] Later in the month, on Corpus Christi, 28 May, Father Francis blessed another statue for the shrine. This one, recently imported from Europe, and positioned in the grotto, near the spring, was of Saint Walburga, the eighth century abbess who was the monastery's secondary patroness.[93] With this addition the setting was completed. Father Felix was happy, and Leo Haid had been displayed to his best advantage.

Soon after the grotto blessing, Felix Hintemeyer presented to the bishop a second design to add luster to the prelate's episcopal labor—and image. In this scheme, the Very Reverend Prior was able not only to promote the abbot's interests, but to secure invaluable benefits for the Church in Carolina, as well.

It had been the custom in the United States, that wherever there was established an abbey of Benedictine monks, a convent of the Order's sisters was invited to join the work. By 1891, the men had been in the state for fifteen years, but no sisters had yet appeared.[94] Bishop Haid decided it was time to remedy the situation. He enjoyed cordial relations with the Benedictine Sisters in Richmond, and it was presumably to that convent that he proposed to appeal.[95] One of the bishop's sisters, apparently Margaret,[96] taking the name "Sister Augustine," was stationed there, and the Richmond sisters of the Order of Saint Benedict had proven themselves dedicated and conscientious religious and educators. The plan was to grant these women the southern portion of the Caldwell land, and buy additional adjoining acreage. The sisters, in turn, would establish a motherhouse, school for girls, and an orphanage for females.[97]

Father Felix liked the outline of the plan, but he recommended an alternative to Haid's proposal: Hintemeyer suggested that rather than Benedictines, the Sisters of Mercy should be invited to the ninety-seven acres in Belmont set aside for the bishop's female coadjutors.[98] Besides, the Mercies were already working in the vicariate and thus had familiarity with the problems and needs of North Carolina.

The Sisters of Mercy were more ideally suited to the needs of the Vicariate Apostolic of North Carolina at that time. The special charism of the Order was a willingness to undertake any service that met the needs of the Church and poor. Thus they were as likely to be found working in prisons and pauper-houses as in schools and hospitals. Gibbons had invited the Mercies of Charleston and Baltimore to establish a convent in Wilmington, North Carolina. The new foundation, from Charleston, was started in 1869, when the sisters began what the Belmont chronicler Anselm Biggs, O.S.B., called "their magnificent work in the care of the poor, sick, and ignorant."[99] Though their growth had not been spectacular since moving to North Carolina, their service was noteworthy indeed. And by October, Hintemeyer had convinced the bishop that the invitation should be tendered to the Mercies rather than the Benedictines. As the sisters' annals recorded the day, "something like the shadow of a new institution appeared on the horizon."[100]

Mother Augustine, the sisters' superior, went to Belmont early in November to consider the details of the bishop's invitation. Haid and Hintemeyer showed her the abbey, land, and the proposed site of the new convent. The abbot also made clear his inability to assist the women financially, but he "manifest[ed] a kind disposition, intimating that he and the Fathers would give any help in their power." It was estimated that five thousand dollars would be needed immediately, half for land. The Mercies courageously voted to undertake the move, and Sister Mary Charles sketched a plan for the grounds, walks, and the convent. This and all other communications regarding the project were handled by Father Felix. On 3 February 1892, at half past one in the afternoon, construction work began under the direction of Brother Gilbert Koberzynski, O.S.B. It followed the general design of the sister's sketch, but was more ambitious. Throughout construction and in all facets of planning the school, Hintemeyer was the bishop's agent.[101]

The Mercies had decided to name their new convent in honor of the Sacred Heart of Jesus, an idea warmly endorsed at Belmont.[102] In the spring, the bishop and Mother Augustine exchanged visits, and the foundation of cordial and pacific relations was established.[103] Perhaps Haid's most eloquent endorsement of the sisters was his gift of Father Felix, his own most trusted assistant, as their chaplain and advisor.

On 1 September 1892, at about half past four o'clock, the Sisters of Mercy stepped off the train at Belmont and proceeded to their new convent. There they found

> about two dozen men inside the house, at work, no doors either back, front or side and no way of fastening up for the night, except in the dormitory at the top of the house. We went to work at once to prepare for the night, put up a bed for each of us, with Reverend Father Felix at our side to see that it was done right, and the entire Catholic congregation of Belmont looking on, at least the ladies who had come to help, but who in reality were rather a hindrance.[104]

Hintemeyer arranged for Brother Philip to take the sisters their meals until a kitchen was ready for use, and the women settled in to the far from routine existence of erecting a new house of religion.

The dedication of Sacred Heart Convent and Academy was scheduled for the afternoon of 8 September. Father Felix, as *ceremoniarius*, arranged for his bishop an entrance befitting the important enterprise being initiated. By half past three the convent grounds were generously populated with sisters, area Catholics, ladies from Charlotte, and children, when the crowd was silenced by the beating of drums, at some distance northward. Finally the afternoon sun touched the processional cross; behind that was the brass band of the college; it came into view, then the school's colors, the entire student body, all the brothers, the clerics, the priests, and finally Bishop Haid himself, vested in the livery of his office. The nine sisters greeted their Ordinary with lighted candles, and accompanied by the other "men folk" followed him through the building where each room was blessed individually. In the chapel Abbot Leo spoke, and officially welcomed the Sisters of Mercy to their new home: *Crescat! Floreat! Vivat!* "Grow! Flower! Live!"[105] The lumber for the new orphanage was already on the grounds, so the progress of the sisters seemed inevitable.[106]

The festivities ended with an impromptu reception, that was carefully recorded by the sisters' historian:

> The band took its stand in the hall and played, refusing to go till they got refreshments which we had to prepare for them and which, not only the band, but everyone of the priests and Brothers enjoyed like boys. I never saw so many men's heads and limbs in one place in all my life, everywhere you turned, it was the same, men, men, men. The band is composed of priests, lay-Brothers and a few of the College boys. They wound up playing "Good-bye, my Lover, Good-bye," gave "three cheers" for the Sacred Heart Academy, which nearly took the roof off the house, and to our relief took their departure at about half past five in the same order in which they came, with colors flying and band playing while we had to go to work to clean up the litter of cake crumbs, and lemon-peels, which men-like, they let fall all over our nice clean floors and halls. After this we were left for a little while to ourselves which was indeed a relief, as we were completely worn out. . .[107]

In October, the sisters accepted the odious burden of opening a "steam laundry" to serve the college and monastery. This was so large a task that their well went dry in the second week of operation. Then the sisters learned that the laundry used so much water that the convent would have to forgo steam heat that winter. But there must have been some comfort in the solicitude the Benedictines sought to manifest on behalf of the welfare of the Mercies. Hintemeyer personally designed their grounds; Brother Philip planted a vineyard for them; and the bishop reportedly tried to visit daily. "He is indeed a kind Father to us," wrote Sister Agatha, "and I do regret and take back all I so often said about him and the Benedictines."[108]

The sisters had twenty-one pupils that first year, twelve boarders and nine day-students. By the second year, there were thirty-two students. Saint Anne's Orphan Asylum was opened in Belmont. On 26 February 1906, the Sisters' operation of Mercy Hospital in Charlotte commenced. In 1910, Saint Leo School for Boys began serving students too young for the abbey. Their schools and hospitals assisted Haid throughout his territory, and they granted him an unfailing loyalty that, in his troublesome years as Vicar Apostolic, was as welcome and appreciated as it was unique.

While the Mercies were the most important of Hintemeyer's gifts in the early 1890's, they were not the one that received the greatest attention. This most favored project was, of course, another new building.

The abbot seemed always to have at least one construction project in progress. And if the work was not actually at the abbey, it might just as well be in the nine Benedictine counties of the vicariate.[109] The many construction efforts throughout the state laid the foundation for instituting an ambitious policy in Haid's territory: new churches were to provide for what at that time was considered racial integration; that meant that in all churches, pews would be reserved for blacks, and separate houses of worship would no longer be constructed. The policy was only a partial success, and some parish activities such as the choirs did not ordinarily become biracial. But the bishop did have the courage to let his decision be published in the papers.[110] Nevertheless, the constant news from his pastors, detailing the objections of the laity and insisting that the "good of religion" demanded condescension to the standards of the day, successfully forestalled through the years any significant progress toward full integration. And Haid himself thought it reasonable that races should prefer separate churches, just as the Germans liked to have their own congregations, apart from the Irish.

At the abbey, monastery wings arose[111] in 1880, 1891, 1894, and a special area for the brothers appeared in 1893. Sections of the college were erected in 1886, 1888, 1898, and a college wing was tacked on to the Brothers' Building in 1897. Facilities for the farm consumed the laborers' time in 1887; there was a bakery to build in 1890. Later there would be another brothers' wing (1904), also intended to house the library, and other independent structures. For these projects the abbot gave the general direction; the prior was engaged in the construction efforts primarily during Haid's absences. But for the principal project of the 1890's, Hintemeyer and the bishop shared more equally in the effort to secure a structure of the quality and dimension they required.

That project was the erection of a church that would be appropriate to a Benedictine abbey. Even beyond the inadequate quantity of pews, the frame church had proven unsuitable for pontifical ceremonies such as were expected of a prelate in residence. The monastery's church was not a cathedral—it would not achieve that rank until 1910—but because of the bishop's presence it was popularly identified by that term. At first Abbot Leo had exploited the modesty and the primitive mien of the church, but as the brick college and monastery increasingly dwarfed the house of God, the bishop decided it was necessary to acquire a more suitable structure. The current church—"our little cabin"—the abbot said, was little more than a "[bowling] alley"; it "is really a disgrace."[112] And so he embarked at the beginning of 1891, on an extended begging trip. "Never did I enter on a more distasteful work," he lamented with his usual hatred for solicitation, "and I would not do it for anything but a church in poor North Carolina."[113] It was, he said, "a very disagreeable outlook."[114] Haid began by approaching the other Benedictine monasteries in the country,[115] then traveled through the

North.[116] His goal was to raise sufficient funds for a new, larger, wooden church that would last until a brick one could be afforded.

The trip was not his most successful. Despite being absent for more than a month, he was constantly worrying about the classes he was missing and the overall problem of his subordination to poverty.[117] He was seeking only a few thousand dollars, enough to build only a modest church out of lumber. It would be "something like a decent church,"[118] he said, though not what he wanted. But the money would not appear. The present church had again been outgrown, and the abbey "could not let the church go any longer."[119] Alone, however, he was powerless. The bishop returned to North Carolina without sufficient funds for a new frame-and-board church. He discovered, however, that in his absence, Father Felix had made other plans, anyway.

The place where the permanent church was eventually to stand had been determined several years earlier. The "U" formed by the monastery-college was to balance this, the supreme structure, flanking it on both sides, with the monastery stretching behind. Its site was comfortably north of where the frame church stood, so the first would not have to be razed until the final building was ready for use. But Father Felix, determined that his abbot-bishop should have an appropriate western cathedral, had already decided that the permanent church should be constructed immediately. Finding his abbot returned without even enough money for a lesser edifice, and knowing the man as well as he did, the prior argued that the funds had not been supplied because the abbot was aiming at practicality over God's will. Hintemeyer told Haid to start building the grand brick church he really wanted, knowing he could not possibly meet the expense, but having the courage to trust God to provide. It was the kind of logic that always appealed to Haid—the same reasoning, indeed, that sparked his decision to have vicariate pastors do their own begging. As he had already resolved, "What success will attend my efforts I don't know—but I must try, praying God and our Blessed Lady to pity our poverty and help us."[120]

And so, at Hintemeyer's insistence, Leo Haid embarked on the construction of a sixty thousand dollar "cathedral," the largest Roman Catholic church in the state, with no earthly means of financing it. F. Dietrich of Detroit was architect; J.H. Thore of Charlotte was hired as the contractor. Saint Vincent would not give permission for Brother Wolfgang to go south; Saint John could not spare their builder, Brother Andrew, O.S.B.,[121] so Brother Gilbert Koberzynski, age fifty-two, of Belmont, formerly an apprentice boatwright, coordinated the brothers' contribution to the building effort, working under Mr. Thore's management. Brother Charles Eckel took charge of executing the interior woodwork. On 9 February 1892, the bishop contracted with Lentz and McKnight, a local partnership, to "deliver to site three hundred thousand good, smooth brick of exact size three by four by eight inches at four dollars per thousand."[122] Leo Haid was about to build a cathedral.

Groundbreaking ceremonies, postponed from Saint Patrick's Day, were scheduled for the Solemnity of Saint Benedict, 21 March 1892. The Pontifical Mass of the day was celebrated at nine o'clock, and the bishop preached, taking as his theme the call to personal holiness in Benedict's *Regula*. A luncheon followed; then the monks, students, and guests reassembled in front of the frame church.[123]

For commencing work on the church there was a simple program. The party processed the several yards from the first church to the site of the new one, with the band, of course, leading the way. Bishop Haid dug the first shovelful for the foundation, then each of the monks followed. Next the guests were invited to ply the spade, and the Mount Holly *News* reported, "it was very amusing to see the ladies swinging the shovel, or rather attempting to do so." The students, who followed the guests, proved both more adept and enthusiastic at digging, and the whole affair acquired something of a festive air as the band played continuously through the ceremony.[124] As had happened in 1886, with the College Building, the boys stayed at the site afterwards, sacrificing their free-day and games to work on the new building. The commitment had been made: Maryhelp Abbey, already in debt, was building its most expensive building ever, with available cash reserves of barely one hundred dollars.

To bring the building to the attention of the public—and of potential donors—Hintemeyer volunteered to choreograph the laying of the cornerstone. This, he decided, would be as opulent a ceremony as the groundbreaking was subdued. Gibbons, unfortunately, was unavailable,[125] so once again Bishop Haid had to be the featured attraction and principal speaker.

The activities surrounding the benediction of the cornerstone followed what by this time was the ordinary sequence for abbey celebrations. The preceeding evening featured a presentation by the college's dramatic association, at which the orchestra performed during the intermissions.[126] High Mass was held at mid-morning the next day. There was a luncheon. The special ceremony occupied the afternoon. And a Grand Illumination in the grotto (on some occasions replaced by another play) was presented in the evening.[127]

The church cornerstone ceremony was scheduled for 4 May 1892. The boys performed *The Recognition* on the third, assisted by the orchestra. Mass at half past nine the next morning was squeezed into what the Charlotte *Chronicle* called "the present little house of worship."[128] But the afternoon ceremonies featured the best Hintemeyer could arrange.

Press coverage by this time was taken for granted. The Mount Holly newspaper even invited a regular column from the students, let the college author its own articles, then published them verbatim. In addition to the press, Hintemeyer had arranged for a special train to bring people to Belmont from as far away as Wilmington. Reportedly, several hundred made the trip, and met in front of the old church at half past three o'clock as the procession was forming.[129]

There was no more distance to be covered than at the groundbreaking, but this time there was not only a brass band, but banner-bearers to precede them; there were the several hundred guests, a full contingent from Sacred Heart, representatives of the clergy, the entire monastic community, and finally, of course, Leo Haid in full episcopal regalia.[130] At the site, the abbot performed the blessings, including the foundation, the place where the main altar would stand and finally the cornerstone itself. There he sang in Latin, "You are Peter," and the assembly responded, "And on this rock I shall build my church."[131] The stone—a granite block in which were carved a cross, motto, the date, and an eight by eight inch cavity for various papers, medals, and coins[132]—was then set in place, and the bishop ascended the dais to begin his address.[133]

The talk was uncommonly personal in tone, an indulgence of his own involvement which translated into a forum for ideas the bishop had failed to emphasize during the immediate past. He began by noting that only six years earlier he had laid his first cornerstone, and started work on the College Building. But this, the church, was his special dream, reaching now for fruition. He stated he wanted the liturgy to be performed here as it was nowhere else in the state, with grandeur, solemnity, and the full richness of the Catholic and Benedictine ceremonials. He wanted the students to hold in their hearts for years to come the beautiful liturgies that would take place here, and seminarians to imbibe a flavor of ritual that would inspire their whole lives in the ministry. These ambitions were important, but they did not represent what this building meant to him, however. For Leo Haid, the church was primarily and above all else the heart of his monastery. And to the assembled missionary clergy, the faithful who saw him primarily as a bishop, and to his own monks, Leo Haid clarified himself as well as his building. He said,

> But to me—a monk before I was either priest or bishop—this church is doubly dear because it will resound with the prayers of men dedicated wholly to God in the monastic state. Day after day, ere the sun gilds our mountain tops, the voice of prayer will be raised to God in this church; day after day when darkness and silence cover the earth the same voice will praise our good God!

The abbot continued,

> Some people only love and value or tolerate monks for what they can do in active life—as tillers of the soil, learned men, artists, teachers and pastors of souls. I love them more for what they can do immediately for God—for their quiet lives of prayer and meditation. This is the first and greatest ideal striven after by those who founded them—by the Church who has nourished and loved them as her special, most dutiful children. If then all have reason to rejoice today, surely our joy—children of Saint Benedict that we are—should be greatest, because we know that our labor and prayers in erecting this abbey church will build a house of prayer especially for those whose lives are altogether dedicated to God.

In conclusion the abbot made his usual commendation, summoning the protection of God, Saint Benedict, and the Blessed Mother. In particular he prayed, "May our dear Lady—to whom this Abbey and College are dedicated—our Lady, Help of Christians, be our help and stay in the work we have today begun."[134] If the monks of Belmont were still worried that their abbot planned to move them all from cloister to parish, this address should have arrested their fears.

Typically, Father Felix had already quietly endorsed the abbot's sentiments. The document he included in the cornerstone ended with a prayer of its own, asking "that this church may become a perpetual monument of religion in these districts."[135]

The Grand Illumination at eight o'clock that same evening was in no way dwarfed by the opulence of the ceremonies that preceeded it. The orchestra and band led a torch-light procession to the grotto,[136] where Chinese lanterns illuminated the whole cove. The crowd watched the colored lights reflected on the grotto. Then while the band continued playing, a giant balloon was released, and the people watched it drift toward Charlotte until nine thirty-five.[137]

There was an unexpected postscript to the evening, of which the crowd did not learn until later in the week. It seems that the Belmont festivities had incited a considerable stir in the Paw Creek section of Charlotte. As a local newspaper reported it,

> Disquiet and unrest prevailed in Paw Creek Wednesday night. About nine o'clock, some [people]. . .described a peculiar looking object in the field. Every now and then it would rise up from the earth and remain in the air a

few minutes, and then "flop" back again. It was too dark for anyone to tell the size or manner of being of the remarkable thing, and the [citizens] soon became alarmed and began to raise a terrible commotion.

The Paw Creek residents then armed themselves, only to be frightened away as the thing began advancing toward the reconnoitering party, presumably on the attack. Later, braver souls appeared and engaged in their own reconnaissance mission, only to discover the alien matter was nothing more than the remnant of the balloon the abbey had sent aloft the previous evening.[138]

Construction of the church was expected to last at least a year, during most of which time Hintemeyer acted as the local superior. The abbot was absent for his vicariate visitations and on Congregation business; there were begging trips and the mission to Rome. The new church in Charlotte was also under construction. But Hintemeyer kept all the work moving. When large trusses collapsed on the abbey's new church, causing serious damage to the recently constructed walls, Father Felix checked for injuries, surveyed the destruction, and ordered the work recommenced immediately. He was determined that this greatest monument to his abbot-bishop would not be thwarted.

Actually, it was Leo Haid who seemed to be failing the project. In addition to the abbey's church and Saint Peter Church in Charlotte, he was also building the brothers' wing of the monastery, and by the summer of 1893, Abbot Leo returned from Rome to find that there was no more money. Rumors began spreading among the employees that work was soon to be halted, and it seemed, if only for the nonce, that Leo Haid's greatest monument was to stand uncompleted, its open shell testifying to failure rather than triumph.

Francis Meyer, who by this time, his health restored, was the energetic, construction-minded pastor of Saint Peter Church, had acted while the bishop was in Rome to secure extra funds for the new Charlotte edifice. The abbot upon his return expressed pleasure with the priest's initiative and promptly informed Meyer's donor that he could "see no reason why I should not gratefully accept your generous offer."[139] The only condition on the gift was that the church include an appropriate number of pews for the exclusive use of blacks,[140] a requirement that enhanced the commitment already made by the bishop. Accordingly, after consultation with Fathers Felix and Francis, the abbot decided to approach this benefactor on behalf of his beleaguered abbey "cathedral", too.

The gracious donor Father Francis had uncovered was Katharine Mary Drexel, a Philadelphia heiress. Katharine, who would turn thirty-five in 1893, was the second of three daughters born to Francis Anthony Drexel. A fabulously successful financier, Mr. Drexel's net residual estate was valued in 1885, after his death, at fifteen and a half million dollars. One-tenth of that was left to charity. The remainder was apportioned in the elaborate and rather famous Article VII of his will. This proviso allowed each daughter to draw income equally from the remaining principal, valued at approximately fourteen million dollars. And if, as proved the case, a daughter died without issue, the remaining sister(s) would divide the income each time equally. Elizabeth, the eldest sister, died without issue in 1890, leaving Katharine and Louise—a younger sister through Drexel's second wife—to divide the income from the fourteen million equally, so long as they should live to draw it. Louise died—without issue—in 1943, after which Katharine drew the full income. She managed to live and draw on her inheritance until 3 March 1955, when at age ninety-seven she finally died—also without issue—and the fourteen million dollars was given to charity according to the dictates of her father's will, first probated seventy years before.[141]

Katharine had a decided religious bent, and after dealing with considerable objections, founded the Sisters of the Blessed Sacrament for Indians and Colored People on 12 February 1891. From that time forward, her substantial income was devoted to the needs of Catholic Indians and negroes. Mother Katharine was a tough businesswoman, and one of the few people who could regularly outmaneuver Leo Haid at the bargaining table. But whether she was charging him the "extra fee" of preaching a "Crusade" for the Indian missions—as a condition for a fifteen hundred dollar gift for the Gastonia church[142]—or debating whether or not blacks really wanted to use the same churches as whites,[143] there was a bond of mutual respect in their correspondence that was surpassed only by her generosity. This 1893 bequest was the beginning of their long association.

In later years, the famous Drexel "conditions," requiring separate pews for blacks in churches, were criticized, even to the point of suggesting that she and accomplices like Haid furthered segregation. For its time, however, such schemes for securing black admission to what would otherwise have been all-white churches, was considered daring, and in some places—Wilmington, North Carolina, in particular—proved inflammatory. In perspective, Katharine Drexel provided a far greater service than can be evaluated within the generous totals of her financial munificence. North Carolina was not anxious for even so modestly integrated a church as Mother Katharine required. But by the well-publicized "conditions"

Katharine Drexel imposed when she helped build a church, leverage was given to people like Haid who sought to secure this relative racial unity, which he considered important—though often uncomfortable for people on both sides—for the Church.

The bishop wrote Drexel on 24 June 1893. His proposal was that not only would pews be reserved for blacks, but he would close Belmont's Saint Benedict Church—converting it to a school—in order to insure integration. But the abbot also begged Drexel's donation on the grounds of the larger effect that would follow on the bishop's own church inviting the presence of negroes.

> The *Moral effect* on the Catholics in North Carolina especially, and in other Southern States, would be a great gain. If the Benedictines at the Abbey and in Charlotte break down the ugly prejudices against Colored people—it would go far to enable the Bishop to insist on building all future churches large enough to make decent room for Colored people. This last reason seems to me the principal motive. There is no use in butting the head against the hard wall of prejudice—but we may climb over the wall or go around it slowly—especially by good example.
>
> There are other reasons—but let these suffice. . . .It would do my heart good to see some black faces there too—in the body of the church at that.[144]

Mother Katharine responded more generously than Leo Haid dared to expect. She offered four thousand dollars under the usual conditions.[145] The bishop executed a document on 1 July, affirming that the "Benedictine Fathers gladly [promise] to give the Colored Catholics the same care they bestow upon the Whites," and of course a row of pews in the body of the church.[146] Fittingly, the document was co-signed by Father Felix on behalf of the monastic Chapter.

Work on the church never had to stop. Mother Drexel sent a check for the whole amount on 16 October,[147] a full three months ahead of schedule. Haid responded,

> I was made very happy by your great kindness, as I can now finish the church, and hope to have the First Pontifical High Mass in it December eighth which I will offer to God for you and your Community. May God reward you all! I do hope that after we again unite the Colored people we will have greater fruits to be grateful for.[148]

Construction delays kept Haid from meeting that schedule, unfortunately, but he did offer Mass for Mother Drexel that day, even though the setting was "the dear old Cabin [church]." Finally on Sunday, 17 December, the bishop offered the first Mass in the (still unfinished) new Church of Maryhelp. His intention for the Sacrifice covered not only Katharine Drexel, but all the building's benefactors.[149] Immediately, the abbot's mind turned to the blessing of the church. He managed to secure Cardinal Gibbons for the ceremony, then conveyed the whole affair—including the appointments for the interior of the edifice—into the waiting hands of the real father of the brick church, Felix Hintemeyer.

Leo Haid's new "cathedral" was only about one hundred twenty-five feet in length, but with its rugged facade of hand-pressed brick and Carolina granite trim, its towers and spires of one hundred fifty and one hundred feet, surmounted by celtic and filigree crosses, the building stood in dramatic contrast with the fields and farmlands that composed its vista. The monks had not only built the largest Catholic church in the state; they had built the most resplendent, as well.

The final form of the church did lack some of the ornamentation Haid had wanted. For example the abbot-bishop had quietly delayed the purchase of new Stations of the Cross, merely translating the ones from the frame chapel.[150] But all the essentials had been provided in some form, and reflected the rather Florentine tastes of the prior.

The church[151] was a modified Gothic-Revival structure, brick with granite trim. Designed in the form of a Latin Cross, its length was divided into eight bays with a width roughly equal to two. The front featured a granite arch, surmounted by a large tracery window. There were projecting front corner towers, one about fifty feet higher than the other; each had an octagonal belfry and a spire. The higher tower, at the southwest corner, included the bells and was intended to symbolize the active apostolate of the monks. The "quiet" tower, lower in heigh and lacking bells, represented the monks' hidden life of monastic prayer. Exterior ornamentation consisted of pinnacles, buttresses, and trim. The most serious stylistic deviation in the cruciform structure was the squared eastern end, where an apse would have been more appropriate.

The interior of the church, at an elevation of four steps, was entered by massive wooden doors with iron 'frogs'. The arched ceiling was painted light blue, and covered with gold *fleurs-de-lis*. The sanctuary, another three steps higher, was bordered by a gilt railing of butternut. A luxurious crimson carpet covered the center aisle and pointed the visual line toward the main altar. In the sanctuary, on the north wall, was an episcopal throne, twenty-six feet in height, approached by three oak steps. The throne's canopy of oak and gilt was topped with a spire ascending almost to the ceiling. Padding was deep burgundy. The main altar, and this too was of gilt oak, stood thirty-six feet in height and included three niches, with blue ceilings dotted with stars. Father Joseph Jessing, an orphanage priest in Columbus, Ohio, furnished the woodwork.

The main altar featured at its highest pinacle an arresting statue of Maryhelp in support of the Christchild. The *Catholic Mirror* singled out the image for its "delicate beauty."[152] Maryhelp was flanked by images of Saints Joachim and Anne. Scholastica and Benedict had altars to the side. The Saint Joseph altar in the left transept had statues of Joseph, Augustine of Canterbury and Edward the Confessor. The baptismal font stood nearby. An altar dedicated to the Sacred Heart dominated the right transept, with statuary images of the Sacred Heart of Jesus, Aloysius Gonzaga, and Rose of Lima.

Seating in the nave was divided by three aisles. There were two gothic confessionals of polished oak, "undoubtedly. . .enumerated among the handsomest in the South," according to a Washington, D.C., newspaper, the *Church News*.[153]

In the choir stood a pipe organ by A.B. Felgemaker, of Erie, Pennsylvania. It had a white oak case, and its thirty-three pipes were decorated with bronze and gold. The instrument had two manuals and twenty-five stops and couplers.

But the crown of the church was its extraordinary windows.[154] Measuring five by eighteen feet, and designed as gothic arches, they contributed a striking, rich luster to the interior of the church. Four single-figure windows by Schneider of Ratisbon, Bavaria, decorated the transepts. But the main body and the chancel featured ten windows from the Royal Bavarian Establishment of Francis Mayer and Company in Munich. Mayer's artistry, shown at the Columbian Exhibition, the World's Fair in Chicago, had taken four gold medals for the manufacturer in 1893.[155] That display had included windows destined for North Carolina and other parts of the country.

Each of the two hundred eighty dollar windows[156] for Belmont featured a single saint in the center light, with ornamentation in the side panels. Not really stained glass, they were painted, in the manner of much of the European glass at the time, with pigments that were fused with the host surface by a heating process, making them portraits on glass, and far more life-like than ordinary American work of the period. The efforts of different artists were obvious in the renderings. The renaissance styling in the hands of Saint Maurus contrasted with the gloved, quasi-Byzantine effect of Saint Anselm. The best windows were the richly embellished Saint Patrick, featuring magnificent detail in the face and robes, plus a depth of color that was unsurpassed; and the Saint Placid window, an engaging study with a powerful and provocative face set off by an undetailed cloak that seemed almost unfinished. The Saint Leo the Great window, copied from the designs Mayer executed for the Vatican as a gift for Pope Leo XIII, was of special interest, also, although its parallel, Saint Gregory, was more perfectly rendered.

The windows were positioned with Gertrude opposite the monastery's secondary patroness, Saint Walburga. Saint Patrick (most local Catholics around Belmont were of Irish lineage) faced Saint Boniface (apostle to the Germans, and thus to the forefathers of most of the monks); Anselm (patron of Benedictine schools) gazed across at Bernard (for Benedictine prayer). Popes Saint Leo (the abbot's patron) and Gregory (the first Benedictine pontiff) stared at one another, as did Saint Benedict's disciples, Maurus and Placid. The Schneider windows placed Martin of Tours and John the Baptist (to whose honor Saint Benedict had built chapels) at the Joseph altar, and the Guardian Angels (as patrons of the American Cassinese Congregation) and Saint Michael the Archangel (as patron of Belmont's grandmother house and of the baptismal consecration of the abbot and prior) on either side of the Sacred Heart altar.

The Gothic-Revival church of Leo Haid was further accentuated by its placement on the grounds. The buildings that would frame it were not yet completed, but the expanse of lawn on either side already lent a natural definition to the space. The bricks united the structure with its surroundings, and the elevation of the ground combined with the spires—which made effective use of the contrast in a square tower, beneath an octagonal base, that ascended to a perfect point surmounted by a cross—enthroned the new church as the focal point not just of the cloister and campus, but of the surrounding countryside.

The blessing of the Abbey Church of Maryhelp was described in the press as "a fair and grand day—a day ever [to live] in the Catholic history of the South."[157] Even rain could not restrain Hintemeyer on this occasion. He simply ordered the sisters and young ladies at Sacred Heart to start praying for sunshine. The prior was so excited as the time of the blessing approached, that he absentmindedly left poor Father O'Connell, only a few months from his death and already enfeebled by this time with a "trembling palsy in the head,"[158] standing out in the rain,[159] waiting to offer his welcoming speech at the abbey, while the Cardinal was being awaited at the depot.

Father Felix had arranged a special railroad car—a "train de luxe"—for Monday evening, 9 April 1894, to bring James Cardinal Gibbons to Belmont for the dedication. The train stopped in Charlotte the next morning, where the Cardinal had breakfast with Doctor Denis O'Donoghue, the wealthiest Catholic in the area and an old acquaintance. At one o'clock the Gibbons entourage reached the abbey. And despite the inclement weather—"the very bowels of the clouds seemed to empty themselves"[160] (the effort at Sacred Heart did not succeed until the following day)—the festivities began.

As usual, the preliminary celebration began with a play. An all male cast of Abbeymen presented *Saint Caecelia*. The *dramatis personae* included two future priests of the vicariate,[161] two future monks of the abbey,[162] and a future abbot of Maryhelp.[163]

On 11 April 1894, the feast of Saint Leo, the abbot's patron, with the proud ladies of Sacred Heart reportedly beaming as brightly as the sun they had summoned, the dignitaries and people assembled for the dedication of the Abbey Church of Maryhelp of Christians. Though admission to the church required a ticket, Haid had distributed his invitations generously, and the building was filled to capacity. The ceremonies progressed smoothly, however, as Gibbons performed the blessing, and Haid officiated at the Mass. The choir sang Mozart—the abbot even permitted a choir of "mixed" voices—and Father Ganss, a Pennsylvania priest imported for the occasion,[164] presided at the Felgemaker console.

Cardinal Gibbons preached that day, reminding all assembled that he had chosen the Benedictines for this site in North Carolina. He did not mention that he had done so only after the Redemptorists had turned him down.

The frame chapel had been demolished before the Cardinal reached Belmont, and the new church, only one hundred twenty-five feet in length, and fifty feet wide, may have seemed less imposing without the comparison. But the memory of the frame structure, once dubbed "the poorest cathedral in the world," was a reminder to the Benedictine monks of the generosity of Providence and Katharine Drexel. If the abbot was not pleased with the new church, he concealed that fact.

The blessing was a grand day for Leo Haid. And through Hintemeyer's efforts it was witnessed by people from throughout the state, brought to Belmont like the Cardinal on special trains. Bishop Northrop also attended, as did Archabbot Leander (Saint Vincent), Abbots Alexius (Saint John), Innocent (Saint Benedict), Hilary (Saint Mary), and Benedict (Saint Bernard). At half past one, the prelates enjoyed a festive meal, followed by the play *Saint Walburga*, performed by an all female cast at the girls' academy.[165] The dignitaries dined that evening at Sacred Heart.

The next morning, the Cardinal had breakfast with the boys, who were so excited by his condescension that they followed his carriage to the limits of the campus when he departed. His Eminence cracked a rather classical joke about the Greek calends, and as he disappeared down the road toward Belmont, one of the boys belatedly realized the Cardinal had just given them a free-day. For once they did not spend it in construction work.

Haid made few changes in his church during the years of his reign. Not until 1896 did he even succeed in erecting new Stations of the Cross. The ones he finally acquired stood six feet three inches when framed. Executed in bas relief, they featured tender images in subdued colors. Though undistinguished artistically, they were particularized by the sensitivity of their subjects. The eighth Station, in which Christ turned to the ladies of Jerusalem to give his blessing, was the most notable of the images.

In 1897, at the prior's suggestion, Haid hired A.F. Sauerwald of Richmond to add "frescoes", but on the whole the abbot did not tamper with the structure. Only Felix Hintemeyer made changes, slowly accumulating donations of vessels and candalabra of gold and silver, and vestments of silk and velvet. To Hintemeyer, nothing was too good for Leo Haid.

Saint Leo, Florida

The missions in Florida, more than five hundred miles from the abbey, were always treated with abstraction by Abbot Leo. He had heard the old myth that the state was merely floating, and would some day break loose from the panhandle. "Eventually," he mused, "Florida will no doubt float to North Carolina—as that is the opinion I generally hear."[166] Until it did float away, however, the abbot used it as a place to send infirm monks. He invited Saint John Abbey to send consumptive clerics there, too,[167] and Haid sent his own weaker members, like Meinrad Buechling[168] and Lawrence Wiegand,[169] there for reasons of serious infirmity. Another monk, Alphonse Conrad Metzger, died at the Florida monastery in a rifle accident.[170]

The territory given by Bishop Moore to the Benedictines had originally been accepted by Boniface Wimmer, who in his last months offered this most distant of southern missions to Leo Haid. But the archabbot's death delayed the official transfer. Andrew Hintenach, the second archabbot of Saint Vincent, re-endorsed the idea after assuming his throne, and asked Abbot Leo and the Chapter at Belmont to accept responsibility for the Florida work as soon as possible. As a bonus, Father Gerard Pilz, O.S.B., who was the chief Benedictine missionary in Florida, asked to transfer his stability to Maryhelp, as an alternative to abandoning his work. He had founded the Benedictine mission there, and by transferring his stability to the new proprietor, he insured some measure of continuity in the administration of the parishes. But in the summer of 1888, Haid's episcopal consecration was the primary concern, with the Walter Leahy affair in close competition; these conspired with Florida's yellow fever epidemic, which inhibited travel. Finally all these factors were joined by an unfortunate encounter with poison ivy—which "disfigured [Haid] beyond recognition"—so that the abbot resigned himself to submitting the proposed acceptance of the Florida missions to his Chapter before even going south to see the place. Nevertheless, on 10 October 1888, the Belmont capitulars accepted the Florida missions, "with all the bonus and onus," and the transfer of Father Gerard. The abbot advised Pennsylvania of the Chapter's decisions, and Belmont found itself in possession of its third dependency.[171]

Acquiring the services of Gerard Pilz ranked among the more propitious aspects of the new endeavor. Father Gerard, at age fifty-four, was one of the most respected monks of the archabbey. A Bavarian native, he had been trained as an artist, and Wimmer had even sent him for advanced studies in Munich. Pilz was a gifted speaker, too, and had published a volume of sermons. Wimmer had also given him experience as a missionary and administrator. Pilz was prior of the New Jersey monastery when it was promoted to the rank of an abbey. After that he was assigned to the priory in Chicago, where on 12 April 1886, he received an invitation to enter the mission fields of Florida. Boniface Wimmer apparently had not responded to Bishop Moore's letter of 1 February, so the Ordinary of Saint Augustine wrote directly to Pilz, who he hoped would be Wimmer's candidate for the work anyway.[172] The archabbot sent Father Gerard to Florida, and Saint Vincent acquired its valuable mission territory there. Pilz, assisted by Cyprian Creagh and Brother Francis Zwiesler, soon added a school to his responsibilities, achieved the bishop's approval for erecting a permanent Benedictine foundation, and instigated the territorial donation of 1887.[173]

No sooner was this venerable monk and gifted administrator incorporated into Maryhelp, however, than he found himself immersed in scandal. A county commissioner, it seemed, had observed the priest on the previous 10 August in the company of a postulant for the sisters. The official "accused [them] of sinning in a buggy on the road side." By November, word of the incident had spread and become general knowledge. Legal action against Father Gerard was even being considered.[174]

Haid was greatly alarmed and left North Carolina immediately for Florida. Concerned also that the story should not surface at the abbey, he sent his communications with Bishop Moore first to Pennsylvania, where Hintenach posted the missives to Saint

Augustine. Abbot Leo explained, "I don't want too many letters to go out from me," as that might create suspicions at Belmont.[175] Although the charges of impropriety proved to have been greatly exaggerated, the notoriety and its effect on Pilz's nerves and reputation required the priest's removal. He was sent to make an extended retreat with Father Joseph,[176] and then assigned to teaching duties at the abbey. Belmont's prior, Father Roman, took over the work in Florida, thus occasioning the promotion of Father Felix to the prior's office at the abbey. After investigating the situation in Florida, Haid surmised that Father Gerard's work had been destroyed for no greater reason than his having "made enemies and give[n] them whips with which to punish him! How mercifully people treat their priests," he lamented. "I am getting so used to storms breaking out somewhere that I am getting used to them."[177]

The gentleman who had expanded the Commissioner's complaint and village scuttlebutt into a *cause celebre* was himself no stranger to controversy, and he would continue for the next few years to be a thorn and a drain on the resources of Leo Haid. He was Edmund Francis Dunne.[178] A New York native, just one year younger than Father Gerard, he had gone to California as a young man and studied law. During the Civil War he moved to Nevada where he eventually became a District Judge. In 1874, he entered a brief tenure as Chief Judge of the Territorial Court at Tucson. Amid various, and mostly unresolved factors (of an unpleasant nature), President Grant apparently relieved the judge of the burdens of his office. Through his wife, Josephine Cecelia Warner, of the Vicksburg gentry, there was some money at the judge's disposal, and with his children, of whom there were at least four, he relocated randomly in search of opportunity. He acquired through the years a reputation for "Irish intransience" and for being "a militant Irish Catholic."[179] But from his religious interests he won a Knighthood of Saint Gregory from Pius IX, and Leo XIII created him a Papal Count.[180]

Good fortune finally visited Dunne in 1881. As the judge told the story, the state of Florida, in order to retire its considerable debt, had determined to sell fifteen million acres of land. Hamilton Disston of Philadelphia agreed to purchase four million acres, and chose Judge Dunne to act as his representative in selecting which four million acres he would take. As his payment, Dunne was given the right to any section of up to fifty thousand acres he desired from the four million he purveyed for Disston. In this way, the Count, as Haid liked to call Dunne, became the principal land owner in the area of San Antonio, Florida. He used his land to establish a "Catholic Colony."[181] It was because of this concentrated Catholic population—in 1883 there were about one hundred thirty colonists[182]—that Bishop Moore invited a Benedictine missionary to journey southward.

As a federal judge, Papal Knight, Count of the Apostolic Palace, and the trusted representative of Disston, Dunne's business dealings must have seemed above question. And Moore, Haid, and the colonists recognized the judge as a generous benefactor of religion in the South. He had reserved a section of land totaling more than thirty acres for the Benedictines,[183] and Haid was enthusiastic about accepting it and redesigning the Benedictine parish commitment into a monastery and college. The land fronted on a sink hole, but included a right-of-way to Clear Lake,[184] and was picturesque and presumably to be of future value. Haid accepted the land, and later built there the monastery—originally called "Saint Benedict", but finally known by the school's name, "Saint Leo", in honor of Leo XIII.

On 18 October 1888, Bishop Haid and Judge Dunne entered a legal agreement, whereby in return for one hundred thousand square feet of land in San Antonio, about three acres with potential as a lemon grove, Maryhelp agreed to educate the two Dunne sons, Eugene[185] (who styled himself a Papal Viscount) and Brian[186] (who was apparently resigned to being the commoner of the family). The agreement was to run for a period not to exceed twelve years, covering all expenses attendent to education and living, except clothing and pocket money.[187] It was an expensive bargain, as Brian took the full regular studies, and the "viscount" not only completed the ordinary educational program, but decided on a Master's as well. Considering that the land had reportedly cost the Count only a dollar and a half, or fifty cents per acre, he made a substantial profit. But Saint Leo Priory, which acquired the property upon receipt of canonical independence, enjoyed the greatest benefits, obtaining valuable land in the city of San Antonio, while Maryhelp was left with the bills for the education of Eugene and Brian Dunne.

The other business transaction between the abbot and the judge ended less cordially. Dunne's ambitions for hosting, and selling land to at least a thousand, Catholic colonists were slowly disintegrating as dissatisfied customers, led by a retired naval officer, leveled charges of varying degrees of fraud in an increasingly vociferous manner.[188] His personal finances exhausted by the slump in business, the Count appealed, around 1890, to Leo Haid for a loan of three thousand dollars, for up to three years at eight per cent interest. Already fleeced once, and wary of the dealings in which Dunne engaged, the bishop insisted on proper collateral. Finally the loan was arranged, apparently in the form of a mortgage on the one hundred acres the judge had reserved in the colony for his own home.[189] During the next three years, the parties differed over the details of their agreement, but when the loan went unpaid, Abbot Leo was forced to act anyway. At first he refused to employ the courts, lest a bishop suing a Count of the Holy See should create scandal. Dunne, however, was not only declining to pay his debts, he was also allowing the mortgaged land to ruin. Accordingly, Haid, after consulting with Saint Leo and with the Maryhelp Chapter, decided early in 1893 to foreclose on the property. The monks were not the first party to make that decision, however. A firm in West Virginia, due to the judge's debts in that state, already had a lien on the land. The Benedictines, it was explained, had to pay Dunne's prior debt in order to take possession of the acreage in satisfaction of his more recent dissolvency.[190]

In the meantime, George B. Williams, a former student, claimed to have heard the full story of Dunne's supposed business irregularities in a classroom lecture delivered by Father Charles. Williams told the viscount; Eugene told Edmund; and the Count began threatening the Florida prior with "terrible looking documents" that demanded a public apology, and held out the probable exaction of pecuniary compensation unless restitution were made freely. Father Charles asked the abbot, who by this time was totally infuriated with the Count, to remain aloof. The prior then enlisted the aid of a friend who sat on the bench in Tampa, and this man succeeded in quieting Dunne.[191] The monks executed the foreclosure, and severed all association with Judge Edmund Francis Dunne.[192]

The abbot of Belmont was greatly impressed by the service rendered by Father Charles in the Dunne affair. That, the undeniable progress of the Florida work, and the fact that the Catholic Colony of San Antonio was causing a seemingly endless succession of crises, led Haid to consider promoting the house to canonical independence. It was not yet ready to be an abbey, but he thought it could stand as an autonomous monastery with the rank of a priory.

At the core of Saint Leo's prospects was Charles Mohr. Though only thirty years old in 1893, he was experienced in pastoral work, teaching, and administration. He had not rated particularly high in the bishop's esteem until recently, however. He had been assigned to parish work, then to Florida mostly because of his delicate health. Indeed, the abbot's first choice for establishing the Saint Leo Military College had been a New Jersey monk, Father Frederick Hoesel, O.S.B. This thirty-nine year old priest had been loaned to the Florida missions by Saint Mary Abbey. On his way to Florida in July of

1889, Hoesel stopped at Maryhelp to discuss with Bishop Haid the proposed foundation. While at Belmont, however, a hemorrhage of the lungs cut short his life. The next year Charles Mohr was transferred to Florida to take charge of the newly erected school that was to have been Father Frederick's responsibility. Under Father Charles' administration, the school was self-sustaining at the end of its first term.[193] At least two years earlier than expected,[194] in 1890, the priory was already strong.[195] In 1891 choral recitation of the Divine Office was instituted, and the bishop was boasting of his "Baby," all of whose "running expenses are paid, and besides many improvements made. I am quite satisfied so far," he said.[196]

Haid decided, as abbot of the monastery's motherhouse and as *praeses* of its Congregation, to petition for the independence of Saint Leo Priory. The *praeses* also decided to request the appointment of Charles Mohr as the first conventual prior, a decision later ratified by vote of the capitulars in Florida. Originally, the petition was to be submitted in the spring, after the close of the school term. In January, Mohr almost blocked the effort, however, by tendering his resignation.[197] The abbot was able to dissuade him, fortunately, and the effort for autonomy began in earnest soon thereafter, before further problems could arise.

The formal petition was finally sent to Rome on 28 June 1894, requesting erection of Saint Leo as a conventual priory, with Charles Mohr as superior. A term of five years was recommended, at the end of which the *praeses* believed[198] a petition for abbatial status might be made. Bishop Moore wrote an enthusiastic endorsement of the Benedictine effort in Florida.[199] Fathers Roman, Charles, Benedict, James Schabacher, and Louis Panoch, and Brothers Thomas, Anthony, Gerard, and Leander asked to transfer their vows to the new priory.[200] Rome granted their petition without problem in mid-September.[201] Two weeks later the documents were in hand.[202]

As father of the new monastery, Leo Haid wrote the Abbot Primate, "the new Priory promises to become an honor to our Order. May God's blessing always rest on it."[203] In only nine years at Maryhelp Leo Haid had brought honors and achievements to his monastery that surpassed even the boldest of expectations. And he need not be faulted for boasting of his first daughterhouse. But these had not been halcyon years, and the progress had left scars and cast the frame of future conflicts. Even with Saint Leo promoted to independence, Maryhelp was left in 1894 with dependencies in Georgia and Virginia, nine counties in North Carolina, and scattered missions beyond that territory; there were schools at Saint Mary's and Maryhelp; there were impressive new buildings and a sizable debt.

By this time, however, Abbot Leo had settled into a pattern of diversity and over-commitment that would mark the remainder of his career and the future of his abbey. His popularity and his prestige, both in Rome and America, did not translate as security but as a challenge. Even when the opportunity arose for consolidating his efforts, focusing his monks, and insuring the status of his monastery and its charges, he fell back repeatedly on the crutch of activity. In founding monasteries, he believed, the monks of Maryhelp would always be focused on Benedictine values and not fall into the allurement of purely clerical commitments. Thus even as Saint Leo left the embrace of Belmont, a new dependency in another state was already being designed.

ChapteR V:

the Linton Legacy

Canonical independence bestows autonomy on a monastery. Thus even though Saint Leo acquired its independence not as an abbey, but with the rank of a priory, its separation from the North Carolina monastery meant that, for affairs of the cloister and apostolates, permissions or approvals from Maryhelp were no longer a necessity. Similarly, the Belmont motherhouse no longer had to supply monks, teachers, monies—other than educating the Dunne boys—or supervise the conduct of the monastery, school, and parishes in Florida. Independence allowed the daughterhouse to establish its own customary and to particularize its observance and identity. For the founding abbey, it was a time to reemphasize the work within its own cloister, and to breathe quietly while rebuilding its manpower after the loss of the monks—in this case nine in number—who had transferred their stability to the new canonical priory.

Since Belmont, though a small abbey, was already staffing Saint Mary in Richmond, the foundation in Savannah, the nine counties in North Carolina, random parishes in the vicariate, and the schools, there would have been no stigma attached to a comfortable period of inertia, or of reconstituting and strengthening the resources of the monastery. But Leo Haid, drawing his example from the expansionism of Boniface Wimmer, had already determined the site and character of his next venture, even before Saint Leo was officially released. Haid liked the function beginning monasteries could fill in keeping monks focused on the principles of the *Regula*. So even though this new project was not an opportunity the abbot had sought, once the invitation appeared there was never any doubt but that Leo Haid was anxious to negotiate acceptable terms.

The new foundation was the first major fruit of Bishop Haid's growing reputation in America. Sister Mary Baptista Linton, of the Georgetown convent of the Visitation Nuns, selected Maryhelp as the recipient of her largesse on the recommendation of friends who had heard of the abbot-bishop, and the intriguing *eclat* that attended his reputation and image. Linton and Haid had never met, but the donation at Sister Baptista's disposal was of sufficient magnitude that she had no difficulty winning the abbot's attention.

The Lintons were descended from English nobility. Having fallen from favor when their support of Charles I culminated in the loss of that monarch's head, they—and a good deal of their fortune—took refuge in Scotland. Unfortunately, the absence of court life proved a bore for succeeding generations, so around 1760, several of the Linton descendants decided to move to America, where land was inexpensive, plantations were seats of fashion and aristocratic indulgences, and where misfortunes of the past would not impede the privileges of their class. Among those who left Scotland for the New World were William and Moses Linton, brothers.[1]

Moses settled in northern Virginia, where he purchased at least two plantations. In Prince William County, near the land that would later be designated the District of Columbia, he established his permanent residence, and had a proper manor house constructed.[2] The Lintons survived the American Revolution with their fortunes intact, and thrived in the newly created independent nation. However, the marsh land that surrounded "Lintonsford," as the estate came to be known, was less kind than the economy, and strains of malaria began to afflict the heirs. Moses' grandson, John Augustine Elliot Linton, was among those who fell victim to the fever, and the estate, which by antebellum times had grown to nearly two thousand acres, finally passed to John Augustine's only son, John Tyler Linton.[3] More land came to the family, but their fortunes were otherwise destined to decline.

In this heir, John Tyler, the Lintons had a man of unusual promise. He was young, vigorous; he held a degree in law, and had married well, taking the beautiful Cecilia Graham as his wife. With her at his side, Linton assumed command of Lintonsford, and a golden age seemed in the offing for the family. But John Tyler too fell prey to malaria. It seemed at first he would recover, but consumption complicated his problems, and at age twenty-six he lay dead, leaving Cecilia alone to run the estate, at age twenty-three. The young widow Linton was pregnant at her husband's passing, and soon after, on 12 January 1822, gave birth to their child, a girl, named Sarah Elliot Linton.[4]

Unable to handle the burden of the plantation, widowhood, and her maternity, Cecilia yielded, before even a year had elapsed, to the entreaties of Lintonsford's overseer, R.H. Phillips, and wed the employee. But at age twenty-four, Cecilia Graham Linton Phillips was, for the second time, a widow, pregnant, and the administrator of the estate. Once again her bereavement was interrupted by the birth of a daughter, this one being named Anne Cecilia Phillips.[5]

Mrs. Linton-Phillips' brother served as guardian of the two children. Young Sarah developed as a lively, determined girl, intelligent and dominating. Anne was her balance, painfully shy and easily threatened. It was Mr. Graham's decision that Sarah should be sent to the exclusive boarding school in Georgetown, operated by the Visitation Nuns. She went reluctantly; nevertheless, her considerable talents were gradually channelled by the nuns into constructive employments, and she was graduated with distinction at age sixteen. Sarah had not, however, modified her willfullness during the years at Georgetown, and much to her family's chagrin she marked her return to Lintonsford with the announcement of her intention to embrace Roman Catholicism. Her uncle successfully forestalled her conversion for four years, but her determination had not dimmed as she approached her majority, and in 1842 she was baptized.[6]

To compound her family's anxiety, Sarah elaborated on her advent to Catholicism by proclaiming her desire to become a nun. Once again the young lady's intentions were not greeted warmly at home, but on 1 August 1844, Sarah took up residence with the Visitation Nuns at Georgetown. She was received into the Order on 2 October 1844, and professed the vows of religion on 21 November 1845. Henceforth she was a vowed Catholic nun, Sister Mary Baptista Linton, V.H.M.[7]

Lintonsford did not prosper after Sarah's departure. Mrs. Phillips and Anne built a smaller house for themselves on another part of the property, but soon after its completion Cecilia died. The original mansion burned, then the second house. After the Civil War, Miss Anne Phillips found herself among the land poor, and in consultation with her much stronger sister, the painful process of dissecting the Lintonsford plantation, and selling parcels as separate farms began.[8] Of course, Sister Baptista, secure in her convent home, and indeed distinguishing herself in Visitation convent assignments in various localities, did not really share the anguish of her half-sister's penurious spinsterhood. She did, however, experience the pain that attended the vivisection of the Linton heritage and her father's legacy.

In the early 1890's, reportedly after reading Montalembert's *Monks of the West*, Sister Baptista conceived a plan that would keep the remainder of the Linton lands intact, and secure for the family home a future of honorable use. If Benedictines accepted the estate, she reasoned, and established there an educational and charitable enterprise, supporting themselves as mediaeval tradition dictated by farming, Lintonsford would suffer no more dismemberment. The greatest obstacle to the plan lay not in securing religious to accept the property, but in obtaining for Miss Anne a sufficient endowment to cover her remaining years. Phillips, who had also become Catholic, was willing to endorse her sister's dream, but this timid maiden lady had very reasonable fears regarding her own well-being.[9]

The manner in which Miss Anne's dilemma was resolved remains mysteriously shrouded. An anonymous benefactor appeared, offering Phillips an annuity, reportedly fifteen hundred dollars.[10] There were rather unusual conditions on the gift, however, which resulted in the supposition that Sister Baptista, through one of her many contacts, had arranged her sister's good fortune. In return for the annuity that would endow her remaining years, there was to be no violation of the sanctity of the benefactor's identity; no contracts or other legal devices were to document the gift, and Lintonsford was to be consigned to trustees who would settle the future of the land according to the wishes of Linton and Phillips.[11] Miss Anne agreed, and henceforth received in biannual installments, issued by a bank in Baltimore, her regular support.[12] With the creation of the trust, Sister Baptista, her vows notwithstanding, directed the future of Lintonsford.

Sadly, despite her income, Miss Anne Phillips did not find happiness in her declining years. After Sister Baptista died in 1901, the spinster had no dominant force to guide her business dealings. In 1903, Miss Anne summoned her courage and purchased two tracts of land, one of a hundred four and a half acres and the other of thirty-two, that had been sold as small farms in the postbellum years.[13] Here she planned to spend her remaining days. But her insecurity and poor business sense quickly drove her to accept the hospitality of a woman in Prince William County; supposedly, the hostess was a disreputable matron, who local gossip contended had killed her own father. A virulent anti-Catholic, the woman refused to let a priest on the property, and made every effort to debar Miss Anne from the sacraments. According to Julius Pohl, the hostess was "dosing that aged lady with castor oil and calomel."[14] Phillips finally passed out of her misery in the summer of 1917. She had lived for more than ninety unhappy years. Her one hundred thirty-six acres were left to the Benedictines.[15]

In 1893, Sister Baptista had retained M.J. Colbert of Washington as her attorney. She assigned him to draw up the trust for the remaining one thousand seven hundred thirty-six acres of Lintonsford, but she apparently did not intend to encourage either his advice or counsel. As trustees, the sister nominated Martin F. Morris, Imogen B. Lyons, and Nannie Lomax Green;[16] then she added the name of Emily V. Mason.[17] Selecting the trustees had apparently presented no major difficulties. It was the issue of the powers to be at the trustees' disposal that revealed to Colbert how exasberating Sister Baptista could be, the strength of her resolve and opinions, the invincibility of her will. Colbert's draft of the trust document, for example, included the power to sell land according to necessity. Baptista Linton demanded the removal of that clause. As she later told Haid, "I was inflexible."[18] Colbert pleaded his position even after the clause had been removed from the proposed document.

> I send you herewith the draft of the proposed agreement and deed concerning the Virginia lands. I have. . .stricken out the provision relating to the power of the Trustees to sell. I do this against my own better judgment. As the deed stands with this clause stricken out, there is no power on this earth, no matter how great the emergency may be, which will authorize any living human being to sell this property, prior to the incorporation [of the Benedictines in northern Virginia], or one foot of it. But I yield to your wishes in the matter.[19]

Colbert's agrument was based on legal practicality, but Linton's sprang from the general experience of religious founders. She wrote Haid that Colbert

> *insisted* upon giving the Trustees the power of selling portions of the seventeen hundred acres for the benefit of the Schools. On this point, I was inflexible. . .My motive for resisting his judgment, was to secure the *fee simple* of seventeen hundred acres to the Benedictines *after* their incorporation, and not to risk sales that might, in the long future, be regretted. Again, I used this argument against yielding the fee simple to the Benedictines on the outset. Were they to solicit contributions from parties of wealth, these later might say—"sell your lands, and raise money"—If the Fathers can reply, we have no power to sell, until our schools are in working condition, and this condition we cannot attain without assistance, then the case is in favor of gratuitous contributions.[20]

Though Haid appreciated the sister's practicality, and though he in no way anticipated a situation such as had arisen with Judge Dunne, the abbot had legitimate reservations about committing himself to an enterprise before he held clear title to the lands at issue. He wanted a fee simple deed from the beginning; Sister Baptista—citing concern for Belmont's sake, not her own—thought that imprudent.

Another factor that faced the bishop as he considered accepting Lintonsford was the conditions imposed on the recipient of the estate. Phillips (Linton) had instructed the trustees in the deed of 14 January 1893, to find an Order willing to

> hold, manage and use the said land for the purpose of establishing thereon an industrial and training school for poor and friendless white boys and youths, and for the further purpose of establishing thereon a school for the training and education of poor and friendless white girls in habits of industry and virtue, and in learning useful occupations suitable to their condition of life, in such manner and under the direction and control of such religious or charitable order or organization as the said trustees may deem most suitable.[21]

Industrial schools were not considered the ideal work for a monastery. And since only one monk of Maryhelp, the abbot himself, held a commercial degree, the prospects for Belmont's success were slim. Nevertheless, Haid expressed immediate interest in the project in Prince William County. Sister Baptista received the bishop's favorable response on 21 March 1893, the feast of Saint Benedict, when "this dear Saint sent me as his love token" both the news of Belmont's interest and "a desperate attack of vertigo."[22]

Despite Maryhelp's willingness to undertake the Linton project, negotiations regarding the form of the deed caused a considerable delay. In company with Mother Edith, O.S.B., of the sisters in Richmond, the bishop visited Lintonsford that spring. The Benedictine women, it was hoped, would operate the girls' school, and both the monks and sisters wished to see the property before accepting this adventure at the hamlet of Bristow, near Manassas, Virginia. The trip north seems to have convinced the superiors—since they "were both of a pioneering spirit"—that the project was worthwhile. Thus the two superiors announced that the terms of the trust were accepted in principle.[23]

Two technical preliminaries had to be resolved before the actual commencement of the Benedictines' new schools, however. Curial approval from Rome was necessary, and a state charter had to be obtained before the trustees could execute the transferal of title.

The prelude to securing the approval of the Holy See was a mandate from the monastic Chapter at Belmont for acceptance of the

Bristow work and property. The abbot contacted the monks outside the monastery and won their endorsement of the project. Then, on 29 March 1893, the Chapter of Maryhelp was convened. As Haid presented the offer, the monks were to receive seventeen hundred acres of land near Manassas, in fee simple. A moral, but not contractural, obligation accompanied the gift, whereby the monks were to operate an industrial school for boys. The bishop announced that he hoped the Benedictine sisters from Richmond would operate the desired companion school for girls. It was also mentioned that the monks would have to mortgage the property if insufficient donors were discovered who were willing to endorse the expense of starting the new school; after all, "with an empty purse little can be done," he said. Eight of the Belmont fathers attended the meeting. Haid did not vote. Of the others, six favored the new apostolate and one remained uncommitted. "The Bishop then stated that he would, on his visit to Rome, have all confirmed."[24]

Carrying with him the permission of both the monastic Chapter and the bishop of Richmond, in whose territory Bristow lay, the abbot-bishop met no friction in Rome. As Haid described the work in northern Virginia, it was promising, practical, and should advance the good of both the Church and its members. De Propaganda Fide endorsed the project, and on 20 June the Cardinal Prefect of Propaganda advised Abbot Leo that approval was "herewith graciously granted." The Holy See even accepted the proposed future erection of a college and academy on the site.[25]

Immediately thereafter the abbot moved to incorporate the Order in northern Virginia, so the land could be transferred and held. A charter for the Benedictine Society of Linton Place, Prince William County, Virginia, was issued on 1 August. It specified

> That the purpose for which the said company is formed are: The establishment and conduct of an industrial farm and school for the maintenance and education of youth in the arts and sciences and in the different branches of industrial and agricultural instructions.[26]

Only at this point, when the abbot thought he had fulfilled all the preliminaries for obtaining Lintonsford, did the painful encumbrance whose cloud would hang over the estate for years to come begin to emerge.

Haid had insisted from the beginning that he was not interested in the Bristow project unless he received the indenture for the land through a fee simple deed. A clear title, free of encumbrance, was demanded, and in no way negotiable. As for the conditions imposed by Sister Baptista, Abbot Leo considered them to be moral in nature, not legal. They were accepted by Maryhelp as a moral obligation, but the abbot feared that if they were expressed in the deed, an unnecessarily precarious situation would be created, in which the monks' title to the property was sure to suffer future challenges. As Haid understood the matter, and thus as he presented it to his Chapter and to Rome, Sister Baptista and her trustees comprehended and accepted the abbot's adamantly held position.[27] He was greatly chagrined to find that, apparently, the sister thought that the conflict had been resolved according to her standards. And with the abbey having already sought and secured its various endorsements, approvals, and legal faculties, it was the Linton trustees, unofficially but truly at Sister Baptista's disposal, who held both the deed and the command of the situation.

From this struggle over ownership of the land there emerges the real foundation of Bristow's importance in the history of Maryhelp and of Leo Haid. This priory was never among the abbey's more favored ventures; it was never even the object of much apostolic enthusiasm. Rather the significance of Bristow lies in the microcosm it presents for the style of leadership that was uniquely Leo Haid's. Because this mission always functioned on such a small scale, it came to embrace more perfectly than any other single endeavor both the weaknesses and strengths of Abbot Leo's administrative gifts and facility.

Unfortunately, it is not strength of leadership that is found in this first, critical juncture of the Lintonsford project. So long as it had been a matter of accepting the adventure, of inspiring enthusiasm for the project—among the monks, in Belmont's missions and priories, in the Chapter, in Rome—the abbot was in his element and progressed along a smooth course. But then Sister Baptista became obstreperous, and Leo Haid found himself helpless. He did not like to fight. A hearty quarrel with Leo Haid usually found the bishop's side to be no more than a perpetual repetition of his position, surrounded by raw wonder at why people were not doing what he wanted. He was skilled at bargaining; he could inspire and lead, but there was at his command little facility for countermanding, persuading, or fighting. The abbot was ill-suited for dealing with Baptista Linton, who did indeed have no intention, it seems, of giving Maryhelp a fee simple deed.

The Visitation nun was not the only party pressuring the bishop in the late summer of 1893. The monk who would head the Bristow mission had desires of his own to urge and promote. Haid had appointed Julius Pohl as director of the northern Virginia work. He was to be prior of the monastery (Saint Maur), and director of the industrial school (Saint Joseph), and chaplain to the sisters and their school (Saint Edith).[28] For the first year, only two other monks, Brothers Gilbert and Louis, could be spared to assist in the new project, but this did not dampen Father Julius' fervor. Pohl was a missionary and a founder at heart, and life at the abbey, where post-independence success was obvious, and his nine—really very successful—years as director of Saint Mary's College, had caused a serious and prolonged depression. He was loved by the students, but the lack of adventure in an established monastery was for Father Julius a heavy burden. His appointment as founder of Saint Maur Priory, however, was a vivifying tonic, restorative in every way. Leo Haid had no talent for dealing with disobedience and a bad spirit, but from the roots of a profound sensitivity to his monastic children, he was remarkably gifted at channeling monks into avenues of productive and spiritually satisfying labor. Felix Hintemeyer was ideally suited for a life as the loyal lieutenant; Bernard Haas, the monk the bishop later sent to activate the Savannah monastery, proved one of the best administrators in Maryhelp's history; young Charles Mohr in Florida surprised everyone, including himself, with his paternal insight; even Walter Leahy belatedly realized that the bishop's intention to consign him to parish work was insightful and provident. Julius Pohl was in the same class of wise assignments. He was invigorated by the primitive conditions of Bristow, and the fact that the mission never did really thrive kept the prior fresh in the work that would be his passion for more than a quarter of a century.

Immediately after his appointment, Father Julius had journeyed north to see the estate. He visited other industrial schools to learn what Bristow needed, and he traveled extensively seeking financial support for Saint Joseph.[29] He returned to Belmont then, rejuvenated, anxious to take up residence in Virginia, even though the land had not yet been transferred. And Haid, ever partial to his role as father to the monks, and despite conflicts with practicality and elementary standards of administration, did not squelch his prior-elect's enthusiasm. He argued for the reasonable course—"If you insist on going to settle this fall," he advised Pohl, "the promised Fee Simple Deed must be in our hands"[30]—but before the end of September Pohl was in Bristow. He would start the school, Brother Gilbert the buildings, and Brother Louis the farm. But the deed was not in hand; instead, Linton acquired her best bargaining strength yet: the Benedictines had commenced their work without first acquiring a fee simple deed.

The demand for the promised form of indenture dominated Belmont's first year in northern Virginia. Yet despite obvious and constant delays, the bishop seems not to have doubted that the title, as he believed it had been promised, was forthcoming. He wrote Father Julius on 13 September, reminding him to "demand that promised" deed,[31] and letters with the same message were still being addressed to the Bristow prior in June of 1894.[32] Pohl and the brothers were busy erecting buildings, designing the school, working the farm, while Abbot Leo in North Carolina was growing impatient. "I acted in good faith in the face of promises repeated time and again," the abbot wrote Pohl. Trusting in the nun's assurances, the chapter had accepted Linton's conditions on the land. But it was mandatory that nothing encumber any additional projects. "I insist on elbow room to do other things,"[33] he said. But still no fee simple deed appeared.

M.J. Colbert, as attorney for Linton and the trustees, finally sent a deed on 4 June 1894, but it was not fee simple, and Haid found it "a great disappointment—no less than a breach of promise and original contract."[34] Colbert tried to soften the disappointment. Sister Baptista was distraught over the bishop's displeasure, Colbert wrote after his 3 June meeting with Linton, but feared the possible effects of weakening their position; in particular they expressed concern that Miss Anne might lose her annuity if the conditions were not explicit. Moreover, the Linton trustees, it seemed, had wearied of the struggle as much as the abbot had, and thus the lawyer's tone changed from gentleness to ultimatum. If, Colbert wrote,

> you should conclude that under the conditions which I have mentioned, you cannot go on with this great and good work, we would regard it as a most unfortunate ending to a most propitious beginning, and we would have to look elsewhere for some religious organization to accomplish the work.[35]

So violent was the discrepancy between the proposed indenture for the land and the proposition submitted to the monks of Maryhelp a year earlier, that the abbot thought it necessary to convene a new Chapter to consider the proposed project. But confronted by insistent demands, Haid's prudence collapsed. The monks met on 6 June; Abbot Leo read them Colbert's letter, then surprised the assembly by endorsing what he had consistently represented as absolutely untenable demands by the Linton trustees.[36] Despite all that had transpired, Leo Haid stood before his monks and proclaimed that on the merit of Sister Baptista's original commitment, it was his "understanding that we would [still] get a Fee Simple Deed" at some future point.[37] The capitulars, probably in no position to know the full scope of the battles of the past year, endorsed their abbot's wisdom, and committed Maryhelp to a course the abbot regretted but accepted.[38] Leo Haid's trust had exceeded his prudence.

The indenture for the land was executed on 23 June 1894, and included all of Linton's conditions, the "friendless white boys," the industrial school, everything.[39] When the sisters went to Bristow they exceeded the monks—as would so often prove the case through the years—in wisdom. At a cost of nineteen hundred dollars, they purchased the ninety-two and a half acre Kincheloe farm. It was formerly part of Lintonsford and was a walk of perhaps seven minutes from where Father Julius built Saint Maur Priory. And since the Kincheloe land was not part of the Linton gift, the sisters were free to "erect [there] whatever kind of building they chose."[40]

Saint Joseph, Saint Maur, Saint Edith

Associating himself with the Benedictine sisters of Virginia ranks among Bishop Haid's wisest and most provident commitments. Resolute in their intentions, experienced in their work, hearty in their efforts and thoroughly enveloped in their religious ethos, these women were ideal missionary companions. The two Benedictine bodies, the monks and the sisters, were compatible and overwhelmingly cordial in their relations, and their labors proved mutually advantageous.

This branch of Benedictine sisters, like Maryhelp's own pioneers, had proceeded south from a motherhouse in Pennsylvania. The sisters settled in Richmond in 1868, then they began educational work at Saint Mary Parish. In 1874, they requested canonical independence from the Pennsylvania convent, and acquired their autonomy.[41] Their first three novices entered in 1875, and the enterprise began to grow and flourish.[42] Bristow was their first permanent foundation outside Richmond.[43]

The sisters voted to participate in the Linton project on 4 October 1893, soon after Father Julius established residency.[44] Brother Gilbert supervised the necessary construction projects on their behalf, starting immediately so that the women could take up abode by the spring of 1894. Both the monks and sisters planned to open their new schools that fall. All proceeded on schedule, and at the Richmond convent, on 30 April 1894, Mother Edith posted a notice assigning Sisters Mary Alphonse Bliley, Mary Clara Vogel, Mary Maura Wendl, Mary Evangelist Loehr, and Mary Agnes Johnston, to the new foundation. They were to begin their work the following day. The sisters greeted the news "with wondering awe and tear-dimmed eyes." Sister Alphonse, as superior of the mission, coordinated the arrangements, and the adventure began.[45]

In Prince William County the sisters easily found their residence, but only a bat—hovering near the doorway—seemed to have anticipated their arrival. The monks eventually spotted their coworkers, however, and greeted the ladies with small gifts, mostly provisions for the new convent. Then through the courtesy of Father Prior Julius, the Benedictine men and women celebrated their new collaboration by sharing a can of peaches.[46]

Father Julius served as chaplain, adviser, and "never failing friend" for the sisters.[47] His exuberant spirit was as much of a help at Bristow as it had been a decade earlier at Maryhelp. The sisters planned to operate two schools. Saint Edith was to be the girls' academy. It opened in the fall of 1894, with sixteen boarding students and a small number of day pupils.[48] Saint Anne, the required girls' industrial school, was to come later; work on its building began in May of 1897;[49] the blessing was bestowed on 22 August of that same year.[50] The sisters resisted threatening fires;[51] they dealt with some unstable personnel;[52] they gave concerts,[53] did their work and prayers, and in every way promoted the work in northern Virginia. A more industrious, practical, and edifying set of compatriots for the monks cannot be imagined. So successful were the women at Bristow, that "under pressure from Bishop Van de Vyver,"[54] the Ordinary of the Richmond diocese, and with the warm encouragement of Father Julius, the motherhouse itself was transferred from Richmond to Bristow on 21 November 1901.[55]

Interestingly enough, Pohl seems to never have had any complaint against the sisters—at least none more serious than their inability to communicate quickly. Saint Maur and Saint Edith were convenient to one another; vision was unobstructed, and the walk was minimal. But Father Julius was always desirous of greater convenience when he needed to speak with one of the sisters. He used his telephone for the first time on 21 August 1900, and proudly recorded in his daybook that it was a "Success!"[56] But on the twenty-second of the next month he replaced the mechanical device—apparently for a mercifully brief period of time—with megaphones.[57]

Sadly, Pohl was not to reveal himself to be as fine an administrator as he was a friend and promoter of others' work. Though he had been a pioneer and founder at Maryhelp, and had directed Saint Mary's College for almost a decade, he had never served as a religious superior before. Pohl did prove more direct than had Haid at dealing with recalcitrants and problems, but his subordinates quickly learned that in a confrontation he buckled as readily as did the abbot. Then too, Father Julius was usually reluctant to recognize that difficulties even existed, a hesitancy that caused him to lose control in the midst of turmoil. Father Julius' letters through the years constitute an endless litany of disobedience and languid administrative responses. The quality of monastic observance remained undistinguished thereby, even while the prior exhibited a singular facility for restorative work with his weaker brethren.

In the early years at Bristow, Pohl's inexperience at being a superior was so marked that he tried to exercise administrative prerogatives that did not attend his office. He thought he possessed the same powers as Charles Mohr had acquired in 1894. But there was a difference, a serious one, between Saint Leo and Saint Maur, the former being canonically independent of Maryhelp by this date, and the latter remaining a dependency of the North Carolina abbey. Not until the spring of 1897, after exchanging a series of detailed and technical arguments with a New York canonist, did the prior of Bristow concede that his service was totally subsidiary, and existed only within the peripheries established, and according to the pleasure of the abbot of Belmont. Saint Maur was not governmentally independent.[58]

Julius Pohl was not particularly adept as a superior of men, or at least not as skilled as he was at guiding educational institutions. Nevertheless, his abbot retained him in office through the next quarter-century. This seemingly unjustified tenure was expressive of the hierarchy of values that marked Bishop Haid's style of leadership, coupled as it always was with his spiritual paternity. Firstly, the abbot never forgot why he sent the man to Bristow. That need in Pohl for hardship and struggle, that talent for beginnings, they were seen as intimately connected in Father Julius with the course whereby his spirit was to flourish. Leo Haid wanted to focus Julius Pohl on channels for which God seemed to have given him the talents. Once the man was installed as prior of Bristow—in the position for which Haid believed the appointee to have special, God-given faculties—he was granted the freedom and support to execute his office. These were the same prerogatives the bishop would allow Bernard Haas in Savannah, and Thomas Oestreich in the College at Belmont; Hintemeyer already enjoyed them as prior of the abbey and as Vicar General of the vicariate. Those men who served Leo Haid as lieutenants invariably discovered that even when in error, even when their actions caused displeasure and earned them a correction, the abbot still trusted them. For Haid, this was the sensible manner for fostering their growth—as monks primarily, but as practical leaders of charitable enterprises as well. The abbot had made their appointments in response to what he believed to be the Divine will, and outside of creating scandal, the subalterns of the Belmont prelate held the sort of liberty of office and jurisdiction that could only proceed from a superior's genuine trust. Julius Pohl, as he executed his offices in Virginia, received the unfailing support—or at least non-interference—of his abbot in matters of internal governance, particularly in the rather wild personnel issues that developed. The abbot was concerned, of course, especially by Pohl's dreams of costly construction projects and his facility for winning diocesan disfavor. Nevertheless, though Haid's advice was readily available when requested, for internal matters he was reluctant to impose his abbatial prerogatives.

There were two spheres, however, in which the abbot would not stand at his appointee's side: the threat of potential scandal, always the bishop's great fear, would invariably elicit intervention. And in diocesan conflicts, when the powers of Richmond and the Virginia Benedictines were at odds, Haid would again prove nonsupportive of his prior. As a mitred prelate and the true superior of Bristow, Bishop Haid was the most appropriate party to negotiate with the Ordinaries of Richmond. Nevertheless, it fell to Father Julius, who could be pleasantly cordial but seldom diplomatic, to handle most of his disputes with the diocese. Perhaps in this instance in particular, the abbot's trust in his prior may have exceeded caution.

For each of the four men in whom Haid placed such extraordinary confidence, there was always a different substratum of motivation. Oestreich had genuine expertise for his work; Haas earned his respect through his natural inclination for careful administration; Hintemeyer had the loyalty and the touchingly simpatico spirit that both buoyed and when necessary shielded his abbot. But Pohl appealed to Leo Haid for other reasons, and because of this, even as often as he disappointed the bishop, he retained the man's support. Unlike the other three administrators, Pohl was not a figure of competence but of faith. Leo Haid believed Julius Pohl was a man of virtuous aspirations, with potential for great holiness. And the abbot was reluctant to impede that disposition for beatitude in any way. Unfortunately, it may have won the prior at Lintonsford too much indulgence.

Concurrence with Haid's evaluation of the prior was given by the Bristow sisters. Father Julius was "pre-eminently a monk," the Benedictine women wrote in their official history. In particular they found his love of the liturgy noteworthy. The sisters liked to remember the fervor with which Julius Pohl would lose himself in the *Opus Dei*.

> To have seen and heard the Lamentations of Jeremias as sung by Father Julius was a unique experience in every sense of the word. Accompanying himself on a small reed organ, his zeal would reach such an intensity of expression, that it seemed to those who were trying to follow the text that either the voice or the instrument must surely reach the bursting point before it was over."

The abbot was also aware that Pohl's friendships, his compassion, and his charity spoke of the movement of God in his soul. Pohl was always devoted, for example, to the monastic theories and insight of James Zilliox, even supporting them in debates with his beloved Boniface Wimmer.[60] Only Abbot James' untimely death in 1890, terminated the letters of spiritual guidance Pohl so gratefully received.

One incident in particular, from Bristow's early history, illustrates the sort of spontaneous charity Haid found so appealingly abundant in Pohl. In the summer of 1898, when the Spanish American War was dominating the minds of military leaders, a contingent of twelve to fifteen thousand troops[61] was marched from Camp Alger, Maryland, to Camp Thoroughfare, Virginia.[62] Pausing *en route*, the men, by this time estimated at twenty thousand in number,[63] encamped at Chapel Springs, a couple of miles from the priory. "Incessant visits" followed, as officers paid courtesy calls[64] and soldiers of lesser rank came for food—especially to the convent[65]—as well as for articles of piety, the Sacraments, and the quiet of a Benedictine chapel.[66] So busy did Lintonsford become that thirty military guards were posted at the priory[67] and a dozen at Saint Edith.[68] Despite the security, the men still went to the chapels, and on the second, and supposedly the last, evening in Bristow, "the Seventh Illinois Volunteers came up to serenade us," Father Julius wrote, "the bands served fine music."[69] The next day, 9 August, the encampment was dissolved, and the soldiers marched past Saint Joseph toward Thoroughfare Gap, the bands playing, the men refreshed.[70]

Yet not all the military personnel departed; a substantial contingent of the men remained, victims of an epidemic of typhoid fever that had erupted in the camp before its dissolution.[71] That fever was then joined by malaria, measles, and mumps. Technically, the spiritual ministrations of the Church should have been offered through the parish clergy—Fathers Kelly and Sherman, secular priests, had tended the men at Camp Alger—but "it became impossible for these good priests to attend to them all." Accordingly,

Father Julius recorded, "The officials waited on me and desired me to look after these poor, soldier boys."[72] Pohl visited the remnant of the encampment, now a pitiful field hospital. He was deeply moved by the suffering he saw, and implored the officers to seek the local pastor's permission for the Benedictine to share in this work. The parish priest gave Father Julius full authorization to function on behalf of the Catholics within the army's camp. On his own, Pohl quickly expanded his ministry to include the needs of non-Catholics, as well.[73]

He wrote the abbot,

> I am kept very busy. Every day I spend hours in the Camp with the sick soldiers....Night before last...the Major and Doctor sent for me at one a.m. I reached [the camp] in time to give every rite of the Church—when my work was finished—[Corporal Murphy] breathed his last. Late yesterday I heard confessions and anointed another who had been away so long from the Church that even the "Lord's Prayer" and "Hail Mary" were no longer at his command. The officials, at my request, have kindly consented to have my wishes respected in every way. Confession is facilitated by my having the sick carried to private tents, etc.—the boys anxious to hear from home consume a little more of my time by desiring me to pen their letters.[74]

And so Father Julius expended himself, in a ministry that would extend from August until October.[75] Each day he visited the camp for at least three hours,[76] and whenever necessary, the ambulance was sent for him at night.[77] By 5 September, so much time was being spent at the field hospital, that the army offered him quarters on the site.[78] He declined the courtesy, however, lest he neglect his spiritual and administrative obligations to the sisters and students.

The next day, perhaps to no one's surprise but his own, Julius Pohl reluctantly recorded in his day-book that he too had been forced to submit to treatment by the military doctors.[79] A weak body could not restrain an indefatigable spirit, however, and the priest refused to slacken his work. Part of his fortitude was lent by certain members of the Protestant clergy who deeply scandalized Father Pohl. "The preachers came invariably to preach to the Nurses," he wrote—not without bias. And they just "stood in astonishment," he said, "[when they saw] the priest move about among the sick!"[80]

Julius Pohl was much like Leo Haid in his uncompromising blindness to any suggestion that he was acting with special virtue. A priest's duty, as the prior saw it, was intrinsically unparticularized. So Pohl was genuinely surprised to receive a letter from Major J.K. Weaver, commander of the Bristow encampment, and a surgeon, wherein the priest's "gentle manner and sincere sympathy with the boys, your kind words and religious ministrations"[81] were acknowledged and praised. Pohl was also deeply touched when a group of convalescent soldiers asked to be photographed with their Benedictine chaplain.[12] Typically, however, instead of recording his accolades or his own efforts, the prior wanted to praise only the soldiers. "Not one of us [at Saint Edith or Saint Joseph]," he proudly wrote the abbot, "has heard as much as a profane word." The army personnel tendered every gesture of respect, and there was such piety and thirst for religion, Pohl noted, that "our very rosaries were stripped of crucifixes."[13] Then the soldiers left; a new school year began in earnest, and apparently the prior of Bristow never wrote another line regarding his work on behalf of the military. Neither his humility nor his charity escaped the abbot's attention, however.

Of course the prior's industry was already well known, since like any good, pioneer monk, he was devoting considerable time to erecting buildings. Indeed on his way to settle at Bristow, Pohl had stopped in Richmond where he induced Fritz Sitterding, who was knowledgable concerning construction materials, and had contributed to the erection of the parish school at Saint Mary, to journey north and offer advice. The gentleman surveyed Lintonsford's "rather desolate scene," a hugh expanse of flourishing, untended blackberries, "covered with brambles and briars." He suggested razing the existing, woefully inhospitable building in favor of a more servicable edifice that might utilize the original foundation.[14] Pohl thought that to be a sensible recommendation, and lost no time or enthusiasm before starting. Sitterding, meanwhile, hastily departed.

Despite the return of his old high spirits, Father Julius was in no way insensitive to the miserable condition of his priory in 1893. He later wrote Belmont,

> We reached here with next to nothing. From a worldly point of view nothing to encourage—everything to discourage us. An abandoned shack housed us and our few belongings. The land had not been tilled since the Blues fought the Grays.[15]

What more could there be to secure Julius Pohl's pleasure? The first building arose so quickly that the new school opened on schedule in 1894, a few students even appearing earlier. In 1895, he added an east wing;[16] he acquired a printing press;[17] there was an addition to the living quarters;[18] the chapel and refectory were finished, blessed, and inaugurated,[19] all in that one year. In 1898, Pohl spent the summer hauling stone for his next project; he also placed an order for twelve thousand bricks in anticipation of erecting his first non-frame-and-board structure.[90] The hope of a building with a more permanent facade had been extended by Bishop Haid himself who visited Bristow at the beginning of June and suggested that the time had come to build a real church.[91] So Pohl built a brick chapel; then before it was finished, he started a west wing for the school—this being intended for use as a dormitory.[92] On 10 May, Bishop Van de Vyver of Richmond and Abbot Leo went to Bristow. The Richmond Ordinary blessed two bells, "Benedict" and "Scholastica", for the new church.[93] The next day Haid dedicated the oratory; Van de Vyver gave the Sacrament of Confirmation, and both bishops preached.[94] But still Prior Julius did not rest: work on new buildings continued, and on 28 October he helped the boys move into their new dormitory.[95]

There was so much construction work in the first years of Bristow, that even though the buildings were mostly rough, frame designs, by mid-July 1900, they were insured for fourteen thousand five hundred dollars.[96] In September of that year, another wing of the school was blessed,[97] and on 30 September the new chapel in the cloister of Saint Maur was dedicated.[98]

Of course Father Julius was not just erecting buildings in these years. There were also the duties of the school, farm, and parochial work to occupy his time, to say nothing of the demands of his monastic vows and the administration of the cloister. Agriculture had begun immediately upon the monks' arrival—or at least clearing the land for cultivation commenced. This sequence, with the farm preceding the educational institution, was important since the income from the crops was thought to be the most stable earnings the monks could expect in the early years. But agriculture served yet another purpose at Bristow. Bound to open an industrial school, but having no prospects for acquiring any professors who could teach the trades or practical sciences, farming seemed as close to industry as Saint Joseph was likely to reach in its first days. So land was a high priority when affairs were being set in order. And when boys did arrive, the farm served to keep them busy. It lent some semblance of reality to the "industrial school," too. But as at Maryhelp, farming was never really profitable financially. In particular, immoderate rain, which seemed addicted to granting either superfluity or drought, destroyed crops.[99] So after the first few years when the farm and school produced relatively equal income, the agricultural enterprise's financial prominence was replaced by the generosity of donors.[100]

Saint Joseph Institute, the boys' school at Bristow, was more successful than the farm. For the first school year there were sixteen boys, served by nine monks (two priests, one cleric, six brothers); Pohl also listed one professor and one candidate as being in residence.[101]

The boys studied elementary and secondary subjects, emphasizing commercial rather than classical studies. They had household and grounds duties—designed to promote their practical skills—and all learned (and practiced) farm labor. There had originally been hopes of erecting a college at Bristow, but by 1897, Washington had become such a centre of well-funded Catholic higher education, that a fledgling Benedictine college in nearby Bristow would have been a ludicrous endeavor, and Haid—still wary of the difficulties about the deed, too—announced that he had "dropped all ideas of founding a College at Saint Joseph."[102] But the institute served a valuable purpose, nonetheless, and enrollment was surprisingly steady. There were slight increases in numbers through the first eight years, and after 1905, attendance figures began centering around the seventies, where they remained throughout Father Julius' time. Of these students, approximately one tenth were usually day pupils; the rest were boarders.[103] The school was never a first-rate educational institution, and it was never really an industrial school at all. But Julius Pohl ran it with such good will that its value as a charitable institution, at least, remained strong.

The third sphere of work Pohl wanted to see instituted at Saint Maur, after the farm and school, was parochial responsibility. Father Julius wanted a single parish to be attached to the priory to promote apostolic zeal, local contact and interest, higher liturgical standards, a useful diversion for the teaching fathers, and auxiliary income. Haid quietly assented, and even consented to visit Van de Vyver with Pohl in an effort to secure parochial jurisdiction.[104] Bishop Van de Vyver in turn endorsed the idea of parochial work by the Benedictines, and he expressed no objection to lay Catholics attending the priory's church.

Later, the appointment of Father Patrick Donlon, O.S.B., as pastor of Warrenton seemed to secure the Benedictines in their pastoral work in northern Virginia. Warrenton's parish and missions included Manassas, Nokesville, and Bristow; so the Benedictine pastor had broad local authority, and of course enjoyed cordial relations with his confreres at Saint Maur. Unfortunately for the monks, however, Van de Vyver seems never to have committed his permissions to paper; thus the timing in particular was left vague, and the critical point—that permission for parochial work preceded and did not directly relate to the nomination of Donlon to Warrenton—fell into obscurity.[105] Bishop Van de Vyver never gave the Bristow Benedictines any parochial rights or privileges in perpetuity, but no one seems to have anticipated just how ephemeral the monks' pastoral assignment in northern Virginia was to prove.

After Father Patrick's death in March of 1913, when he was only fifty-one years old, the monks expected to be called upon to supply the new Warrenton pastor. Etiquette, however, left the procedure for the appointment uncertain. Had the parish been held in perpetuity, the abbot would have been expected to nominate from among his monk-priests a new pastor. The Ordinary of the territory would then either name that monk-priest to the pastorate, or instruct the abbot to submit additional nominees until there was an acceptable candidate. But since this parish was not really assigned to the Order, but rather had been entrusted to a particular Benedictine pastor, Haid could not presume to nominate a successor unless the bishop of Richmond invited such a submission. In the interim, while matters were being discerned, a secular priest was appointed pastor *pro tem*, ending—temporarily, it was then thought—fifteen years of Benedictine governance in the parish.

Another change had also taken place in Virginia, however. In the previous year, 1912, Denis J. O'Connell had succeeded Augustine Van de Vyver on the episcopal throne of Richmond. The new Ordinary knew the Benedictines reasonably well—he was Jeremiah O'Connell's nephew—but because of his predecessor's penchant for oral instructions, he had no documentary resources to elucidate the situation at Warrenton. Understandably, he did not act hastily, but gathered the opinions of his Consultors.

Apparently, the story developed that the Benedictines had decided to abandon the parochial assignment, and thus "*our* parish died with [Father Patrick]." Diocesan memories also revived the apparent fact, unknown to the monks until this time, that when Van de Vyver had first assigned a Benedictine pastor in 1898, his failure to consult his Council had earned him criticism "for exceeding his rights."[106] This incident—perhaps united with some wistful or proprietary yearnings regarding the Benedictines' flourishing and perpetually held (through Roman approbation) parish in Richmond—helped spark what was to be a painfully long and vibrant history of strained relations between the monks and their secular counterparts, Richmond's diocesan clergy. The unpleasantness seldom reached the episcopal level in the early years, but it did extend to the Ordinary's most trusted advisors. Most notable among these in 1914, was the Very Reverend Felix Kaup, the particularly unfriendly chancellor of the Diocese of Richmond.

In this situation both Pohl and Haid were powerless to secure Benedictine parochial rights near the priory. Neither of the monks was consulted. There were no written records to consult either, except a detailed narration written after the original appointment and negotiation of parochial rights in 1898.[107] And although the narrative account was extant and in Leo Haid's possession, the abbot either forgot about it or could not locate it at the time. Of course, this contemporary item of testimony might have been difficult to submit anyway, since the Benedictines—either at Bristow or Belmont—had no inquiry submitted to them in advance of the bishop's decision.

The Diocesan Consultors assembled in Richmond, by order of Bishop O'Connell, on Holy Thursday, 9 April 1914. Father Thomas E. Waters, as secretary, sent the Virginia bishop a copy of his priests' recommendations, and one month later, after the Ordinary had ratified the decision, Richmond wrote Belmont. For advising the Benedictines of the action of the Council as endorsed by O'Connell, word should have been addressed to the abbot, and since in this case the abbot also enjoyed the episcopal character, O'Connell should have signed the communique to his peer in North Carolina. Protocol not withstanding, however, in an intriguing variation on ecclesiastical propriety, the letter was issued by Richmond's Vicar General, Father J.T. O'Farrell, and addressed to Felix Hintemeyer, the Vicar General of the vicariate. Haid thus received his official notification from a subordinate (Hintemeyer), as issued by an inferior (O'Farrell), and as addressed to an ecclesial entity that was totally uninvolved with the affair (the *abbey* was responsible for the northern Virginia work, not the *vicariate*). Understandably, Abbot Leo accepted the manner of the promulgation as a deliberate insult. And O'Farrell's admission that, "I now take pleasure"[108] in forwarding this effrontery, only added to the ire of the Lord of Belmont. The phrase was, of course, a standard convention of the time, but it seemed too well chosen.

The Consultors' resolutions, which had passed unanimously, were lucid in every way, and certainly did not soften the rude manner in which they were transmitted to Maryhelp. Bishop Haid must also have noted that the Benedictines' ever present adversary, Chancellor Kaup, had taken the trouble to authenticate the copy sent to Carolina.

> *Resolved:* That outside of their Monastery grounds at Bristow, Virginia the Benedictines have no jurisdiction either parochial or personal;
>
> 2. That the arrangements heretofore existing between the Diocese and the Benedictines both at Bristow and Warrenton were of a temporary nature and only for the purpose of administering to wants of the Catholics living within that territory;
>
> 3. That the Parish of Warrenton, within the boundaries of which Bristow is located, should not be divided for the purpose of creating a Benedictine parish.[109]

Having been forwarded to Belmont as a *fait accompli*, and already promulgated, the decision was inviolable, unless scandal were to be risked. There also weighed heavily the factor of Haid not having been consulted, even while advanced word regarding the limits to be imposed on the Benedictines' work had been allowed to circulate freely throughout the diocese. Julius Pohl had written his abbot five days before the Consultors met, reporting then, with perfect accuracy, what was about to happen.[110] There was nothing Haid or Pohl could do to remedy the situation. Heresay did not constitute evidence or notification of impending episcopal acts. The abbot saw the manner in which the whole affair had been conducted as ungracious and provocative.

Actually, except for its value as a medium of contact with area Catholics, and the insulting manner in which the decision was executed, Warrenton was not a great loss. It had "never been remunerative;"[111] it required a monk to live outside the cloister;[112] but the document of limitations, as phrased, reached farther than the geography and jurisdiction of a congregation. If strictly interpreted, the Saint Joseph "parish"—people who looked to the fathers at the priory for the Sacraments, since Bristow had no other Catholic clergy nor even a church—would be considered a congregation of renegades if it continued to assemble, and its clergy would be usurpers. And far more importantly, the Benedictine sisters, whose convent was situated on the Kincheloe land, rather than on the donated acreage of the Linton-Phillips trust, would not lie within the restricted territorial remnant in which the monks could function. A Benedictine could not automatically serve the women as chaplain or confessor. This in particular was painful to both Pohl and the abbot.[113]

By 1914, Leo Haid had grown considerably in the exercise of political acumen. But the radical step he announced in this case surprised virtually everyone. Keenly aware that the Diocese of Richmond, despite its recently inhospitable actions, depended on Saint Joseph Institute to take care of the sort of boys required by the Linton conditions, the abbot of Belmont summoned a meeting of the monastic Chapter, to be held at the conclusion of the annual retreat—the time when the greatest number of monks would be at the abbey. The announced agenda had one item: consideration of a proposal to terminate all the Maryhelp Benedictines' involvement in Bristow, Virginia.

Apparently, as had been the case in Richmond that spring, word of this meeting and its agenda somehow "leaked" out, and circulated freely among the parish clergy. Unfortunately, among those who heard the news on the level of a rumor were not only the gentlemen of the Richmond chancery, but the monks of Bristow. And Father Julius, not yet advised of the meeting by Haid, was distraught, especially since he had already requested and received permission to make his retreat separately that year, and thus absent himself from the conferences at the abbey. Unaware that the proposed meeting and vote were intended primarily as a message to Richmond's clergy, Father Julius wrote a letter to the abbot and capitulars at Maryhelp, explaining the situation and pleading for the future of Saint Maur Priory. Pohl admitted that he was "aggrieved" at the diocese's decision. But "to abandon [Bristow]," he argued, "when neither financial nor other failure haunts," would be "dig[ging] not *another's*, but our own graves." The prior found it "regrettable that there should be hostile feeling between the Seculars and the Religious Clergy," but the friction should not supersede the good that had been and was yet to be accomplished. The sisters were also to be considered, since they would never have settled in Bristow had not the monks done so. With the many commitments already made, to say nothing of the complexities that would attend abandonment of the indenture of the Benedictines under the trust deed, the prior concluded, "the divorce seems far from easy."[114]

The Bristow work was not terminated in 1914, but relations with the Diocese of Richmond continued to suffer from chronic irritation. This agitation constituted less of a new beginning than an intensification of what was already the norm. Many of these conflicts proceeded from personal disfavor toward Pohl, but the readily perceived support of the abbot for his unpopular—at least among the diocesan clergy—prior expanded the peripheries of the original animosity to encompass Belmont Benedictines in general.

Several instances are available which are highly illustrative of the character of diocesan relations in the Pohl years, some rooted in diocesan impropriety, and some in the prior's more abrasive eccentricities. But in one of the earliest conflicts, it was neither of these factors, but the interference of a confrere that ministered to the prior's detriment.

From the beginning of the work at Bristow, Pohl had taken considerable annoyance from Father Willibald Baumgartner, O.S.B. The Richmond pastor liked to make unannounced visits to Saint Maur, where his interest was perceived to be excessive rather than charitable. Father Willibald was the senior Benedictine in Virginia, both in terms of profession and tenure, and by that merit he enjoyed precedence. But Pohl, as prior, outranked Baumgartner at Bristow. Nonetheless, Father Julius was disturbed by the regular visits of the senior monk from the well-established priory in the capital city. Both monks were conscious of Bristow's primitive conditions. A spirit of competition, undistinguished by overtones of friendliness, resulted.

There was further friction from Father Willibald's interest in the sisters. He was, of course, the pastor of their motherhouse in Richmond, and thus he was cordially available to accompany new sisters transferred from the Richmond convent to Saint Edith.[115] Baumgartner continued to maintain a conspicuous interest in the sisters' welfare even after they reached Bristow. In all fairness to the Richmond Benedictine, he had a solid reputation for pastoral zeal and personal kindness—some conflicts with the sisters notwithstanding.[116] But although he was venerable in many ways, he was also, by temperament, inclined to indulge his curiosity, and his involvement in Bristow's affairs did not settle well with the insecure prior in Prince William County, managing his first assignment as a monastic superior.

In 1896, Father Julius' day-book records a slight increase in the frequency of Baumgartner's trips north. Of particular note was the visit of 3 October, on which day the Richmond pastor was accompanied by his brother Leonard, a recent immigrant. Pohl was persuaded to hire Leonard as a factotum and construction worker. The man proved very helpful with the sisters' buildings, but incompatible with Father Julius personally.[117] The Reverend Superior and Mr. Baumgartner engaged in frequent disagreements, centering mostly around the prior's observation that his employee "was a slow-poke and a scandal," and above all a "rotten egg."[118] Father Willibald also entered the fray because he disliked the treatment his brother received, as well as the gradual shift in loyalty among the sisters, who seemed to have started preferring the services of their Bristow chaplain over their Richmond pastor's ministrations.

At the same time, the Richmond priest noted that Father Julius was guilty of a technical impropriety with the sisters: he was serving simultaneously as both the women's chaplain and their confessor, two duties that would not ideally have been filled by a single priest. Word somehow reached Bishop Van de Vyver, and the Richmond Ordinary recognized his obligation to correct the situation. On 26 May 1897, Father Willibald paid a surprise visit to Saint Maur,[119] and rather than offend his confreres by a hasty departure, decided to stay the night. The next day the bishop of Richmond also appeared; he made an official, if unscheduled, visitation of the convent, and relieved Father Julius of the office of confessor for the sisters. According to Pohl's account, Baumgartner, who departed with the bishop, "feasts on my defeat."[120] On 2 July Leonard also took his leave, despite his construction work for the sisters being unfinished,[121] and Father Willibald's visits north subsided dramatically.

In 1900, there was another conflict with the diocese, this time a disagreement with the secular priests of Richmond. According to Father Julius' account, the diocesan School Commissioners approached Bishop Van de Vyver and convinced him Saint Joseph Institute should be subject to the same visitations as any other school within Richmond's territory. Precedence was cited by the commissioners from the fact that Walter Leahy had permitted diocesan visitations during his brief service as principal of Saint Mary High School in Richmond. Pohl objected to admitting the commissioners to Bristow, however, since the Richmond academy had been a parochial school, subject to the pastor of the parish, and thus to the diocese. Saint Joseph, however, was not parochial; indeed, it was not even diocesan, but the project of an exempt religious Order: so long as faith and morals were unimpugned there, the running of the institute in Bristow did not lie within diocesan provenance, he argued. And Patrick Donlon, who happened to attend the commissioners' meeting, informed the clergymen that they would not be received at Bristow if they tried to visit in their official capacity.[122]

With Haid's concurrence, but without his intervention, Pohl fought for his exemption from the commissioners' investigation, and finally won the point. The victory was secured from the manner of the school's erection. Van de Vyver had endorsed the project, of course, but it was the Holy See which had actually permitted the endeavor to be undertaken. In issuing their approval, the Propaganda had empowered the Benedictines with authority, not the Ordinary of Richmond.[123]

The next quarrel into which Father Julius fell was of a more personal nature. On the whole, Van de Vyver enjoyed warm relations with Bishop Haid, but in the Bristow prior he found a grating and annoying presence. Pohl's lamentations were frequent and vocal. He was also convinced that the Benedictines should be granted any number of special concessions without permitting the slightest challenge to his rather broad interpretation of the principle of exemption. Bishop Van de Vyver tired of Pohl, his complaints and requests, and in 1910, he finally erupted against Father Julius' constant nagging:

> Instead of harping everlastingly on poverty would it not be much better to take some of your thousands on hand, clean up your premises and keep them clean, furnish your house properly, have your priests not hewers of wood and drawers of water, but gentlemen and religious, saying the office in common, etc. You as the head, a kind, gentle, considerate, sympathetic

father. If you cannot do these things then ask for the most humble place in
the college [at Belmont] or elsewhere.[124]

Two days later, Van de Vyver was still fuming. This time he wrote
Leo Haid, giving the contents of the rebuke to Father Julius. "Do you
blame me, my dear Bishop," he asked, "for being sick and tired of this
disgraceful place?"[125]

That same day found Pohl also busy reproducing Bishop Van de
Vyver's "insulting letter,"[126] and he too appealed to Haid. But if the
bishop of Richmond thought Julius Pohl would respond to the
correction with a spirit of contrition or amendment, he knew the man
very little. Instead, the prior, in perfect obedience to the Ordinary's
instructions, sent Van de Vyver's missive to the abbot with a cover
letter "ask[ing] for the humblest place."[127]

Not to be outdone, Haid, who received Van de Vyver's letter a day
before Julius Pohl's, himself spent 11 March carefully copying the
bishop's communication, then sent it to the Bristow prior for a
response.[128] But there was no doubt what the resolution would
ultimately be. Leo Haid did not condone quarrels between monks
and Ordinaries. He refused to support the priest's protestations of
innocence and mitigating circumstances, and he also declined to
permit a good man to withdraw from his work. Instead Abbot Leo
"bade me do as I was told," as Pohl remembered the incident, and the
prior spent approximately fourteen hundred dollars on improvements
at Saint Joseph, as a result.[129]

But the worst of Father Julius' diocesan disputes came in 1917,
again with Denis O'Connell, Augustine Van de Vyver's successor,
who the prior believed, "dislikes Benedictines."[130] Actually several
factors converged to constitute this contretemps, and Bishop
O'Connell was not as singular a factor as the prior presumed. The
first issue to arise was the minimum age for students at Saint Joseph.
For at least seven years, Abbot Leo had been instructing the prior to
receive no students under the age of twelve. Pohl disliked the
decision, but accepted it under obedience. His complicity, however,
was imperfect since, "I never had the heart to say 'no', and I always
feared that if I did, God's blessing, which counts more than money,
would be withdrawn."[131] Haid admired Father Julius' generous heart,
and quietly indulged the disobedience. In the interval, Pohl would
send occasional reminders to the abbot concerning how unreasonable
the minimum age requirement was. The letter of 8 July 1917 is
perhaps his best.

When I entered Saint Vincent's I was under twelve, and I was not the

> youngest. One of [Belmont's] members of the Chapter wrote me a year or so ago asking me to take one *five* years of age. I refused. . .One of our Fathers—without a line to me—encouraged a lady who adopted a boy—aged ten years (!), who has neither father nor mother—without any mention of terms, to send him to me. He came practically clothes-less. I wrote the lady to recall him. A most piteous reply. If we were not able to clothe them like College-bred boys—we always *fed* them. The lady fears she must now send him to a non-Catholic home! Heavens, must these little waifs lose even their Faith!![132]

As waifs and orphans began filling out the classrooms of Saint Joseph, the situation began growing steadily beyond control.

The second factor in 1917 was the filth and disrepair that again marked Bristow. Father Julius cared little for amenities, and the deterioration of his domain was uninterrupted, progressive, disedifying, and potentially dangerous. So bad did it become that the monastic Chapter at Maryhelp convened on 15 June 1917, censured Father Julius, and ordered specific improvements.[133] The threat—implicitly at least—was that failure to improve conditions would require the priory's termination. Accordingly, the Bristow monks appealed, even before the Chapter had officially acted, to salvage their mission from suppression.[134] The entreaty won its point, but no sympathy. The Chapter issued its mandate, unanimously approved, and stated in the strictest possible terms. Pohl was to take "stringent and immediate steps" to initiate the long delayed industrial school; practical and sanitary renovations, including "toilets, plain sanitary wash-stands, shower-baths," window screens, clean sleeping facilities, and "a liberal application of whitewash," were to be executed and the expenses charged to Saint Joseph, not to Belmont; no boys under twelve were to be admitted for any reason; the cleanliness of the students was to be nurtured, maintained, carefully supervised and frequently checked. Finally the Chapter ordered that an inspection be held so that the improved circumstances at Saint Maur could be verified.[135]

The tone of these resolutions notwithstanding, the Chapter still expressed its desire to assure Father Julius,

> that the aforesaid resolutions are made in the spirit of fraternal kindness with the hope of assisting those members of our Order at present engaged in this great work of charity and in carrying out the object of the Founders of the Institution which was to aid poor boys in their struggle to become useful citizens and good Catholic Christian men.[136]

On 20 June, Prior Julius acknowledged receipt of the resolutions. The letter, only one sentence in length, assured the Chapter, "I will endeavor to act on [the resolutions] to the best of my ability."[137]

And he "worked wonders with the place." Father Bernard Haas, O.S.B., who conducted the investigation on behalf of the Chapter, could make no more serious complaint than the fact that he found the placement of some pipes was "not ornamental." He also accepted "Father Julius' castigation very patiently." Haas' report was particularly amazing, given that he had viewed Bristow less than three months after the Chapter's vote, a full seven months before the deadline imposed on the prior. Pohl was pleased with Father Bernard's observations. "Then you can report [the] progress of the 'recalcitrant monk,'" he suggested, "to the great monastic Chapter."[138] At no point did Leo Haid inject himself into this affair, since it was a matter of internal governance. He declined even to be the party who forwarded the Chapter's resolutions.

The real crisis of 1917 came when Father Julius was exhausted and peeved from the controversies concerning the age of students, local hygiene, and the Chapter's mandate. As these matters began to subside, Pohl managed to seriously offend Bishop O'Connell. The incident was a small one, but its repercussions contributed more than any other factor to the exhaustion of the Benedictines' commitment to the work of Bristow.

In 1893, Sister Baptista, V.H.M., had written Mother Edith, O.S.B., assuring the Benedictines that the Bristow schools did not have to accept their students *gratis;* indeed, the schools did not even have to be started until "they have means to meet the expense." Mother Edith had communicated this news to Leo Haid—in the same letter in which she reported her acceptance of the Linton offer.[139] The abbot had saved this communication; he not being noted for filing his papers, however, the important document lay undiscovered from around 1900 until three quarters of a century later.[140] The bishop of Richmond seems not to have been familiar with the aspect of the Saint Joseph arrangement that authorized the charging of fees, and Haid was not in a position to substantiate it as a specific indulgence of the agreement with Linton.

The prior had already annoyed the Ordinary of Richmond in the fall of 1917 by not attending a diocesan meeting, to which, as it happened, he had not been invited.[141] The next month, the diocese tried to send some orphans to Bristow. Pohl had in the past accepted students whose fees were never paid. His usual approach was to solicit the child's support from the party who sent the "friendless boy" to Bristow. The Diocese of Richmond was expected to pay five dollars per month for boys it sent to Saint Joseph; that amount went toward board and tuition; clothing and other expenses were not included in the regular fee. Saint Joseph was a school, not an orphanage, and based its charges on that principle. Richmond, however, was not particularly comfortable with that distinction, and in 1917, when relations were already strained from the affair over the diocesan meeting, the prior was informed that the O'Connell administration would no longer cover the various expenses for the boys they sent to Bristow: the five dollars would have to cover everything. When Father Julius suggested that even that payment, in an amount settled before the horrible inflation of the period, was already inadequate to cover even tuition costs,[142] the bishop and priests of the Diocese of Richmond strenuously objected to Pohl's extravagant financial demands. Then—quite suddenly—the chancery fell silent. The prior thought the matter had been resolved, but the bishop did not. An investigation was quietly initiated into the legal conditions under which the monks held Lintonsford. The seeming quiet of the next five years, at least as far as the diocese was involved, left Father Julius free to concentrate on other matters, placidly ignorant of the tempest that Denis O'Connell was preparing to set in motion.

Prior Julius and Abbot Leo

Perhaps one reason the abbot of Belmont gave so little attention to Pohl's diocesan woes was the unhappy reality that they paled beside the internal battles of Saint Maur Priory. But there was also the confidence Haid placed in Julius Pohl, and the support he believed must attend the priest's assignment. Speaking of Father Julius as rector of the college at Belmont, the abbot had observed, "I know the responsibility of your position—spiritually and temporally. It is taking away half my own cares to be able to go to rest with the assurance that you are [at work]."[143] This faith in Pohl was virtually above challenge; the chaos at Bristow, as the hapless prior lugged the impedimenta of his responsibilities through what seemed a maze of endless conflicts, was divorced in Leo Haid's vision from the person of the local superior.

The prior's perpetual innocence proceeded in part from his deft responses to queries Haid directed at Bristow. For example, when the abbot told Pohl where to build the priory's church, the superior's response had been a perfect version of the sort of attitude toward the bishop's authority that had achieved such a vogue in the vicariate. Father Julius wrote,

> I note what you say regarding the location of the future Chapel. I desired to speak to you about this also. I will not wait for your insistence about this. As you merely say "you think it would be better", etc. If you do not object, I would certainly prefer having it on the other side.[144]

And "the other side" is where it was built. The abbot, after all, had not ordered; he had merely recommended. The logic was there, but it was at least not the classic interpretation of the niceties of a vow of obedience.

In dealing with his superior, the prior also exhibited a remarkable talent for turning corrections to his own advantage. On one occasion, after a wrestling match among a couple of inmates, followed by letters of complaint to Belmont, Father Julius was questioned by Abbot Leo regarding monastic discipline at Saint Maur. The prior responded,

> If men of a *religious* bend should complain to you, dear Father Abbot, I should cordially not only thank *you* but *them*, for enabling you to correct me; but for men who use knives, fists, etc., on each other and wrestle with even negroes—this is much! Yet, even here I cheerfully bend.[145]

Of course, he had not bent at all, but the *savoir faire*—in the literal sense—which attended his response succeeded in rescuing the prior from yet another correction.

Between these approaches, and his requests for penances for whatever he had already justified in his previous sentence, Julius Pohl seldom lost a dispute with his superior. But on the rare occasion that his own will went without indulgence, he would not only give the Carolina bishop what he wanted—probably accompanied by a request for some compensatory act to be assigned in reparation for his delay or incorrigibility—the prior would also leave Leo Haid with a dose of guilt to spoil his victory. The boldest of these was written in May of 1900. The scene was this: disaster had struck Maryhelp, and the abbot had seen two-thirds of his beloved college razed by fire. Desperate for reconstruction to begin at once, the presence of Gilbert Koberzynski at Belmont was imperative and had to be secured post haste. The venerable brother was at Bristow that spring, however, helping with one of Father Julius' buildings. It was the low point of Abbot Leo's dreams, and of course, Brother Gilbert was dispatched to Belmont without delay. Pohl wrote the abbot, "As we ourselves are just building we will, of course, miss him very much.[146]"

Because of the skill with which the prior could handle Bishop Haid, and because of his submersion in temporal and personnel matters—a condition the superior of Bristow denied—Father Julius never made real strides toward securing a true monastic observance at Saint Maur. As late as 1901, he was still having to post reminders to keep seculars out of the cloister.[147] He assured the abbot that he sought to serve the interests of the Order,[148] and there is no reason to doubt his good intentions, but he seems to have been distracted from his holy purposes. As early as 1897, Leo Haid was calling this problem to the prior's attention, but Pohl always successfully blamed the extenuating circumstances that surrounded him.[149]

The longest running problem regarding monastic observance in Bristow pertained to the *opus dei*. The abbot first instructed Father Julius to start having the Divine Office recited *in choro* in May of 1900.[150] Half a year later, Haid wanted an explanation for the delay in compliance. "Never for a moment since you mentioned 'choir' to me did I think of not complying with your pleasure," Pohl explained. What follows was not one of his better efforts, but at least it worked temporarily:

> Even now I am desirous of doing so....I fear, however, that the "choir" business will work very poorly. *One* must be absent as boys cannot be left without [a] prefect. That would make us three; that means two on one side—and one on the other. It will prove rather hard on the one. The recitation of the tenebrae has shown this. Not a chance for a cough, a sneeze, a yawn—a call of nature, etc. My voice is high—the others low. ...I cannot do more than assure you of the most perfect readiness to introduce this monastic, Benedictine feature. Kindly let me know if despite these drawbacks you wish us to hold "choir".[151]

The abbot did not insist on immediate institution of choral recitation of the Divine Office, but ordered instead that the effort begin as soon as possible. Two years later, on 28 December 1902, the four priests at Bristow finally convened for prayer in common.[152] But the effort did not last. They were ordered in 1908, to start again,[153] but to no avail. In 1910 both the bishop of Richmond and the abbot of Belmont reminded the prior of the importance of the Benedictine *opus dei*, and its recitation in choir.[154] But soon afterwards the number of priests assigned to Bristow was reduced to three, a total never again exceeded, and the idea was allowed to dissipate.[155]

Perhaps matters of observance could slip from prominence in the prior's mind, and after a decade of reminders even Leo Haid seemed resigned to this non-observance. But personnel problems[156] never left the forefront at Bristow. In this sphere of governance, Father Julius' gifts functioned in a manner that reversed Haid's, even though the results were often similar. Whereas the abbot's authority seemed to increase, the greater his presence;[157] for Bristow's prior, the more his subjects came to know him, so too did their ability to ignore the man grow stronger.[158] Monastic order and discipline did not profit by such circumstances. When possible, the abbot granted the several changes of personnel Father Julius requested.[159] But there is no extant case—outside of granting faculties for absolving brothers from the censures that followed some of the more malevolent acts of violence—in which Leo Haid interfered in his prior's hyperactive domestic environment. He expected his appointee to do the job, and waited for more than a quarter-century for Pohl to impose order on Saint Maur.[160]

Unfortunately, affairs at Bristow finally exceeded Father Julius' ability to compensate and make amends. The final spark was not some new villainy, but a factor that had surfaced repeatedly through the years. No one, however, anticipated the ultimate trauma it would cause. The culprit was cleanliness—or more precisely, its absence. The bishops of Richmond, the monastic Chapter, Haid himself, each had commended this problem to the prior's attention at various points in Bristow's history; nevertheless, Saint Joseph continued to be maintained with substandard hygienic conditions. Two major campaigns, one in 1910 (requested by Bishops Van de Vyver and Haid) and the second in 1917 (mandated by the Maryhelp Chapter), had already been waged in the interest of cleaning and maintaining the premises. But Pohl, whose interests did not rest in housekeeping, allowed the property to revert each time to its previous state of neglect. This caused increasingly serious problems, that were most virulently manifested in an outbreak of typhoid fever at Saint Joseph in the summer of 1922.

In its earliest days, the prior did not write the abbot about the presence of the disease. After all, when typhoid had first appeared at Saint Maur in 1900,[161] Pohl had thought it minor enough not to be mentioned to Abbot Leo, and that time even a monk had fallen prey to the fever.[162] So this time, when no monk had yet proven susceptible, the prior found no necessity, apparently, of worrying the bishop. It was an internal matter pertaining to the students, and the authorities in Belmont would not expect to be troubled, he reasoned.

The typhoid did not long confine itself, however. By mid-July five of the boys who had elected to stay the summer were bedridden with the fever. Father Raphael Arthur, O.S.B., was nursing them with all diligence, but at least two of the students, the Barnes brothers, were critically ill. On 26 July, Father Julius journeyed to Washington to enlist the aid of a nurse. Mrs. F.M. Kane was hired, and agreed to begin the following day. Before leaving the city, Pohl took time to notify Mrs. Barnes of the gravity of her children's illness. Apparently, though the boys had been bedridden since the eighteenth, the woman had received no previous word of her sons' perilous condition, nor indeed of the fact that they were ill.[163]

On the next day, 27 July, while awaiting the nurse, Father Julius was surprised to see Mrs. Barnes arrive. She had journeyed to Bristow in order to cheer her boys, but her first sight of the priory changed her mission from charity to mercy. The children were found with

> temperature[s] running at that time 105°. . . .My two boys and one other boy was [sic] just covered with flies, lice, and bed-bugs; it was a terrible sight for me to see my poor boys. . . .I feel as though my boys were neglected at the beginning. Because they were very ill, have been anointed. This is a very unsanitary school as the flies are terrible around the food. And that is where the germs are.[164]

Barnes stayed at Bristow to help in the nursing duties, until she arranged the transfer of her sons to a Washington hospital. Based on her observations while at the institute in Bristow, she was finally moved to excuse Father Julius from charges of deliberate negligence. As she saw the full scope of the priory and school she concluded, "Father Julius' health is very bad;" the prior "is not able to attend to things."[165]

This letter of 3 August, written after Mrs. Barnes had spent two full weeks at Bristow, was a triple shock to the abbot—his first word of the epidemic, of the return of the unsanitary conditions, and of the decline in Father Julius' health and competency.[166] A frightening portrait emerged from the Virginia farm, and Mrs. Kane was quick to corroborate and substantiate the story. "Father Julius," she wrote, "is ill, and not able to cope with duties and youth."[167]

Both women also mentioned an auxiliary difficulty at the priory, one of which the abbot had not previously heard from an objective source. This problem was a man named Denis Smith, who was commonly called "frater," a title appropriate to monks preparing for ordination. "Frater" Denis, however, was neither a monk nor preparing for Holy Orders. Smith had gone to Saint Maur in 1914. Father Julius grew fond of the man and allowed him to stay and work as a prefect—later even as a professor—in the school. Denis asked to be admitted to the Benedictine Order, and Pohl did as much as he could, receiving him as an oblate. Anything more, without appealing to the Chapter at Belmont, would have been impossible. Smith slowly increased his influence at Bristow, while convincing Father Julius that despite imperfect health his role as prior was still being properly exercised. Denis Smith regularly assured Julius Pohl that everything at Saint Joseph was in good order.[168]

In 1917, "Frater" Denis had announced his ambitions regarding the priesthood.[169] Father Raphael tried to tutor him in Latin, but Smith proved "deficient."[170] Therefore, the effort was conveniently terminated at the first opportunity—when the first World War produced an edifying moment of patriotic fervor, and Denis Smith enlisted for duty in Panama. The military were reportedly displeased with the man's lungs, sight, and hearing, however, so Frater Denis returned to the priory, by this time in full Roman collar and monastic habit.[171] It took Pohl until 1919 to arrange for Denis to be received at Belmont. That summer the incipient novice was dispatched to Carolina to enter the clerical novitiate. He made his pre-novitiate retreat, but then mysteriously returned to Bristow. Smith lied to the prior regarding the reason for his hasty departure from the abbey, but Felix Hintemeyer wrote Father Julius, advising him that Denis Smith had been tested and his academic credentials found so elementary that he had been refused admission. Pohl, of course, forgave Denis for his dishonesty, presumably out of compassion for the blow of thwarted ambitions. Smith next decided to become a missionary in Africa. That objective endured for even less time than had prefecting, military life, or monasticism, and he finally settled in at Saint Joseph, where he took for himself the religious habit, the title "father" this time, and worked as Julius Pohl's assistant.[172] Other than the abbot's usual confidence in his prior, and particularly in Pohl's ordinarily wise discernment in friends, there is no evidence to explain Haid's indulgence of these irregularities.

After 1920, "Father" Denis acquired a prurient interest in a teenage girl, the daughter of the priory's cook, a laywoman. Unbeknownst to Father Julius, this romance between his erzatz cleric-assistant and the sixteen year old Baptist girl was flourishing, and stirring great interest among the townspeople, diocesan authorities in Richmond and the District of Columbia, and others. When the pair would rendezvous in the evenings, "the boys at the Institute [who knew] of his relations with the girl, [would] watch them go through the grounds."[173] But no one told Pohl. Mrs. Kane reported the situation to diocesan officials when she returned home;[174] they wrote Bishop O'Connell in Richmond;[175] in August the dioceses, Mrs. Kane[176] and Mrs. Barnes[177] all sent word to Bishop Haid. But Julius Pohl, ill in bed, unaware even of the gravity of the school's epidemic, was allowed to remain oblivious of the situation.

So dramatic were the Bristow revelations that showered on the abbot's office in the summer of 1922, that Haid was left in a quandary, stymied by the complexity of these previously unsuspected conditions. He was reluctant to modify his trust in Pohl, and yet his worst phobia, scandal, was breeding with a vigor too real to be ignored. Accordingly, the abbot of Belmont decided to send an emissary to Prince William County to investigate conditions there. Ordinarily Haid's inquisitor was Bernard Haas. In his long career at the abbey, this priest was assigned to govern, investigate, or conduct visitations at each of Maryhelp's major enterprises. But Haas was so well known for undertaking such missions, that Father Julius would have immediately perceived the purpose of Father Bernard's visit. Also, since Haas had conducted the Chapter's review of Saint Joseph just five years before, the possibility of friction was high.

No such suspicions would attend the man Leo Haid did send, however. He was young—not even ordained yet—and in no way identified as one of the abbot's special assistants. The man, Frater Joseph Tobin, O.S.B., was a studious, observant young cleric, with an eye for detail and an instinct for propriety. Tobin had gone to Belmont as a boy, and had never left, completing his classical, philosophical, and theological studies at Maryhelp. As his seminary training progressed, or so the situation was represented to Pohl, Frater Joseph's health had grown delicate. A month of rest in Bristow seemed the ideal remedy.[178]

On 4 August 1922, Joseph Tobin wrote his abbot a twelve page letter describing the state of Bristow and its prior. As in the several other reports correspondents submitted to Haid, Denis Smith was closely associated with the current crisis. In Frater Joseph's analysis, Smith "can wiggle Father Julius around his finger." Tobin also gave the details of Denis Smith's liberties with the cook's daughter, their "auto riding at night, returning late," the man's masquerade as a cleric. "It is a disgrace," Frater Joseph observed, "and is disgusting." But the most frightening aspect of the situation was Pohl's total acceptance of whatever Smith testified or suggested. "He has Father Julius bluffed that everything is perfectly all right around here," Tobin warned, and that meant conditions—even after the crisis—were destined to "go right ahead as before." "Dear Bishop," he finally pleaded, "wake [Father Julius] up or somthing," And that required tending also to Denis Smith.[179]

If, however, Frater Joseph's report merely confirmed the presence of the problems in regard to Smith, it found other matters worse than expected. Hygienic standards were deplorable. Tobin was given the prefect's room, "and it was filthy. . . .I don't know how many years ago it was since it was washed," he said, but when he cleaned it, "the water was muddy when I finished." The stories of bed-bugs and lice were confirmed, too. A doctor and nurse inspected the premises and threatened to condemn the whole institute. A water inspector forbade continued use of the well for drinking purposes, so Father Julius, from his sick bed, ordered the water in the reserve tank to be employed. Frater Joseph inspected that receptacle and found it "all slimy inside, and full of mud." The outhouse, he discovered, had not been cleaned for two years, and there was evidence that some of the more impatient residents had not bothered to journey to its facilities.[180]

The centre of infection, however, was the refectory, which Tobin found "infested with flies." Father Julius had permitted conveniences for human waste to be maintained just beyond the windows, and the food—which the frater found good and prepared with proper standards—could not even reach the table before the flies pounced on it. Conditions were so severe that Tobin feared for his own health, and begged to be removed. He was so disturbed that instead of returning to Belmont, he implored a real rest—perhaps in Pennsylvania—as a necessity when he was permitted to leave Virginia.[181]

Before departing, Joseph Tobin arranged for everyone at Saint Joseph to be vaccinated against typhoid,[182] and he had the refectory fumigated. But he was at a loss for what to do with poor Julius Pohl. The prior was weak, suffering from dysentery; it was feared he showed signs of the fever. Yet the nurse could win no cooperation from him. Gradually, Pohl had reverted to the marks of depression that had so seriously scarred his last years in Carolina, complete with whining and closing himself in his room.[183]

The abbot had no choice but to intervene. He wanted to go to Virginia in order to relieve Father Julius of his duties as gently as possible. But by the summer of 1922, Leo Haid no longer had the health to endure any but the most necessary travels, and had to resign himself to merely writing the pioneer monk for whom he had developed such affection.

With his usual innocence, Julius Pohl was totally surprised by his abbot's letter. He wrote in response,

> I just received your letter, and while the contents were quite a shock I write to thank you for its kind tone....I wish my successor Heaven's best blessings. I fear for myself. My inefficiency is my great drawback, having for the past twenty-nine years taught small boys only—so that I am all thumbs only. I can but try to do your will—and leave the result—even if failure—to God.

It was a poignant end to the priest's administrative career. Before leaving Virginia for Carolina, the former prior—and again, here was Julius Pohl at his most genuine level—begged a few days' grace so he could render services requested of him by the sisters and the secular priest in Warrenton.[184] He scheduled his arrival at Belmont for Friday, 25 August 1922, a few days short of his twenty-ninth anniversary as prior of Saint Maur.[185]

Some years earlier the pioneer monk of Belmont and Bristow had written his abbot of the submission he wished always to offer his monastic superior. Leo Haid was to him, and in this Father Julius found great comfort, a true "father", the *pater familias* of his monastery and home.[186] On that occasion, Pohl wrote also of pain, the serious pain he drew from the delicate balance of Abbot Leo's trust against the weakness he knew to be his own.

> I am at your disposition. I now feel more than ever my deficiencies. Bristow was about the lowest rung in our ladder. I was fairly equal to its demands—but I am no more fitted to undertake any other duty than was the great Bishop England to teach vocal music—and College work is so different from what it was in my day; and I am no longer young—hardly teachable—though I could not be more willing. Here we had but lowly classes. Where I was fingers before, I am now all thumbs! God help me—and aid you! Bless me![187]

It is, of course, arguable that Bristow was Haid's failure as surely as it was Pohl's. The uncompromised support the abbot granted the prior—a man clearly unequal to his burden—constitutes irrefutable substantiation. For this same reason, however, Bristow's history serves as one of the most eloquent testimonies of Leo Haid's values, and the levels of priorities he considered in administering his dependencies.

Saint Joseph was not a favored apostolate of the bishop's; he gave it only minimal sustenance. But it did serve its purpose. In Abbot Leo's vision, the monastery of Saint Maur and its school were invested with the task of reformation. That was a real and valuable contribution to expect, and because that was the abbot's perspective, the seeming neglect may not be as severe as it at first appears. It is particularly interesting that at Bristow, a foundation he possessed—at least as far as the land was concerned—because of its apostolate (the industrial school required by Linton), Leo Haid placed less emphasis on the state of the monks' external works than was the case at any of his other houses. Equally intriguing is the fact that it was not really on the monastery, *per se*, that the focus rested either: it was on the monks. Perhaps it is unfair to say that Saint Maur gravitated into a school of remedial monasticism, thus allowing the institute to be undernourished from lack of attention. But it is undeniable that Leo Haid consistently sent his weakest monks there—brothers with bad tempers that needed soothing, fraters who required tutoring; there was the flutist priest who was lazy and obstreporous; two of the priests, because of their particularly undistinguished intellects, worried their abbot, so to save them the embarrassment that might attend them in a school assignment, he sent the two men to his largest farm; there was the newly ordained cleric who feared preaching, the gifted educator with the undisciplined will. Leo Haid entrusted these men to Julius Pohl. The men in his monastery who were weak, and whom he had not successfully advanced in monastic values and standards, he entrusted to the prior who he thought was a holy man. For Leo Haid, that was the value of Bristow, and it was the rationale by which he considered Julius Pohl among the foremost of Maryhelp's resources. The prior was not a great administrator, not even a good one. But he was gifted as a pastor of souls. And the gentle, somewhat negligent, marginally competent monk-priest-prior achieved remarkable success in that sphere of activity. Many of the subordinates he suffered did not amend; some—mostly the ones who developed that talent for ignoring the prior—even left the Order. But in the men Father Julius guided back or into useful monastic observance, there was a far more impressive total.

Leo Haid must be faulted for poor administrative judgment in this regard. Saint Joseph Institute was indeed a failure; its boys were not always well served; it brushed all too closely against the corpus of serious scandal. In terms of the values to which the abbot-bishop of Belmont had committed the priory, however, in the midst of this deplorable lack of ambition for practical success, there was a small ray of light that exposed a wise *abbas*, a compassionate father. By that measure, at least, Haid succeeded in meeting the standards of his own profession, if not those which held a more pervasive influence. The failure of Saint Joseph should not be praised, but it was not a complete loss.

a final Effort

Father Julius lived for two years after his return to the abbey. Cancer of the throat caused him great physical pain, but the abbot made every effort to ease his mental anxieties. Poor health was given as the official reason for the priest's return, despite which Father Julius served generously in the vicariate and at Belmont, until he grew incapable of sustaining the effort any longer. Bishop Haid spared Father Julius the pain of knowing of any of the official complaints registered against him by the Church in Richmond[188] and in Washington.[189]

As the new prior of Saint Maur, the abbot appointed Father Ignatius Remke, O.S.B. This was a sound choice on several counts. Remke was a practical man who had served as procurator of the abbey; he could be expected to oversee the restoration in Bristow with dispatch and economy. He was also a native Virginian, scion of a prominent Catholic family in Richmond, and Belmont's first vocation from Saint Mary parish. This, it was thought, would create an advantage for the Benedictines in seeking to improve relations with the diocese. Remke's appointment to Bristow was also timely, since after long years of investigating and under the influence of the institute's most recent excitement, Denis O'Connell was finally ready to challenge the whole manner of the monks' work in Prince William County. It was a struggle Pohl could never have met.

Upon his arrival in Virginia, Father Ignatius first tried to solidify finances. Father Julius' annual reports[190] had not shown a deficit since the 1890's, and cash reserves had been recorded as increasing at a fantastic rate. Indeed Pohl's final report, dated 19 August 1922, showed his legacy as eighteen thousand five hundred forty dollars and ninety-six cents, with eight thousand eight hundred twenty-two dollars and fifty-six cents of that actually on hand. There were also three priests, one oblate [Denis Smith], seventy-seven boarding students, eleven day scholars, eight horses, two mules, one bull, thirteen cows, four heifers, three calves, thirty swine, about three hundred fowls, and two brothers.[191] But conditions were not as comfortable as this report made it seem. There were over four hundred Mass intentions, too many for Bristow to handle, even over a period of years. The Masses and their stipends had to be assigned elsewhere.[192] Income was found to be rooted not in the school or farm but in donations; these disappeared when Father Julius' charm was replaced by Father Ignatius' practicality.[193] There were repairs to be made on all the buildings, of course;[194] these were a financial drain. Then Remke discovered that in his own impractical way, Pohl had been a rather creative bookkeeper. The large surplus of funds existed only on paper. The prior had each year dutifully recorded the services of the monks and sisters, since they drew no salaries, as income.[195] All these variants were adjusted and in January, Father Ignatius reported that instead of eighteen thousand dollars, the priory had one hundred seventeen dollars and ninety-eight cents, and no anticipated income capable of meeting expenses.[196] Haid was so shocked that he later ordered Fathers John Smith and Wilfrid Foley to audit Remke's accounts. These men vindicated the new prior's accuracy.[197]

Physical conditions were no better than financial ones. "You have heard so much about the dirt, filth, etc. of this place," Remke wrote the abbot, "It was all true." Despite the presence of two wells, there was no water acceptable for human consumption.[198] Then when Father Ignatius thought he had finally uncovered all of Bristow's problems, he was shown the sewer line which was broken, and had been spilling its contents under the priory for as long as three years.[199] In an effort to restore hygiene, Haid decided to limit school enrollment to only twenty-five or thirty pupils per year.[200] Living conditions were eased by the decision, but income evaporated, and the school neared death. Bishop O'Connell and Father Kaup could not have found a more opportune moment to challenge the Benedictines in Bristow.

Ignatius Remke, when on his way to assume control of Saint Maur, had visited the Ordinary in Richmond. The two men spoke frankly, and the prior was able to perceive the strength of O'Connell's annoyance. The bishop

> reviewed the whole history of Bristow and his dealing with Father Julius, told me all the complaints he had to make against Bristow and all the trouble and worry this place has caused him....The general condition of the place, he said, was a reflection on his diocese and a *personal* reflection on himself....He feared all along that the Board of Public Health would close up Saint Joseph....He was very plain-spoken and rather severe in his criticisms. Still, he was...delighted that the change of Superior had been made and hoped that a change of conditions in many things would soon follow.[201]

In a perceptive, if impolitic, response, the ever practical Remke left the meeting and secured the abbot's old friend Thomas Lion as the priory's attorney.

One month later, Father Kaup announced his intention to send two orphans to Saint Joseph. The struggle of five years earlier was immediately revived, and Remke informed the priest that he would only consider accepting orphans if the diocese not only paid their fees and expenses, but also agreed to take back the boys should they prove incorrigible. Kaup's response took an ominous tone. He said, as Father Ignatius reported it, "that he could not send the boys on the conditions which I had made, that the Bishop had read my letter with deep regret, and that [O'Connell] 'will call for an official interpretation of the trust attached to the Bristow property.'"[202]

In December, Remke met with O'Connell in Richmond. Their discussion lasted more than an hour, as the bishop praised "good, good Bishop Haid's *intentions* to erect shops, to start a choir, etc." But neither the institute nor the monastery seemed to be functioning properly, and at least regarding the former, "the law requires more than intentions." The Ordinary seemed concerned throughout the meeting that, by violating the trust agreement, Maryhelp was in danger of losing the Bristow property. O'Connell did not mention, however, that it was the diocese that was considering a challenge to Saint Joseph's conformity with the Linton conditions. "I have been [expecting] trouble," the prior wrote Belmont, "since I came here, and now I have it." Remke's one request—and this echoed Mohr's of almost three decades before—was that the gentle-hearted abbot would not enter the fray.

> I beg you not to worry about this matter, and don't write to Bishop O'Connell. I am, in fact, I have been in consultation with our lawyer for some time past, and I am in hopes that we will straighten out matters to the satisfaction of everybody. So please don't worry about it. I shall write to you again before long, perhaps before the end of the week. Just keep cool. Don't worry.[203]

With seventeen hundred acres of land, a priory, school, farm, to say nothing of justice and related virtues at stake, the abbot may have been imperfect in following Remke's injunctions. Nevertheless, keenly aware—albeit somewhat belatedly—that he should have pressed for that fee simple deed Sister Baptista had promised in 1893, Haid did stay quiet, and let this very competent priest act without restraint or interference.

Lion decided that the monks should take the initiative in the case, and introduce a petition to the Circuit Court in Prince William County asking the appointment of new trustees, who could then clarify or reconstitute as necessity might demand, the terms of the trust deed. By appealing to the court, Remke and Lion hoped to exclude the diocese from legal interest in the case,[204] but Richmond petitioned the court for the same purpose—though with a different end envisioned.

At the same time Father Ignatius applied himself to a statement of the case that could serve in an appeal to the Holy See. Here too there was a determined effort to win the initiative, so that the issue would be the intrusion of the bishop outside his rightful jurisdiction, rather than whether or not Saint Joseph met the conditions of the Linton trust deed. The argument was three-fold: First, the Holy See, not the Diocese of Richmond, had indulged the monks' acceptance of Bristow; second, the property of the Benedictines, since they were an exempt Order, was not subject to claims of this sort, made by the local Ordinary; therefore, lacking the prerogatives of origin and authority, Richmond could make no ecclesiastically founded claim on Lintonsford, no matter what civil irregularities were thought to exist.[205]

In February, O'Connell sent two gentlemen to Lion's office to discuss the case. In this meeting the bishop's representatives apparently conceded that diocesan interference would not be sustained by ecclesial law. Remke wrote the abbot, gloating over his success: "That was quite a different tune. Quite a change, eh, Bishop? A little firmness at times doesn't do any harm. It prevents people at times from running over you." In a quieter vein the prior also admitted that the diocesan representatives declined to deny the probability of a struggle in the state's courts.[206] And before the end of the month, the litigation was in progress.

Hoping to bring pressure on Kaup and his Ordinary, Remke called on the Apostolic Delegate in Washington before the civil judgment was at issue. Actually, for reasons that were not understood by the prior at the time, the Pope's representative appeared as eager for a meeting as did the Belmont monk. Apparently when they met, the Delegate was able, without Remke realizing the full scope of their conversation, to elicit the information he needed regarding another Belmont matter that had come to Rome's attention.[207] Father Ignatius perceived the talk of Bishop Haid and the abbey—at that time, at least—as cordiality, and since the Apostolic Delegate assured the monk that O'Connell "has no rights in the matter" of the Bristow acreage,[208] Father Ignatius left satisfied.

The Circuit Court in Prince William County heard the case at the end of February. Because the fear of scandal was so prevalent—as two bodies within the Roman Church challenged one another in civil suits—the litigants kept the affair as subdued as possible, and there seems to have been a tacit agreement that the court's decision would not be appealed. According to Remke's account, Richmond argued that the conditions of the trust deed had not been fulfilled: there was no "industrial school, shops, etc.;" the work was "educational rather than industrial," and, of course, the monks declined to take *'friendless* boys free of charge." Remke argued that there was legitimate endorsement of the character and substance of what was undertaken by the monks at Bristow, noting that not Linton, not Phillips, nor any of the trustees had ever complained. This was important, since Lion had uncovered an obscure Virginia statute that required any "protest against a non-fulfillment or change" of a legally binding pact, to occur within twenty years of the contract's taking effect. "If none is made within that time the change becomes an actual fact."[209] This invalidated Richmond's claims against the Benedictines' apostolate, and also undermined the petition for the appointment of new trustees. Indeed, in the court's judgment, the trust itself was "exhausted." Accordingly, it ruled, "there remains no necessity for, and the Court doth refuse to appoint, substituted trustees as prayed for in the petition of the plaintiff."[210]

Unfortunately, though the land was saved, the apostolate was not. When Saint Joseph determined to reduce its enrollment in the interest of improving living conditions, the sisters consented to operate a boys' school, and Saint Joseph was allowed to die of attrition. The sisters' work with girls returned to its Richmond focus; Saint Edith Academy was closed, and the Linton Hall Military School for boys opened in Bristow.[211] The Benedictine women were consistently efficient and prudent in their administration, and acquired a reputation for sound academic standards, as well as high moral, disciplinary, and cultural values. Thus Linton Hall, unlike Saint Joseph, became a successful and respected school for boys.

With its small enrollment, Saint Joseph Institute was a constant drain on Belmont finances; with a larger quantity of students, proper and necessary standards could not be maintained; manpower at the abbey was insufficient to cover enlarging the school; Belmont Benedictines had never been noteworthy farmers, either, of course. So the monks' value, and thus their future, in northern Virginia faded quickly after 1922. Haid took no action to discontinue the work, but in the years after his death the resolution of the situation became imperative.

On 18 May 1927, the monastic Chapter at Belmont passed five *dicta* regarding Bristow:

1. The lands covered in the Linton-Phillips trust deed were offered without charge to the Benedictine sisters. The acreage from Anne Phillips' will, however, was to be retained at least for the present.

2. Belmont agreed to help the sisters with the taxes for at least five years.

3. All buildings were offered without charge to the sisters.

4. All chattels and livestock were given to the sisters. Only the library, which included *incunabula* and rare and autographed books as well as ordinary volumes, was excepted from this gift, as were nonconstitutent items like the automobile.[212]

5. Father John Smith, O.S.B., was approved as chaplain-for-life.[213]

The sisters voted to accept the gift. The bishop of Richmond, Andrew Brennan, O'Connell's successor, also endorsed the plan.[214] And on 1 July 1927, the status of the Benedictines in northern Virginia was submitted to Rome. The petition was terse and presented its point without embellishment or elaboration:

Existing conditions render it advisable and necessary for the Benedictine Fathers to withdraw from this work, and to relinquish the operation of the school to the Benedictine Sisters, exclusively. . . .With the consent of the Chapter and [the bishop of Richmond, Belmont] humbly petition[s]. . .for permission to withdraw the Fathers from the above mentioned work, and that the Benedictine Sisters be allowed to continue its operation.[215]

The petition was approved, and Belmont withdrew, leaving the sisters—whose work had always been beyond challenge and whose prospects for future success were no longer tied to their less efficient brothers or to the defunct "industrial schools"—to their labors.

In late October Mother Agnes, at the convent in Bristow, received a letter from Belmont. In some small measure it acknowledged the bonds established between the monks and sisters during the past three decades. Abbot Leo's successor, Vincent Taylor, wrote, "I expect never to lose interest in Bristow and your community there."[216]

It was 1927, and Saint Joseph Institute was forever gone. Also dead was Leo Haid's vision for the Bristow monastery. All his other monastic foundations were conceived and executed along more conventional lines.

These photographs show Haid in the three stages of his tenure at Saint Vincent: As a twelve year old Scholastic (ABOVE, left) in 1861, a newly professed monk in the clericate (center) during a visit with his mother in 1869, and as a young priest-professor in 1879.

Saint Vincent Abbey (Westmoreland County, Pennsylvania) in 1880.

LEFT: Haid's first formal portrait as abbot (1885).

ABOVE: The Abbey-College in early 1887.

ABOVE: The College faculty for 1886-1887 included (seated, left to right) Felix Hintemeyer, Patrick Donlon, Julius Pohl, Leo Haid, Eustance Sonntag (loaned to Carolina by Saint Vincent), George Lester, Charles Mohr, and (standing) Benedict Roth, Francis Meyer, and Bernard Haas.

BONIFACE WIMMER, O.S.B.
Archabbot of Saint Vincent

JEREMIAH O'CONNELL
secular priest

JAMES CARDINAL GIBBONS
Archbishop of Baltimore

HERMAN WOLFE, O.S.B.
monk-priest

JULIUS POHL, O.S.B.
Prior of Bristow

OSWALD MOOSMUELLER,
O.S.B.
monk-priest

WALTER LEAHY, O.S.B.
monk-priest

WILLIBALD BAUMGARTNER,
O.S.B.
monk-priest

FELIX HINTEMEYER, O.S.B.
Prior and Vicar General

MARK GROSS
secular priest

GILBERT KOBERZYNSKI,
O.S.B.
monk

MICHAEL McINERNEY, O.S.B.
monk-priest

LEFT: The Abbey and College in early 1892.

RIGHT: The Lourdes Grotto in 1894. Father O'Connell is seated on the bench at right.

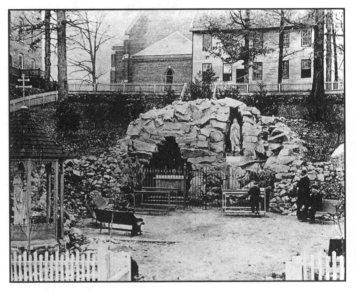

LEFT: The Abbey Church of Maryhelp, under construc-\.on in 1893.

ABOVE: Julius Pohl (third from left) posed with soldiers convalescing near the Bristow priory in 1898. RIGHT: Bishop Haid's first episcopal portrait (1888). BELOW: The sanctuary of the Abbey Church (c. 1899), as decorated under the direction of Felix Hintemeyer.

ABOVE: In 1908, the Abbey's Pilgrimage Shrine was the focus of celebrations in the mid-South commemorating the fiftieth anniversary of the apparitions at Lourdes.

ABOVE: The future of Saint Maur Priory and its school was never sufficiently secure to merit brick buildings. In this photograph (undated, c. 1915), students who remained in Bristow during the holidays posed with their Benedictine faculty. Pohl is centermost of the three priests.

Brick shell of the College Building at Belmont, after the Great Fire of 19 May 1900.

LEFT: Photographs of Haid show him aging at an accelerated pace after his elevation to the episcopacy. This photograph was used in fund raising efforts after the fire of 1900.

RIGHT: These were three of Haid's favorite monk-priests. Bernard Haas (seated, left) was Belmont's most gifted administrator. The cure of Francis Meyer (standing) resulted in construction of the Lourdes Grotto in 1891. It was Meyer who introduced Haid to the philanthropy of Katharine Drexel. Aloysius Hanlon (seated, right) shared the abbot's love of theatre; he wrote plays, and even appeared as Hamlet. This photograph was taken in

ᴛhe college
aᴛ belmoɴᴛ

LEFT: On 8 June 1913, the Belmont seminary celebrated the largest ordination class in its history. Five of these nine men were ordained for the monastery: Martin Schoettle (second from left), Edmund Meister (third), Lawrence McHale (fourth), Maurus Buchheit (seventh [actually ordained six months earlier]), and Richard Graz (eighth).

RIGHT: While baseball was required of all students, only the best players were on the team that competed off campus. Four future monk-priests are included in this 1901 photograph: Vincent Taylor (seated, third from right), Joseph (Michael) McInerney (front, second from right), Jerome Finn (standing, third from right — apparently posing as a student), and Ambrose Gallagher (standing at right).

RIGHT: *The Evidence of the Blood-Stained Dagger* was presented in 1897, to celebrate both the new theatre on campus and the visit of Cardinal Gibbons. Dramatics served as the most popular extracurricular activity on the campus at that time. This cast included two future priests: George (Vincent) Taylor (standing, left) and Patrick Marion (seated).

CDARYhELP CATHEDRAL ABBEY

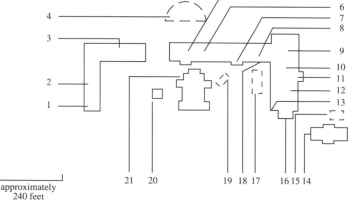

approximately
240 feet

1. Jubilee Hall (1897)
2. Brothers' Clausura (1893)
3. Library wing (1904)
4. Pilgrimage Shrine of Maria Lourdes (1891)
5. Monastery Annex (1894)
6. Monastery Annex (1891)
7. Monastery Porte Cochere (1902)
8. Monastery [originally college] (1880)
9. College Building (1886)
10. College Annex (1888)
11. College Portico (1902)
12. College Annex (1898)
13. Site of beginning of fire (1900)
14. Saint Leo Hall (1906)
15. Site of O'Connell Cottage (1886)
16. College Tower (1898)
17. Site of original Chapel of Maryhelp (1877)
18. Pilz's main entrance of Saint Mary's College (1880)
19. Site of O'Connell House (1885)
20. Bakery (1890)
21. Abbey Cathedral of Maryhelp (1892)

– J –

LEFT: Thomas Oestreich, working at his desk in the monastery. BELOW: Novices posing for a Christmas photograph in 1915. They are (seated, left to right): Patrick Conroy, Gregory Eichenlaub, and Cyril McElhatten; the monk standing (right) is not identified.

BELOW: Leo Haid, undated photograph (c. 1892).

RIGHT: The second floor corridor of the monastery was decorated in the autumn of 1910 for the distinguished visitors who came for the erection of the *nullius* and the bishop's jubilee.

– K –

The State of North Carolina

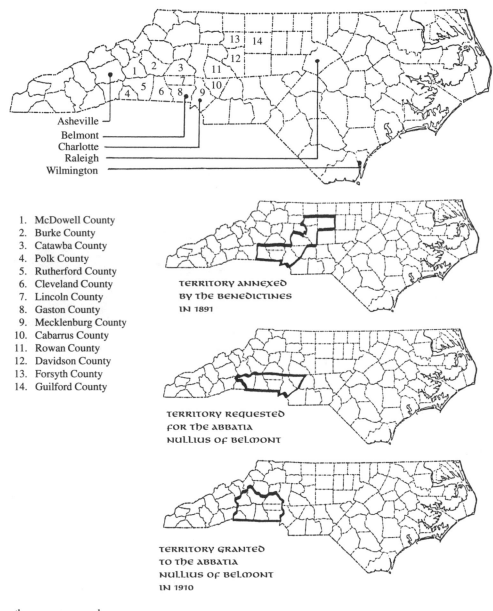

1. McDowell County
2. Burke County
3. Catawba County
4. Polk County
5. Rutherford County
6. Cleveland County
7. Lincoln County
8. Gaston County
9. Mecklenburg County
10. Cabarrus County
11. Rowan County
12. Davidson County
13. Forsyth County
14. Guilford County

Asheville
Belmont
Charlotte
Raleigh
Wilmington

TERRITORY ANNEXED
BY THE BENEDICTINES
IN 1891

TERRITORY REQUESTED
FOR THE ABBATIA
NULLIUS OF BELMONT

TERRITORY GRANTED
TO THE ABBATIA
NULLIUS OF BELMONT
IN 1910

these maps are used
courtesy of the Department
of Cultural Resources of
the State of North Carolina

τbe aBBATIA NULLIUS

Photographs on this page mark the erection of the *abbatia nullius* in 1910. LEFT: Official portrait of Bishop Haid, used for materials related to the *nullius'* erection. BELOW: The procession for the Mass at which the *Bulla* formally erecting the *nullius* was proclaimed. BOTTOM: These were the priests who attended the controversial retreat for the Vicariate's clergy that August: (seated, left to right) Thomas Frederick Price, Felix Hintemeyer (retreat master), Peter Marion, (standing) George Watkins, (unidentified), Joseph Gallagher, Patrick Marion, Michael Irwin, Louis Bour, Francis Gallagher, Christopher Dennen.

MONKS AT THE ABBEY IN DECEMBER OF 1910

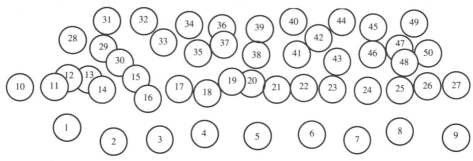

1. Father Alphonse Buss
2. Father James Buchholz
3. Father Thomas Oestreich
4. Father Felix Hintemeyer
5. Abbot-Bishop Leo Haid
6. Father Ignatius Remke
7. Father Augustine Ecker
8. Father Eugene Egan
9. Father Michael McInerney
10. Father Raphael Arthur
11. Frater Philip Fink
12. Frater Benedict Rettger
13. Frater Maurus Buchheit
14. Father William Regnat
15. Brother George Poellath
16. Father Richard Graz
17. Brother Richard Kleiner

18. Father Mark Cassidy
19. Brother Wolfgang (?)
20. Frater Andrew Stauffer
21. Brother Mark Poegel
22. Frater Theodore Zink
23. Frater Lawrence McHale
24. Frater Edmund Meister
25. Frater Martin Schoettl
26. Brother Ambrose (?)
27. Father Francis Underwood
28. Brother Felix Keilhacker
29. Brother Celestine Wiegerle
30. Brother Christian Hierl
31. Brother Aloysius Foerenbach
32. Brother Benedict Marschall
33. Brother Leo Kopp
34. Brother Charles Eckel

35. Brother Boniface Schreiber
36. Brother Louis Marschall
37. Brother Francis Zwiesler
38. Brother Simon Keilhacker
39. Brother Fidelis Kuhn
40. Brother Aegidius Seier
41. Brother Francis Buss
42. Brother Maurus Lobenhofer
43. Brother Albert Popp
44. Brother Joseph Ringlestaetter
45. Brother Leonard Metzger
46. Brother Philip Lobinger
47. Brother Frederick Schleid
48. Brother Gilbert Koberzynski
49. Brother Lawrence Bittel
50. Brother Bernard Geil

ABOVE: McInerney's design for the school building in Richmond (1910); it was a variation on his original plans for Savannah (1902). LEFT: Monastic and lay farmers in the fields (c. 1913). BELOW LEFT: Some Bavarian candidates for the brotherhood at Maryhelp; boys were still journeying to Belmont in response to Baumgartner's visit of the previous decade. They are (left to right): Philip Lobinger, Joseph Ringlestaetter, (unidentified), Richard Kleiner, Frederick Schleid, and Wolfgang (?). The photograph is dated 1911

RIGHT: Bishop Haid (third from left) and Thomas Oestreich, during the 1914 journey.

LEFT: The funeral of Bishop Haid at Maryhelp Cathedral, 29 July 1924.

RIGHT: The Abbot-Bishop's tomb, designed by Michael McInerney, showing the two croziers.

BELOW: Leo Haid's grave.

Chapter VI:

the mitre exceeds
the Crozier

On 22 January 1897, American newspapers[1] began carrying a story that placed Maryhelp Abbey in the forefront of the day's religious news. James Cardinal Gibbons, archbishop of Baltimore, was reported as having received a cablegram from Rome the previous day. The communique, released by an unidentified chancery worker, carried news of two episcopal appointments: One was the assignment of Father Edward P. Allen to head the See of Mobile, Alabama; the other saw Felix Michael Hintemeyer, O.S.B., prior of Belmont and Vicar General of the Vicariate Apostolic of North Carolina, named to the throne of Wilmington, Delaware. The following day the Baltimore *Sun* announced that it had confirmed the story through its correspondent in Rome. The alleged appointments acquired credence.[2]

The Holy See's nomination of Allen aroused little discussion. The priest was a respected seminary rector in Maryland, and his elevation to Mobile was received as a wise judgement, recognition granted a proven administrator. The candidate for Wilmington, however, incited considerable comment. At age thirty-four, three months short of the minimum age, Hintemeyer was considered too young for the post. Also Father Felix's name had not been placed on the provincial *terna* for Wilmington, causing suggestions that the appointment was gratuitously insulting to the metropolitan in Baltimore and his suffragans. Furthermore, Hintemeyer was both Bavarian-born and associated with the conservative branch of American Catholicism, two factors that evinced a detachment from the party of Gibbons and his adherents, and thus alerted the press to potential dissatisfaction. Also, Felix Hintemeyer was virtually unknown to the powerful prelates of the urban East, and was thus assumed by them to have been inconsequential. The newspapers immediately began investigating this unexpected bishop-elect. Periodicals like the *Post* in Pittsburgh, the *Herald,* the *World* and the *Journal* in New York, as well as the Baltimore *Sun,* offered a variety of suppositions regarding the prior of Belmont, and the rationale behind his episcopal nomination.

Little could be contributed from North Carolina, however, where nothing was known of the appointment beyond the journal coverage. Until Gibbons received documentation of the Holy See's pleasure regarding the vacancy in Wilmington, the news of the nomination was considered unsubstantiated. Nevertheless, at the abbey the story was being watched closely as newspaper clippings were received from throughout the country. Haid was shocked by the announcement, and greeted the loss of his friend and prior with serious reservations.

Despite the obvious speculation, Abbot Leo was not the power behind his Vicar General's promotion. Indeed both Haid and Hintemeyer were ignorant of Rome's motives in the case. The newspapers, however, had no shortage of theories, and they were convinced that Leo Haid and his Benedictine cohorts were the perpetrators of this grasp for power. The *Sun* characterized the abbot-bishop as a "prominent member of the Order in this country," and recalled hearing Mark Gross speak of the North Carolina prelate. The Benedictines were described as "strong in Europe," where they presumably "influenced the appointment of Father Hintemeyer."[3]

In New York, both the *Journal* and the *Herald* went even further and presumed to identify Haid's Roman friend who had advanced the name of Father Felix. Francesco Cardinal Satolli, noted for both his Roman conservatism and his opposition to increasing liberal and Irish domination of the American hierarchy, was the supposed force behind the nomination. The *Journal* criticized the appointment on all these points and more. "The new Bishop is a German, a Benedictine monk, and a staunch supporter of [New York's] Archbishop Corrigan's conservatism," the paper lamented, as if those qualities expressed the worst possible aspects of Romanism in America. It continued, "In fact he is all that Cardinal Gibbons' candidate [for

Wilmington]...is not." Hintemeyer, like the Pope, was identified as "radically opposed to the new Catholicism" of prelates like Gibbons, Ireland, and Keane.⁴ The *Herald* noted that Satolli, when in this country, had "displayed a predilection for the views, influence, and opinion of the German element of the Church in America which is largely represented in the Benedictines."⁵ So much confusion and consternation was aroused by the surprise appointment of Hintemeyer, that the Cardinal in Baltimore was supposed to have even denied knowing the Maryhelp prior.⁶

The Wilmington vacancy had been created by the resignation of Bishop Alfred Curtis,⁷ whom the *Sun* reported to be a foe of the Order of Saint Benedict, "as he was under the impression they labored too much for the Order and not enough for the general good."⁸ The bishops of the province had been summoned to Baltimore in September 1896, to create the *terna* for the Delaware See. Three names were selected on the twenty-fourth,⁹ none of which was Father Hintemeyer's. Gibbons sent the list to Rome on 9 October.¹⁰ Leo Haid had been absent from the provincial meeting.¹¹ Nevertheless, rather than insisting that Felix Hintemeyer be nominated, as the newspapers seemed to suggest, the Carolina Ordinary submitted to the Cardinal a letter endorsing the provincial *terna*; the communique from Haid made no mention of Belmont's prior.¹²

Now, since it appeared the appointment had been made, however, Haid was reluctant to comment at all. If the Holy See had named Father Felix to Wilmington, Abbot Leo could not presume to express displeasure, no matter how much he wished to retain his prior. Hintemeyer, too, remained silent, being unwilling to comment on a matter that was technically unofficial, despite the general credence it received. The taciturnity of the two Belmont monks was further encouraged by the controversies aroused by the nomination. Haid, more conservative than his metropolitan, and more sympathetic to the German-born Catholics, had been careful throughout his reign to avoid the national issues of American Catholicism, lest his positions create friction with Cardinal Gibbons. Instead he maintained silence on the larger questions that affected the Church, and took an active voice only in the interest of his own territory and subjects. In this way Haid neither compromised his positions nor offended the other bishops. At the same time he created a more practical following, in terms of his needs, among the laity—who were spiritually and financially supportive of his works. The abbot-bishop also cultivated Roman channels through the Benedictine Order. Accordingly, Bishop Haid had emerged before the American hierarchy as a respected figure, highly regarded at the Vatican, too, yet non-adversarial at home, and thus in all ways inoffensive. But the Hintemeyer controversy implied the interference of Leo Haid in ecclesiastical politics. Even worse, it appeared the abbot had won a victory over Gibbons and the regular consultative processes of the Catholic Church in the United States. Haid had not committed the breach of etiquette of which he was accused, but the newspapers had indeed stumbled upon the identity of the abbot-bishop's positions on important and controversial issues. Even when the furor had dissipated, Haid correctly surmised, the suspicions would not fall from the bishops' minds. Hintemeyer's episcopal nomination promised its greatest impact with the obstructions it would create in the path of Leo Haid, a path that could never again be credited with the innocent, impartial, anonymous selflessness that attended his image in the first decade of his episcopate.

The rise of Father Felix met a quick and embarrassing end when Rome sent the official papers for the Wilmington throne. The documents, received on 15 February 1887, proclaimed John Monaghan, not Felix Hintemeyer, the third Ordinary of the Diocese of Wilmington.[13] It was an announcement that should have provided a facile escape for both Haid and Hintemeyer. But instead of revealing that the unofficial announcement of Father Felix's appointment had been unfounded, and the attendant rumors false, the elevation of Monaghan to the See of Wilmington was popularly interpreted as a change of heart at the Vatican. Rome, the story suggested, had cowed under the impact of the adverse reaction to Hintemeyer in America. Thus the Holy See had retreated, abandoning Felix Hintemeyer in favor of John Monaghan. Humiliated by the new controversy which should have ended their problems, the abbot and prior continued their silence. Three months later, when Gibbons consecrated Monaghan, Leo Haid decided to avoid a potential resurrection of the controversy: he did not attend the ceremony.[14]

A full year later, Hintemeyer was still mortified at having been affiliated with a situation that embarrassed his abbot; thus he submitted his resignation as prior and Vicar General. Reluctantly, Abbot Leo accepted Father Felix's petition. In an extraordinary move, then, instead of appointing a successor, Haid ordained that the Maryhelp Chapter be summoned to elect the new prior. The abbot received the ballots at six o'clock on 11 June 1898, but he declined to count them in the presence of the capitulars, and retired to the abbatial apartments.[15] The next day, Abbot Leo, to the surprise of no one except the nominee, named Felix Hintemeyer prior of Maryhelp and Vicar General of the Vicariate Apostolic of North Carolina. The whole effort, of course, had been a ruse. The abbot was not willing to lose his faithful prior, and through this elaborate scheme, the Chapter was made to seem as enthusiastic about retaining Father Felix in office, as was Haid. If Abbot Leo consulted the ballots, he failed to note the totals.

It seemed there was little Father Felix could do to bolster the abbot's reputation in the aftermath of the Wilmington confusion, but few people could surpass Hintemeyer in an effort to display his Ordinary's best qualities. And the prior had been applying himself to that end throughout the past year. The most notable effort had commenced on 26 June 1897, when in the abbot's absence, Father Felix presumed to convoke a meeting of the monastic Chapter. Hintemeyer reminded the monks that the abbot was nearing the silver anniversary of his ordination, and suggested that a celebration be planned that would facilitate the desires of Haid's many friends "who wish to honor the occasion by their presence." The Chapter endorsed the idea, scheduled the festivities for 25 November, Thanksgiving Day, and appropriated two hundred dollars for new pontifical vestments.[16]

The prior did not mention that the abbot had already vetoed such a commemoration. In 1894, Haid's jubilee of profession had been ignored in order to focus the year on the blessing of the new church. The sacerdotal anniversary was to suffer the same fate, this time for reasons of expense and humility. But Hintemeyer circumvented the jubilarian and argued that "the good of Religion and our Order and the universal esteem in which he is held demanded action contrary to his pious and humble wishes."[17] Returning to the abbey from his summer episcopal visitations, Haid found the event scheduled, the vestments ordered, and a new college wing being appended to the Brothers' Building. The construction effort, called "Jubilee Hall", proved the most prized gift of the sacerdotal celebration because it finally gave Saint Mary's College the dramatic hall the playwright-abbot had so long desired.

Even for a Felix Hintemeyer gala, the silver jubilee celebration was extravagant. The prior had determined that the commemoration of the abbot's anniversary would "be the means of infusing renewed life and energy into the Church and afford consolation and encouragement to the scattered Catholics throughout the State."[18] And he planned an occasion extensive enough to suit those grandiose purposes. Cardinal Gibbons consented to attend, as did the bishops of Richmond and Syracuse. Even more important than the Cardinal this time, however, was the appearance of John Monaghan, bishop of

Wilmington. The Ordinaries of Philadelphia and Rochester sent personal envoys to the celebration. Abbots journeyed from New Jersey, Kansas, Alabama, Minnesota, Illinois, and Florida, and the Archabbot came from Pennsylvania. Thomas Frederick Price, the first native North Carolinian to be ordained for the Vicariate, gave remarks on behalf of the clergy; Frank Bourke, of Saint Mary's class of 1897, conveyed the greetings of students and alumni; Gibbons spoke on behalf of the Church and the Holy Father. Regis Canevin, a priest who since his childhood had known Haid, and had studied under him in Pennsylvania, gave the festive homily. Canevin had attended the jubilarian's ordination twenty-five years earlier; he preached for the silver anniversary in 1897; and twenty-five years after that, by which time he also was a member of the episcopate, he would return to Belmont to deliver the address at Haid's golden sacerdotal jubilee.[19]

There were gifts, too, all selected by Hintemeyer and financed by the bishop's various constituencies. The students gave a gold crozier; seminarians, a silver ewer; the priests and people of the vicariate gave a pectoral cross and chain, both of gold; from Sacred Heart Academy and the Sisters of Mercy, there was a waiter of sterling and a new *cappa magna*. As a special treat for the bishop, two dramas inaugurated the facilities of Jubilee Hall: *Sir Thomas More*, a new play in five acts, written for the occasion by Father Aloysius Hanlon, O.S.B., gave the theatre a religious hue, while *The Evidence of a Blood-Stained Dagger* appealed to other interests. There was a torch-light procession in the evening, capped by pyrotechnics at the grotto. The next day was the students', and was given to track and field sports.[20] Gibbons and the bishops were treated royally throughout their visit, Father Felix having thoughtfully arranged to punctuate any movement by the prelates with cheering students and suppliant monks.[21] The celebration gave all the appearances Hintemeyer desired, and the Ordinaries and their representatives were appeased if not convinced by the prestige Haid seemed to enjoy. The *Catholic Mirror* acknowledged the abbot-bishop to be "a profound theologian, an able administrator, and an eloquent preacher," and marvelled at him for ruling a "Vicariate [that] embraces the whole state of North Carolina."[22] With greater modesty and from a more practical interest, the abbot advised the primate that the celebration had been "very grand," and had elicited "the good will of so many friends."[23]

The carefully orchestrated convocation at Belmont in November of 1897, through the efforts of Father Felix, succeeded in surrounding the bishop with adoring subjects and appreciative peers. The various constituencies were, it appeared, virtually vying with one another in the effort to pay homage to Haid. The members of the hierarchy were given every opportunity to perceive this adulation, so they might remember it whenever they should think of Leo Haid in the future. The celebration was a success, even if it did not assuage the prior's self-imposed guilt.

The occasion also exposed the prelates and journalists to the imposing institution Maryhelp had grown to be. Jubilee Hall stood as the northwest extension of the central buildings. It connected with the Brothers' Building at the east end, to form one balance of the "U" that embraced the Abbey Church. The next wing, which would extend the Brothers' Building, and complete the north to south facade behind the church, had not yet been constructed; all the buildings that would border it had been erected, however, and its intention and placement were obvious. The main monastery, running behind the church in three wings, was finished already. The College Building which proceeded east to west, and started at the south end of the monastery, had two wings in use, and the final extension was under construction. When Leo Haid had first seen Maryhelp eleven years earlier, there had been a single brick building, a frame chapel, and an assortment of temporary wooden houses. Plentiful evidence of the abbot's successful tenure was on exhibit in 1897, and the transformation the Haid years brought to the old Caldwell place could not have escaped the eyes of the influential Cardinal who in 1875 had seen on this site a barren farm with a board cabin.

When completed in 1898, the College Building was particularly impressive, and expressed the scope of Saint Mary's College. The abbot even added electric lights, courtesy of Miss Rose Frauenheim of Pittsburgh, and on 20 November 1898, Maryhelp was "a vision of electric brilliancy."[24] The building was well-planned and functional. It stood three and a half stories high, and had a basement of forty by fifty feet to house the kitchen.[25] For years, Haid had embellished the building by promulgating the illusion of greater expanse than reality provided. He accomplished this through an artist's rendering of a full two hundred ten foot building, only two-thirds of which stood. That drawing adorned the cover of the college's catalogue and enjoyed various general references, all of which obscured its lack of existence. But in 1898, when the third, and final wing was nearing completion, it was determined that the building would be stretched to two hundred forty feet, and a hitherto unanticipated crown would be added at the west end: a four storey tower, possessed of various gothic inclinations, boasting pointed capitals, granite trim, and housing the western stairwell. The tower would provide a more monumental character to the dreams Leo Haid had realized.

The completed building hosted the dormitories, dining room, parlor, chapel for one hundred thirty-two students, sacristy, art and music hall, lockers, infirmary, class rooms, study rooms, director's quarters, society hall, laboratory, lecture halls, and even a museum. All the rooms were completely furnished. The Charlotte *Observer* encouraged its readers to visit the museum by reporting the presence of "a counterfeit foreign coin." There was electrical lighting throughout the building, and even a "massive telescope" for astronomy. Haid combined the dedication with the celebration of Frater Charles Rettger's solemn vows on 25 September 1898, as the monks and students dedicated the building "for the glory of God."

It was a proud and happy abbot who officiated at the ceremonies that day. And Hintemeyer vested the occasion in the usual livery of solemnity.

> A lengthy procession, composed of students, seminarians, Benedictines, priests and lay brothers, Sisters of Mercy, pupils of the Sacred Heart Academy and members of the congregation, followed Bishop Haid, as in cope and mitre and assisted by attendants, he blessed the structure from basement to turret. Never had North Carolina beheld the like, and the most unimpressionable heart must have quickened at the final picture as the beautiful new chapel was reached. There the solemn blessing was bestowed, the litany of the saints chanted, and Benediction given by the Right Reverend Bishop. As a conclusion, Bishop Haid addressed short but appropriate remarks to those present.[26]

The gothic tower at the building's west end was promptly adopted by Haid as the ornament that would illustrate his achievements. Visitors were escorted to its uppermost windows, above the level of a fourth storey, and allowed to survey the abbot's domain. To the west there stretched abbey farmland; to the north, abbey buildings; to the south there was the country road on which Leo Haid had first walked to the old Caldwell place. To the east, neglected now and virtually hidden by the grandeur of Saint Mary's College, there still rested the old granite slave stone on which Abbot Leo had stood twelve years before when he took possession of Maryhelp. The damage of January 1897 seemed an insignificant episode of the distant past when compared with the edifices that adorned Haid's abbey in September of 1898.

Little of note happened in 1899. College enrollment exceeded one hundred students for the first time in seven years. There was a minor disaster when the water tower burned, but in general, the completion of the College Building signaled for Maryhelp a period of quiet and security. Haid was so satisfied that not even a storage shed arose that year within the usually contruction-minded Ordinary's domain.

In the spring of 1900, a new century was greeted with all the beauty Hintemeyer could summon to adorn the abbey. Easter that year was celebrated as the "Solemnity of Solemnities," complete with the grandest pontificals since Haid had assumed the throne. Through it all, Father Felix stood at Abbot Leo's side, not only as *ceremoniarius*, but as friend and chief assistant. Despite the dry winter, the prior ordered the brothers to plant fruit trees and evergreens in the monastery courtyard that year, so that the buildings would be enveloped in blossoms and greenery each spring. Maryhelp was to display every possible sign of success and promise.

On 19 May 1900, the fathers and clerics arose at forty-five minutes past three o'clock as was their custom. At four, they assembled in the monastery chapel for Vigils. The Office was solemnly intoned; the monks stood through the invitatory; they sat as the first psalm began. But just then, outside the chapel, from the wooden floors of the monastery corridor, the sound of someone running could be heard. Abbot Leo nodded to the prior who rose and started for the door, seeking to halt the disturbance. He had barely left his choirstall, however, when his progress was arrested by the peeling of the church bells. The monks froze, silent and stiff in their places as Brother Englebert, the night-watchman, burst into the chapel and pronounced the verdict in a quiet, level tone: "Fire."[27]

Once outside the abbot had a clear view. Thick, dark smoke was being emitted from beneath the eaves at the northwest corner of the new College Building; the wind was blowing the smoke toward the church and monastery. Overcome with the sheer terror of the situation, Haid—with a muted voice and gestures of his hands—dispatched monks to hasten into the building and escort the boys to safety. The fire itself was over the chapel, but the dormitory of the youngest boys, the "minims", was just across the hall. Bishop Haid sent Father Eugene to rescue the Blessed Sacrament from the chapel, and ordered him next to the Abbey Church to offer the Sacrifice of the Altar. Then the abbot stood back, and Hintemeyer took command. By this time, flames had burst into sight on all levels of the building.

Bernard Haas awakened the small boys, who slept closest to where the fire had appeared, and led the procession of thirty-five minims—each carrying an armload of possessions—out of the building, "without a break in ranks, even after they learned of their extreme peril. . .so thorough was their training." The older boys had exited on their own. The wind drove the flames eastward and sent sparks northward. Hintemeyer directed the monks to fight the flames in the college while Haas sent boys to the monastery and church to pack valuables. Even while Eugene Egan was offering Mass at the altar, students were spread through the church packing vestments and liturgical appurtenances.

In every building of the central complex the work proceeded. In the first hour, the students saved a few valuable books, paintings, and assorted curiosities, while the flames grew and widened their course. Chemical extinguishers were employed and bucket brigades were formed, but they were no match for the fire. So as the flames spread and the sparks flew through the air more wildly, the work squads' approach was changed, and items were thrown from the windows to students at ground level.

At half past five, Haas telephoned the Charlotte Fire Department, begging assistance. But the city's firefighters declined to attend the Gaston County disaster, suggesting that the lack of water made such a trip useless. Hintemeyer interjected himself and protested. The water tower had not been rebuilt, but the bathrooms and water supply were ideally located at the centre of the building, he suggested. There were two wells close to the endangered structures, a cistern, tanks, and the lavatory. Nevertheless, no firemen were sent from Charlotte.[21]

When Hintemeyer went to report the city's reluctance to assist the Benedictines, he saw the bishop for the first time since the delegation of command more than an hour before. A story appeared later of the majestic figure presented by Leo Haid, his beard blowing in the wind, his booming voice threatening the Heavens, "God, save my monastery!" The contemporary accounts give a very different picture, however. Father Felix found his beloved abbot at the front of the monastery. "The disaster was a terrible blow," Hintemeyer wrote; the bishop was "crushed by the catastrophe." The prior approached his superior.

> At this juncture the saintly Bishop and Abbot Haid, crushed by grief, heartbroken and almost a mental and physical wreck, stepped upon the abbey porch and with arms outstretched towards the pitiless flames, like Moses on the mountain, called upon God's mercy and begged that his monastery and church be saved.

The prior did not address the abbot, but turned, and found his eyes in contact with the exact perspective required for studying the onslaught of the flames. Immediately the prior began barking orders. The time was six o'clock and it was clear that the building would be destroyed, the only remaining question being the extent to which the fire would be allowed to progress.

From Haid's side on the monastery porch, Father Felix had spied the crucial juncture for the progressing flames, the site on which the monks and students must make their final effort. Hintemeyer "directed all available help to one vulnerable spot in the main building." The only way to save the remaining third of the college, the prior had decided, was to separate it from its flame-infested wings. Five bucket brigades composed of boys on the ground and monks in the building were formed at the former exterior wall (now a fire wall) that had ended the 1886 section of the building. Each brigade doused its own level (ground, first, second, and third floors, and attic), while the younger boys crawled around, trying to plug all the air-holes in the wall. As the boys worked at that, monks took axes and chopped at the beams that connected the burning building with the original section.

It worked. The fire was contained in this way. Seventy-five feet of the College Building still stood. At half past six the first volunteers ventured into the smoldering middle section of the structure to try to extinguish the small, smoky fires that still dotted the remains of Saint Mary's College. At seven o'clock, Haas sent his boys to eat breakfast, hastily cooked by the brothers, while the priests and clerics tended the fire. Girls from Sacred Heart Academy came at eight o'clock to carry "delicate items" into the water-damaged, but safe, monastery.

Later that day, the grateful monks gave up their rooms and beds to the tired boys. Milo Dodd, a student from Norfolk, Virginia, was given a life-time scholarship in recognition of his bravery in fighting the fire. As it happened, however, Master Dodd was graduated two days later.

No lives were lost, but more than three thousand books, the boys' possessions, and all the furnishings of the rooms were gone. Electricity was ruled out as a possible cause of the disaster. The conflagration was believed to have resulted from spontaneous combustion in a sparrow's nest under the eaves. But the cause was never definitely established.

At forty-seven minutes past eleven, Father Francis wired the *News,* Charlotte's afternoon newspaper, "The fire is under complete control." The Gastonia *Gazette,* whose reporters did not reach the abbey until noon, reported that "the fire had about finished its work, but a gaping mass of crumbling brick walls stood where we had often seen a stately college building."

Through all of this, Leo Haid had been standing in silence in front of the monastery. As the commotion ended, he ordered Father Francis to buy new trunks for every boy in the school as a gesture of appreciation. Then he allowed Father Felix to conduct him to the abbatial apartments. Hintemeyer, upon his return, approved Meyer's plan to canvass Charlotte raising funds, assigned Father Aloysius to chaperone the Pittsburgh boys on their trip home, sent Father Joseph to photograph the ruins, dispatched telegrams to abbots, newspapers, and parents stating, "College destroyed by fire. No lives lost. Complete loss. Bishop Haid." To the brothers, Father Felix expressed the abbot's appreciation and his own, then as prior he advised them that reconstruction should begin the following day. Also, it was Father Felix, not Haid, who wired Pohl to send Brother Gilbert immediately. Felix Hintemeyer did not rest then, and it was not only because students occupied his cell and bed, but because of the ashen figure of Leo Haid. The prior "grieved over the blow" to his abbot-bishop.

Felix Hintemeyer was not the only persons to note the impact of the disaster on Abbot Leo. The Charlotte *Observer* carried a story describing the bishop as "prostrated at seeing the work of twenty years taken away in a few hours." Haid was indeed distraught. "I am nearly despairing,"[29] he wrote Katharine Drexel. To Abbot Peter Engel at Saint John Abbey he admitted his overwhelming depression. "Had my Monastery burned [too]," he said, "I would have given up; I am getting too old to begin over again as the struggle of the past has worn me out."[30] Even three weeks later, Abbot Leo was continuing to entreat Engel to, "Pray for me sometimes, for I am still so nervous and fearful. May God strengthen me, and give me a little of my former courage!"[31]

When the monastic Chapter had assembled on the front lawn that day, before the raging fire, the absence of the abbot had dominated the meeting. Father Felix took charge, of course. The Minutes recorded that, "our Right Reverend Abbot was grief-stricken at such a terrible blow." The monks passed three resolutions as a testament of faith in their superior and his abbey:

1st - That the rebuilding of the College, should be begun at once.
2nd - That all should do their best in obtaining help with means to defray the expenses incurred.
3rd - To empower the Abbot to act and do in rebuilding what he thinks the very best under [the] circumstances.[32]

The assembled monks did not realize until the following day that their rather public Chapter had been overheard by newspaper reporters. The Charlotte *Observer* had used the meeting to further illustrate the abbot's condition. "Whilst the fire was still raging," the paper noted, "the Reverend Fathers met, expressing their sympathy to the Right Reverend Bishop, and consoling him in his affliction."[33]

Hintemeyer ran the abbey for the next few days, without consulting the abbot who mostly kept to his own cell. Hintemeyer ordered Haas to assemble the faculty and dismiss school for the year. A brief commencement ceremony was held on the twenty-first, at the close of which the students presented their premiums (their awards for scholastic excellence) back to the rector "as a nucleus for a new College library."[34] The prior had Father Francis organize the solicitation of funds. What Father Felix could not order, however, was the restoration of Leo Haid's spirit and zeal.

The losses were staggering, with two-thirds of the College Building gone, most of the rest damaged by smoke and water, appointments and furnishings destroyed. Frances Meyer estimated the damage to the library alone—a "magnificent college library, the collection of twenty years, and containing many records and authoritative works, especially on history and sciences"[35]—at one hundred thousand dollars. The total loss was placed—and probably somewhat extravagantly over-estimated—at four hundred thousand dollars. Insurance coverage totalled just fifteen thousand dollars. The only advantage in this dearth of funds was the leverage it gave Hintemeyer in occupying the abbot's mind by sending him on the most important begging trip in his career. Haid was in Pittsburgh within the week, and the summer included journeys through much of Pennsylvania, Illinois, and Virginia. He implored help from all sides, then earned additional sums by giving retreats, lectures, and missions.

The bishop saved many of the messages of sympathy that came to Belmont in the aftermath of the fire. And a cordial correspondence developed with Peter Engel, the Abbot of Saint John, as a result of that prelate's compassion and interest. Haid wrote the Minnesota monk, "God only could save what was saved," and promote the appearance of "so many friends...to aid us."[36] Even the Abbot Primate in Rome wrote, sympathizing if not comforting:

> ...I was grieved by this painful news...Yet, as it is, it is bad enough when considering that the work done within a few hours by the fire will entail upon you, my dear Lord, years of toil and care. May Divine Providence give you both the patience and the means to meet the emergency.[37]

The generous and charitable response of so many people, coupled with the round of activity Hintemeyer imposed on him, served more than any other factor to raise the abbot from his despondency. "I am more than thankful for your brotherly help,"[38] he wrote Engel, "Your message of consolation and hope in our great trial was most highly appreciated."[39]

But the disasters of May were not yet completed. Reconstruction work began on 22 May, while the abbot was in Pennsylvania. Several of the college boys decided to forego their summer recess, and spend those months at the abbey assisting in the restoration. To save time, Hintemeyer decided to build the structure over the burnt timbers of the original, employing also the brick shell that remained standing. Brothers running the sawmill staggered their hours to maximize efficient use of tools, machinery, and time. Haid was buoyed upon his first sight of the abbey in the following week, when he found progress already in evidence.

On 26 May, Brother Andrew Huemer, O.S.B., a forty-two year old Bavarian native, just nine years professed, was directing the abbey sawmill alone. Leo Haid, surveying the restoration of his property, was approaching the mill when he heard faint cries—not for help, but for a priest—coming from inside. The abbot, who customarily carried the Holy Oils on his person, rushed inside and found a blood-spattered room, and the pitiful Bavarian writhing in pain on the floor. Haid immediately knelt at the man's side and gave

> poor Brother Andrew Extreme Unction—weltering in his blood! Sawing wood, he put on too much steam; the saw exploded and a piece nearly cut the whole left shoulder off. He could not speak after calling for the priest—I was quite near and gave him all I could. He had gone to Holy Communion this morning. [May he] rest in peace![40]

From this trial the abbot did not retreat as he had one week earlier. He wrote Father Francis, "Oh may God in His mercy, have mercy on us!...Pray for me especially." Haid officiated at Huemer's requiem. Then, solemn faced, the abbot set off on the work that awaited him. "My poor nerves were again terribly shocked,"[41] he admitted, but this time he surfaced not shattered, but hardened and determined.

Paul Haid was summoned from Pittsburgh to act as superintendent of the construction project. Brother Gilbert was assigned to be the master carpenter. As the architect, the abbot-bishop appointed one of the students who had sacrificed his summer vacation to accomodate the college's needs.

The student architect was Joseph Vincent McInerney,[42] who at age twenty-three was one of the older scholars in the college. McInerney was born 18 March 1877, in Lockhaven, Pennsylvania. Both of his parents were Irish Catholic immigrants. As a child, Joseph had attended Saint Peter Parochial School in McKeesport, and had assisted his father in his work as a stone contractor. The fascination with buildings arose at an early age, and at fifteen, while attending the High School of the Holy Ghost in Pittsburgh, where the family had moved, Joseph McInerney was accepted as an apprentice by W.A. Thomas, former professor of architecture at King's College, London. Thomas supervised the boy's training for the next eight years, and finally named him a partner. Young Joseph also managed during this period to complete two years of liberal arts studies at Duquesne. Seeking to broaden his education and experience, McInerney resigned his position with Thomas, and moved in January of 1900 to Belmont, where he enrolled in the classical course at Saint Mary's. Older and more accomplished than his classmates, Joseph McInerney was soon identified as a leader among the students. He was noted for his piety; he was an honor student;[43] and perhaps most importantly in terms of his popularity, he was a "stellar" first baseman.[44]

Such was the young man's modesty, that not until the fire of 19 May did "school authorities [discover] that he knew a thing or two about architecture and design."[45] Working with the monks through the summer, Joseph McInerney began to wonder if the search in which he was engaged and which had led him to resign his promising position in Pittsburgh, might be a quest for God rather than for classics and culture. So in 1902, when he took his degree, Joseph Vincent McInerney determined to enter the monastery. There is little to document his move to religion;[46] as he remembered it a half-century later, after working with the men of Maryhelp in the summer of 1900, he simply knew he "was called to become a Benedictine monk."[47] So Joseph McInerney, taking the name "Michael" in religion—which was his father's name—entered Maryhelp as a novice on 20 August 1902. He was professed the following year, and ordained in 1907.

The importance of McInerney in the developing dreams of Leo Haid has no parallel. No other creative force at Maryhelp could even approximate the contribution he would make through the years. The "Great Fire", as the happenings of 19 May came to be called, brought at least one benefit to the abbey: it incorporated Michael McInerney into the Haid story.

So for that summer, Felix Hintemeyer ran the monastery; Meyer and the abbot sought funds; Haas managed finances; and McInerney, Koberzynski, and Paul Haid supervised construction. Under the architect's direction, the old design was improved, and at the end of August Father Bernard published this notice: "We are happy to announce to our patrons and friends that Saint Mary's College will reopen September 15."[48] Not only did the monks manage in the space of one summer to resurrect the college and restore the building, they even managed to emerge in the fall of 1900 with an increased enrollment, the second highest in the school's history.

Episcopus

Although the setbacks of May had proven mercifully ephemeral, their impact on the abbot himself was strong and lasting. There was a perceptible change in Leo Haid after the fire of 1900. The disaster of the nineteenth, followed by the violent death of Brother Andrew just one week later, summoned to the surface images of challenge and menace the abbot could not fight. As the primate had suggested, "the work done within a few hours by the fire" destroyed a project that had consumed Haid's entire reign of fifteen years. By attacking the edifices Haid used to symbolize his progress, the fire had shown how frail that success actually was. The fire destroyed the most tangible symbol of Haid's accomplishments. And yet while this was a painful loss, it did not defy restoration. The loss of the gentle Bavarian, however, did exceed the limits of the abbot's authority. And since the death had occurred while the brother, with excessive zeal, was trying to resurrect the images of his abbot's dreams, it was easily recognized that Haid—or his impatience—was at least partly at fault. Suddenly Abbot Leo found himself faced with a crisis that affected him on an uncomfortably personal level.

Not making friends readily, and convinced that his offices demanded a certain reserve from intimacy and common conviviality, Haid remained somewhat aloof from most of the crises he faced. The problems of his reign were ordinarily concerned with either finances or personnel. For each case, the abbot sought to maintain distance between himself and the situation, making responses that were clearly professional rather than personal. This was not always compatible with the obligations of his spiritual paternity, however. The compromise between these two principles—professionalism and paternity—that finally surfaced came from the core of Haid's personality, from that balance of personal reserve and fatherly care that marked his relationships throughout his tenure: Though the abbot was genuinely compassionate, he gave sympathy more readily than empathy; his involvement ordinarily reflected the reserve that indicated. He loved his subjects, but did not share their pain. He was not accustomed to being intimately involved in their problems, and thus he experienced Brother Andrew's death—where he found he was more directly involved—not only on a more personal level but also in a way that underscored his helplessness.

But falling images and human sensitivities were not sufficient to bring about the bishop's transformation on their own. There was another factor that influenced Haid, one that emerges with a surprising clarity when the sundry articles of correspondence, coverage, and commentary are assembled. Leo Haid recognized in his initial response to the fire an overwhelming weakness, a deplorable lack of fortitude, edification, and episcopal virtue. In theological terms, God had given him the grace, but the abbot had not manifested the strength of will to use that Divine gift. Even by more conventional standards Haid reasoned that he had failed: He was ordained to lead, but had not led. He had shown weakness that was unbecoming his rank.

There were obvious reasons for reaching his conclusion. But what is peculiar here is the difference between the standards applied to himself and those the abbot invoked against his subordinates. Leo Haid, after all, was not noted for seeking the more conventional qualities in administrators. He is the man who admired Julius Pohl, the ineffectual prior of the chaotic monastery in Bristow, more than Bernard Haas, an administrator possessed of skill, stability, and virtue.

The abbot was deeply affected by what he perceived as cowardice and what he believed others found to be weakness. He realized he had not been heroic when heroism was asked of him, and he was pained by that realization. He also did not see in his acts the strength of paternity that was the core of his administrative approach. Neither did he perceive that these fatherly virtues had become so integral to his personality that he practiced them even when shattered and disoriented by the fire. No, Leo Haid had not gone in and chopped wood or carried buckets of water; he had not assumed command nor even coordinated the efforts of his subordinates. But what he did manage to do was more expressive of both his character and his standards than ordinary heroics would have been. Leo Haid was the man whose first response had been to secure the safety of the little children; who sent a priest to offer Mass before it occurred to him that a bucket brigade might help, too; who though in debt, with his apostolate out of operation, and his main building smoldering in ruins, had ordered new valises for all the boys who had lost their possessions.

There was a second perspective to be considered regarding Abbot Leo's pusillanimity. But the man would see only one side. To his mind it seemed that at a time when circumstances called for his greatest strength, he had been weak. For once, misfortune had struck his own heart, and he had found himself lacking the love, grace, and fortitude that were necessary for exercising his paternity. He expected to know his frailty better than anyone else, of course. But he lacked the comfort of exclusive command of that knowledge. The newspapers had announced his enervated performance to the world. Even more painful, his monks had written his failure into the Minutes of the monastic Chapter. There is no evidence to suggest that anyone other than the abbot himself interpreted his response—this supposed weakness—to be cowardice. But the abbot believed he had humiliated not only himself, but his abbey. On this there followed the resolution to amend, and he began the effort to toughen his character and his reign by giving himself to the more imposing of his positions, his episcopacy. The effort was largely futile, of course. Haid could change his actions, but not his whole character and personality. In 1900, the externals that attended Haid began to change; the velocity of his apostolic labor increased. He tried to reach for a style that was both aggressive and marked by a cool professionalism; he wanted to manifest the regal bearing, broadly focused concerns, and fervent activities that were regarded as episcopal virtues. From his more placid and paternal mien as an abbot, he sought to move into conformity with the popularly conceived image of a bishop.

The first signs of a changed outlook were subtle. For example, he began styling himself "Bishop Haid" rather than "Abbot Leo", even when at his monasteries. This was a slight change, of course, and since the episcopal title outranked the abbatial dignity, the shift was not wholly inappropriate. But this small alteration reflected a far more significant transmutation in his priorities. The episcopal duties began acquiring prominence in Haid's schedule. For the monks too, missionary work expanded dramatically, as weekend parochial assignments became commonplace. During the summers, monks were sent for prolonged periods of time to parishes—some in states as far away as New York and Pennsylvania. Leo Haid's desire for a more aggressive approach to his responsibilities caused him to emphasize his role as bishop, and thus take himself and his monks into a decidedly more active mode of apostolic labor. It was a change that not only affected the abbot-bishop, but influenced the character of his monastery, as well.

Even the images of Haid's success began to change in 1900. He no longer possessed the fervor for construction projects that had marked the previous fifteen years. After 1900, the bishop wanted his monuments not to be in red brick, but in the black ink of debt-free apostolates. He encouraged the Mercies to expand their work throughout the state, too, most notably with the opening of Mercy

Hospital in Charlotte in 1908. Father Thomas Oestreich, O.S.B., recently returned from doctoral studies in Rome, was named the bishop's secretary; that priest handled routine paperwork while Felix Hintemeyer ran the monastery. For the first time, Leo Haid did not seek to balance his responsibilities, but gave the Vicariate Apostolic clear precedence. Even in the staffing of his abbey, there was a distinct orientation toward assignments that would free the abbot for his episcopal duties.

In the monastery the change of perspective had an immediate impact. The young monks found that they were to be educated with an increasingly clerical emphasis that conflicted both with the senior Benedictines' orientation and with the character Abbot Leo originally had imparted to his monastery and disciples. Of himself, Haid began to think less "Abbot-Bishop" than "Bishop". And for his monks, he reasoned, "To be mere teachers can never satisfy good Priests!"[49] The abbot did not abandon his monastery, and in his words, at least, he still gave unfailing emphasis to the demands of the Benedictine vocation. But he developed the theme differently after 1900, using a theory that said Benedictine identity, if well learned and inculcated, was itself sufficient to make a monk true to his vocation, despite duties that were apostolic in orientation and exclaustral in manifestation. Educating men for this new direction in Maryhelp's monastic ethos undermined the original tenor of the house, and compromised the spirit the abbot had worked so hard to create. But Leo Haid was absent too much during these days to really perceive the change that was taking place, and when, years later, he belatedly recognized the grasp this activity had acquired on his monks, Abbot Leo would be severely—albeit, belatedly—shaken.

In the vicariate, the apostolic fervor Bishop Haid brought to the first decade of the twentieth century, produced a period of extraordinary growth. According to statistics in the *Catholic Directory*, the century began with only nine secular priests, just one of whom, Frederick Price, had been at work in North Carolina when Haid was consecrated vicar. The 1910 figures showed seventeen priests, almost all products of Belmont's seminary. In this same period though only two additional churches had acquired resident pastors, eight new church buildings had been erected, most designed by Father Michael McInerney. The Catholic population had increased by forty-three percent.

Various small groups of sisters were brought to Carolina in these years,[50] and the Josephites became the first non-Benedictine male religious to take up residence in the state. Katharine Drexel assisted in securing those clergymen.[51] Haid's travels became increasingly extensive and prolonged. In December 1909, just a "little trip through a part of Eastern North Carolina" required him to dedicate four churches and deliver eighteen addresses.[52] To economize his efforts he began carefully dating and identifying his homilies and speeches to facilitate their use at a greater variety of locations, and thus streamline his preparations. For example, one address on the Eucharist is listed as being delivered five times in six weeks in three states.[53] A sermon first prepared for Forty Hours devotions in 1908 was delivered during the next twelve months in Pittsburgh, Greensboro, Raleigh, Wilmington, Charlotte, Savannah, and Asheville.[54] Speaking tours routinely covered Georgia, Virginia, and both Carolinas; extensions into Pennsylvania and New York were common. New Jersey, Ohio, Maryland, Florida, and the District of Columbia were also on the schedule with some regularity. Even after suffering through a train derailment in 1907, an event which must have conjured images of his father's death, the bishop did not limit his journeys. He treated that accident philosophically, venting his new coriaceous facade, saying it was just "one of those 'fool' wrecks which might easily have been avoided,"[55] and so he continued his hectic scheduling.

So infectious was the abbot's enthusiasm that he found surprisingly little trouble this time in converting his monks to the work of missionaries. Of course, until he had succeeded in educating a new generation of Maryhelp monks, the fathers' ardor for the missions may have been imperfect, but the Benedictine priests were at least supple under his guidance. The flurry of activity that began to centre around the abbey, as it developed, melded nicely with the bishop's conviction that the followers of Saint Benedict should be kept busy. "Get nearer and dearer to God, Busy Worker." This was his new theme. Duties were to be weighted on the balance that was God. "The Church needs you!", became his battle cry.[56]

The abbot argued that there was no real conflict in this change of values on behalf of his Benedictine subjects, because the monk's self-sanctification was to continue to hold priority; only its environment had been modified. After all, he suggested, sanctity was promoted in the missions, as it was in the monastery, by being "true to their first duty—to God," through prayer, meditation, and "self-conquest."[57] Indeed, because of the "intercourse with our people," he theorized, a strength of character would be developed by the missionaries, summoning an even greater perfection than would be promoted in the cloister alone. "The greatness [and] holiness [of priestly service] demanded *dignity*," he said, and "the lowly condescension [which is] charity."[58] Through these virtues the monks were to speed along the road to beatitude, bringing edified and spiritually comforted souls throughout the vicariate along with them.

Remarkably, the monks accepted the new spirit and its muddled logic which Haid had so suddenly and unexpectedly proposed, and they embarked on missionary labors as assigned. It appears that in the beginning they did not fully comprehend that the changed perspective was to be permanent, but other factors seem to have figured into their adaptability, also. Most significant among these influences was the movement it permitted into mainline Cassinese monasticism. The houses of the Order in America had been noted for their missionary zeal and priestly endeavors. Saint Meinrad (Indiana), Saint John (Minnesota), and Saint Benedict (Kansas), like Maryhelp, had even contributed to the missionary episcopate. At Belmont, however, although the monastery had shared in that reputation for apostolic zeal, it had not really manifested the full evangelical spirit before 1900. Once the monks of Maryhelp engaged in the essentially priestly work, they found that it was congenial and satisfying, nonetheless. It gave prominence to their presbyteral character and provided an immediate gratification the cloister neither supplied nor was intended to supply. This adaptation was also supported by the stability of the monastery; whereas, in the first days of Haid's reign the mere survival of the abbey required urgent attention, by 1900 the demands of stability seemed to permit a broader scope. This was illusory, of course, since Benedict had not designed his monasteries to support a broad scope of exclaustral endeavors, but in an age of missionary monks this change seemed to pass for logic, nonetheless. There was, finally, a theological argument, too, that supported this prominence of the clerical character: priesthood was a state of life consecrated by a Sacrament, instituted by Christ himself; whereas, monasticism's vows were sacramentals, pledged to God, but not attributed to Divine promulgation. This seemed to justify the prominence ordination began receiving; unfortunately, it was a perspective against which Benedict had specifically warned. In Chapter sixty-two of the *Regula* he had said, *''Nec occasione sacerdotii obliviscatur regulae obedientiam et disciplinam''* ('Reasons of priesthood should not allow them to evade the obedience and discipline of the *Regula* ').

Maryhelp had changed during Haid's fifteen years; it had grown stable and comfortable; then in 1900 the abbot called for a new surge of activity and a fresh spirit. As in his first days, he sought to infuse spirit through busyness and labor. And as proved the case in 1885, the flurry of activity did inspire excitement and many satisfying endeavors, but it also fragmented once again the monks' focus. And this time, through its impact on cloister and stability, the effects were more serious. The groundwork for Maryhelp's new perspective had been laid inadvertently, perhaps, but it had efficaciously prepared the monks for the change. They embraced the new perspective, and reaped benefits that served their Church responsibilities in the immediate more than the eternal sphere.

Pleased by his Benedictines' willingness and adaptability, the bishop appealed to the Ludwig-Missionsverein in Munich,[59] the Society for the Propagation of the Faith at Lyons,[60] and even De Propaganda Fide in Rome to help underwrite the fervent activity of his missionary priests, both secular and religious, in the Carolina apostolate. Michael McInerney designed churches, schools, convents, and hospitals, many of which Katharine Drexel and other wealthy friends of Haid's helped build. Attention the abbot-bishop received in the press encouraged further gifts. And little time was wasted. The Church reaped immediate rewards; the abbey's more enduring fruits from this period proved harder to evaluate.

The character and prolific output of McInerney's work quickly developed a national reputation for the monk.[61] This won commissions, lecture fees, and other income for the abbey, but more importantly it earned for both the Benedictine and his monastery a large, wide-spread following and considerable prestige. He taught, designed buildings, wrote, did pastoral work,[62] until an ocular disorder in the 1920's finally required that his schedule be revised.[63] So he stopped teaching, and virtually terminated his parochial work, but his attention was soon claimed by a variety of other duties.[64]

McInerney's broad service and national reputation came to epitomize, popularly at least, the new spirit of Leo Haid's monastery. In Michael McInerney, the bishop discovered a co-worker who was unquestionably apostolic-minded, without ever losing his identity as part of the abbey at Belmont. And Father Michael's image was actively promoted by the abbot and his subordinates, casting the priest as an emissary from Maryhelp to a larger audience. It was a mantle McInerney wore for decades. He was portrayed in this way:

> Simple and modest of habit, reticent but kind of speech, humble and sympathetic of approach, this gentle monk with unassumed dignity plies his daily tasks at the Abbey, an example to all of what a Christian may be when genuine art and genuine religion find lodgment in the heart and mind of one individual.[65]

With this image, McInerney was expected to represent Maryhelp. And just by supervising the construction of the buildings he designed, the monk-priest was given frequent and broad exposure. In his architectural career, which eventually totalled more than sixty years and almost five hundred buildings, Father Michael produced more than two hundred institutions (dormitories, schools, laundries), one hundred large churches, over one hundred smaller churches and chapels, twenty-seven hospitals or infirmaries, eighteen convents or monasteries, ten gymnasia or recreation centers, and countless residences, barns, storage and mechanical facilities, renovations, and consulting jobs.[66] Here was the embodiment of Haid's revised monastic image: a monk-priest who was pious, hard-working, of unimpeachable character, and thoroughly devoted to Maryhelp Abbey.

Unfortunately, while McInerney was associated with the sort of man Leo Haid wanted for his apostolic work, he was not really typical of either the religious or the seculars whom the bishop usually received. And only through a fortuitous mesh of publicity, personalities, and Providence, did the popular image of Bishop Haid, his work, and his aspirations, come to center on outstanding men like Michael McInerney.

In the apostolic decade with which he initiated the new century, Leo Haid found his personnel problems compounded at an alarming rate. No amount of travel could give the bishop sufficient presence for inspiring the scattered Catholics and clergy of the vicariate. The territory was too vast, the people too few. Indeed, the dominant factor in his missionary tours was travel itself. The Vicar Apostolic was in transit more than in contact. Moreover, as the bishop extended these journeys and assigned his monk-priests to undertake an increasing burden of missionary labors, the Benedictines too were cost the presence of their abbot. Activity increased; the carefully developed focus of Maryhelp was fragmented, and discipline had no abbatial example on which to base its response and course. Increasingly, Haid had to resort to giving orders in place of example. But as a giver of mandates, he was no more successful in the twentieth century than he had been in the nineteenth. So it fell to Felix Hintemeyer to maintain order among the monks whom the abbot left at the abbey. Fortunately, the prior proved effective and competent at that work, encouraging a stricter monastic observance and more unified spirit than Haid had been able to produce on his own resources. Here, in Hintemeyer once again, the abbot and Maryhelp found the perfect force to amend and counteract the abbey's weaknesses. Father Felix was able to maintain order at the monastery, and secure the proper observance despite the abbot's absences. In the expanse of North Carolina, however, where the clergy lacked such an opportunity for immediate supervision, discipline continued to suffer.

Leo Haid still maintained the necessity of mingling "as much paternal affection with severity as the due preservation of discipline will permit."[67] But because he also believed and practiced the principle "humility alone can lead to God," the bishop was characterized by his subjects as a weak superior. Even his new expanse of activity could not counteract this image, and Haid found himself "severely censured for over-kindness."[68] He chose to ignore that criticism, however, and insisted that gentleness was so integral a Benedictine virtue that it could not be abandoned without compromising his Divine vocation. No matter how often the problem was brought to his attention, Leo Haid believed it would be wrong for him to replace abbatial paternity with a more assertive approach. That was not the sort of aggressiveness Bishop Haid wanted. Action and example were preferable to declamations.

Familiarity with Haid's style of leadership became so extensive, and its character so controversial that reprimands were sent to the abbot-bishop, even from other states. A monk from Saint Bernard, for example, wrote to warn Abbot Leo, "You are... *too good* to some of those whom you love."[69] In another case, Julius Pohl received what the bishop intended as a strong correction for emphasizing temporal affairs over spiritual duties; as usual, however, its impact was destroyed by the gentleness that surrounded it; accordingly, also as usual, the Bristow prior, after studying the letter, saw no need to amend. After all, he wrote, "While this is a painful surprise...I thank you all the same–as you do not make an accusation–but merely inform me of public opinion."[70] The abbot accepted none of the signs or warnings that suggested his leadership was proving ineffective.

The problem rested less in Haid's theories than in his practice. "Let the Abbots keep sternly to the rules."[71] he wrote Archabbot Andrew. Abbot Leo, however, did not translate that principle into his own jurisdictions, either in the monasteries or the vicariate. And simply recognizing that "Malcontents will always be found,"[72] provided no answer to what had become a major problem.

When Haid did try to enunciate his theory of governance, its paternal character was obvious. He recognized that quality to be appropriate to his office, of course, and accepted it as a virtue. His monks recognized its clear, Benedictine character. His secular priests, however, while apparently respecting their Ordinary's inclinations toward sanctity, accused his "paternity" of being mere "gentleness," an excuse that allowed him to evade flexing the authority that duty demanded a bishop to exercise. This basic Benedictine virtue was cast as a principle that could not be reconciled with episcopal responsibility. But if a choice were demanded of him, Leo Haid sided with the monastic standard.

The bishop analyzed his role as a superior according to this schema:[73]

>   1. God is the Absolute Superior;
>   2. Authority is, thus, Divine in its source, delegated from God;
>   3. Responsibility goes in this order:
>   a. to God,
>   b. to Church,
>   c. to the Order [for the Benedictines] or Vicariate [for   secular clergy]
>   d. to parents,
>   e. to the people in general;
>   4. Abuse of authority is criminal, and will usually appear in   one of these ways:
>   a. exaggeration,
>   b. minimizing (which is itself an exaggeration).

To prevent such problems, superiors should "note and examine [their] conduct, [their] tendencies," looking especially for any of these dangerous inclinations:

>   a. vanity [because] of possessing authority;
>   b. injustice in exercising authority;
>   c. ignorance, or too great demands;
>   d. unwillingness to share the burdens of...subjects;
>   e. want of sympathy in...manner, voice, etc., whole nature;
>   f. lack of sensitivity—especially by demanding respect;
>   g. suspiciousness, watchfulness, and deception respresented as "prevention";
>   h. unforgiving nature;
>   i. jealousy, envy, crankiness...;
>   j. lack of reason, too great severity;
>   k. failure to pray for...subjects.

The bishop treated the same subject from another perspective in an address to his novices in 1918. In this instance, he was concerned with what subjects should realize regarding their superiors:

> First, the Superior must look to the *general good*, [which he] often cannot help.
> Second, [it must be remembered] no Superior acts without sufficient reason; he is only too glad to give to every one the work for which he is best fitted, [or which is] most advantageous to the Community. No Superior wishes to make anyone unhappy, etc. Superiors have a wider, clearer understanding of all [the] circumstances [with which they deal]. [They] must use the Cloak of Charity. Superiors are *human*—but as a rule—really reasonable—and often would most gladly grant what is wanted if they only could!...[Thus]
> a. Let our obedience be for God's sake—meritorius.
> b. The greater the sacrifice—the greater the reward.
> c. Let us all work for the common good—not our personal advantage.[74]

In Haid's mind, these principles about the natural benevolence of superiors were so clear that the seemingly disobedient conduct of his subordinates acquired for him a frustrating and ever increasing incomprehensibility. For example, one monk sent him a note saying, "Being driven to desperation, I leave."[75] To the abbot this message made no sense. It appeared to be in response to an abbatial effort to provide income for the priest's mother, and to save the family from uncovering the youngest brother's "crimes against nature." The abbot could not grasp that the priest was exasperated with what he perceived as a lack of direct, strong responses to serious problems. For Haid nothing was visible except the effort to bring charity and Benedictine gentleness to a difficult and unpleasant situation. In another case, an apprentice monk decided to abandon the monastery when the chance of inheriting a fortune arose. Facing a man leaving the cloister for pecuniary reasons, the abbot was totally mystified. There was, he believed, no logic in the young man's decision.[76] Repeatedly the abbot was found longing to help his subjects, but unable to understand their problems or their dissatisfaction with their superior. He seldom managed to bear much empathy for them in their discontent, nor could he anticipate the resolution this augured.

While the monks failed to evince stability and perseverance, the secular clergy under Haid fell into various ill habits of their own. One cleric was arrested for drinking. It became commonplace to find Catholic clergy "airing their views in public print."[77] So many priests left the Vicariate Apostolic of North Carolina that Bishop Haid reported he was "suffering agonies" trying to keep staffing at minimum levels. Nevertheless, he told Gibbons, so poor were the candidates he had received, that he resolved, "I will take no more Priests [who had been ordained originally for other jurisdictions], no matter who recommends them." He was just thankful, "My Fathers in the Abbey are more than willing to help me."[78] Haid did not realize that Gibbons had been forced to resolve to keep higher standards in selecting vicariate priests during his own tenure as Vicar Apostolic.[79] He did not succeed either.

Leo Haid did not persevere in his intentions regarding the selection of personnel. Neither of his jurisdictions seemed able to afford that luxury. His apostolic endeavors were expanding too rapidly for the demands of discretion to be indulged. His commitments were too broad. "Our work is increasing much faster than the workers," he wrote the archabbot at Saint Vincent, and especially in the vicariate this was "leaving me trying to fill holes, sometimes *round* holes with *square* pegs."[80]

In both jurisdictions, Haid's age of activity produced an odd balance of spectacular statistical success weighed against disciplinary decline. "The idea of liberty, etc., goes too far," the bishop suggested to the primate, speaking of the American Church in general and the vicariate in particular. "Hence it is much more difficult to govern."[81] That did not really explain the Vicar Apostolic's problems with his missionaries, but it was as sophisticated a theory as he cared to create. For the monks who failed to persevere, however—and because of Haid's informal approach to record keeping the exact figures cannot be ascertained—the abbot gave a different analysis. Here, he thought, American acculturation rather than misguided democratic ideals produced a large measure of the problem. Benedictine priests abandoned their vocations, he reasoned, from these motivations:[82]

1. There's human nature...;
2. We educate many *gratis*...The novitiate doesn't kill, so they follow the crowd...become discontented, find fault with 'cranky' Abbots...;
3. Some had a vocation, but through worldliness...lost it;
4. ...Parents, etc., are really without support;
5. Most frequently this [No.4, *supra*] is only a 'Plea,' a desire to throw off the yoke of vows is the real cause—but there must be some taffy to serve up to Rome—and off goes, this *'obligatio naturalis;'*
6. Some successfully hide their meanness...and when they get 'big enough' to stand alone they want to shake off their monastery...;
7. Some lack humility...;
8. The condition [and spiritual needs] of the Church in America has little [influence] with these discontented monks...;
9. ...A few...got into the wrong car and should be helped out gently.

It is unfortunate that the abbot discerned these reasons at the peak of his commitment to active life. For he had no time for dealing with such serious monastic problems while distracted by the effects of having the quantity of workers so liberally distributed, though so frugally in supply.

The abbot did make one effort to deal with the problem, however; unfortunately it was not the most prudent gesture of his reign: he instituted an astoundingly open policy of admissions for Maryhelp. Monks from Pennsylvania, Minnesota, New Hampshire, several from New Jersey, members of other Orders, men whose vocations had failed elsewhere went to Belmont for their second chance. To Haid this policy became a source of special pride. He saw it as both charitable to the monks who transferred south, and practical in terms of his own needs. But Abbot Leo received so many rejects from other places that by 1909 Hintemeyer had to caution other monasteries to slow the pace, lest Haid be embarrassed. "We have received many good men," he wrote, "but we must be careful, and it is [suddenly] harder to get through our Chapter for vows than probably in any other monastery—just now."[83] Several good men entered Maryhelp in this way, men who would later serve as priors, rectors, headmasters, monks gifted in music, education, and various necessary services of the cloister. But there also appeared a generous number who wasted little time before showing exactly why their vocations had been brought into question elsewhere. For these men, the abbot discovered he could save time by simply dismissing them. He possessed faculties to handle that; whereas, a dispensation would require an appeal to the Holy See. "Why carry to Rome what can be fully settled here?," it was queried.[84] Nevertheless, Haid's personnel problems remained a constant feature of life at Maryhelp. His several Bohemians proved "a restless people."[85] The secular priesthood frequently lured men away,[86] because "so many advantages are held out to secular priests and so few to religious."[87] Despite the number of men who entered, there was always an insufficiency.[88] Not only did many leave the monastery, especially for positions among the secular clergy, but death was also claiming Belmont's monks. Some men died young, too, "just when life's earnest work seems to be waiting for them."[89] And it took so long to educate the monastic clerics that Haid wondered if the future ever really held enough years of service after ordination.[90]

To these problems was added Abbot Leo's endless expansionism. "Our work is growing faster than our means of doing it," he lamented to the prior of Saint Vincent, "as candidates in the South are as scarce as blackberries in December!"[91] Secular priesthood candidates did not appear in abundance, but they did at least apply with some regularity. With them, the bishop mused, the problem came later, when there was no way to support them.[92] Yet through it all, Leo Haid's compassion dominated, and men who wanted to leave Carolina could expect to find the abbot looking after their temporal welfare, even as they abandoned their Church vocations.[93]

To encourage perseverance from the monks, Abbot Leo held, the emphasis had to be placed not on stability, but on *conversatio*. Without that quality, there would be no reason to abandon all the allurements of the world in favor of the promise of God under the austerity of the monastery. If there was no depth to the monk's *conversatio*, there would be no real commitment to his monasticism as a true, life-long vocation, and in turn there would be no stability. Abbot Leo commended six points in particular to the daily attention of the monks of Maryhelp, as an aid in encouraging the basic elements of *conversatio* which would in turn promote stability. Their key was daily manifestation:[94]

1. Actual determination and effort;
2. God's aid....Avoid above all, our hearts and minds getting away from spiritual things—from God;
3. Pious reading...;
4. Regularity in [the] Monastery. Don't excuse yourself too easily... [particularly from attendance at the] daily recitation of [the Divine] Office;
5. Honestly keeping our Vows;
6. Assiduous Prayer.

These principles applied to all the monks. After ordination, however, additional standards were necessitated, including true "devotion to duty,...toiling day and night," a "spirit of sacrifice," "infinite patience," and "poverty/disinterestedness."[95] Even when vocations were scarce, and as always the abbot associated the shortage with the comforts and amenities that surrounded the secular priesthood, Leo Haid emphasized that monastic life and its priesthood—both in intention and actuality—were more rigorous, more demanding, and more lacking in consolations than other courses young men might embrace. To some that emphasis on sacrifice did not seem the theme to attract American men to Maryhelp. Yet that is the essential principle—sacrifice—in Haid's understanding both of why young men would enter the monastery, and how after entering they could embrace such work as the missions without either losing God or compromising their vocation. Sacrifice insured a place for God in the soul, and thus allowed a broader scope for monks' activities, even outside the cloister. Abbot Leo also maintained that sacrifice was the quality that *should* awaken the movement of the soul toward God. And even in the midst of his most active period, and the greatest dearth of vocations, he was willing to expel men whose motivation fell short of the person of God Himself. No matter how active he might make their lives, Abbot Leo believed it was all part of the search for God. The monks simply had to trust the superior, who had "a wider, clearer understanding." The union, then, of sacrifice and obedience allowed Abbot Leo to avoid total compromise of monastic principles. And in establishing his new priories and clarifying the vision of his schools, Haid continued to evince the Benedictine standards and influence that marked his earlier years. When the changing attitudes finally achieved dominance, even in the Savannah and Richmond dependencies, it was less the result of Haid's theories than of the new orientation taught the young monks in their studies at the motherhouse.

Interests Broaden

The brothers were not completely overlooked in Haid's emphasis on his two staffs of priests. But their vocations, if not their discipline, tended to be somewhat quieter, and their activity—except in its fruits—less conspicuous. Nevertheless, because Hintemeyer, assisted by Alphonse Buss and sometimes by Ignatius Remke, took charge of the non-ordained monks, the abbot's relationship with the brothers gradually became rather generalized, in that he responded to them more as a group than as individuals. For that reason, though he was apparently paternal and compassionate toward them, there is a certain air of detachment in evidence. Typical of the stories that survived through the oral tradition is this one:

> Frequently in the afternoons [Abbot Leo] would walk around (with his cigar) the Abbey property inspecting the work of the Brothers on the farm, in the vineyard, in the shops, etc., giving them a word of encouragement and showing that he was interested in their tasks. He is recalled with deep gratitude and admiration.[96]

When, through the years, the brothers—outside of Bristow—melded into a relatively quiet group, the abbot gave them surprisingly little attention at all. Rather than their observance (an issue that kept Haid attentive to the priests), with the brothers the main problem was the discovery of sufficient candidates to fill their ranks as necessity demanded. Since German was the language used by the brothers most commonly—even in devotions—American candidates seldom applied for the brotherhood, and throughout Haid's time almost never persevered. Accordingly, just to keep the numbers stable, it was necessary to recruit in Bavaria. In 1889, Father Felix made a successful enlistment appeal while visiting his native country.[97] But a decade later, the expanding work of Maryhelp, plus the deaths and departures, necessitated delegating yet another Belmont monk to solicit candidates in Bavaria.

The abbot decided to send Willibald Caspar Baumgartner, one of the founders of Maryhelp and a Bavarian native. That priest was only forty-seven in 1900, but he showed signs of exhaustion, plus nervous and other minor ailments. Almost half his life had been spent in the Benedictines' Richmond parish, but in the new century a change was necessary. There were three reasons that supported the deputation of Baumgartner for the Bavarian assignment: His native status and language skills, the change of venue demanded by his health, and the proprietary attitude he had developed toward the Benedictine sisters, a propensity which—it was suggested—threated the sisters' progress and security in the Diocese of Richmond.

Haid announced the "retirement" of Father Willibald from Saint Mary at the close of 1900, and immediately found himself besieged with protests. A petition[98] was submitted to the abbot in January. A parish forum was convoked in Richmond by the laity on the thirteenth of that month. They sent a copy of the notice for that meeting to the abbot. It contained an ominous, hand-written appendix: "It might be of considerable importance to the future interests of the Southern Benedictine Society here to give this matter further consideration."[99]

The meeting featured an address by John J. Steinbrecher, a parishoner, who dramatically moved that Father Willibald should

> remain with us until his hair turned as white as the sands of the sea, and...when God, in his Omnipotence, shall see fit to take him away from us, we want the privilege of erecting a monument to him, that will be as lasting as time itself.[100]

A committee consisting of Gerhard Ross, Herman Evers, Henry Holzgrefe, John Amrheim, and Joseph Bliley was deputed to call upon Haid in North Carolina,[101] but the parishoners, though unaware of the fact, never had a chance of achieving their objectives. For although it was the abbot of Maryhelp who had ordered Willibald Baumgartner to his new post, it was Augustine Van de Vyver, bishop of Richmond, who had pressed for the priest's removal. The threat was that land in Richmond, intended by Van de Vyver for the Benedictine sisters, would be sold unless the meddlesome priest were eliminated.

When Baumgartner departed, Van de Vyver wrote Bishop Haid commending "the wisdom of your action....Now we will, I trust, be helped and not hampered in our work."[102] That apparently was the case, since before the year was completed, and with Baumgartner on another continent, the Ordinary succeeded in encouraging the sisters to remove their motherhouse to Bristow, and keep only their schools in the capital city.

At the same time, in Bavaria, Father Willibald was far too busy to interfere. He found it "very difficult to get candidates, at least desirable ones."[103] But in what evolved into a four year effort, he finally won enough postulants to Maryhelp to supply for the losses, and even raised the number of brothers from twenty-three (1901) to thirty (1906).[104]

It was the stabilization of the brothers' work force that enabled Leo Haid to further expand his influence beyond Carolina. The brothers cared for most of the household duties at the abbey, the farms, mechanical chores, and skilled labor and crafts. They were the domestic support on which the more externally employed monk-priests depended. So successful was Baumgartner, both in immediate results and in the initiation of valuable contacts, that for the remainder of the abbot's reign the brothers, including their candidates, never fell beneath a total of twenty-seven, an adequate number for covering their duties.[105]

At the turn of the century, clerical monks were present in quantities roughly equal to the brothers'. From 1900 through 1911, the ordained priests totalled around thirty, after which time the numbers began increasing, centering around the low forties by the last decade of the Haid years.[106] The quantity of priests was closely watched by the abbot, especially as he expanded the abbey's commitments.

Yet the number of available workers is only a secondary concern when monastaries analyze their quantity of members. In more apostolically oriented religious communities, growth in numbers may be a definite sign of success. But for monastics, the same standard does not apply. Because of the stable and familial environment a Benedictine monastery was supposed to create for its inhabitants, only a limited degree of growth would ordinarily be indulged. When the quantity of members changed substantially, either by increasing or decreasing, the quality, tenor, and manifestation of the monastic community were altered, too. Accordingly, each abbey tended to center upon a certain ideal size, particular to its own goals, potential, and facilities. When a monastery grew substantially beyond its ideal size, it founded a daughterhouse, and encouraged that foundation to seek autonomy and its own identity. If a monastery fell substantially below its ideal number, there would be insufficient personnel to cover its labors or to conduct the monastic routine in the abbey's customary manner. In either case—increase or decrease—the changed numbers would alter the flavor of the abbey's community life, as well as the manner of relationships and stability of practice which were so essential to Benedictine monasticism.

From the buildings, choir facilities, and actions of the abbot, it appears that Leo Haid envisioned Maryhelp as having (ideally) approximately thirty choir monks (ordained monks, or those preparing for ordination) in residence at the motherhouse. In that size monastery, a variation of about seven members—either up or down—would be the limit of toleration, lest the character of the community be affected. Ideally, in 1900, Maryhelp should have had an additional five priests for vicariate assignments, two for Bristow, and at least three each for Richmond and Savannah, for a total of forty choirmonks. But the 1900 *Ordo* indicates only one abbot, twenty-six priests, five clerics, and four novices. Most of the adjustment came from charging the Belmont monastery its personnel so that all assignments elsewhere could be covered. And of course the choirmonk figures did not include the twenty-four brothers who cared for most of the domestic work at Belmont.[107]

In 1902, Maryhelp was at its ideal size. The *catalogus* for that year listed one abbot, twenty-nine priests, eight clerics, and two novices, exactly forty choirmonks. There were, in addition, the twenty-two brothers. But that was also the year the abbot re-entered the pursuit of daughterhouses, and determined to erect the Savannah work into a fully operative priory; Benedictine College—a military-preparatory school—arose there that year as well. This was the boldest gesture of Haid's post-1900 expansionism. For although the move paved the way for consolidating the Benedictines' activity in the city—spread at that time among the town, Isle of Hope, and Skidaway Island—having a priory and school, required that a minimum of six monks be assigned to Savannah, and the ideal quantity would have been ten. The abbot withdrew one monk from the vicariate, but there was little else he could do to juggle his manpower. There were simply not enough monks, and Savannah itself would not develop into a generous source of vocations until several decades later.

Sacred Heart Priory in Savannah, however, did become— statistically, at least—the most outstanding apostolate at Haid's command. But its success reflected the abbot's maturation as an administrator, more than his prudence in insuring the priory's staffing. The plan for Savannah was simple and rather ordinary, but it orchestrated success for the foundation efficiently and expeditiously. This was the schema:

1. An academically sound boys' preparatory school, Benedictine College, was initiated immediately. McInerney designed a generously sized building that could be readily enlarged. The educational program was given four special aspects that lent distinction: military training (for discipline), forensics (to readily exhibit academic prowess), athletics (to encourage popular support), and thorough religious and moral instruction.

2. A parish, Sacred Heart, was accepted in perpetuity. For this, a rough copy of the Abbey Church was built, complete with Mayer windows. The presence of a parish provided both a convenient outlet for the ministerial inclinations of the monk-priests and a ready body of Catholics who could be expected to support the monks in their good works. The switch here was important: these were parochial duties Haid accepted, not missionary ones, and that meant few if any men had to be sent away from the Savannah monastery for regular

assignments. There was also, however, the unfortunate fact that the parish tied the monks to an urban setting where land was limited, and farming impossible.

3. A monastery was erected, Sacred Heart Priory, where the monks could live the common Benedictine observance. To one side of the priory building stood the Benedictine College, at the other side Sacred Heart Church was built. All the apostolates were close, and some fidelity with the *Regula's* prescription restricting the monks' work to the environment of the cloister could be maintained.

4. Regarding leadership, Haid showed the true extent of his administrative maturation. For the 1902 project, Leo Haid initiated none of the idealistic standards that had distinguished and would eventually help destroy Saint Maur. Sacred Heart Priory was founded along conventional lines. As for immediate jurisdiction, Bishop Haid planned to remain aloof from questions of internal governance. To take charge of the project, he sent the man who was then serving as rector of Saint Mary's College, Bernard Haas—who was, incidentally, the best administrator at Haid's disposal. Prior Bernard was a gifted, widely respected man, noted for his practicality and business sense, who was particularly beloved since he gave the abbot little trouble. At various times in his monastic career he transformed unproven schools in Belmont, Savannah, and Richmond into successes. But Savannah's was his most masterfully executed achievement. It opened in 1902 with twenty-one scholars; by 1905, Benedictine College had as many boys as Bristow; in 1908, only its seventh year, its student body exceeded even Belmont's. That same year, Benedictine enrolled more than a hundred students for the first time, and only twice fell below that number through the remainder of Haid's life. No single project of Abbot Leo's career ever matched the unqualified success of Bernard Haas and the priory, school, and parish in Savannah. The plan was Haid's; the execution was Prior Bernard's; the achievement was without parallel.

In 1910, Abbot Leo designed another monastery/church/school, and once again he did it without the necessary manpower. At the decade mark, Maryhelp needed fifty-one choirmonks (thirty, Belmont; ten, Savannah; four, vicariate; four, Bristow; three, Richmond). However, there were only forty-three priests on hand, plus the thirty-six brothers.[108] But it was in that year that the opportunity appeared—admittedly less auspiciously than had been the case in Savannah—to erect a real monastic foundation in Richmond, and Bishop Haid was not the man to allow such possibilities to pass untried. So the monks of Richmond, already fifty years in possession of their parochial domain there, finally moved toward the canonical erection of the dependent priory of Saint Mary's. Until this time, though the rectory was called a "priory", it technically lacked that status—as had Maryhelp from 1876 until 1884—because notarization of its creation had not been sought from Rome. The new arrangement in Richmond was to be similar to Savannah's, having a parish, boys' college-preparatory school, and the priory which would double as a rectory.

The sequence, however, was different. In Savannah, the Benedictine College opened in September of 1902, in temporary quarters—an old building erected during Moosmueller's time. The next month, the construction of Sacred Heart Church was endorsed.[109] Foundation work was undertaken immediately, and Bishop Benjamin J. Keiley of Savannah laid the cornerstone. But in December, finances required a delay in the project.[110] Since the parish was more than twenty years old and had a wooden church building on Habersham Street already, there was no real urgency, and the delay could be readily tolerated. One year later, it was voted to proceed with the church,[111] and a bid of about thirty-one thousand dollars was accepted.[112] While the church was under construction, the new priory building was started at a cost that would total in excess of eight thousand dollars.[113] On 1 November of that same year, 1904, the Chapter at Maryhelp met to discuss Father Michael's plans for the permanent school building in Savannah. The cost was estimated at twenty five thousand dollars, a sum the Chapter would not approve; the monks also voted down a payment of twenty-three thousand, before finally authorizing construction of a twenty thousand dollar school building. Abbot Leo wrote Prior Bernard, "Nothing remains but to suit the building to the money allowed."[114] The students were in the new Bull Street college building in the fall of 1905. An additional floor, then an annex, were added subsequently. This was an uncommonly swift progression for any new monastic foundation to enjoy.

Richmond was unable to advance quite so rapidly. Indeed, at almost every juncture the Virginia monks found obstacles that existed only minimally eight years earlier in Georgia. In 1910, the Benedictines purchased a full city block of property in Richmond's west end. McInerney designed the school, and it was built immediately. Classes began in 1911. While awaiting funds, the parish held services in the school, and most of the monks stayed in residence at Saint Mary, downtown. Father Michael designed a fifty thousand dollar priory,[115] but it was not built until the 1923-1924 school year, more than a decade after the educational structure. The parish church did not appear in Haid's lifetime.

But the progress was not as smooth as even the list of dates might seem to imply, because unpleasant diocesan relations incessantly impeded the advancement of the Richmond project. In Savannah there had been problems with parish boundaries,[116] and Bishop Keiley wrote occasionally to complain about priests being seen at the circus,[117] about homilies,[118] insufficiently zealous pastoral undertakings,[119] the parish choir,[120] personnel,[121] the offerings in the school,[122] and any number of other, equally minor matters. But in Virginia the indelicate dealings between the chancery and the priory were more serious; they threatened the whole project, and they began at the very first contact in 1909.

Bishop Van de Vyver had recognized that the need for a German church was not to be perpetual; whereas, the western section of the city of Richmond was developing rapidly, and would need a new parish to serve long-term needs. Accordingly, he invited the Benedictines to establish the new and more promising parish, with the understanding that Saint Mary, which the Benedictines held in perpetuity, would eventually be terminated,[123] though it would continue as long as necessary.[124] Haid found the proposal appealing for several reasons, particularly the prospect of growth and the chance to deal with the unsalubrious environment of urban Richmond.[125] There was a possible impediment, however, found in a recent Roman decree that severely limited the liberty monasteries possessed for contracting debts;[126] indeed, Haid rejected Van de Vyver's first overtures regarding the project because of these strictures imposed by the Vatican. The new parish promised to be a very costly project for Maryhelp. Finally, to insure that the undertaking would be worth the effort, the abbot insisted on being granted the new parish—first called "New Saint Mary", and later "Saint Benedict"—in perpetuity, and he wanted permission to erect another Benedictine college (really a boys' military, college-preparatory school). Van de Vyver agreed, but reserved to himself the right of approval over the land the Order of Saint Benedict would purchase for the new church.[127] The two bishops, Haid and Van de Vyver, were amicable and confident of the benefits to be secured through this agreement on behalf of the Catholic Church in Richmond.

The clergy of the diocese were less cordial about the concordat, however; Father Julius, described them as "hostile."[128] The Diocesan Consultors met to discuss "the feasibility of establishing...[the] new parish to be given to the Benedictine Fathers;" the measure "was voted upon unfavorably."[129] But Van de Vyver ignored the priests' advice and on 10 January, by his own authority, approved the parish and school for the Benedictines.[130] Reportedly the secular clergy were furious, remembering the Warrenton affair earlier in the Ordinary's reign. But matters progressed too quickly for the secular priests to impose their reservations on the agreement. On 23 January, Abbot Leo instructed his Benedictine agents in Rome to see that Van de Vyver's petition was expedited.[131] The land was purchased on 10 February; the Holy See acted on 10 June;[132] construction of the school began immediately.

By the time Old Saint Mary was to be closed, however, Van de Vyver—who as usual had not committed his intentions to paper—had been succeeded by Denis O'Connell, and Father Kaup was directing the chancery. Regarding the technicalities of terminating the German church and removing the Benedictines from downtown, there was a profitable discussion with Bishop O'Connell,[133] then the expected contretemps with Felix Kaup.[134] Father Mark Cassidy handled some of the negotiations, but whenever possible Bishop Haid himself went to Richmond to conduct these interviews and arguments, a move necessitated by their complexity and tone. Financial quarrels continued for years,[135] until Saint Mary was finally closed, and the Benedictines' operation was restricted to Saint Benedict on Sheppard Street.

In matters of monastic discipline, the abbot was also willing to occasionally intervene in Richmond and Savannah; at least he seemed to do so more than in the special conditions at Saint Maur. But on the whole such action occurred infrequently. And his reprimands usually passed as general principles. For example, he wrote Bernard Haas a lengthy call to greater fervor using this approach: "Childlike love for our Holy Religion, our Holy Order, etc.,"[136] he said, was sufficient to motivate assiduous attention to the standards of monastic life. If that were present, abbatial intervention should be unnecessary. A right attitude in a cloistered setting—as he believed he had arranged through the compact design of both priory/school/church situations—should serve to assure that Benedictine environment.[137] Then, "if we observe the Spirit of our *Holy Rule*," and this directive he sent to all three of the Georgia and Virginia priors, "we will sanctify ourselves and be a source of edification to our people."[138] The interventions of Leo Haid were not readily recognized as commands.

It was typical of the bishop's shifting emphasis in these years, that frequent instructions were not forwarded to his priors regarding monastic observance. Instead, the bishop most often wrote regarding financial matters. He also began emphasizing the theme that had intrigued him in the mid-1880's—theories of education.

In creating the schools of 1902 and 1911, Leo Haid aimed at a more focused program than had been possible during the early days of the college at Belmont. The two high schools had identical daily schedules;[139] each was a non-boarding institution, without provisions for dormitory facilities. Each had a neo-Romanesque building, and a classical course of studies. The first catalogue in Richmond, for example, listed offerings in Latin, Greek, English (composition, rhetoric, literature), history (ancient, mediaeval, modern, American), civics, physics, and chemistry.[140] So important was this design for studies that the bishop even cautioned the Savannah monks that if they instituted the commercial course Keiley asked them to provide, they must "be careful [lest it] ruin your Classical Course!!"[141] The preparatory schools administered by the Belmont monks were to "educate, in the genuine sense of the word. The course of studies has been planned to educate a boy, to test and develop all his natural faculties, to develop habits of industries [sic] and thus to insure the acquisition of a thorough training and education."[142]

By "thorough," the Benedictines meant that there should be a breadth of training that exceeded academics and ordinary classwork. It needed to be, as Haid promoted the concept, both "mental and moral education...[by] conscientious teachers."[143] "Thorough" education became a key element in the abbot's designs for the proper enrichment of American youth.

The environment the abbot-bishop thought would best encourage this thorough training was a cadet corps. A military program was primarily designed to teach discipline, but it also directed the student's attention toward the development of beneficial personal habits, while offering "every opportunity for the proper training of mind, heart, and body."[144] The abbot maintained that the cadet's duties would develop the boy "physically and mentally. It creates habits of promptitude and order, fosters self-reliance, and inculcates in the student, as part of his nature, manly ideals of obedience, loyalty, discipline and courtesy."[145] The result he expected was the growth of the boy into a moral, educated, disciplined young man who had acquired strength of will through obedience, while also being given "health and physical propriety and beauty [of] the body."[146] The boys at Saint Leo had first dressed in their grey uniforms on 10 December 1891.[147] A decade later, and again in the decade after that, the new preparatory schools established by Maryhelp incorporated the military atmosphere and influence into their program. While discipline and character development were emphasized as the rationale for the military program, the abbot was, of course, also conscious of the government monies such a program put at the disposal of his schools.[148]

Although a cadet corps was not an appropriate adjunct for the offerings of Bristow's industrial school, the abbot did long to institute a military program at Belmont. Only the lack of a drilling room prevented that innovation.[149] In its absence Leo Haid was forced to conceive a more sophisticated plan to insure the progress of his educational objectives.

The governance of Saint Mary's College had proceeded along lines similar to the priories' schools. Haid was president of all his educational institutions, by which office he reserved to himself jurisdiction over policy, and over all major changes of program. But at Saint Mary's, no less than in Richmond and Savannah, the daily affairs of the schools were handled by a rector. Felix Hintemeyer, who taught in but did not administer the school at Belmont, tried to create the image of the bishop at his desk in the college, considering every element of minutiae that was at issue. But even if the abbot had been present enough to do that, it would have been inconsistent with his concept of governance. The rectors were the true administrative officers. Leo Haid did, however, maintain a taxing schedule as a teacher in the Belmont school, especially the seminary, but he taught only a fraction of the schedule attributed to him in the catalogue. And during the bishop's frequent and often prolonged absences, Father Felix usually tried to instruct the Haid classes as well as the Hintemeyer ones. Only later, in an effort to relieve the prior of some of this burden, did Abbot Leo begin leaving special projects for his students to complete or problems for them to solve in his absence. Hintemeyer's appreciation of the gesture has not been recorded, but a student later noted that this practice kept the young scholars from being "over-glad to see [Haid] depart for his missions."[150]

Julius Pohl had run Saint Mary's College as a small, familial institution. William Mayer, the rector during the two year interim that followed Pohl, made no substantial alterations. Bernard Haas' seven year administration saw enrollment and income soar, but produced little academic innovation. His successor, Eugene Egan, was a prudent, scholarly man, noted more for his charm and grace than his initiative. The one-year term of James Buchholz, the bright, young, Roman-educated monk who succeeded Egan, was overshadowed by personal concerns. But finally, in 1909, Saint Mary's College received the type of rector it had long needed. The new administrator was Thomas William Henry Oestreich, O.S.B. Working in concert with Leo Haid, he made the bishop's dream of "thorough" education come closer to reality than either Haas' practicality or the military ethos and environment had been able to do.

Father Thomas was thirty-six years old in 1909. A native of Reading, Pennsylvania, he had attended Saint Mary's College before entering the monastery. When he announced his desire to embrace the religous life, his mother sent a message to the abbot, "Willie Oestreich belongs to you. If God gave him a Vocation he must stay with you...[We] give him to God and trust that God's Providence will provide."[151] It was a gift Leo Haid valued highly. He respected the faith and spirit of Frau Oestreich, but he also admired the son, who was scholarly, uncommonly mature for his age, and showed undeniable promise for the Benedictine life and work of the schools. As "Frater Thomas," he professed his vows on 30 June 1893; in 1897, he was ordained a priest. The abbot then sent Oestreich, accompanied by James Buchholz, to study in Rome, where his intellect permitted an accelerated sequence of courses. He was the first of Belmont's monks to earn a doctorate, a degree he took with honors in history. His particular expertise was the reform movement under Hildebrand. The abbot would not allow his young scholar to accept a position in Rome, naming him instead to the faculty of Saint Mary's College and the seminary. He was also the abbatial-episcopal secretary. Oestreich continued his research while teaching, did some writing, and like Hintemeyer became noted for his loyalty to the abbot and to Maryhelp. He was also committed to Haid's vision of thorough education, and sought to advance that concept through Saint Mary's College from the time of his assumption of the rectorship in 1908, until poor health mandated his relinquishing the position in 1924, in favor of less taxing duties as head of the seminary.

At Saint Mary's College, as Haid and Oestreich directed the institution, admission could occur at any point in the academic year. The student was simply "placed in the class for which his previous attainments may qualify him."[152] Most students came from points no farther south than Richmond.[153] After the opening of the academy in Georgia, it supplied a number of students, but the vicariate of North Carolina never was generous with its boys. Preferably, candidates for the schools were at least fourteen years old,[154] but students as young as ten, and sometimes eight year olds, were not uncommon. It was not required that students be Catholic,[155] but the boys did have to "present satisfactory testimonials of good moral character."[156]

Indeed, President Haid was primarily concerned, in receiving his students, that the boys gave evidence of moral rectitude. The academic prowess was to be developed once the boy was at Saint Mary's. Upon admission, the bishop was satisfied to find he had "average student[s], with fair opportunities."[157] But during a boy's career at the college he was expected to seriously strive for discipline and strength of character, and thus to manifest the learning, culture, and "thorough" development Haid associated with a Benedictine education. "Conduct of students" was to be motivated and regulated "by the principles of Christian morality and honor." That meant there should be evidence of diligent application, too. And "no pupil whose industry, progress or conduct is unsatisfactory [was to] be permitted to remain at the College."[158] In particular the boy who exerted a harmful influence over the other scholars, or one who proved "incorrigibly idle" was subject to expulsion.[159]

The students followed a set horarium:

6:00 a.m.		rising
6:30		morning prayer, Mass in the College Chapel
7:00		breakfast and recess
7:30		study period
8:30		class recitations
10:45		extra studies (drawing, typewriting, music, etc.)
11:45		dinner and recess
1:45 p.m.		study period
2:45		class recitations
4:15		extra studies (cf. *supra*)
5:00		reading
5:45		supper and recess
7:15		study period
8:45		night prayers and retiring

Classes filled six days per week, but on Wednesday and Saturday afternoons the boys could enjoy recess until four o'clock. On Sundays, the schedule was different, and the boys were not required to arise before half past six o'clock. Students were permitted to go home for Christmas, but not for Holy Week or Easter.[160]

Haid, as the definitor of policy, insisted on these moral and disciplinary standards, but he gave Oestreich the liberty to develop and refine the educational program. Originally the school offered three divisions of study. There was a one year preparatory course for the youngest students. A commercial course, two years in duration, for boys interested in business careers, or a classical course of six years was available for the older boys.[161] At first the commercial and classical programs had enrollments that were approximately equal;

the classical then came to be associated with men interested in the seminary, and the commercial division enrolled substantially more students. Around the turn of the century, however, that trend reversed, and boys went to Saint Mary's College for academics more than business training.

In Oestreich's time, the whole organization of Saint Mary's was refined. The Commercial Department offered "a practical business education." The Academic Department was a secondary school, college-preparatory sequence. At the summit of Saint Mary's offerings by this time was the College, where Abbot Leo and Father Thomas sought to provide the breadth of studies and opportunities they thought so integral to good and thorough education.

> The Collegiate Department aims at giving the student such a general, vigorous and well rounded development of all his faculties, mental and moral, as will enable him later to enter upon his chosen life's work with ease, pleasure, and profit. Each of the studies pursued in this course has a distinct and peculiar educational value. History, Language, Mathematics and the Natural Sciences are complementary studies, and the mental discipline given by one cannot be supplied by another. The studies are carefully graded, and so classified as to be adapted to the mental growth of the student.[162]

For following these courses of studies, Saint Mary's would grant a Commercial Diploma, carrying the title "Master of Accounts," to business students; classical studies could win a Diploma in Letters. The College would grant a Bachelor of Arts degree to its students, but only if their scholarship included at least two full years of work in the department of philosophy.[163]

Haid and Oestreich later created a revised division of Saint Mary's offerings, in order to better accent the presence of the seminary.[164] Then modern educational developments required a final rearrangement by the two monks in 1922. In that schema the school had four divisions:[165]

1. The School of Sacred Sciences (the seminary)
2. The College of Liberal Arts and Sciences (degree granting courses in philosophical, scientific, classical, or literary studies)
3. The Academy of Liberal Arts and Sciences (high school department, emphasizing ancient and modern languages, English, mathematics, the sciences, and history)
4. The Upper Grade School (a special preparatory program for students who did not meet the entrance requirements)

Various special programs augmented the course offerings. In music there was private instruction (especially in strings and keyboard), the brass and reed band, the orchestra, and the Cathedral Choir. Father

Joseph erected a photography studio and laboratory.[166] Dramatics and forensics were Haid's favorites. Once Irish-Americans started entering the monastery in quantity, athletics achieved increasing emphasis. For religious activities there were five separate groups in which to participate. Publications, literary and library interests, a variety of sports: the president and rector encouraged the broadest possible scope for their students, all built around the stable guiding force of discipline, obedience, and all necessary coordinants for granting the boy a strong, moral, God-centered character.

Oestreich's special interest at Saint Mary's was the library. And he was devoted to the development of its holdings. While in Europe he had bought many volumes, especially reference and history works for the library. In order to save money he purchased the volumes unbound, and had the monks prepare the books for the shelves.[167] Henry Ganss, the organist at the dedication of the church in 1894, was persuaded to leave part of his large collection of books to Maryhelp.[168] In 1914, and again after the First World War, Father Thomas toured Europe acquiring books in exchange for alms. At the same time, Julius Pohl was obtaining rare volumes with exquisite bindings through his wealthy friends, but Oestreich oversaw all efforts to bring books to Belmont, and even took responsibility for the works once they appeared. Through all these sources, Haid and Oestreich were able to place at the students' disposal a superior library for a college with fewer than one hundred fifty students. The history and theology collections were especially strong; philosophy was also good. There were *incunabula*; manuscripts were acquired. Marbled, gold-leafed, "ivoried," volumes entered the Saint Mary's library. There were works bound in leather, volumes with overlays of brass. Even after Thomas Oestreich retired from his college office he continued to send books to the library.

Father Thomas served Saint Mary's as the librarian in a tenure that exceeded the length of his rectorship. With the sort of administrative standard that was so typical of Abbot Leo, Father Thomas was retained in the librarian's position, throughout the sixteen years the priest served as rector. Lest the breadth of responsibilities prove too burdensome, the monastic Visitators in 1910, 1914, and again in 1920 instructed the abbot to remove Oestreich from his second job.[169] But Leo Haid could not bear to relieve his librarian of such congenial responsibilities. To soothe the Visitators, a "student librarian" was appointed to assist Father Thomas.

The abbot's most ambitious statement of educational vision came in the last major building of his life. It was a thirty-five thousand dollar postscript to the Saint Mary's College design, and was named "Saint Leo Hall".[170] Erected from McInerney's plans in 1906,[171] and designed to house a gymnasium, three hundred seat theatre, orchestra room with a full complement of music studios, photography dark room, and various academic and recreational facilities, Saint Leo Hall was intended to reflect Haid's ambitious vision for the path of higher education.[172] The building was not the sort of achievement that would incite admiration and national acclaim. It did not even receive the publicity or attention that greeted the grotto in 1891. But when it opened in 1907, it was a genuinely remarkable contribution to a county that had not been noted for its attention to the fine arts and culture. Because of the focus McInerney and Haid gave the building, it became a monument in its own right. And since Bishop Haid had positioned Saint Leo at the southwest tip of the college complex, anyone journeying between Belmont and Mount Holly had to pass by Saint Leo. Thus the new building became a landmark, as well. A Charlotte newspaper marveled,

> Belmont Abbey grows more stately as the years pass. The tree planting of days past has developed into the landscape effect that was anticipated, and the shrubbery and flowers give the appearance of "ancient grandeur." The Catholic monastery is one of the pleasure sights of Gaston County.[173]

These monuments that Haid erected spoke primarily to outsiders. But while the bishop enjoyed the awe his facilities inspired, and wasted few opportunities for promoting that effect, his own infatuation with edifices had faded since 1900. By this time, the bishop was expounding a far more sophisticated, theologically based, theory of education. And it sponsored priorities that buildings alone could not actualize.

The intellect, in Haid's conception, was the "soul's unblemished gift." God gave man intellectual faculties; as the possessor of reason, man was constituted more God-like than other beings by the very form of his creation; in turn, the thinking person made the ideal use of his intelligence when it was employed to bring the soul "near to Him." Properly developed and disciplined, while being augmented by the influence of faith, the intellect would not only assist in learning but would teach as well. Intellect and faith were the two principal forces for enlightening man. And in proper union, they also became appropriately ordered and oriented. That was especially important since "God Himself demands the first and principal use of my intelligence for Himself." The student had to be encouraged to avoid the "danger of burying ourselves in temporal studies," since the ideal development of human intellect and potential required, firstly, a solid foundation in philosophical methodology, followed by serious, disciplined application aimed 1) toward the grasping of some knowledge of God, 2) toward studying God, 3) toward meditating on the external mysteries and precepts. These, in turn, led to the incorporation of eternal values into the boy's adult life, and thus to an edifying, Christ-centered maturity. Just as each course was integral to the whole academic program, so every activity, rule, building, dormitory, and instructor figured into the whole educational schema. The church, the dramatic hall, the playing fields, the presence of the monks, the dedication of the faculty, each element was purposeful and integral in creating an environment that encouraged the union of faith and intelligence, and thus of man and God.[174] "The young man with a trained mind has ten chances where others have only one," Abbot Leo wrote.[175] Accordingly, his teachers were charged with instilling the discipline, knowledge, and rightly oriented values that would promote such an end.

The professors in the college were Bishop Haid's key to a sound educational program. To as great an extent as possible, those who taught should be those who had developed their intellects and acquired advanced knowledge through scholarship; but those who taught in a college should also evince a true dedication to God as the ultimate object of the intellect, of life, of the soul. In his own circumstances, this usually meant that the teachers were monks. "Many rules [have been] given to teach us how to teach," the abbot told his novices, "Yet Saint Benedict in his intercourse with God found the foundation." The lesson Leo Haid drew from the monastic patriarch was strikingly similar to the instructions he had found there for monastic superiors: the approach should be reasonable ("an intelligent treatment of our scholars"), the essence of which was an example of compassion and understanding. This had to be shown in the monastery, classroom, pulpit, and confessional. And only through the monks' good example and their life of sacrifice would the breadth of knowledge the student acquired be transformed, and thus "improve [the] Divine gift of understanding" that was held by each young scholar—not equally, but—in a measure "sufficient if properly cultivated."[176]

To accomplish this good the instructors were to practice the proper "means of increasing [students'] interest." These were study, prayer, patience, fatherly care, humility, strength and justice[177]—a list, once again, that was similar to the mandate received by superiors. These were the official instructions the abbot gave his professors:[178]

1. Remember you must not only teach your class, but you must prepare your scholars for a good and useful life on earth and for everlasting happiness after death.
2. Be a model in words and deeds to those under your care.
3. Be just and impartial...
4. Don't be loud or boisterous...
5. Avoid familiarity...Mingle the dignity of the Superior with the kindliness of the Father.
6. Answer all appropriate questions; never argue...
7. Never talk of matters not concerning your scholars. Guard your own reputation and the good name of others—College and Monastery.
8. Be even tempered. Your humors, etc., should never be intruded on your scholars.
9. Work in harmony with the Faculty. Personal disagreements must never appear.
10. Adhere strictly to your class periods. Don't steal from one branch to favor another.
11. Assist the backward student; the more talented require less aid.
12. Be prompt and punctual in performing all duties...
13. Prepare well for every class...Boys must have full confidence in your ability to teach.

Whilst God rewards our work in the present, it prepares us to carry on His designs in the future!

These standards for professors were intended to work in concert with the expectations imposed on students. Both objectives, with their vision and union, gave Saint Mary's College a clearly defined philosophy. There was some distinction in these theories, and a quality that made Haid appreciate his college's success even when enrollment was modest. Saint Mary's never developed the estimation that attended the Savannah school where the abbot was annoyed to have to report an "increasing reputation" that centered on the boys' "good looks and football."[179]

Because of his strong emphasis on the theory of education, manifested early and promoted by Oestreich, Haid was able to encourage an integration of philosophy and practice from the beginning. Saint Leo Hall was the grandest symbol of the bishop's educational intentions, but the message went deeper and was often expressed with subtlety. Father Thomas' and Abbot Leo's conviction that every dimension of the school participated in the boys' development came to be reflected in a variety of even very minor forms. For example, in a gesture typical of their approach, the award for excellence in mathematics, bestowed at the graduation exercises in 1902, was not a slide-rule, geometric table, nor even a theoretical work in the field. The mathematics prize—won, incidentally, by McInerney—was a volume of Milton's poetry. No opportunity for promoting well-rounded, "thorough" education was disregarded.[180]

When the time came to place the educational achievements of Saint Mary's College and its president on exhibit, Hintemeyer conceived the first alumni reunion, and invited all the Old Boys to journey to Belmont for a common celebration on Thanksgiving Day, 27 November 1913. There were to be Masses, speeches, athletics, and of course tributes to Saint Mary's College and to Leo Haid in particular. The reunion was the sort of public praise the prior loved to arrange for his abbot. By the time of the Solemn Pontifical Mass of Thanksgiving that highlighted the celebration, Hintemeyer had accomplished his goal: "When Bishop Haid entered the procession from the front of the church, he passed hearts filled with love and gratitude."[181]

As the major announcement of the gathering, the abbot informed the Old Boys that the name of the college was to be changed. Originally, when the alumni reunion had been tentatively scheduled for 1911, the new name selected was "Belmont Cathedral College." But in 1913, the abbot decided upon "Belmont Abbey College"—justified in the official programme as "a pretty title" that was "absolutely distinctive." The name also gave the college a clear association with the popular—though never official—name of the monastery, "Belmont Abbey." Of course, in making the change for the school, the abbot was careful to specify that the Mother of God, as Help of Christians, would continue to be recognized as the principal patron of the college, monastery, and church. The abbot-bishop's filial piety remained uncompromised; only terminology had been altered.[182]

the GRanÒ touR

The expansion sponsored by Haid was unchecked in the first decade of the twentieth century. The abbot became a familiar figure in the American Church, noted for zeal but not controversy. His problems in the Vicariate Apostolic were largely attributed to the jurisdiction's heavy burden, which had driven men as gifted as Gibbons to accept comfort elsewhere. The monastic troubles were mostly unknown outside the Order of Saint Benedict, and in many cases reflected difficulties common to Benedictine monasteries at that time. Bishop Haid expanded his interests to include political contacts in North Carolina, cultivating cordiality with men like the state's chief justice, Walter Clark, and an attorney who later won the governor's mansion, Locke Craig.

Politics was not worthy of the abbot in Felix Hintemeyer's opinion, however; so in 1903, when the bishop was expected in Rome anyway, Father Prior Felix expanded the journey into a tour of the major Benedictine monasteries on the continent. This was intended to cast the Haid reputation in a more distinctly religious context.

The original purpose of the trip was the execution of Haid's decennial visit *ad limina*, required of him as a reigning Ordinary. This consisted of an appearance at the Vatican where the bishop would report on the stewardship he had exercised over his territory since the last *ad limina*. Every bishop in the universal Church was expected to undertake his visits *ad limina* as scheduled, and even signed an oath in testimony of that intention at the time of his elevation to the episcopal throne. While at the seat of Catholicism, there were also certain required church visitations, an appearance—if it could be arranged—before the Holy Father, and in Haid's case, interviews with the primate and figures of influence in the Order of Saint Benedict.

This was an auspicious time for Haid to undertake such a triumphant tour. There were trusted subordinates at work both in the abbey and the dependencies; Hintemeyer took charge of the vicariate in the bishop's absence. There was, to the abbot's credit that year, an impressive statistical report, too, that promised to make for good conversation when asked how matters were faring in America. At his monastery, buried in the country's most Protestant state, there were sixty-eight monks (one abbot, thirty-two priests, eight clerics, two novices, and twenty-five brothers).[183] In the 1902-1903 school year, his educational work had flourished, too. The college at Belmont had one hundred eighteen scholars, its third highest enrollment to date; Bristow had sixty-eight boys, its second highest level; and the Savannah school, in its first year, had attracted twenty-one pupils, before jumping to thirty-six in the Michaelmas term of 1903. The Richmond high school at the German parish had closed, of course, but the parochial work there was flourishing. Saint Benedict, in the west end, was yet to appear. The peregrination would be attended by all the trappings of the abbot-bishop, his dignities, his prominence, and his success.

Father Felix designed the itinerary. The bishop sailed from New York on 23 May, the vigil of Maryhelp. After being at sea for two weeks he finally reached Naples. From there he went to Cava and to Montecassino. In Rome he fulfilled the obligations that attended the decennial visit *ad limina*, and sought approval for the American Cassinese Congregation's constitutions.[184] He also had the pleasant surprise of a private audience with Pope Leo XIII. To Father Felix the abbot wrote,

The Holy Father recognized me and received me most cordially. He seemed little changed from ten years ago; [and] spoke plainly and very freely...He gave [the apostolic benediction] *"ex intimo corde."* Indeed he could not have been kinder—He asked me to be seated, but I preferred to kneel—as he was so very kind.[185]

From Rome the abbot continued through Italy, passed through Switzerland—giving Maria Einsiedeln a full week so he could fulfill the primate's request for a scrutiny of the monastery's prior[186]—toured Austria, Bavaria, and Prussia. He touched on England before returning to New York, more than three months having passed since he had last seen America. During his absence, the abbot had also visited the Shrine of Saint Walburga, sought Bavarian brothers,[187] sent instructions regarding governance[188] and assignments[189] to Maryhelp, and written the prior almost daily.[190]

The triumphal tour was exhilarating, and certainly complemented Leo Haid's new, active orientation. But on a more personal level, it enabled the abbot to secure something else he wanted very much—a special honor for Felix Hintemeyer. It was a gesture of friendship and consolation for Father Prior, and also, the abbot thought, an act of justice. The manifold duties Father Felix had accepted under Leo Haid had precluded pursuit of the academic distinction for which his natural gifts seemed to argue. He had accomplished some writing, both creative and scholarly, taught in the college, was the principal instructor in the seminary. But Hintemeyer had not been given an opportunity for pursuing a doctoral degree. That was the condition Haid wanted to remedy or at least acknowledge.

Accordingly, at his first opportunity for a private interview with the Abbot Primate, Haid announced that he "wanted the doctor's hat for my Prior."[191] Apparently the primate responded with little enthusiasm. He did not presume to suggest doubts regarding the prior's worthiness, of course, but he also did not wish to initiate a precedent that might ultimately cheapen the other (earned) degrees the Benedictine college in Rome, Sant' Anselmo, gave under its pontifical charter.[192] Abbot Leo responded graciously, assuring the primate that the honor was sought through the Roman prelate's offices only because it would please the prior to have the degree issued by the Benedictine institution. However, the Carolina abbot announced, not wishing to cause difficulties, he would have no qualms about securing what he wanted from "the Holy Father directly."

Rather suddenly, the primate found all obstacles removed, and assured Abbot Leo that Sant' Anselmo would grant Father Felix the diploma and four-cornered biretta. Leo Haid immediately sent the news to Maryhelp, advising the prior, "You must keep your head from swelling or the Hat might be too small."[193]

Eight days later, on 16 June 1903, the abbot was annoyed that the degree had not been issued. But the primate was again concerned about the possible precedent to be inferred, and he delayed acting on his commitment. Months later, back in America, the letters from the bishop to the primate were growing increasingly terse. "You did not yet grant my faithful Prior and Vicar General the honor I requested for him!", he wrote in November.[194] And that same theme was still being emphasized the next spring. By this time, Abbot Leo was more determined than ever that Father Prior Felix was to be named a Doctor of Divinity.[195] And under pressure the Abbot Primate finally acquiesced and sent the honor—begging that Father Felix would "not [make] too public use of the honorable act of Sant' Anselmo, especially among the Order of Saint Benedict." Hintemeyer took the doctoral oath and donned the hat on 14 June, at which time he reportedly cried at this evidence of his abbot's munificence, charity, and affection.[196]

pateR familias

Approaching the twenty-fifth jubilee of the abbey's erection and his own elevation to the abbatial dignity, Leo Haid might have expected the veneration appropriate to a Benedictine patriarch. The abbot of Belmont, whose children were spread through three states, whose monasteries were thriving, whose episcopal character enhanced his prestige, whose daughterhouses stood in all but one of the southern states of the eastern seaboard, was the most influential abbot then reigning in America. Many factors had conspired to secure his reputation: the joint office as abbot-bishop was unique and distinctive; his vast territory seemed beyond ordinary Church governance, and his perseverance as Vicar Apostolic seemed to border on the heroic; the foundations in Bristow, Richmond, Belmont, Savannah, and Florida had all flourished and grown and earned respect; in Carolina the Catholic Church and the Benedictines in particular had for the first time won a permanent place, and had increased in numbers despite the thoroughly Protestant environment in which they existed; Haid's schools were all solid, and Hintemeyer had enhanced the bishop with a reputation for scholarship and pedagogy; the speaking engagements across the country had won for Haid repute as a man of orthodox theological tenets that were activated by a deep, vibrant spirituality; the occasional productions of

Major John Andre drew further attention to the abbot's versatility and even brought that work back into print; frequent mention in the press imparted to Bishop Haid credit for success and distinction. Even the abbot's long, white beard, his monastic habit, his gentle eyes, those powerful, long-fingered hands, seemed to accent the venerable and fatherly essence that was his image.

Only back in North Carolina were the signs of trouble in evidence. The Hintemeyer publicity of 1897 had invited hierarchial suspicions upon Haid's activities and growing influence. In the vicariate, however, where Hintemeyer like Haid was deeply loved, such accusations had seemed unwarranted. And yet, the Vicariate Apostolic of North Carolina was not at peace. No large issues surfaced, but there was a sense of impending turmoil, hiding beneath appearances and propriety that were still polite. The restlessness of the clergy was the most obvious sign, but there were others, too. Lawsuits peppered the Haid years, mostly over issues of finances, and these too indicated a persistent problem.

Indeed, financial matters constituted a sphere in which the bishop was particularly vulnerable. Income and expenditures were juggled by the abbot-bishop through a central repository. There was an episcopal account in Wilmington and an abbatial deposit in a Charlotte bank, but for purposes of practicality, the needs of the monastery, vicariate, and college were all handled in common. Bills were paid by funds on hand, and since all three institutions were in the service of the Roman Catholic Church in North Carolina, the bishop's principle was that God would provide for all the needs, and neither the Lord of Heaven nor the Lord of Belmont needed to worry about which particular dollar was intended for which particular institution. There was income that went to Haid's jurisdiction as abbot/bishop/president; there were bills that went to him because of the monastery/vicariate/college. God had given him these jobs; God made provisions for the necessities that attended his work; from those provisions the bills were paid. As for the priories, the abbot cosigned the loans, and accepted the debt, but the payments were expected to come from the daughterhouses themselves. On that, the abbot most strenuously insisted. He also expected each dependency to forward an annuity to Carolina. The monastery contributed manpower, educational personnel, McInerney's services, and certain monastic necessities like habits and breviaries to its daughterhouses. But on the whole, the priories were expected to support themselves and contribute to the founding abbey.

There were various charges of malfeasance through the years. But in fact, matters were even worse than that evidence suggested: The complications from Bishop Haid's irregular land acquisitions did not surface until after his death, when it was discovered that the abbey usually paid for lands, which were then placed in Haid's name personally, but with intentions left lamentably unspecified regarding their eventual incorporation into the vicariate for employment.

Legacies also provided difficulties. For example, the estate of Lawrence Brown, a wealthy Catholic in eastern North Carolina, granted Maryhelp some income, but the gift was challenged by the family. The abbey lost in court, then Haid felt so sorry for one niece who had been excluded from Brown's beneficence, that Maryhelp began paying her an annuity—for which she did not reward the abbot with either gratitude or civility.[197] Dr. O'Donoghue's estate also proved to be a problem, and the secular clergy grew increasingly suspicious of the bishop's financial dealings.[198]

There were also small lawsuits that proceeded from problems with land, other inheritances, and contributions that fell to Abbot Leo's jurisdiction. But Haid was simply too irregular in his bookkeeping to ever justify or definitively disprove the charges leveled against him. Despite subsequent suggestions to the contrary, North Carolina usually got less from Propaganda, Drexel, and other sources than was needed for its projects. Once the money came, the bishop paid bills as they appeared, regardless of the origin of the funds or nature of the need. He used the monastery as collateral and sponsor for the vicariate's many loans. When the monastery had money, it repaid debts; when the vicariate did, it paid. The accounting was simply too desultory, and the approach too pragmatic, however, for a realistic charge of misappropriation of funds to be substantiated. Conflict of interest is a more legitimate accusation, but Haid believed that since without priests there was no Church growth, and since Maryhelp was the cheapest place for him to educate priests—to say nothing of sacrificing his monks to this inappropriate labor in order to take up the slack—the whole Church in Carolina profited by making Maryhelp a good and attractive school. At the same time, it was the abbey's duty to support and encourage the growth of the vicariate. Money received was granted to any project of Haid's that suggested the most immediate need.

The financial dealings, more than any other issue, however, served to erode the secular clergy's confidence in their bishop. Open quarrels were mercifully rare. Nevertheless, the tensions continued beneath the surface, as Haid's apostolic decade brought quantitative growth to the vicariate, much as it did to the monastery. But Leo Haid was not sufficiently present to either constituency for his own peculiar and charismatic style of leadership to earn its best response. Then came the jubilee year of 1910; Haid and Hintemeyer campaigned for new honors and prestige, of course. But there was no honor great enough to quell or overshadow the animosity that finally surfaced over Benedictine expansionism.

Chapter VII:

a Grasp on Security

Benedictine monasteries, from the demands of their nature as expressed in the *Regula*, exclude themselves from the ordinary avenues of societal intercourse. Their sense of separation, precisely because it does pertain to the nature of monastic life, is considered essential to their integrity. Benedictine abbeys are not intended—on the ideal level, at least—to fill an immediate role in secular life; accordingly, they seek a practical level of expatriation, so that their monastic ethos may thrive without the encroachment of alien influences. Charitable responsibilities toward "the world" are met through hospitality, sacrifice, edification, apostolates like education, and primarily by prayer. For monasteries that accept missionary duties, these standards are usually compromised somewhat, but these adaptations are considered delays, temporary in their impact, and not actual changes.

Maryhelp, especially as her missionary obligations grew, made most of the adaptations incumbent on monks engaged in essentially priestly responsibilities. There were the absences; the horarium was modified; parishes were accepted, and the Abbey Church itself received some parochial responsibilities. Yet like other Benedictine monasteries, Belmont was also conscious of two additional objectives within the goal of corporate detachment: autonomy and separation. The first was easily accomplished. Erection as an abbey on 19

December 1884, granted autonomy automatically. As an abbey, Maryhelp—though part of the order of Saint Benedict—was self-governing and was expected to develop its particular observance and ethos. The American Cassinese Congregation sent visitors at intervals of approximately three years to inquire into the preservation of the Benedictine spirit. But unless there were flagrant or scandalous practices or the presence of factors that were antipodal to the Catholic faith or to morals, the visitors could make recommendations—supposedly morally binding though not juridical in character—but they had little actual power over an autonomous monastery.

The other factor to which Benedictines were so sensitive was more subtle in form: The Order of Saint Benedict traditionally sought some separation not only from the world but from the interference of bishops as well. This last aspect was an uneasy effort for the monks because it pertained primarily to Church politics, and rested on a rather weak theological foundation. Essentially, there were two factors that influenced this desire for separation even within the Church: First, stabilization in a monastery's post-missionary period required redefining an already well-established relationship with the local diocese; the revision of this propinquity between the local church headed by a mitred bishop, and the monastery with its mitred abbot, raised pertinent questions of responsibility and apostolic legitimacy; these issues, in the monks' view, were not appropriately scrutinized by "the world" (those outside the monastery). The second factor was also recognized—and generalized—after centuries of Benedictine experience: to the same degree as the local bishop was permitted to exercise his influence *within* the cloister or on its members, would the monks find themselves called upon to function *outside* of their monastic clausura. In other words, if a diocesan bishop had authority over monks, he would probably use that authority in a way that would draw the monks outside of their cloister. For both of these factors, then—the need to redefine the relationship, and the danger of yielding too much practical recognition to the local bishop—the monks feared that too close an association with the diocese would compromise their freedom to pursue traditional, Benedictine values within the environment of the monastery. Autonomy was considered essential to the integrity of monastic observance; thus the abbeys of the Order of Saint Benedict sought and valued a genuine independence from the jurisdiction of the local bishop. They could not really support this desire within traditional Catholic ecclesiology (the theology of "church"); so they cast it as an essentially practical issue, created from the need to secure the integrity of the monks—who were vowed to a special and particular form of service within the universal Church.

By Haid's time the monks of the Order of Saint Benedict possessed "exemption" as a universal privilege. This was a principle in Church law that, on the level of practice, recognized the symbol represented by the abbot's mitre. The head of the abbey, like the Ordinary of the diocese, wore the mitre as a statement of his legitimate prelacy. There was also a ring that reflected constancy with his jurisdiction; the crozier made reference to his responsibility for governance and thus for stewardship of the judicature assigned him; the mitre indicated rank and implied authority. Ordinarily, only bishops and abbots were invested with the mitre. The bishop reigned as a successor to the apostles, head of the local church. An abbot's reign reflected a patriarchal rather than an apostolic tradition, but as the mitre suggested, he was blessed as a prelate of the Church, and he held a real authority over his subjects, the monks. From the perspective of ecclesiology, it was an antinomy to have two mitres, each possessing the crozier, existing within a single diocese. Exemption satisfied that conflict, however, by constituting the abbot as head of an *ecclesiola*, a "little church." Whereas, the head of a diocese was an Ordinary of both people and place [his jurisdiction had its own territory and subjects], the abbot was primarily an Ordinary of persons. The monastery existed territorially within the diocese, but the monks were subject firstly to their abbot. The monks' exemption removed them from the bishop's direct governance in most matters, and subjected them to a mitred abbot instead. The bishop could legitimately intervene in the internal affairs of their monastery only if faith or morals were threatened, usually with an overtone of scandal. But this last factor, of course, scandal, was recognized as bringing the issues into a larger sphere, beyond the environment of the cloister anyway. The bishop could also act legitimately in matters that were within the prerogatives of his apostolic commission, such as insuring sacramental discipline, liturgical propriety, or doctrinal fidelity. While some details of exemption varied somewhat through the ages, the basic principle stood: an abbot exercised legitimate authority—reserved from episcopal intervention—over his monks in monastic matters; to the degree that the monks sought to extend their influence beyond their liminal status and character which Benedict had created on their behalf, bishops (as territorial Ordinaries) had greater authority and responsibility for supervision.

In general, this was moot for the residents of Maryhelp. Since the abbot and bishop were one, there was no practical or immediate need to emphasize the monks' exemption from the diocesan Ordinary. But in 1903, the abbot and prior began devoting their attention to the transitory quality of this placid condition. Perhaps Haid might reign for another decade, possibly even for two. But with his death, when in all probability a non-Benedictine would be consecrated as bishop, conditions would change radically. No American monastery was more intimately involved in diocesan affairs than Maryhelp at that time. What would happen when that diocesan territory was governed by a secular clergyman? What would be expected of the Benedictines? These were highly threatening prospects for monks to face. The heightened missionary life of the Belmont Benedictines since the dawn of the century multiplied the problems. And as Haid surveyed the fervor with which apostolic duties were being embraced, and the activity-oriented vocations that were being attracted to Maryhelp—especially from among Irish-American boys in the Northeast—he would have been remiss had he not taken some steps to insure the independence of his monastery when the governance of the vicariate passed to other hands.

Haid and Hintemeyer maintained that there were two possible courses. The first was that Abbot Leo should restrict the monks' pastoral activity. This was no longer feasible, however. The new spirit of the monastery, the needs of Haid as Vicar Apostolic, and the impracticality of again—and so soon—reversing himself on this delicate issue rendered an abdication of the Benedictines' pastoral activity impolitic. The territorial grant of 1891 also argued against this course, since abandoning those nine counties, barely more than a decade after they had been granted, would have required Roman approval and would have reflected unfavorably both at the Vatican and in America on Maryhelp and her abbot.

The second option was even more difficult to arrange. It required a petition to Rome asking that the abbot of Belmont and his successors be granted a territory, constituting the head of the monastery an *ordinarius loci* rather than a mere ordinary of persons. This was the ultimate form of exemption, because it removed the monastery territorially from all existing dioceses. The head of the abbey was then no longer just an "abbot", but an "abbot-ordinary", capable of exercising a quasi-episcopal jurisdiction within his territory. The abbatial church would be invested with cathedral rank; the monastery would acquire an unparalleled security that should provide the environment for a maximum degree of monastic integrity, free from outside demands and intervention.

This also represented the ultimate status an abbey could achieve. Whereas, titles like "archabbey" were essentially honorific and carried little more than rights of precedence, erection as a Cathedral Abbey carried actual power, authority, heightened rights of exemption, and practical faculties, as well as honor. It was a privilege Rome rarely granted, and it would be extraordinary for more than fifty such territories to exist in the world at one time. Indeed no abbey in North America had ever been raised to that rank. Haid and Hintemeyer agreed, however, that this status was the best answer for averting Maryhelp's anticipated problems with exemption, and they decided to seek it as the foundation of their monastery's future security.

Under Church law, erection as a Cathedral Abbey constituted the monastery *vere nullius diocesis*, territorially and juridically "of no diocese."[1] A monastery and its territory formed an "abbatial 'diocese'"—actually it was on a par with a diocese rather than composing one in the fullest sense[2]—usually small in size, sometimes comprising only the grounds of the monastery.[3] At this time, an abbey *nullius* still held a subdiocesan character under the law, but the revision of the *Codex Iuris Canonici* had already begun (1904), and with the promulgation in 1917 of the new code of Church law, these monastic territories became quasi-diocesan.[4] Nevertheless, under both the old and the revised codes, the essence of what constituted a *nullius diocesis*—separation—was sufficient to achieve the ultimate exemption, and thus that assurance of an environment for monastic integrity that the Benedictines wanted.

Especially because of the situation that followed on Haid's service as both the abbot and the local bishop, Maryhelp could not request the *nullius* status on the basis of a need for an abbatial 'diocese'. A petition for the separation, if based on reasons of need, would necessarily imply that in his dual jurisdiction Haid lacked the concinnity his reputation suggested. If the monks intimated a current condition that was bifurcated through contention, the abbey's reputation and that of the abbot would suffer. Accordingly, Hintemeyer recommended that the bestowal of the *nullius* should be sought primarily as an honor, the crowning achievement of Leo Haid's monastic administration. The rank and the deserved prestige were to be emphasized. They argued that the American Cassinese Congregation already had an archabbey, and a second with that title would be inappropriate. They also observed that since Haid already possessed the episcopal character, to grant him a benefice inferior to his rank would be contumelious. Thus the *nullius diocesis,* constituting Leo Haid an abbot-ordinary, and carrying quasi-diocesan character, was clearly the appropriate honor for Belmont.

Both the abbot and prior thought the *nullius* status would be readily granted Maryhelp. Haid considered requesting it during the decennial visit *ad limina* in 1903. He thought the Pope would honor him with the title of "abbot-ordinary", and he would carry that prestigious designation with him on the Grand Tour. So great was his confidence that he did not even bother to submit a preliminary petition in anticipation of his arrival at the Holy See. This proved fortuitous. The Pope was already considering two other petitions for the erection of abbeys *nullius*. And in Rome the primate and other Benedictines with curial contacts and influence all advised Haid against such a cavalier approach to so great an honor. It would be embarrassing enough that Haid, as his monastery's local bishop, would have to be the party who submitted the petition requesting honors for his abbey and thus himself, but at least the groundwork could—and should—be laid by others. And when Haid went to the Propaganda to grant his superscription to the request of the Canadian Benedictines for some missionary rights *in perpetuum*, he discovered just how reluctant Rome was to grant territorial concessions to the Order of Saint Benedict during those final days of the reign of Leo XIII. Accordingly, Haid prudently filed no petition on behalf of himself or his abbey.[5]

The Benedictines in Rome advised Abbot Leo that the petition seeking the *nullius*, since it was being cast as an honor more than as a necessary pastoral arrangement, would be more favorably received in connection with some occasion of special significance at Belmont. It would be more appropriate and opportune for Rome to bestow an honor as a specific recognition than as a general acknowledgment. Accordingly, Haid focused on 1909, the silver jubilee year of the abbatial erection of Maryhelp, as the occasion for Rome to honor the American Church with its first *abbatia nullius*.

The missionary character and the determined effort on his part to stabilize finances enhanced the reputation of the abbot-bishop and his two jurisdictions, and thus added plausibility and rationality to the request for an honor. The extensive journeys and public appeals, the daughterhouses and schools, all of these heightened Haid's visibility and appeal on a national level. He was increasingly identified with the sacrificial character of a missionary and the mystery of a monk, an image that was enhanced by the long, white beard that dominated his appearance. His face was marked now by deep lines; his voice was still strong and his presence charismatic. The abbot-bishop looked and acted the part of the venerable *vir dei*. All of these factors reinforced his popular image. There was also the admirable statistical record of his reign, of which he had boasted in Europe in 1903. It was an ideal time for Leo Haid to appear as a candidate for special recognition by the Holy See.

One of the most notable achievements to the abbot's credit in this period was the redemption of Maryhelp from serious debt. In 1898, the abbey's accumulated deficit was almost twenty-nine thousand dollars,[6] and that total did not include the debts owed at the dependencies and on loans for churches in the vicariate. But in the missionary period Haid gave close attention to the solvency of his monastery. In 1900 his expenditures for travel more than doubled. In 1901, he spent more money seeking aid than he received in contributions. But by 1902, his efforts began to bear fruit; donations were reported in black ink, and more than two thousand dollars could be applied to the debt. The abbot was indefatigable in this effort, and in 1909, though individual parishes had outstanding liabilities, and the Savannah priory alone was trying to satisfy a debt of fifteen thousand dollars,[7] of the monastery and vicariate—the mother institutions—Haid could write the Abbot Primate, "We are nearly free of debt."[8] Concerted effort won a dramatic reversal of his abbey's financial status.

Solvency further legitimized the growth of which Belmont boasted. And in 1908, as scheduled almost five years earlier, contacts were initiated as paviors for a *nullius* diocese of Belmont. Felix Hintemeyer, as Vicar General of the vicariate, was deputed to present the petition in Rome, and all of his organizational and diplomatic skills were applied to this effort to supply "our Monastery [with a] solid future foundation."[9] He departed from the abbey in late spring, even before the school term ended, in order to promote the petition.

The first stop was in Baltimore where Hintemeyer was Cardinal Gibbons' guest and was permitted a lengthy audience. The breach of etiquette from 1891, whereby the metropolitan of Baltimore had not been properly advised of the Roman petition of his Carolina suffragan, was not to be repeated. Hintemeyer played on the Cardinal's vanity throughout the interview, and through that approach achieved considerable success. Gibbons argued that a Diocese of Charlotte would constitute a better petition than an *abbatia nullius*, since he doubted that an abbatial 'diocese' would work any better in America than it had in England. Father Felix corrected the inaccuracies of the Cardinal's historical reflections—noting "that England *never* had such an arrangement"—then

> made it plain to him, what we want, and what we *deserve*. I laid special stress upon the fact, that he was the "Founder" and he should crown his work with getting for us, what we ask for. Then like by spiration he lightened

up—and said, "Yes, I will do what I can." He asked me to remain in Rome, till he arrives—which will be about July 30th.[10]

With Gibbons' support so handily won, the Vicar General envisioned a clear path to Roman approval. In order to expedite matters he decided to abbreviate his proposed excursion to Bavaria, and announced to the primate his intention to reach Rome as soon as possible.[11]

The Baltimore Cardinal had suggested that Hintemeyer, once in Rome, should seek local advice, formulate the petition in Haid's name, then submit it "through proper channels" to De Propaganda Fide. Thus the curial officials could already be familiar with the request before Gibbons reached Rome and made it "his principal business."[12] Unwilling to trust too exclusively in the non-Benedictine procurators whom James Gibbons preferred, Father Felix advised the Abbot Primate to be prepared to use "Your Lordship's influence in Rome to accomplish what with the consent and good will of Cardinal Gibbons our dear Abbot and Bishop is aiming at."[13]

Hintemeyer also sent instructions to Belmont advising Haid to write the Cardinal. "Dwell especially," he advised, "on the fact that this would be the crowning act of his work for North Carolina and *add new glory* to the Province of Baltimore–that Benedictines have ever been faithful in the Church, the support of the Church in centuries, etc., etc." Father Felix placed unerring trust in the susceptibility of the Cardinal's ego, but the abbot was also advised to respond to Gibbons' more trenchant objections. It was necessary to assure Baltimore, and thus Rome

> (a) that [the proposed *nullius*] will not cut up the state, and that future dioceses formed, will not be interfered with;
> (b) that this arrangement will not exclude secular priests, as the future *Abbas Ordinarius* may employ both religious and secular clergy–only that they belong to the Abbey;
> (c) that for the present the administration of North Carolina should remain as it is, though the *abbatia nullius* should be established.[14]

Father Felix then left for Rome, while at Belmont Leo Haid commenced the second phase of the *nullius* effort, his own letter to Gibbons. By virtue of Hintemeyer's success, the abbot was able to avoid the usual gestures of supplication and petition, and write instead a benign letter of appreciation for the Cardinal having "graciously expressed a willingness to aid the Benedictines...in their efforts to have [the Holy See] declare Maryhelp Abbey an *'Abbatia Nullius.'* "[15]

The abbot's presentation followed his prior's recommendations. Maryhelp, Haid wrote, "owes its existence to your Eminence," and the *nullius* would "crown your good work." The abbatial 'diocese' would encourage "renewed good will and self-sacrifice" among the monks, he reasoned, and lend "certainty [to the idea] that the Abbey will always remain the centre of an assured and definite field of labor." Also, the territory proposed would be more reasonably apportioned than the 1891 grant had been, in order to assure clear territorial responsibilities and access when North Carolina saw other dioceses erected. After the fifty years of the first grant had expired, the Benedictines could relinquish Rowan, Davidson, Guilford, and Forsythe counties; the proposed *nullius* would include the other five counties—Mecklenburg, Cabarrus, Lincoln, Cleveland, and Gaston—and append Rutherford. The additional territory, the bishop noted, had virtually no Catholics. This geographic distribution would cause no interference when Rome created the Sees of Wilmington and Asheville in North Carolina. Indeed, Haid reminded the Cardinal, the future cathedral for Asheville was already planned, and Wilmington's was soon to be erected. As a final note, Haid expressed his willingness, according to the pleasure of the Holy See, "for the present [to] attend to the whole State as I have been doing," even after Rome created an abbatial See for him.[16]

Hintemeyer attended to his Roman mission until September, but without success. Although Cardinal Gibbons endorsed the idea of a *nullius* diocese, he did not fulfill the commitment to make it his "principal business" that summer. Accordingly Haid advised his prior to entrust the matter to the more expeditious intermediaries of the Order of Saint Benedict, and return home. The abbot also announced that the date of the jubilee celebration would be postponed until 1910—so the abbatial erection could be commemorated at the same time as the jubilee of his abbacy; thus he also provided the Benedictine agents in Rome with an extra year for pursuing the creation of an *abbatia nullius*. With the change of intermediaries and date, the third phase of the petitioning process began.

For the annual celebration of the Solemnity of Saint Benedict, Maryhelp usually scheduled one of its grandest observances of the year. That day, 21 March, was both the patronal feast of Western monasticism and the college's annual "Founder's Day," so the students and monks commemorated the feast in tandem. In 1909, Bishop Haid decided to further enhance the solemnity by inviting Archbishop Diomede Falconio, O.F.M. This prelate was the Pope's representative to the Church in the United States, with the rank of Apostolic Delegate. Coincidentally the responsibilities of his office included evaluating and recommending proposed diocesan changes and erections.

By this time the Belmont Benedictines had decided, as Hintemeyer expressed the point, "It is useless to ask any favors from American bishops for Religious!" So with Falconio—a more direct line to the Holy See—at the abbey, Father Felix recorded, "we have not been idle." The monks saw that the delegate was exposed to the full expanse and grandeur of Maryhelp and to the adulation enjoyed by the Ordinary. Then, as the Vicar General wrote the primate, "Our good abbot-bishop and your humble servant had a long conversation with His Excellency [regarding] the *Abbatia Nullius*." Hintemeyer had been in contact with Denis O'Connell who knew both Falconio and curial processes extremely well, and had already arranged for the archbishop to be apprised of the many benefits an abbatial 'diocese' would bring to North Carolina and to the donation of O'Connell's uncle. O'Connell had also informed Father Felix of certain pertinent details of Falconio's background, so that the conversation could be nostalgically focused on the archbishop's happy early days in Italy, where he resided in the *abbatia nullius* of Montecassino. On 22 March, the day after their interview, Felix Hintemeyer recorded, the delegate "is heart and soul for [the *nullius*]; he sees the poetic part of it."[17]

Falconio advised the monks that they were right to trust the Benedictines to get the petition approved; the primate, he reasoned, would serve far better than the procurators used by the American bishops. The delegate even offered to receive the document of petition personally, "for perusal and endorsement." He said he would immediately begin "to interview the bishops of the Province of Baltimore, but he will *not* mind it, however, if they should be against it—*'The Delegation,'* he says, *'is for it.'* "[18]

On 8 April, with the petition phrased and forwarded, Bishop Haid wrote the primate. As custom required that the party requesting a Roman favor should cover all expenses incurred, he enclosed three hundred *lira,* to help with "any...trouble you may undergo now." And "later," referring to the *taxa* the Holy See would impose if the request were granted, he suggested, "we will be glad to defray all expenses."[19] As a token of this willingness, the prior was instructed to forward another three hundred *lira* just two days later. "We will do our best," Father Felix promised.[20]

To the primate, Abbot Leo emphasized the importance of the security a *nullius* diocese would provide.

> ...In order to encourage our religious for the future and preserve the spirit of sacrifice, under the present circumstances, their future should be secured permanently. This can now be done by making the *"Abbatia Nullius,"*...All this can be properly explained to the authorities to prove that we are not selfish, but only desire what will really benefit the Church now and in [the] future.[21]

Hintemeyer, who was still coordinating the *nullius* effort, sent corroborating documents to assist the primate in forwarding the case. There were photographs, a copy of the Brief from 1891, a map. In his usual manner, Father Felix also wrote a letter keyed to the special concerns of his audience. This included a deft but specious argument regarding why the *nullius* petition requested two counties that had no Catholics in residence; this, he noted, was not really as *outre* as it might seem, since "someday the good Benedictines in Europe, driven from their homes, [may] want a quiet, healthy locality in the New World, where they can devote their life to God—here it is!"[22]

The Hintemeyer petition, submitted by the Abbot Primate, signed by Haid, and endorsed by Falconio, was dated 11 April 1909. It had the usual balance of diplomatic ameneties, prefacing a concise statement of the request, followed by effluent aspirations suggesting God's will and glory as the source of the request and the fruit of its approbation. The Benedictines wanted a *nullius diocesis* of Maryhelp to be erected for the perpetual glory of God, the good of religion, and the well-being of the faithful. Its territory should consist of Mecklenburg, Cabarrus, Lincoln, Cleveland, Rutherford, and Gaston counties in North Carolina. Leo Haid was willing to accept, according to the will of God and the pleasure of the Holy See, the duties of an abbot-ordinary. Until the North Carolina dioceses of Wilmington and Asheville were created, he would also continue as Vicar Apostolic if Rome desired that service of him.[23] The primate submitted the petition, and the usual long silence began. By November, with no word received, Abbot Leo instructed his Benedictine agent to begin applying pressure. "The monastery," he noted, "is anxious."[24]

It was only at this point, seven months after the petition was submitted, fourteen months after Hintemeyer's Roman visit ended, that the investigation began. On 16 December 1909, Cardinal De Lai wrote Gibbons. The Baltimore prelate had already endorsed the idea of an *abbatia nullius*, and that in conjunction with the approval of the Apostolic Delegate, Abbot Primate, and of course the diocesan Ordinary in Carolina, seemed to virtually assure Rome's *volo.* De Lai's letter sought confirmation of Gibbons' satisfaction, as metropolitan, with the specifics of the arrangements for the abbatial 'diocese'.[25]

It is unclear whether Cardinal Gibbons had been uncertain of the territorial delineation the Benedictines had submitted, or whether he had merely remained tacit on the subject. The latter appears to be the case, since Haid had listed these same counties in his letter to Gibbons of 24 June 1908, specifying them as desired for the *nullius*. [26] Available documentation also fails to note whether or not the metropolitan expressed his reservations about the proposed territory of the *nullius* when he was in Rome that summer. But on 25 January 1910, Gibbons clearly stated his objections.

He began by praising the Benedictines. Perhaps reflecting Hintemeyer's influence. Gibbons acknowledged himself as the father of the Benedictine mission in Carolina, then he recognized the labors of both the monks and their abbot. "They have performed the work most faithfully," he said, and "the present Vicar Apostolic, Monsignor Haid, is a zealous Prelate, and has done very much to spread the faith in that territory." Nevertheless, he argued, "after serious reflection I feel it my duty to say that I do not believe it expedient to grant the request of Monsignor Haid."[27] The reason for his objection rested on the proposed territory. As in 1891, when Mark Gross took umbrage at the Benedictines' acquisition of his parish, Mecklenburg County and the city of Charlotte were the focus of dissension. Gibbons found no fault in Haid's reasoning, but he did challenge the premises on which the arguments were based. The archbishop believed that when a diocese was finally created for North Carolina, the cathedral city would be Charlotte rather than Asheville or Wilmington. The See of the vicariate, Wilmington, was too far east; Asheville was not as accessible as Charlotte. That left the Mecklenburg city as the obvious choice for the future See of North Carolina; accordingly, its county should not be incorporated, he argued, into the *abbatia nullius*. The Cardinal did allow, however, that "if an *abbatia 'nullius'* be conceded...this should embrace" a real territory. Mecklenburg, he insisted, had to be removed for the sake of future diocesan growth, and if that county were excluded, Cabarrus also should be eliminated since it would be left bordering on no remaining portion of the abbatial 'diocese'. In place of these two counties, Gibbons recommended conceding four others, ones that were not on either the Benedictines' lists of 1891 or 1908—Catawba, Burke, McDowell, and Polk.[28] Territorially this was generous, although since the Catholic population of the four additional sections was less than that of Mecklenburg alone, it was not as liberal a gift as it might first appear. The extraordinary element of the Gibbons proposal lay in the addition of Burke and McDowell; these caused the proposed *nullius* to virtually sever the state. If with this territory the abbey were also to acquire either Yancey or Mitchell counties, or subsequently the county of Avery that was erected in 1911, the western end of the state—at least eleven and perhaps thirteen counties—would be completely isolated from the rest of the vicariate, the Diocese of Charlotte, Asheville, Raleigh, Wilmington, or whatever jurisdiction Rome erected for those parts of North Carolina outside the abbatial territory.[29] Gibbons' recommendation was, of course, inconsistent with his own conditions imposed on the proposed *nullius* two years earlier.

The Vatican considered Gibbons' recommendation, endorsed his judgment, then instructed Falconio to consult with Haid. The delegate wrote on 20 March, naming Gibbons as the adversary, and asking if the eight counties recommended by the Cardinal were acceptable to Belmont.[30] But the "good Bishop would not *listen to it*," Father Felix recorded, "and wrote a strong yet *kind* letter to the Apostolic Delegate." The Benedictines, it was mentioned, "have done *everything* in *Mecklenburg County*" and its omission "will greatly interfere with our work."[31] The proximity of Mecklenburg was cited—abbey property touched its border[32]—and it was suggested that "the good Cardinal [Gibbons]...is under false impressions" regarding the centrality of Charlotte to the diocesan development of North Carolina.[33]

The letter from the Delegate was marked "confidential," so the Benedictines were not at liberty to try to persuade Gibbons themselves, nor could the primate be addressed licitly regarding either this development or its details.[34] Thus for the present the Apostolic Delegate had become the monks' only possible channel for arguing for the territory they wanted. The Benedictine agents could, however, be addressed in more general terms. So the Abbot Primate received several letters from Felix Hintemeyer, who rationalized that the confidentiality had been imposed on Haid and not himself. Nevertheless, the prior, while giving instructions to the Benedictine agent, was still careful not to reveal the situation that prompted these directives. Authorization was given to bargain away Cabarrus.[35] The primate, Hintemeyer said, should also assure the Holy Father that secular clergy would be permitted to function in Charlotte. Subsequently, once the Benedictine primate learned of the situation with Gibbons through his own curial sources, the correspondence between the Roman abbot and Belmont became more explicit. The Gibbons proposal, Hintemeyer charged, was "a gift like an empty basket—no Catholics in it."[36] Securing Mecklenburg was to be an inflexible demand. And in that regard, the prior concluded, "We are certain that the case is in the best of hands."[37]

But due to the delay imposed by Falconio's restrictions of confidentiality, the primate lacked the time needed for acquiring Charlotte for the *nullius*. The Sacred Consistorial Congregation, the curial office whose recommendation the Pope would presumably ratify, had already informed Falconio that the Benedictines could not have Mecklenburg. The judgment of Cardinal Gibbons on that issue was not to be considered open to challenge. The Delegate forwarded that news to Haid and received in reply a letter insisting on the necessary role Charlotte played in the abbey's apostolic work. Finally Falconio was forced to explain to the Carolina bishop how limited the remaining options really were.

> In regard to the *Abbatia Nullius*, as matters stand at present in Rome, it is impossible to expect the Mecklenburg County. Hence, should you not be satisfied, there is time yet to stop the proceedings. I fear, however, that if this chance should pass away there will be very little hope for the future to establish an *Abbatia Nullius*. Hence I do think it would be better to accept the terms proposed by the Sacred Congregation mentioned in my last letter, for as I understand it, it is rather for the honor of having an *Abbatia Nullius* in the United States than for the sake of having a large populous diocese. I expect an answer at once. If you think that it is not convenient for you to accept, say so; and I shall ask the Sacred Congregation to stop proceedings in the matter.[38]

Haid resigned himself immediately to the delegate's counsel. The "honor" was sufficient to grant what the Benedictines had actually sought through the petition, namely territorial separation. But Hintemeyer, whose vision was focused on more immediate concerns, objected to the abbot's acquiescence. In the prior's assessment, the loss of Mecklenburg denuded the diocesan character and apostolic prospects of the *nullius*, and reduced it to an undistinguished future.

Father Felix reluctantly wrote the primate, saying that he sent the new petition, whereby Maryhelp "requested" only the territory of which Gibbons approved, under "direct orders."[39] The prior's one remaining hope was that "some future year may present an opportunity of having 'Mecklenburg' added to us, which we ought to have, *I cannot say in justice* for we *Religious* have *no* right to ask for anything."[40] This bitterness implanted itself deep in Hintemeyer's pride, and a month later his rancor resurfaced. "We have no '*jus*' to demand," the prior said this time, and "can only *suggest* and *request* and [be] grateful, if the 'Honor' is given our Abbey."[41]

One other issue arose that spring, and it also vexed Hintemeyer more than Haid. Rome wondered if in separating the territory from the Vicariate Apostolic, the occasion might be opportune for changing the governance of the Church in the rest of the state as well, perhaps by erecting a statewide jurisdiction—exclusive of the *nullius*, of course—of full diocesan rank. The Vicar General sent Falconio a splenetic response stating that "if the Ecclesiastical status of our Vicariate be conclusively settled" the new situation could only succeed if Abbot Leo remained on the throne anyway. The previous year's *Cathedraticum*, he noted, the collection that constituted a bishop's annual income from his territory, was a paltry two hundred ninety dollars. The abbey, not the diocese, served as the support of episcopal activity in North Carolina. Accordingly, whatever was decided in Rome, "matters [had to] be so fixed that our saintly good Bishop could retain the administration *'ad dies vitae.'* " And yet with Rome's current insensitivity to the needs of the Church in North Carolina, perhaps "there may be two bishops in this Protestant State."[42] Then to the primate Father Felix wrote, "Do *try* to have *everything* settled"—and materials for a possible, but never realized, final appeal to the Holy Father himself were enclosed. But Hintemeyer's most urgent request was just "please *don't* let Cardinal De Lai write over to America once more."[43]

Once Belmont agreed to petition for what Rome had decided to grant, no obstacles remained to interfere with the erection of the United States' first Cathedral Abbey. On 11 May 1910, the Abbot Primate cabled Haid, reporting approval of the revised petition.[44] Haid replied immediately, expressing appreciation and an intention to use the separation to support the highest monastic ideals, hoping "that our Abbey may not prove undeserving, as far as we can make it a model Home for Benedictines in America." He also expressed "our earnest desire to pay all expenses in Rome."[45] "But Father Felix, his disposition unchanged, appended a cautionary note reminding the primate that the truncated *nullius* could provide "almost nothing" in terms of "pecuniary income," since "there are not fifty Catholics in the Counties outside of Gaston." And the abbey was poor, and would be unable to make extravagant expenditures.[46]

Benedictine channels were operating more than a month ahead of Falconio's sources. So the Apostolic Delegation was not advised of the erection until June, after which official notice was sent to James Gibbons and Leo Haid. The letters to the two prelates were identical, except for an extra phrase in the Cardinal's notice, assuring him that "the territory [has] been limited to the extent recommended by Your Eminence."[47] Both Haid and Gibbons were satisfied with the results of the *nullius* petition. Hintemeyer began applying himself to the congenial task of organizing ceremonies for the jubilees of the abbot and abbey, and the erection of the *abbatia nullius* of Belmont. Surely this, a student wrote in the college's journal, "is the epitome of [Maryhelp's] history."[48]

The *Bulla Erectionis* was issued by Pope Saint Pius X on 8 June 1910, and its *motu proprio* on 16 July.[49] On the whole, the documents contained nothing extraordinary. The territory was constituted as Gibbons had insisted. Haid was named abbot-ordinary, and permitted to retain jurisdiction of both the monastery and the vicariate, with the privilege of residing in either of the two "dioceses" for which he was responsible. The monastery church of Maryhelp was named a cathedral. The abbots of Belmont were henceforth to enjoy a "dignity like the episcopal." But the key phrase for Leo Haid stated that "the aforesaid Monastery with its attached territory should hence forth be truly and properly of no diocese for all effects of the law and immediately subject to the Apostolic See."[50] That was the victory that justified more than two years of negotiations. In that territorial separation, Maryhelp was granted the security and the chance for integrity that the abbot wished to bequeath as a perpetual memorial.

But there also occured in the *Bulla* a lengthy sentence, written in the obscure Latin for which scholars have so thoroughly criticized Pius X's chancery.[51] It suggested an unusual and unanticipated privilege for the abbots who would succeed Haid.

> Furthermore, We wish that the aforesaid Leo Haid, present Abbot of the monastery of Mary Help of Christians at Belmont...or his successors in the abbatial dignity should exercise also the functions and duties of Vicar Apostolic in the rest of North Carolina at the pleasure of himself and the Apostolic See, by which they can properly acquire this twofold office, namely of Abbot and Vicar Apostolic, and so long as this situation continues.[52]

There was confusion regarding where the emphasis in this long sentence should be found. While it first appeared that Rome intended that all future abbots of Belmont would also hold the office of Vicar Apostolic of North Carolina, that seemed such an extraordinary and puzzling provision that the monks assumed that the phrase "at the pleasure of himself and the Apostolic See" implied that this future or continued union between the Abbots-Ordinary of Belmont and the Vicars Apostolic was merely a possibility Rome chose to mention. Based on that assumption, Hintemeyer assured the secular clergy that in terms of practical jurisdiction, there was no change to affect them or their work—except favorably, since the erection of the *nullius* meant the monk-priests should "be drawn in [from the vicariate's territory] and their places supplied by seculars."[53] Only gradually did the monks come to recognize that Rome had indeed united the *nullius* and vicariate "so long as this situation [the existence of a *nullius diocesis* of Belmont and a Vicariate Apostolic of North Carolina] continues."[54]

Because of their misunderstanding of this key passage, the monks did not at first comprehend why the acknowledgments they received from the hierarchy of the United States and the clergy of North Carolina were phrased with such reserve and caution. But their meaning and the document's would evolve with perfect clarity before the year's end. In the interim there were technicalities of Church law to be met, and though the *nullius* diocese was created on 8 June, it still had to be erected before it could properly function under the common law of the Church. This demanded that the Pope or his representative promulgate the *Bulla* at a public ceremony, part of which included a formal reading of the document. Haid would be officially enthroned in his Abbey Cathedral at this service, and formally constituted abbot-ordinary. Testimonies—actually authentications—that the formal erection had occurred would be taken, and copies of the official documentation were to be prepared and signed in triplicate for retention at Maryhelp, the Delegation in Washington, and the archives of the Sacred Consitorial Congregation in Rome.

The Pope nominated Falconio to preside at the erection of the *nullius diocesis*.[55] There was a solemn pontificial Mass on 18 October 1910, lasting two and a half hours, at which the delegate officiated, vested in red satin made "heavy with gold."[56] Bishops Northrop (Charleston), Monaghan (Wilmington, Delaware), Keiley (Savannah), Owen Corrigan (auxiliary bishop of Baltimore), and of course Haid were also in the sanctuary, as was Abbot Charles Mohr, of Saint Leo in Florida.[57] At the conclusion of the Mass, Abbot Charles read the *Bulla Erectionis*, then "bore it to where Abbot Haid sat on the southern side of the spacious and brightly illuminated altar, and presented it to him, kneeling the while and kissing the ring which is the Abbot's seal of authority."[58] There followed courteous remarks by Falconio: "This monastery, this work here, must become in time the wonder of this country...[Maryhelp stands where] twenty-five years ago there was a wilderness."[59] Next Haid spoke. Equally gracious, he assured the congregation that "the greatest merit belongs to others," not to himself.[60] In conclusion

A solemn *"Te Deum"* was then chanted by the choir. The music throughout was superb and added much to the enjoyment of those who attended the ceremony. Accompanied by Father Francis [Underwood], organist, the orchestra played finely. The choral numbers were rendered by a clerical choir of sixteen select voices, and by a mixed choir, composed of boys and men, numbering twenty voices. Reverend Father Chrysostom [Zoellner] was choirmaster and Reverend Father William [Regnat] leader of the orchestra. The procession after the Papal benediction, retired to the strains of the "March Pontifical."[61]

It was a grand day for Belmont, the culmination of the abbot's dreams for his abbey, marked by unparalleled honors and recognition. So extensive was the celebration that the other Benedictine abbots had been asked not to attend, saving their presence for the celebration on 24 November[62] of the silver jubilee of Haid's abbatial blessing. There was not enough room at Maryhelp to accommodate as many guests as the monks expected—a Cardinal, Apostolic Delegate, eight bishops, numerous monsignori, sixty priests, plus the Benedictines.[63]

But that was a problem that never materialized. The abbey was not as crowded on 18 October as the monks had anticipated. Gibbons, it was thought, would have to attend.[64] He was, after all, not only the supposed "founder" of Maryhelp, and a former head of the Roman Catholic Church in North Carolina; he was also the metropolitan of the ecclesiastical province in which this new 'diocese' was being erected. But the Cardinal of Baltimore, "on account of my many duties," was "obliged to forego that pleasure."[65] Nevertheless, he did send his blessing[66] and allowed his auxiliary, Corrigan, to attend. Others proved equally reluctant to support the Benedictine *nullius* by their presence.

Even within the ceremony there appeared evidence of the tension that surrounded the creation of the abbatial 'diocese.' Haid addressed the assembly, ostensibly speaking to Falconio, with the pointed observation, "You have set your approval upon our Abbey by your presence."[67] But that endorsement was either less obvious to others or counted for very little, because open hostilities were about to surface.

The Response

In seeking the *nullius* Haid had told Peter Engel, "If only I could secure the future in some way, I would be satisfied. As long as I live I have more than enough, but people will come...who 'know not Joseph,' and what may happen?"[68] Yet by 18 October 1910, "Joseph" himself had already fallen from favor, and had taken his followers with him.

The conflict had arisen over that convoluted sentence in the *Bulla Erectionis* that linked in perpetuity the administration of the abbatial 'diocese' and the Vicariate Apostolic of North Carolina. The secular clergy labeled it the "Joker Clause" and accused the Benedictines of "having deceived us." Permanently uniting the two offices had bestowed on the Order of Saint Benedict the right of electing the Ordinary for the entire state. And that ensured that the Vicars

Apostolic would always be one of the monks' own number. It was perceived as the ultimate offense in a long history of the Carolina Benedictines' pursuit of power. The history of Catholicism in North Carolina was interpolated to show the monks' continuous thirst for control. In 1876, they acquired their first missionary responsibility; in 1887, they won the episcopate for their abbot; in 1891, they wrested nine whole counties from the seculars; since their arrival, the Benedictines had been seizing parish after parish, exiling loyal pastors like Mark Gross, all in an effort to promote their own glory and income. "This clause," wrote Christopher Dennen, one of the vicariate priests, "has crushed the zeal of your secular clergy."[69]

Out of courtesy to the bishop, most of the priests waited until after the celebration of 18 October to voice their objections formally, but the word had reached Haid early and had already destroyed the joy he thought the occasion would lend, not only to himself but to the Church in all of North Carolina. This is "some Silver Jubilee," he wrote to Peter Engel, and "I am heartily *sick*! When all is over, I'll be on my knees in humble thanksgiving. I am keeping down to my 'Jobs' in spite of everything. Others are creating the fuss and fury."[70]

The secular clergy was convinced that the Benedictines had requested the perpetual administration of the vicariate,[71] and the furor not only continued past the jubilee festivities, but achieved its full magnitude in the wake of that celebration. "This clause will hurt you more than it will benefit you," warned Father Dennen, because "instead of the few counties named you have the whole State."[72]

Father Michael Irwin, who was one of the secular clergy's most loyal supporters of the work of the Order of Saint Benedict in North Carolina, wrote a charitable yet unfailingly cogent letter to Cardinal Gibbons expounding upon the turmoil in the vicariate. Irwin was at the time among those who believed the abbey had requested the extraordinary privilege. He did not, however presume to impute motives; thus his evaluation was perhaps the most objective of the several sent to Belmont and Baltimore that month.[73] All of these commentaries, however, including Irwin's, suffered from failure to gather all the pertinent facts before applying pen to paper.

Irwin reported that the situation "has given feelings of dismay to myself and my brother priests," because they realize that this was not a new situation as much as a culmination of North Carolina's problems under the reign of Leo Haid. "This service [by the abbot-bishop] of two masters," Michael Irwin reported, "has been the root of all our difficulties."

All of us Missionary-rectors are painfully aware of the blight that has come over the affairs of the Vicariate on account of the divided energies of our abbot-bishop. We are ill at ease in his presence feeling somewhat like step-sons. We love and admire him for his fine qualities even while we say and feel this and would wish for closer union. But it seems impossible.

The bishop's actions in securing the special provisions of the *Bulla*, Irwin believed, were invidious, and had destroyed morale in the vicariate while casting the diocesan and religious priests as competitors rather than co-workers. "He loves his monastery and his monks first," the priest wrote. "We are made to feel our comparative insignificance not. so much by overt acts as by quiet *and I believe unconscious* contempt." Irwin accused Leo Haid of being precisely what the abbot had believed he should be: "Bishop Haid is undoubtedly a grand man, but he is a monk first and a Bishop next."[74]

Irwin also cited a story from earlier in Haid's reign, suggesting that the abbot had once decided to leave the abbey in order to be a bishop full time. However, the monks had reportedly persuaded the abbot against this move. Apparently, Irwin was referring to the proposed resignation during the Walter Leahy crisis, when the objections to the dual reign were proceeding from his other constituency. Fathers Irwin, Dennen, and Price all make reference to this story, but there appear to be no extant materials to document this explanation of the bishop's decision against the resignation.[75]

Irwin proposed that the best way of solving the crisis was to immediately erect the vicariate into a full diocese. He wrote Gibbons that the creation of a diocese would automatically end the abbey's hold on the vicariate, since the monastery could not enjoy the same privilege once the Vicariate Apostolic was suppressed. Father Irwin recommended that the See of the new diocese should be Raleigh, and that the usual argument against the erection–the lack of sufficient income for a bishop–was unfounded. The poor response for the *cathedraticum*, in Irwin's view, was Haid's fault: "The people have been listless inasmuch as they knew that the Vicar Apostolic was not depending on them. Their love and loyalty were not fully aroused." When that changed, he told Gibbons, the support would appear. North Carolina merited a "more vigorous ecclesiastical policy than that which has hitherto obtained." And yet the man who was clearly best suited to lead the new Diocese of Raleigh was still Leo Haid. "He is an able and holy man and we would be glad to see him the first bishop of the See of Raleigh." This would be "a crowning glory to his singularly meritorious life." But he should be bishop without also being abbot, Irwin said, and "I do not think it likely that Bishop Haid will come out [of his monastery]."[76]

Christopher Dennen raised most of the same arguments as Irwin. But Dennen addressed his letter to Father Prior Felix. The response he received, written at the peak of the prior's annoyance with the development of the *nullius* effort, suggested that Father Dennen merely wanted the episcopal throne for himself. Understandably, the secular priest took exception to that charge and wrote Hintemeyer one more time, sending a letter that was frank, honest, and occasionally brutal. "Don't believe all the pleasant things you hear," warned the priest, "they are not always meant."[77]

This letter raised a charge that caused Leo Haid particular pain. The abbot believed he had sacrificed all he possibly could, even the spirit and character of his monastery, in order to support the vicariate and spread Catholicism. But Dennen, suggesting that his words reflected the tone of the whole state, accused the Benedictines of using the vicariate for their own advantage and profit, to the detriment of Roman Catholicism in North Carolina.

> But now man to man let me ask you in all candor and friendship, if the Abbot of Saint Mary's were not the bishop for the last twenty-two years would the conditions surrounding your monastery be enhanced to the same degree as they are at present? Again had we a Bishop for the same length of time separate from the Abbot, one living among us, of missionary zeal, going about with the priests, employing his advantages solely to the interests of the Vicariate, giving that prestige which the episcopacy conveys socially, and spiritually, would not our condition today be far better from a temporal standpoint than it is?[78]

Haid was shocked by the ingratitude of his secular clergy, and their insistence on seeing the fruit of his double reign as a contest for his attention. How could an arrangement designed by the Holy See be criticized for accomplishing what it was created to do? The Church had grown; both the monastery and vicariate had prospered and become secure; bills were paid; the administration of Leo Haid had succeeded precisely where his predecessors had failed. He had persevered, too. The Catholic Church in North Carolina had grown numerically, in its quantity of charitable institutions, of churches, and personnel and members; it had financial stability for the first time since its creation in 1868. This contentiousness and competitive approach toward perceiving the well-being of the Church was abhorrent to Leo Haid; it had no apparent foundation in logic. Then the bishop was advised that James Cardinal Gibbons, the man who was primarily responsible for the union of the two mitres in 1887, and who had instructed Haid on the elements of an ideal balance, was not unsympathetic to the priests' reasoning.

Haid's reponse to these charges was sadly characteristic, in that he had little understanding of the situation from any perspective other than his own. He thought that the monks, not the priests, were neglected. He saw a decade in which he had given himself overwhelmingly to the vicariate and its needs. There were the statistics that seemed to support the success of his work. Yet again, Leo Haid refused to admit the value of his presence, and he could not understand the charges of neglect that were arising from his secular clergy. He could not empathize with men who thought they were ignored, and that he had devoted inadequate attention to their needs. To his mind the vicariate had received even more than the Holy See apportioned when it assigned him the double mitre. The abbot-bishop still maintained that the diocesan clergy was called to a different life than he and his monks, and he did not understand the clergymen's reluctance to embrace, in his view, the sacrificial nature that should be the common bond between missionaries and monks; that was where their vocations met. Why, then, were the priests perturbed at the hardships of their missionary labors? Why did they fault their Ordinary because he had sought to fulfill both the commissions Rome had seen fit to impose on him? How, he wondered, could he be criticized for living vows he had made to God, a profession ratified by the Church, especially when to his mind he had stinted that commitment in favor of his episcopal duties? In essence, the problem was precisely as his priests had suggested: Leo Haid was a monk first. But the insolubility of the dispute did not rest on the fact of Rome's having assigned a divided jurisdiction, as much as it proceeded from the fact that the bishop believed probity and integrity demanded that he be a monk first, while his priests said that the episcopate held precedence. Each side chose the perspective that was to his own benefit, and neither was ever to be satisfied.

The man who had won Gibbons' interest on behalf of the North Carolina situation was Thomas Frederick Price, who had a long history of stormy relations with his Carolina Ordinary. As the senior priest of the diocese, the first native North Carolinian ordained for the vicariate, and the only active missionary whose service in the state pre-dated Haid's, Frederick Price had emerged as the natural leader of the Catholic clergy in North Carolina. Price was relatively short, of ordinary build, with thinning hair, steel rimmed glasses, and a piercing gaze that seldom failed to catch the attention of his listeners. He was also an almost legendary figure in the state. His story included a dramatic rescue and recovery after a shipwreck,[79] and a miraculous cure from deafness.[80] As a child he had served Gibbons' Mass, and that prelate had personally helped the boy in his pursuit of Holy Orders. After his ordination, Price was identified by Mark Gross as having all "the gifts of the good Missionary, good health, good sense, good manners, and a piety as solid as it is zealous."[81] Price was an indefatigable missionary; he took charge of the boys' orphanage that was originally to be situated in Belmont;[82] he founded two Catholic periodicals;[83] but he also gave progressive evidence of eccentricities that caused him to separate from the main course of missionary life in North Carolina. The peculiarities ranged from an "antipathy to bathing"[84] to his extraordinary request to abandon parish life and become a missionary to the state's Protestants; his goal from youth, he said, was to convert the entire state of North Carolina to Roman Catholicism.[85] Haid indulged this last request in 1896, after which Father Price pursued an independent course within the vicariate. He was a zealous missionary priest, but he was not disposed by personality to be part of a team—an unfortunate condition when one has a bishop who considers himself a "father" to his priests, and encourages familial correspondence among their number. In the opinion of George Woods, the last of Price's close associates in North Carolina and his successor at the orphanage, the priest "had a long smoldering antagonism to the wishes of Bishop Haid, which, while it did not result in open disobedience to his Ordinary, was the cause no doubt of many a mistake." In Woods' estimation, Father Price longed to enjoy the rights of a religious superior.[86]

It was that desire that led him toward the creation in 1901 of the *Regina Apostolorum*, an association of secular clergy that was intended to foster missionary vocations for the South. But the *Apostolorum* soon began sponsoring elements of common life for its members, and it acquired an overtone of exclusivity. Father Irwin joined the "Apostolic Company," or the "Apostolate", the popular terms by which the organization was known, and William F. O'Brien was also affiliated. From the beginning there were conflicts over authority, and the group's relation to the Vicariate Apostolic and its Ordinary. The *Apostolorum* shared grounds and facilities with the boys' orphanage, named "Nazareth." And Price sought to exercise the prerogatives of a religious superior over the other priests there. They generally conceded him that privilege, but the bishop did not. When Price and O'Brien had finally submitted the Apostolate to Haid for approval in 1900, the Ordinary had been reluctant to endorse the proposal at all. Apparently, Price proposed himself as founder, fund raiser, and "superior." O'Brien would be the chaplain, and Irwin's service would be as Price's assistant. "The Bishop in deep thought, raised his hand to his head as if to smooth back his hair from his forehead and said, 'Father Price, I am a practical man; I do not have any spiritual light from above that priests should ban together in community life.' "[87] The reservations of the bishop were based on a number of principles. Haid believed, of course, that secular priests had a different vocation than religious, and were not intended to bind together in communities. The vicariate could not afford to commit itself to giving three or more priests to a non-parochial enterprise, either; missionary needs were too great. Furthermore, as was theorized by Father Louis Bour, another of the vicariate priests, as Price proceeded through the various ventures and projects of his priestly career, Leo Haid lost confidence in the man's judgment; Price had persevered in his priesthood, but he had not shown stability in its labors.[88]

The result was that Haid, who reportedly "hesitated to oppose what might be a manifestation of God's will,"[89] neither gave permission for the *Regina Apostolorum* nor did he explicitly forbid it. From the bishop's Benedictine perspective, where a subordinate does "naught but that which is commended to him,"[90] Price should have relinquished his ambitions for a community of priests. But Father Price, educated by the Sulpicians rather than the Benedictines, understood obedience differently, and accepted the bishop's failure to forbid the work as a tacit indulgence to begin it.

The struggle between these two men was archetypical of the problems in Haid's style of leadership. His Benedictine approach was never understood by his secular clergy, and the results—though apparently innocent on the part of the priests—infuriated the bishop. Irwin and Woods both recorded this conflict: "What Father Price wanted was a command—what the Bishop would give was mere advice or counsel."[91] Leo Haid "would not order," then he was "irritated when his counsels were not followed."[92] From Price's perspective, he was not disobedient; he had received advice, not a command, and he treated it as advice, not a command.

Vincent Taylor, who was Haid's successor on the abbatial throne, later agreed that Frederick Price was probably not deliberately disobedient, but neither, this abbot noted, did the priest do what his bishop wanted of him. As Taylor perceived the situation, Haid considered Price irresponsible. Abbot Vincent, speaking for himself, considered the Nazareth priest "very strange." The problem was pride rather than disobedience, however, and Price's fervor was somehow linked to a proud venting of his own will. "Some self-willed people" Taylor stated, "are very zealous [only (?)] when following their own will."[93]

So Price organized the *Apostolorum*, and Haid declined to intervene. The bishop did not, however, consent to bless the cornerstone of the Apostolate's building for Price. He went to Nazareth in April of 1902, gave his benediction to the stone for the orphanage chapel, but according to Price, when asked to bless the building for the *Regina Apostolorum*, the bishop "omitted it through fatigue."[94] Nevertheless, Price's fraternal organization of priests was undeniably indulged by the bishop, who did not order it disbanded and even permitted its listing in the *Catholic Directory*. Thus the organization acquired legitimacy. But Haid did not recognize it as being more than a movement. No priests who might affiliate with the *Apostolorum* could be ordained for or incardinated into its precincts; they would be priests of the vicariate not the Apostolate. This left Haid with authority to transfer the men elsewhere—a power disputed by Price. It also meant that the members of the *Regina Apostolorum* did not owe Father Price obedience under the force of a vow of religion. Frederick Price was never constituted a "superior", in the technical sense, while in North Carolina.

Although the priest and the prelate had regular conflicts over personnel, it was not as significant an issue as it might seem, since of the men Price attracted to Nazareth, and whom he sent to Belmont to be educated, only one persevered. Father Price blamed his losses on the efforts of the Benedictines to undermine his ambitions,[95] while the abbot's perspective suggested that Nazareth was not attracting men with a genuine vocation. Indeed in 1910, when the *nullius* controversy was raging, Haid and Price were also quarreling over that one man who had persevered, George Andrew Woods. Price conceded that the candidate was to be ordained as a priest of the vicariate, then assigned to Nazareth. But Haid was reluctant even to ordain Woods, since the young man was virtually deaf.[96]

Unable to achieve official Church recognition for his *Regina Apostolorum*, Price had a civil charter created. It was formulated in terms that were intended to exclude Benedictine influence. According to Woods' account

> The founding and the ultimate aim for instance of the Apostolate Company was never explained to or ratified by Bishop Haid. The Charter of the Company, the By-Laws, the attitude of the...trustees all showed opposition to Bishop Haid's rights and wishes and it is likewise a fact of legal record that nearly all of the real estate was held *not* in the name of Bishop Haid as Vicar Apostolic but in the name of Thomas Price.[97]

And these land holdings and their buildings, which included the boys' orphanage, were substantial. There were almost four hundred acres, valued by Price at seventy-five thousand dollars.[98]

It was in 1908 that Price began the definitive shift from hoping to convert North Carolina, to a desire to evangelize the world.[99] This movement would eventually culminate in the creation of the Catholic Foreign Mission Society of America, popularly called "Maryknoll." By the next year the priest's depression and dissatisfaction with his labors were growing. "I feel greatly discouraged," he wrote in his diary, "all my men gone, and my spirit broken."[100] In the autumn he conceived a plan to evangelize the students at the University of North Carolina at Chapel Hill, but Haid declined to give permission.[101] Then in October, the priest decided that the goal of the Benedictines was not only to seize his property, but the whole of the Nazareth work.[102] In the following year, 1910, Thomas Frederick Price and Leo Haid reached the critical juncture in their turbulent relations.

At the beginning of May 1910, the bishop went to Nazareth, "disposed to criticize rather severely," according to Price, the plans for a new building at the orphanage. Haid indulged the priest's desires, however, on condition that there be no debt for the vicariate or abbey—the same standard he imposed on his priories and parishes. Even Price admitted that, "altogether the visit was highly satisfactory."[103] But by the end of that month he had heard through a friend in the Richmond chancery of the creation of the *nullius*, and the entente was at an end.[104]

Rumors had first reached Price in the previous autumn, that the Benedictines were seeking the privilege of a perpetual territory. He had inquired of Gibbons at that time, and the Cardinal claimed to know nothing of the effort. Therefore, as the issue resurfaced in 1910, Price believed that "nobody here seems to know of it." So he again wrote the archbishop in Baltimore, who he did not realize had endorsed the idea and even specified the enlarged territory of eight rather than six counties, complaining of the situation. This is to be, he told the Cardinal, "a great injury to the Church in North Carolina."

> It seems that the whole affair was engineered and brought to a conclusion without consulting one single person interested outside of the Benedictines. In fact it looks as if the whole move were studiously concealed from those interested. The history of the Benedictines in North Carolina has been a history of absorption of every thing possible. Steps of some kind should be taken.[105]

Gibbons, apparently, did not choose to dispel Price's mistaken impression. Then in June the news of the erection of the abbatial 'diocese' was made public and official; that announcement coincided with Haid's advising Price that the ordination of Woods, because of his impediment, was less than assured,[106] further arousing the priest's fury. In July, Price was increasingly disconsolate; he was "dissatisfied with my life and work,"[107] and he decided that his foreign mission endeavor needed to be directly subject to the Holy See, and not dependent on any one American bishop.[108]

In August, ten secular priests were summoned to Belmont for their annual retreat. All the vicariate priests could not undertake the spiritual exercises at the same time, of course, since that would leave the state unattended; thus some were brought to the abbey each year, and the rest made a separate retreat. Price was not among those who were to go to Belmont in 1910, but he went anyway.[109] Thus he was present on the morning of 23 August, when Felix Hintemeyer introduced the clergymen to the details of the new abbatial 'diocese', and explained how little difference, in terms of daily governance, it would make to them. Father Price was offended, and began wondering if it would be hypocritical of him even to attend the erection ceremonies in October.[110]

The next month Haid[111] and Price were among the North Carolina representatives to the Eucharistic Congress in Montreal. It was on this occasion that Price and the man who would join him as Maryknoll's co-founder, Father James Anthony Walsh, began seriously formulating the plans for their mission society. After his return to North Carolina, Price wrote Bishop Haid regarding the proposed missionary endeavor; the response was unclear.[112] So on 13 October, just five days before the erection ceremony, Price went to Maryhelp.[113] The next day, Abbot Leo agreed in principle to the opening of a seminary for the missions, presumably at Nazareth, leaving the priest "in an ecstasy of happiness," according to the Price diary.[114] Yet on that same day he wrote Walsh, "I know that Bishop Haid will never concede the necessary conditions in North Carolina."[115]

Despite his misgivings, Thomas Frederick Price decided to attend the ceremonies erecting the *nullius diocesis*. It was an unfortunate choice for the priest to make. He was dismayed at what he saw as unrestricted Benedictine ambitions not only being allowed to subvert the diocesan future and ecclesiastical integrity of North Carolina, but even being celebrated. "It has been a time of rather harrowing experiences," he wrote, and it "confirms me, if I needed any confirmation, in the necessity of getting out of North Carolina as quickly as possible and establishing my mission seminary."[116] He did not, however, want to leave the state without first seeking to avert the proprietary progression of Belmont Abbey and Leo Haid. "There is a storm of protest," Price wrote, "against continuing Bishop Haid, and the Benedictines and their rule ought to be ended."[117] The three Apostolate priests met at Nazareth on 20 October, but O'Brien disagreed with Price's intentions, and nothing was resolved.[118]

Then on the twenty-seventh, Price posted to his friend the Baltimore Cardinal a detailed evaluation of the situation in North Carolina. "The Secular Clergy are intensely indignant," he reported; thus he presumed to "[pour] out to you unrestrainedly my mind and heart." There were six principal points in the thirteen page letter:

> 1. Bishop Haid is held to be well suited for the position of Vicar Apostolic so far as his personal qualities are concerned, but he lives continuously separated from his Priests and people seldom going amongst them and is almost totally under the influence of the Monks. He never consults his Council and the Monks continually influence his actions and the works of the State. The Benedictines hold all the offices of the Vicariate. The Secular Priests who alone belong truly to the Vicariate feel very keenly that they are put below the Benedictines and made inferior to them. The Seculars are made to feel that they are tolerated only as sort of step children who cannot be well gotten rid of. His treatment of them at times has I think been very harsh....
>
> 2. As to the evident fact that the Vicariate has been subordinated to the Monastery: The Bishop does not come out of his Monastery and devote his energies to the upbuilding of the Vicariate but subordinates the Vicariate to the interests of the Monastery by remaining nearly all his entire time in it, governing and upbuilding it and teaching daily classes in it and giving only a fraction of his time and energy to the Vicariate—hardly a fifty at best—directing the Priests mainly by letters. The works in the Vicariate are made subordinate to Benedictine interests....
>
> 3. As to the upbuilding of the Vicariate: It is so clearly impossible for the Bishop to spend practically all his time in the Monastery, governing it, upbuilding it, teaching its classes and absorbed in its interests and at the same time to seriously upbuild the Vicariate and push forward Religion amongst these two million people that it seems idle to dwell on the point....It is a physical impossibility to be in two places at one time. It is a physical impossibility to be given entirely to two different works at one and the same moment....
>
> 4. Regarding the absorption of the resources of the Vicariate by the Monastery: So great is the tendency of the Monastery to absorb whatever is absorbable that Priests and people are very chary of allowing anything to come within the power of the Benedictines. For twenty-three years this absorption process has been going on and it is largely due to this that the Monastery and Belmont Church and College have been built up at the expense of the Vicariate—that is, by absorbing under one form or another moneys and resources that would naturally have flowed into the Vicariate had we a Secular Bishop....
>
> 5. As to the support of a Bishop: It is said by some that this Vicariate is not able to support a Bishop. I would respectfully point out to your Eminence that if we be given a truly Apostolic Bishop—and we want no other—that a question of this kind will never be mooted and that if we are to wait till we can support a Bishop of another kind we shall never have a Bishop of any kind to support as it is only with a truly Apostolic Bishop that we can ever hope to advance Religion in the State....
>
> 6. Another point which I think of great importance: The Benedictine rule has made itself so odious in North Carolina that there is a universal desire throughout the whole State to get rid of it....[119]

Price supported these six points largely with rumor, innuendo, and other stories he had heard and accepted in good faith, but which he was not in a position to substantiate. These included factors related to the territorial grant of 1891, the O'Donoghue and Lawrence Brown estates, the departure of Gross, and finances. The examples were unfortunate choices, since examination of the pertinent documents has virtually disproven his evidence; whereas, his charges alone are far less susceptible to opposing arguments.

His first point regarding Haid is largely correct. The Diocesan Consultors were rarely if ever convened, and the bishop preferred the company and the environment of his monastery. The second argument, also, is basically true in substance, though the subordination theme is questionable. The abbot-bishop was partial to his monastery, but the Vicariate Apostolic of North Carolina was not neglected; it too—like the monastery—achieved unprecedented stability under Haid's administration. If Price's reasoning holds, it could be charged just as accurately that the monastery would have grown more and had a better spirit had the abbot not been required to spend so much time outside his cloister. It must not be overlooked that when the Holy See created the double mitre, it ordained that both the vicariate and the monastery were denied a full-time head. For the third point, regarding the balance of time, the basic contention was valid, and the monks as well as the seculars criticized the bishop on this point. The absorption argument of his fourth contention is untrue. Neither entity, the vicariate nor the monastery, was successful before Leo Haid acquired the double mitre. It was after that distinction arose on behalf of the Catholic Church in the state that income, outside interest, vocations, and the promise of stability began to appear in an appreciable degree. It is not that one body grew at the expense of the other, but that prior to their union neither body was growing as it should. The fifth point, pondering the *cathedraticum*, is conjecture and can neither be proven nor disproven. The sixth, giving Price's assessment of public opinion, is a presumptuous generalization. And of course the fallacy that runs throughout Price's arguments is the image of the monastery and vicariate as competitors. Their Ordinary did not see them in that way, neither did the Holy See when it ratified the joint rule. It may even be the success of that dual jurisdiction that prompted the extraordinary provision of the *Bulla Erectionis* in 1910. Rather than competing against one another, Haid's two judicatures had won their success through their efforts in concert, focused by a single, mitred prelate. Indeed, perhaps the most peculiar aspect of the whole affair is that these complaints did not surface until the close of the most episcopally active period in Haid's career.

All of these points, Price contended, were opinions prevalent among the secular clergy of the Vicariate Apostolic. But he offered his own reaction, too.

> ...Their rule up to the present time has caused me to weep tears of blood and has proven a dagger that has stabbed my heart a thousand times. As to the future, I am convinced thoroughly that thousands of souls will be lost if the present policy be pursued and it seems to me that duty of the gravest kind before God to do all that we can to put an end to it as quickly as possible. That the salvation of a whole people two million in number should be made subordinate to the interests of a few Monks in a back-woods Monastery is so monstrous a proposition that I find it impossible to get suitable expressions to characterize it. That the vicariate of North Carolina should be made an adjunct to a Monastery sucking its life blood like a Vampire and built up largely out of monies extracted from it, that the Vicariate should have placed over it a Bishop of what is now practically another Diocese, who will reside continually out of it, whose attention and interests and work are almost entirely absorbed by other interests than hers, that this Bishop should be so placed that he can neither identify himself with the Priests and people of the Vicariate nor give but a small fraction of his time and energy to the Vicariate's interest so that it is impossible for him to upbuild it, that the salvation of two million non-Catholics should be placed under his jurisdiction when he is so absorbed by other interests that he can give them neither time nor work, that the Vicariate should be crippled by the continuous absorption of its resources and monies into a Monastery, that the continuance of all these evils is upheld under the false plea that North Carolina is unable to support a Bishop—all this forms a status of affairs against which I feel it my bound duty before God to work especially at a time when it is sought to bind the Vicariate hand and foot as long as possible to a policy certain to result in the damnation of thousands of souls.[120]

On 4 November, Price, Dennen, and Father Peter Marion appeared in Baltimore and presented a petition,[121] signed by themselves and the rest of the secular clergy in North Carolina.[122] Gibbons marked the document "unofficially received," but gave it serious attention. A copy was also deposited with the editor of the *American Ecclesiastical Review*, who preserved but did not publicize the document. The petition requested the immediate erection of the Vicariate Apostolic into a diocese, thus effecting a separation from the *nullius* diocese, and ideally forcing Haid, regarding whom "we bear our cheerful testimony to [his] personal qualities," to decide which single jurisdiction he would retain.[123]

This was a very promising approach for the secular clergy to take. It was virtually inconceivable that Rome, after promulgating the *Bulla*, would recall it and impose restrictions on the Benedictines. But the erection of a new diocese was possible, and would allow all sides a graceful extrication from what had become an uncomfortable situation. Unfortunately, Price could not devote his full attention to the matter by this time, because the focus of his concern had shifted toward the creation of Maryknoll. And no other priest of North Carolina had the contacts and influence to advance the cause as effectively among the hierarchy.

On 16 January 1911, as the proposed mission society kept the priest away from the orphanage with increasing frequency, Haid asked Price to submit a detailed report of the assets at Nazareth. The bishop still did not understand the degree to which the priest had sought to exclude his Ordinary from establishing legal possession of the complex; thus Haid acted with reference to his prerogatives and duties according to Church law, and in ignorance of the ramifications or the civil implications.[124] The two men also accepted on that day an agreement regarding Price's future. As he and Walsh created Maryknoll, Price was permitted by Haid to work outside the vicariate, but only on the condition that the Nazareth work continued and the vicariate incurred no obligations.[125] Apparently Leo Haid made no reference to the analogous situation of the bishop and the priest, each trying to cover two Church positions. In March Price circulated another petition, this one to go to Haid, but the other secular priests would not cooperate this time.[126] Then on 27 April, the Council of Archbishops in the United States endorsed the idea of Maryknoll,[127] after which Price determined to personally represent the cause in Rome, granting a welcome cessation of hostilities between Nazareth and Belmont. George Woods was appointed by Haid in June to be the director of Nazareth, and plans for the new building were halted.[128]

Apparently, it was not until 7 October 1911, that Father Price finally wrote Bishop Haid, explaining the legal status of Nazareth, and arguing that Woods could not serve as the superior. Price wanted Woods' services subordinated to his own role at the orphanage,[129] but Haid would not agree, and Price decided to leave the state definitively. Gibbons agreed to receive the priest at Baltimore, and in January of 1912 the incardination was finalized.[130] By April of that year, Price had convinced himself that he had been forcibly driven from his work in North Carolina.[131]

Thomas Frederick Price, with his prestige in the vicariate and contacts in the hierarchy, plus his antagonism and competitive spirit, had managed to destroy the Benedictines' elation upon their erection as a *nullius diocesis*. Far more significant, however, was Father Price's role in advancing a spirit of enmity in the vicariate that would color the remainder of Haid's life, and survive both men. In all charity, Price did not dwell on the antagonism with his Carolina Ordinary after his departure from the state, and there is little evidence that he worked against Bishop Haid during his Maryknoll years. The abbot, for his part, was pleased to see the Price situation subside, but he was left with the legacy of their struggle, a residue characterized by unwholesome animosity between the priests and their bishop, and a mindset that cast the monks and the secular clergy as competitors both for the bishop's attention and for dominance in the missionary effort of the Catholic Church in North Carolina. That tension did not evaporate with Price's departure, but at least his successor as the leader of Haid's opposition, Christopher Dennen, was gracious enough to content himself with reports to Baltimore, and to avoid direct confrontations with the abbot-bishop.

Although the Benedictines had not been allowed to savor their victory in acquiring the *nullius*, the Carolina monks had secured the exemption, and thus the security their abbot had so earnestly desired for the sake of their future. These two men, Price and Haid, were the two greatest missionaries of their age in the Church in North Carolina, and it is regrettable that their efforts were discordant rather than harmonious. This was Irwin's evaluation:

> It seems that it was necessary for a conflict of men to arise between the Venerable Abbot of an Ancient Order with its mellowed traditions, and the starting projects of a holy missionary whose heart was ablaze with fire of love for souls...[There was an] inevitable deadlock [between these] two most virtuous minds of different traditions and outlooks.[132]

Price's efforts created an upheaval that was never resolved in Haid's time; the priest fed suspicions that survived him by decades. Yet, Leo Haid was still willing to concede the sincerity of Price's intentions. He wrote this evaluation in 1921;

> Father Price was a pious self-willed, ambitious man. Without [exception] he would brook no contradiction, nor would he take advice where advice was sadly needed. I gave him a free field to work in—but he always worked according to his own eccentric notions. I put up with more from him than any Bishop should—but I gave him credit for good intentions—and these he certainly had in his own way.[133]

Virtually all commentators give Price credit for being obedient. He did not understand, it is suggested, Haid's approach to governance. The *Bulla Erectionis* for the *nullius*, the document that provoked the priest's ultimate contremps with his bishop, contained a passage upon which Price did not comment in his letters or petiton:

> We also desire and decree that if it should happen that anyone knowingly or unknowingly attacks this document as being tainted by deceit or surreptitiousness or nullity or by Our intention or by any other defect, however much juridicial or substantial, even from this that all who have or

> are presumed to have an interest of any sort in individual points have not
> consented to this, and the reason why all the aforesaid have occurred were
> in no way sufficiently examined and from any other heading whatsoever
> were noted, challenged, nullified, or controverted, they are and always will
> be perpetually valid and effective and acquire and obtain their full and
> entire effects, and must be observed inviolably by all to whom it pertains
> and if other attacks are made upon it by any authority whatsoever, We wish
> and declare that they are void and foolish.[134]

It may at least be conceded that Father Price was not obedient to
that.

a Carolina Diocese

As the post-erection controversy raged, there was more than
sufficient reason for the first alumni reunion for Saint Mary's College
to be delayed from 1911 to 1913.[135] The year 1911 was not peaceful
at Belmont. Much of the bishop's time was consumed just with
writing assurances that Maryhelp had not *requested* perpetual
jurisdiction over the vicariate.[136]

He wrote Gibbons on 28 January 1911, with a tone made
defensive by three months of controversy.

> I may here mention, what no doubt you already know, that in petitioning
> Rome for an *'Abbatia Nullius'* we did *not* ask that the Vicariate should be
> united to the Abbey, so as to make the Abbot *ipso facto* Vicar Apostolic. This
> was made a part of the *Bulla Erectionis* without our knowledge. All I ever did
> was agree to perform the duties of Bishop whilst I was able. That my
> succesor as Abbot was to enjoy the same honor and be burdened with the
> like responsibilities, we never asked for, nor did we know this until, to our
> surprise, we found it in the Bull.[137]

The concern of the hierarchy, first expressed thirteen years earlier,
surfaced again. Leo Haid was made to appear as a prelate with
powerful connections in Rome, capable of winning extraordinary
favors and concessions to satisfy his whims. The linking of the *nullius*
and the vicariate seemed like incontrovertible evidence to support
that contention. Price circulated his opinions as he visited the bishops
of the province seeking to win support for the immediate suppression
of the vicariate and the erection in its place of a see with full diocesan
character.

Haid was forced into a difficult position by this controversy. He
did not want the union of the vicariate and *nullius* perpetuated, since
that condition re-established the confusion he had originally intended
to settle by the creation of the separated territory. Yet it would be

improper for him to apply immediately and directly for the offensive passage to be voided. A Papal Bull was among the Church's most solemn media of proclamation, and both prudence and etiquette forbad a suggestion that the Holy See might have acted unwisely in so serious a matter.[138] Furthermore, Haid was reluctant to act because he believed that the immediate promotion of the vicariate to diocesan status would be harmful to the spiritual welfare of the Catholics and the temporal welfare of the Church of North Carolina. Also it would be embarrassing for Haid to endorse the erection of a diocese now, because of his recommendation of the previous spring, submitted to the delegate through Hintemeyer, against such a move.

It was another sad predicament for the Catholic Church in North Carolina. Its few, scattered adherents had been shunted for a century between the territory of other Sees and the divided attention of its Ordinaries. It had been part of the dioceses of Baltimore and of Charleston; once the Vicariate Apostolic was created, no Ordinary had been allowed to offer exclusive attention to the North State for the full length of his episcopate. Gibbons added Richmond to his duties; Keane had that diocese and the North Carolina Vicariate together from the beginning; there was less than a year for Northrop before Charleston was added to his reponsibilities. Then in Haid's case, it was the vicariate that was appended to his previous mitred duties. Even some of the earliest schemes for a North Carolina diocese had not been centered exclusively in the state. One called for a Diocese of Norfolk, that would include Norfolk, Portsmouth, Petersburg, and Lynchburg in Virginia, and all of North Carolina.[139]

On 23 January 1911, Gibbons wrote Haid, advising him that action should be taken regarding the content of the secular priests' petition of the previous November. The Cardinal had submitted the recommendations contained in the document to the Apostolic Delegate, and those two prelates agreed that the erection of a North Carolina diocese would "not only bring distinction to the Church of North Carolina, but would also be a source of gratification to the Clergy and draw them with closer ties to yourself." Accordingly, Gibbons summoned Haid and the other bishops of the province to a meeting in Baltimore, on Wednesday in the Octave of Easter. The notice made clear the archbishop's intention that the abbot should head the new diocese and that the American bishops, including Haid, should endorse the request for erection. "I hope that Your Lordship sees no difficulty in the way of presenting the petition to the Holy See for the granting of the favor in question," he warned the abbot.[140]

Haid's response, however, was not compatible with the Cardinal's desires. Gibbons' theories went largely unchallenged, but the question of the Ordinary's salary had to be faced before such a petition could realistically be offered. Yet the bishop's position on this question was not precisely consonant with Price's representation of it. Haid agreed with Price, Irwin, and Dennen in the assumption that a secular bishop would receive a more generous *cathedraticum* than did the abbot. But what the priests did not seem to consider was the poverty of the Catholics in North Carolina. The faithful would give more for the bishop of a diocese than they were contributing to Haid's support, but because their funds were so limited, their contributions "would be at the expense of hard-working priests" whose income was already inferior to their needs, and "at the expense of [the] Seminary, Orphan, and other collections. It will certainly be some or many years before North Carolina can support a Bishop along with its other necessary duties." The abbot noted his own good fortune as the prelate of the state, since "I need not trouble [them], as I have my Abbey to fall back upon."[141]

While the bishops prepared for their meeting and Price was engaged with the creation of his missionary society, Christopher Dennen met with Haid. These two men decided that in the bishop's annual Lenten letter, usually reserved for a statement of seasonal regulations, an explanation would be given of the disputed clause in the *Bulla Erectionis*. The abbot committed himself to asking the bishops at the provincial meeting after Easter to agree to erect North Carolina into a diocese upon his death or in 1914—by which time suitable preparations could be made—whichever came first. Father Dennen immediately informed Price,[142] and wrote Gibbons, sending a copy of Haid's letter.

> May I suggest that your Eminence keep this letter so as to be able to remind Bishop Haid of the agreement should it be necessary. I am satisfied he will do all he says. But We [sic] have every reason to fear some of his monks may change his mind.

Despite his misgivings, however, Dennen did endorse this plan as the "best solution."[143] After the Lenten letter appeared, Father Dillon wrote Haid to apologize for the "misunderstanding regarding the Papal Bull."[144] Woods also apologized, and offered a pledge of loyalty.[145] Father Barton, not wanting to be on the losing side, had already written to Price endorsing that priest's efforts,[146] but now wrote the bishop criticizing Thomas Frederick Price and suggesting his own obedience, constancy, and loyalty to Leo Haid.[147] This letter was opportune in an additional way, as Father Price and Bishop Haid were then arguing over the idea of Barton being assigned to the *Apostolorum*.

Father O'Brien addressed to the abbot-bishop a lengthy letter arguing that when the new See was erected, Leo Haid should agree to be its Ordinary, and take up residence at its cathedral. He further proposed that since political influence was so important in the modern Church, Raleigh rather than Wilmington should be the seat of the diocesan territory.

> I do not think that the Church in the capital city can much longer stand the strain under which it is grieving. Nothing less than your presence there can stem the tide, calm the troubled waters, deepen the love of the clergy and hold fast the loyalty of both clergy and laity.[148]

But the correspondence regarding the Haid proposal was not entirely favorable. One dissenting voice has been preserved: that of Frederick Price. That priest had consulted a canonist, and was convinced that "no matter how sincere and true your purpose may be (which of course cannot be doubted)" the erection had to take place immediately. Once again, Price was writing on the basis of hearsay, and had confused the issues. The priest had understood only the three year delay, and had overlooked the fact that the proposal called for the bishops of the province to commit themselves to the erection of the new diocese. Price misunderstood, thinking Haid was seeking to commit his own successor to that policy and intention, an impossibility canonically. "It is painful for me to write this to you," Price assured Haid, "and I do so only under a sense of duty."[149]

Leo Haid was exasperated. There seemed no way to please his priests, especially Price. When the bishops held their provincial meeting, all of Frederick Price's recommendations were approved. The Holy See was asked to erect North Carolina into a diocese immediately. The territory of the jurisdiction was to include the entire state except for the eight counties of the *nullius diocesis*. The See of the new bishopric was to be Wilmington, North Carolina, Price's hometown. But the bishops also announced their desire to see Haid appointed the first bishop of Wilmington. That prelate, however, responded that he would agree only if he retained both his monastery and the abbatial diocese.[150]

The controversy and its manifold entanglements drained the bishop, leaving him discouraged and resigned to whatever fate Rome chose to assign him. The only demand that he expressed with constancy was his intention to keep his monastery. To the primate, he wrote

> The *Bulla* uniting the Vicariate to the *Abbatia Nullius* caused much
> dissatisfaction among the Bishops of the Baltimore Province and also
> among the Secular Priests of the Vicariate. The Holy See will be asked to
> raise the Vicariate to a Diocese, with Wilmington as the Bishop's See. The
> Cardinal and all the Bishops and Priests also wish that I should be the first
> Bishop; I suppose this will be necessary, so that the expenses of the Bishop
> for some years at least will be less by me remaining in the Monastery.
> Perhaps you have already been notified. The whole affair caused me much
> trouble—but it may be for the best, as the future Abbot will have sufficient
> work of his own here....

The endorsement on this letter was more revealing than the
message. *"Episcopus"* was gone, and the signature had reverted to
"Leo, *Abbas*."[151] With this meeting of the bishops, Haid began to shift
his perspective again. The disloyalty of his priests, the innuendo to
which he was subjected, the opprobrium that surrounded him, these
all expressed to the abbot-bishop a sense of failure and defeat. So
great was his resignation by the spring of 1911 that he had even cast
his vote with the majority, putting the bishops on record as
unanimously endorsing the erection of the See of Wilmington, North
Carolina.

The Apostolic Delegate was so surprised by Haid's vote that he
wrote the abbot begging a clarification, and cautioning against
perjury for the sake of peace. "Now, when I saw you previous to this
meeting," he said, "you expressed yourself very clearly as being
against the said erection of the Vicariate into a diocese. I therefore
request you to inform me in conscience in regard to this important
matter."[152]

Gibbons also took note of Haid's dejection, and was careful to
mention his own misgivings about the request for a North Carolina
diocese. Nevertheless, like Haid, the Cardinal believed he "was
naturally obliged to accede to the wishes of my colleagues."[153] The
petition from the American bishops to Pius X was submitted on 31
May 1911.[154]

For the summer, Abbot Leo tried to expedite construction work in
Wilmington. The magnificent church of Saint Mary was being
erected, and since it would be the cathedral of the new diocese, it
needed to be completed post hast so as not to delay the enthronement
of the new Ordinary. And Cardinal Gibbons had already announced
that for this diocesan erection, he intended to be present.[155]

But that was not to be. Saint Mary would never surpass the rank of
a pro-cathedral. For the Sacred Consistorial Congregation of the
Roman curia, the body to which the Holy Father referred the
petition from America, spent little time with the document before
judging it premature. Cardinal De Lai officially "delayed" the

erection of a North Carolina diocese on 17 August 1911. The Apostolic Delegate wrote identical letters to Gibbons and Haid on 1 September.

> ...Cardinal De Lai, Secretary of the Sacred Congregation of the Consistory, has informed me that after a full consideration of the proposed erection of the Vicariate Apostolic of North Carolina into a Diocese, the said Sacred Congregation deemed the project premature, and accordingly gave the response, *Dilata*''.[156]

Gibbons wrote Belmont, this time expressing pleasure "that the matter has been deferred."[157] The archbishop also informed Price of the verdict.[158]

In June Fathers Price and Walsh had won Roman approval for their proposed seminary for the foreign missions. Receiving that endorsement, while facing the effects of the rejection of the North Carolina diocesan petition, Price began to think of centering his labors elsewhere. "It is pretty clear I will be forced out of the state," he confided to his diary nine days after hearing of the *"dilata."*[159] Price returned to North Carolina in the early fall. Haid wrote him on 4 October; Price responded on the seventh. They disagreed on virtually all issues, especially Haid's insistence upon control of Nazareth. The bishop maintained that the diocesan orphanage for boys was not a private enterprise of Price's. The *Apostolorum* was virtually defunct by this time anyway, and of no interest to the bishop. The priest did make one last effort to have it styled a quasi-religious order, however, with himself as major superior, and someone else as the local head. "It would be a position somewhat analogous, I suppose, to that which [the prior] in Richmond occupies in regard to you and the Diocese of Richmond,"[160] he suggested. But Haid had already appointed George Woods, the man who he had thought would be the most pleasing candidate to Price, to head the Nazareth orphan asylum. The bishop was unwilling to negotiate further. On their last point of contention, *Truth* magazine, Leo Haid recognized the priest's ownership, and allowed its sale. Price left the vicariate, achieved his incardination into Baltimore, founded the Catholic Foreign Mission Society of America, reportedly made great strides toward sanctity, and died of appendicitus in 1919 in the oriental missions.

nullius Diocesis

The erection of the *abbatia nullius* seemed to be both the summit of Leo Haid's career and the impetus for its dissolution. It served also to abruptly terminate his active missionary period, which in one decade had brought the state to the verge of diocesan status, only to see that honor "delayed" by the lack of evidence that the people would support the Ordinary. This decade had also shown, of course, how true was the priests' contention regarding the benefits to be won by a full-time bishop.

For Haid the reception granted his *nullius diocesis* seemed a personal as well as a professional criticism. He had spent twenty-five years in North Carolina. In that time he had built a vigorous monastic institution, a boys' college; he had sacrificed himself and his monks for a Catholic vicariate that was finally strong, had grown at a remarkable rate, and which for the first time in its existence of more than forty years was showing the stability that was a necessary prologue to diocesan status. But his clergy seemed to ignore those achievements, and blame him for fulfilling the duties Rome had imposed. "Where one leads *well*," he had written in the year of his episcopal ordination, "others may safely follow."[161] But time had not justified that early confidence. And at age sixty-one, he found that the priests of his diocese did not approve of his work. There were statements of admiration for him personally, but his files show not a single letter that endorsed his policies and his administration, or even recognized the sacrifice and effort of the past decade. The hierarchy too was suspicious, and lent him no support.

The platitudes that surrounded his abbatial jubilee had also fallen short. They had said to him

> Since, with that *"Crescat"* spoken long ago,
> Men have been made to labor and to love;
> Working for God,—a multitude, yet one.
> So His Disciples everywhere have done:
> Knowing not fear nor pain, nor counting loss;
> Planting the Faith, commanding it "To Grow";
> Tending His flocks, counting all else as dross.[162]

He had heard all the conventional praise of such occasions, but he did not accept its veracity. Leo Haid had accomplished for his abbey what no other American abbot had achieved: a separated territory, ultimate exemption, an *abbatia nullius*. He had also freed his monks from debt. There were the independent daughterhouse, three dependent priories and schools, the college and seminary at Belmont with its magnificent buildings. Yet the abbot realized that somehow, inadvertently, he had also drawn upon himself and his monks a virulence and scorn that compromised success and cast it as the fruit of the abbot's villainy. His monks had the care of almost six thousand five hundred souls in three states, more than three hundred students, and they were chaplains to six convents of sisters. Yet they stood accused of trying to destroy the progress of religion in North Carolina.[163]

The last years of Leo Haid's life were quieter. He returned to his monastery and began to practice the seclusion of which he was already accused. For the years that were left to him he decided to give his attention primarily and finally to his monastery, and to the special monastic character of which he had dreamed twenty-five years earlier. But after ten years of intense missionary labors, and a decade of training the young monks for the duties incumbent on priests, the abbot did not find the old spirit still dominant. His remaining years were consigned to witnessing a temper he did not fully understand, but which he knew he had helped implant. Yet there as in the vicariate, he had not the strength to fight what he could not comprehend.

Confused by the ceaseless changes with which he had been forced to contend in life, Bishop Haid wrote Father Felix Fellner, O.S.B., at Saint Vincent, "You historians [will] have a big job before you if you wish to get history straight."[164]

Chapter VIII:

the Dean

Leo Haid had an unremitting devotion to the Virgin Mary. She was the patroness of his abbey and college. In 1895 he won from the Holy See the right for his monks to celebrate her feast as a double major under the title of Lourdes. There was the pilgrimage shrine. Her statue stood before the College Building, atop the monastery portico, and in the Abbey Cathedral, where the high altar was dedicated in her honor.

The Catholic Church assigned many titles to the Mother of God. These were collected in the Litany of Loreto, which was used by the monks during the annual Marian month, May, as part of their devotions in the grotto. From these titles, more than four dozen in number, Leo Haid identified "Virgin Most Faithful" as the one he found most appealing. "Among all the qualities which gain and keep our love and respect," he had told the seminarians at Saint Vincent, "there is perhaps none we value higher than fidelity."[1] And he was deeply pained when, after the diocesan controversy had finally subsided in 1912, he concluded that he had devoted himself to men who had not been faithful, who had proven disloyal, and who seemed to him self-serving, self-willed, and proud. The title "Most Faithful" seemed an inappropriate epithet for his priests, and the bishop rued the fact that he had not inspired in these men the virtue he most admired.

Resuming his full teaching schedule, and seeking to maximize his time at the abbey, Abbot Leo found affairs in good order. Father Thomas was a gifted educator who, like the abbot, believed in the necessity of sound paedeutics on which the boys' college studies and environment would be built. Oestreich sought to integrate Haid's theories with solid educational, theologically founded, disciplined practices. And the school he had developed pleased its abbatial president, and secured for Thomas Oestreich the longest tenure of any rector during Haid's reign.

Hintemeyer's work in the monastery was equally satisfactory. The prior shared his abbot's belief in the necessity of keeping the monks busy. But he improved on that standard by more clearly focusing the monks' activity. Haid tended to fragment the attention of his workers. Much as he had made his abbey responsible for diverse schools, parishes, farms, and monasteries in three states at once, so too would he assign individual monks to countless and disparate tasks. Felix Hintemeyer, however, saw that assignments were better oriented. Ridding the brothers in particular of the factotum orientation that had characterized their daily labors, Hintemeyer invested in individual workers the level of trust and responsibility the abbot reserved for his priors and rectors. Father Felix, for example, assigned a single brother to take charge, as a continuing duty, of the poultry farm; there was one man for the dairy, another for the swine, for the kitchen, the abbey's printery, and so forth through the various jobs; then the younger and less experienced brothers, clerics, and lay workers supplied services wherever help was required. With Hintemeyer's system both morale and efficiency were raised. And the greater responsibility assigned to the individual monks encouraged their stability and solicitude, also.

Prior Felix had also served the abbot by maintaining the discipline of the monastery. This reflected his own professional maturation as prior, a position in which his success had not been immediate. Hintemeyer was only twenty-seven when he took charge of the daily administrative tasks of the cloister. Except for the brief tenure of Father Roman, the abbot had not previously delegated internal administrative duties. So Hintemeyer started without precedents, example, or experience at his disposal. The monks were aware of these hindrances that confronted the young prior; they also knew that the abbot had only apponted a prior as a reluctant step, necessitated and imposed on him by his episcopal duties. Then too, the choice of Father Felix for the position was not at first warmly received. Hintemeyer's nomination was presumed to have proceeded from his role as a school monk, whose intellectual orientation made him an unlikely choice for extended missionary assignments, and thus also made him an appropriate candidate for being present to fulfill the responsibilities of running the monastic cloister. Yet Hintemeyer's appointment as prior still showed the abbot's usual wisdom for placing monks in assignments that would develop and enrich their natural talents. Father Felix's "quiet observance of the *Holy Rule*," the abbot noted, and "his charity towards all, have broken down a certain dislike which some who never understood him had against him." Hintemeyer had immediately established an edifying and wholesome "influence over the brothers" at the abbey. And like Father Patrick, who was procurator of the abbey when Hintemeyer entered the prior's office, Father Felix was recognized as "a good religious with sound sense and indifferent to foolish fault finding. On the whole I am very well satisfied."[2]

Yet it was loyalty that Leo Haid admired above everything else in his prior. "A faithful man," the abbot said, "is indeed invaluable; in fact it is impossible for us to imagine a perfect man unless he is especially a faithful one."[3] As that quality became increasingly evident, the abbot had been drawn with appreciative affection to his prior's friendship. There he found the stability and fidelity, the support, shared interests, and the common love of God, the Order and the Abbey that Leo Haid found so seldom in others. And Hintemeyer's loyalty to his abbot was impervious to challenge. Even when he disagreed with Haid, as in the dispute over the territory offered for the *nullius*, Felix Hintemeyer had not deserted his abbot. The man's devotion, in Haid's perception at least, even seemed to proceed from the proper font: not a personal attachment to Leo Haid, instead it flowed from Father Felix's Benedictine observance and his monastic commitment. "The foundation of all loyalty," the abbot believed, must be "personal service of God."[4] And that was precisely the ordering Haid found in his prior. At this time, when so many of the people around the bishop seemed disloyal, this friendship lent him its greatest support.

Hintemeyer's contribution during this period is especially remarkable because it came at a point when the scope of his activities was particularly broad. In the earliest days of their association, Haid had resumed primary administrative responsibility whenever he was in residence at the abbey. But in the first decade of the twentieth century, Father Felix had been invested with virtually complete liability for daily administrative tasks, a situation comparable to the role filled by the priors working in Bristow and Savannah. Though Leo Haid resumed a more active role domestically and particularly in the college after he began curtailing his missionary work in 1912, he left Father Felix's responsibilities unimpaired. Indeed, as the prior noted the abbot's shift toward greater attention to his interior life, and as the prelate's health began to decline, Hintemeyer began shielding Abbot Leo, seeking to insure his health and felicity by relieving him of all unnecessary burdens. He used his authority as prior in the monastery and as Vicar General in the *nullius* and vicariate to insure that the abbot's increasing needs, both spiritual and physical, might be met.[5]

But the prior also turned increasingly to his duties in the schools and to works of charity. In the seminary his assigned classes concerned dogma and canon law. In the college his specialities were languages and philosophy. His charity functioned both inside the cloister and out. The priests and brothers who had difficulties commonly turned first to the gentle prior of Belmont.[6] This was not only because of his "influence with Bishop Haid;" he was also publically praised for "ever [extending] a kindly word to those in trouble, earnest advice to those in doubt, and a generous hand to those in need."[7] Outside the cloister he gave himself to the welfare of the sisters of Sacred Heart Convent, and devoted himself to the orphan girls there, giving time, attention, and even writing little morality plays for their benefit.[8] Then after the Great War, he expanded his attention to include relief work on behalf of European countries. All of these works and interests reinforced the abbot's regard for his prior. And because the priest also showed that most precious quality, fidelity, even the separation caused by Hintemeyer's expanding interests did not limit or inhibit the abbot's trust of and friendship with Father Felix. This was the man upon whom the abbot knew he could always rely.

A typical example of Father Prior's facility for bringing his regard for Haid into virtually every aspect of his activities occurred at the Alumni Reunion of 1913. Father Felix was instructed to prepare and present an elaborate and lengthy stereopticon exhibition for the Old Boys, regarding the history of the abbey. At the conclusion of the presentation, the event which began and was to set the tone for the whole convocation, there appeared on the screen a portrait of Bishop Haid. "Under his guidance," the prior-narrator said,

> all this has been accomplished. To him under God this progress must be attributed. When he came South his coat-of-arms was inscribed, *Leo Vincit* ["Leo conquers"]. Having witnessed his conquest of ignorance, bigotry and indifferentism, every Saint Mary's student, past or present will join me in voting to have that inscription changed to *Leo Vicit* ["Leo has conquered"].[9]

Of course the surprised and humbled abbot immediately found himself the object of a standing ovation from the monks, students, and Old Boys. The prior had won for Haid precisely the outpouring of respect and devotion that he believed the man deserved, and with which he so often tried to support and encourage his abbot. The Boys found their pride and nostalgia regarding Saint Mary's College focused on its abbot-bishop-president, Leo Haid. And the unsuspecting object of all this attention had received some small evidence of the love and faithfulness he so seldom observed.

One task which the prior may have accomplished too well for his abbot was the creation of the increasingly parochial interest of the monks. Priestly training dominated the fraters' formation by this time. And zeal in the missions was emphasized and encouraged. Part of the ease with which this spirit achieved its rapid ascendency proceeded from the altered ethnic composition of the monastery. Except for the brotherhood, the dominance of Bavaria-born and German-American monks had waned. The greatest numbers among the men who entered Belmont Abbey in the first quarter of the twentieth century came from Irish stock. And though neither the abbot nor his Bavarian-born prior seems to have presumed to theorize about the fact, both men noted that these Irish-Americans were oriented more toward the active and priestly pursuits of the external apostolates than had been their Bavarian predecessors. To a significant degree, this unexplained phenomenon had smoothed the abbey's internal shift of emphasis in the 1910's. And with the usual ability of activity to monopolize attention, it had become a fully constitutive element in the character of Belmont Abbey. Claustral duties, of course, maintained at least a theoretical prominence, but after the prayer, hospitality, and formative duties that implied, only the schools—especially Belmont Abbey College—outranked the missions.

Unfortunately, Frederick Price and the vicariate clergy had succeeded in undermining the abbot's commitment to monks in missionary work, by casting aspersions on its quality and selflessness. At the same time, however, Maryhelp's monks were still resolved to meet the demands of this work. This left Haid with an uneasy situation, which he was not sure he had the strength to amend. The monks expected, as Hintemeyer had told Dennen in 1910,[10] that with the creation of the *nullius* they might allow their vicariate activity to recede, in favor of a clear focus on the territory of the *abbatia nullius.* But in the face of his secular clergy's disfavor, Leo Haid had rethought the wisdom of monks undertaking vast missionary responsibilities. And he returned to the abbey intending to encourage the old, pre-1900 spirit. But the work of the past decade had been implanted in his monks far too well for another change to win favor and support. The spirit and character had been genuinely altered by a decade of missionary emphasis.

In the abbot's evaluation, however, concentrated missionary activity was not an immediate goal. So he sought to restore the old spirit by subtly influencing the monks through his power for making assignments. Thus he adopted toward the territory of the *nullius* a policy only slightly less benign than that which had predominated in the 1891 counties. The spiritual needs of the Catholics were met, though primarily through non-resident monk-pastors who visited their missions on Sundays and Holy Days. McInerney supervised some small-scale church construction, too. But there was little evangelization. The monk-priests were assigned to parochial more than missionary service in the abbatial 'diocese'.

The limits of the monks' liberty for daily pastoral work were strengthened further by the needs of the college, and of the priories and their schools. Despite relatively stable vocations, personnel resources were always limited and the abbey's manpower was utilized to the maximum possible level. The abbot was even able to win an official endorsement of sorts from the monastic Chapter for his cessation of the abbey's expansionism. A policy statement was issued in 1915, in response to an invitation from the Diocese of Superior to work in its territory.[11] The resolution, approved on 18 January, said that "Belmont Abbey absolutely refused to make or accept any Foundation outside the Southern States."[12] This statement served to shatter precedents: the 1920's became the first and only decade in Haid's abbatial career when no new monastery was established by Maryhelp. He had sent his first monks to Florida in the 1880's; Bristow arose in the next decade; Savannah was organized in 1902; then in the 1910's, Richmond had been refocused on the west end. But Leo Haid was older now and less certain of the wisdom of that tireless expansion. Both by temperament and disposition, he was no longer the *Projectenmacher* his past credits suggested.

Tired himself, and concerned by the heavy duties borne by his monks, the abbot even promulgated a new and more moderate horarium. It allowed the fathers to sleep a half hour later in the mornings, until a quarter past four. But Abbot Leo was not wholly comfortable with the new sequence, and was edified to see that Father Felix continued to arise according to the original schedule. The monks still had "rather a busy day" under the new horarium, Haid wrote the prior of Saint Vincent, "but I can't see how to lighten the work!"[13]

The Cassinese Visitators appeared at the abbey at regular intervals and professed general satisfaction with the quality of observance. The library, of course, was criticized, and silence was apparently imperfectly practiced.[14] Yet with equivalent frequency, the Visitators professed respect for "the very good spirit [that] exists here at the Abbey. Choir is well attended, the religious exercises are well made, fraternal charity is observed, and all are filially attached to their venerable Abbot."[15] And that last attribute, personal devotion to Leo Haid, was repeatedly offered as the quality the monastic Visitators perceived to be most singularly edifying. "We find genuine loyalty and deep attachment to the Superior," they noted in 1920; he is truly "the Father of the family." That spirit was, they said, "quite commendable."[16] Indeed the Visitators discerned that so much of the monastery's strength rested in the person and presence of the abbot, that they asked him to "caution Father Prior not to use unduly or imprudently the influence resulting from his many years of excellent service in his present position."[17]

Other than his restrictions through assignments, Bishop Haid did little to deal with the increasingly active tonality of his monastery, especially among the younger fathers and clerics. Instead he sought to inculcate into their training, a very particular understanding of their vows to a life of stability, *conversatio*, and obedience. This seemed, in the new age that those years surrounding the World War appeared to be, the way to deepen the monastic values his monks were to carry with them through all the aspects of their life, prayer, and work. In his monastic conferences the abbot suggested that the realization of the vows should be specifically associated by the individual monks with their loyalty to Maryhelp Abbey. He even characterized the obligation to poverty as an aspect of the common bonds the monks shared with one another and their monastery. Haid defined the practice of monastic poverty as "our mutual obligation to ourselves and [our] brethren—our Monastery, College, etc. All demand that we should be *helpful* members." He reasoned that the monks, by virtue of their vow of *conversatio*, already owned nothing, thus what they had to give was a fullness of common effort in support of the Benedictine spirit at Belmont. "God has given us a beautiful home," he said. "Our exterior work is progress for the glory of God, and [the] Order, and the welfare of our people—education of youth." This focus on Divine glory being realized through the Order and its works, then, was the only factor that could justify the scope of activities undertaken by modern monks.[18]

The abbot urged his monks to engage in a four-fold preparation for the more active apostolates that figured increasingly in the monastic life. First, the monks should seek training for "useful lives," especially for their teaching duties. And, he said, the monk must be willing to "Supplement what is wanting, etc., by personal application"—the same approach he asked of his college students. Then if one were ordained, further effort through reading, study, and self-improvement was necessary—not for selfish ends, but because they would "add to the good reputation of our Colleges, parishes, etc."[19]

The second focus of preparation was an intention to "[go] beyond our mere obligations—everywhere." Thus he chided those who were "sticklers for 'just so much.' " The third facet of preparation was a commitment to poverty, and the liberty it provided. But the fourth and ultimate level of the monks' preparation was intended to summarize all the others. It was, he said, simply "Love of our Monastic Home."[20] Just as he had sought and valued loyalty in the diocesan workers, he expected and encouraged it in his monks. And in both cases he emphasized that the fidelity was not owed to him personally, but to the greater interests he too served. "The fulfillment of our religious obligations has a threefold foundation," he told his Benedictine novices, "The Glory of God," was first, and the other two were merely dimensions of that, "our own salvation, and the welfare of our order."[21]

Increasingly in these last years, the abbot turned his attention to the necessity for his monks to truly "seek God" through the monastery, and to see that their labors were always oriented toward that goal. The monk's *labora*, he feared, could all too easily appear to be worthwhile in its own right, simply because of its charitable and pastoral nature. But the abbot emphasized that *labora* was primarily a means, not an end, and was to be used in educating and advancing the soul in Benedict's "school of the Lord's service." Through that approach, *labora* became not only charitable, but God-centered, and wise. This right ordering and clarity of understanding, he labeled "true wisdom." And as he had told the seminarians at Saint Vincent to remember, "when the soul is called before God's just judgment seat, all else will vanish, but [this] virtue [the practice of 'true wisdom'] alone, will plead our cause before God."[22]

The writings and conferences of this period reflect the pain of the abbot's efforts to grapple with questions of eternal mysteries and the fallibility he knew had marked his stewardship of the two mitres. He was frightened by the burden mortal life imposed on an immortal soul. It was a precarious balance, he said, with reason and free will on one side, while the principal weight on the other was the human soul: "Immortal Souls capable of knowing Life and death—choose!"[23]

Pondering his longing to touch on God he said, "I kneel in spirit beside our Saviour in the Garden—learn from him to be resigned to God's will, etc. When tempted to pride, etc. [I] picture to [the] soul Jesus, especially before the unclean brute—Herod."[24] He would ask his memory to "dwell on God's personal gifts and favors to me."[25] And he would urge his heart, which he associated with man's natural longing for God, to indulge its proper and ever present thirst: "Yes," he said, "the human heart *wants* a Father in Heaven."[26] Leo Haid turned his spirituality definitively in the last decade of his life toward the goal he had first set as a young monk-priest in 1878: "Almighty God, [as] the great Centre toward which all [persons] by their Creation tend."[27] But now, he believed, forty years later, he understood the full effort God required of him. "I belong wholly to God. I must serve him with my whole soul and body."[28]

He recognized the obligation to focus his whole life on God; he pondered his long years of work and effort, the commitments he had made for his monks, the evaluations cast on him by his secular priests. He considered this total service of God, imposed on him by his theology of "true wisdom", and he asked, "Have I done this; am I doing it now?" He instructed his novices to ask the same question of themselves, but to ask it earlier than had he, and to ask it regularly.[29]

And in the end, Leo Haid decided he had fallen short of the obligations God had given him. "My end must be in keeping with my soul;" that was the statement of his resignation to Divine judgement. The burden of man, and of his own spirit in particular, was that regarding God, "we were created to know, and not to reach." And "this," he said, "was to lose all."[30]

final Struggles

The only major journey Haid undertook after the erection of the *nullius* was his third decennial visit *ad limina* to Rome, in the summer of 1914. That year, in which the silver jubilee of his episcopal consecration was celebrated—belatedly, as usual—brought him fresh tributes from outside his jurisdictions: The Pope honored the abbot-bishop on 24 July by naming him an Assistant at the Pontifical Throne.[31] By 1914, increasing infirmity forbad traveling alone, so Thomas Oestreich attended him as companion and episcopal chaplain, while Hintemeyer stayed behind to govern the monastery. There was no "Grand Tour" this time. Together the two monks moved quietly through Italy, Spain, France, and Germany, as Haid saw Europe for the last time and Oestreich bought books for the college library. The two companions were present in Rome when Aidan Gasquet, O.S.B., received the official notification of his elevation to the Cardinalate.[32] And on 28 May, they attended the consistory where Gasquet and others—including Giacomo Della Chiesa, the man who would soon reign as Pope Benedict XV—received the red hat.[33]

Father Thomas also accompanied Bishop Haid when Pius X received the Carolina prelate at the Apostolic Palace on 19 May. The Holy Father's "words of encouragement were earnest and warm," the abbot told his prior. "He looks the Father and Saint he really is....He seems to forget all the grandeur of his exalted State, and remembers only his high dignity as representative of the meek and humble Jesus Christ." The Pope, "with fatherly solicitude" inquired about the monastery, so the abbot showed him photographs and the commemorative booklet from the Alumni Reunion of the previous year. Then, as Haid was about to leave, His Holiness summoned him back, and

> reached over on his table and handed me a red box with his coat-of-arms. When I opened this, I found a most beautiful pectoral cross of gold—a cameo figure of Christ in the centre surrounded by five splendid topaz stones. All he asked was to remember him and pray for him!...We left his fatherly presence as favored children.[34]

There were more honors five years later, in 1919, when the abbot-bishop commemorated fifty years of monastic profession. This time the Soverign Pontiff, Benedict XV, raised him to the ranks of the nobility, creating him a Roman Count, and sent a festive message and the Apostolic Blessing.[35] But Haid was older; the honors meant less, and his most valued gift for the celebration came from Gregory Diamare, O.S.B., archabbot-*nullius* of Montecassino, who offered Mass for the jubilarian on the tomb of Saint Benedict.[36]

The abbot of Belmont also had his usual quota of problems in this period. On 30 April 1917, a tornado destroyed the main barn at the abbey. But McInerney designed a splendid brick replacement,[37] wherein cows could walk through pseudo-gothic arches. That same year, Denis O'Connell advised Haid that he considered the Richmond Benedictines as scandalous as those in Bristow.[38] Father Dennen furtively accused one of his fellow missionaries of misconduct in the vicariate.[39] Then America entered the Great War, and the monastery's German-born monks became a disquieting presence in rural North Carolina; also, the war eliminated the possibility of importing any more brothers for the nonce; and disparaging conclusions were drawn from Haid's reluctance to let all the priests—both from the vicariate and the monastery—who desired military chaplaincies embrace that work.[40] While 1917 was certainly a particularly bad year, the Bristow epidemic was still to come; Richmond would continue to prove slow and costly in getting established; the vicariate priests regularly quarreled, accusing one another of various faults and improprieties, even reporting these to the Apostolic Delegate.[41]

For most of these problems, the bishop had little asked of him beyond mediation. But in 1922, when his attentions were distracted by the typhoid outbreak in northern Virginia and the brewing contretemps with O'Connell, a new effort arose in the vicariate, aimed toward the termination of Benedictine influence. And this effort was peculiarly effective—perhaps because Leo Haid never knew about it.

James Cardinal Gibbons had died in 1921. Leo Haid traveled to Baltimore for the funeral and even performed one of the absolutions for the archbishop.[42] The Cardinal's successor, a surprise choice, was Michael Curley, the forty-two year old, Irish-born Ordinary of Saint Augustine in Florida. Curley was an associate of Giovanni Bonzano, Falconio's successor at the Apostolic Delegation in Washington.[43] The new archbishop of Baltimore was a masterful fund raiser, a powerful homilist, and he earned a splendid reputation as a champion of Catholic education. Yet evaluations of Michael Curley have also been forced to note the lamentable faults that marred his reign in America's most prestigious See. These ranged from his general truculence,[44] to his reputation for a very noticeable disquietude and discomfort when among those whom he presumed to be possessed of a more facile intellect.[45] Moreover, this insecurity was complicated by the popular belief that rather than the nominee's worthiness, it was Bonzano's friendship that won the Baltimore throne for Michael Curley. He was not an ideal successor for a man of Gibbons' stature.[46]

If his dealings with North Carolina are a reliable source, Curley was also something of a politician. His chief compatriot in the North State was Christopher Dennen, who had been a virulent, although usually indirect, opponent of the Vicar Apostolic since 1910. Dennen had first met Leo Haid at Saint Vincent. "I remember the day when Father Dennen," the abbot-bishop said, "then a bright boy, came with others to Saint Vincent's College where I was secretary and chaplain."[47] He was studying as a candidate for the Diocese of Harrisburg then, but in the summer of 1891 Dennen transferred his affiliation to the Vicariate Apostolic of North Carolina.[48] Through the years of his priestly service, Christopher Dennen had proven himself a diligent missionary in the state, and he possessed the ability to win the confidence and trust even of his opponents. But 1922 was not the first time Father Dennen had caused trouble for Bishop Haid. Earlier in his career, the priest had led the opposition to the Haid-Drexel integration plan. Dennen's open hostility toward even so modest an effort toward racial balance aroused the oppugnancy and prejudice of the locals, especially at the church in Wilmington, where he was rector of the Pro-Cathedral. And it was Dennen's efforts, in those volatile struggles of the 1910's, that resulted in prolonging segregation among the Catholics in that city through the remainder of the bishop's reign.[49]

In the first year after Curley's translation to Baltimore, Dennen wrote to alert the new metropolitan to the history of absorption that marked the Benedictines' tenure in the South. It had recently come to the priest's attention that the Benedictines were seeking to expand the territory of the *abbatia nullius,* and Christopher Dennen was determined to see the proprietary policies of the Maryhelp monks terminated.[50]

Leo Haid did "wish to have the limits of the *nullius* changed somewhat before I die." And that, he admitted, created his primary interest in seeing who would succeed to the provincial throne.[51] When Curley was named to the See, a reasonably non-combative attitude toward the Order of Saint Benedict was expected, since he was not known to have caused many major problems for the Benedictines during his Florida tenure. Abbot Leo was also encouraged toward prompt action on the *nullius* by the propitious timing. It seemed fortuitous that the province should acquire a new leader on the eve of 1922, the golden jubilee of Bishop Haid's priestly ordination, an occasion worthy of special favors from the Apostolic See. Once again the public commemoration was postponed a year, and to all appearances the Benedictines were preparing for an effort similar to the one that had won the *nullius* in 1910.[52]

Without even testing the veracity of the charges or seeking their confirmation at Belmont, Dennen implored Curley's intervention in anticipation of the monks' efforts. And the archbishop, also without investigating the crimination or demanding substantiation, immediately allied himself with the Carolina priest's crusade. "I will never give my consent to the adding of Mechlinburg [sic] County to the *Abbatia Nullius,*" the prelate assured Dennen. Then, in the conspiritorial temper the circumstances seemed to beg, he suggested to the Wilmington pastor that the Benedictines might succeed in acquiring the territory without their archbishop's acquiesence. "They may petition Rome directly as they did before," Curley charged, apparently without checking either the history or the facts of the case, "and Rome may act, as it often does, without consulting anyone here." He instructed Dennen to alert the archbishop's friend, the delegate, offering a full account of the situation. All the secular priests of the Vicariate Apostolic should add their signatures to the document, too. But, he suggested, just "keep my name out of it." Nonetheless, the archibishop informed Bonzano himself the next week.[53]

Dennen sent his testimony, signed by the others as the archbishop had recommended, but it seemed at first to be an unwarranted accusation. The anniversary passed quietly in December of 1922.[54] In the spring of 1923 the jubilee was publicly celebrated,[55] but still no petition was drafted at Belmont; no request was posted to Rome. The delegate, however, kept the warnings of Curley and Dennen in mind. Indeed, Belmont Abbey was in his thoughts for other reasons at this time, since Bishop O'Connell of Richmond was making his move against Bristow that spring. Bonzano used the latter situation, which was not really a major concern for him, as a means for obtaining information regarding the *nullius* struggle, the consequences of which were more significant. It was for that reason that in March of 1923, Ignatius Remke found himself so cordially received at the Apostolic Delegation. The Bristow prior wanted to insure the status of his charge in northern Virginia; Bonzano wanted information regarding diocesan administration in North Carolina. Father Ignatius wrote the abbot, "Last Tuesday I called on [the Apostolic Delegate] in Washington. He was very nice and had a dozen questions to ask about you, the Vicariate, the *Nullius*, the monastery, etc., and said that he hopes to see the Abbey some day."[56] Apparently, both men were pleased by the meeting. Remke left with an assurance that O'Connell had no foundation for an appeal to Rome. And Bonzano heard enough about the leadership of Haid, the growth of the abbey, and the activities of the Maryhelp Benedictines, that he asked the metropolitan to submit a detailed report on the status of the Roman Catholic Church in North Carolina. Curley entrusted the responsibility for the task to Christopher Dennen,[57] and did not inform the Ordinary that the report had been commissioned.

Of course Remke had not given a report that was less than glowing regarding the vicariate, *nullius*, and their Ordinary. But he had been unable to take into account what the Apostolic Delegate had been primed to hear. Thus Father Ignatius emphasized the extensive, highly sacrificial work of the Benedictines, and the sterling progress they had made. He gave little attention to the secular clergy. The Bristow prior spoke of the *nullius'* territory, of the even larger grant from 1891. He related how the abbot-bishop was not only giving his time for the administration of the entire state, he was also running the abbey—a network of four monasteries, three preparatory schools, two farms, a college, a seminary, and an industrial school. To the Benedictine this was a description of success, sacrifice, and fervor. To the delegate, it was a rationalized version of the long history of acquisitions and absorption of which Christopher Dennen had already told him.

Archbishop Curley had requested Dennen to submit the usual statistics required for such reports—the number of Catholics, what percentage that was of the total population, the figures for Catholic growth. But he was also interested in obtaining the sort of evaluation Dennen was particularly anxious to give. Curley wondered if the growth of the Church seemed "satisfactory, and if not" he wanted to know why. The archbishop also wanted to learn "the exact status of the *Nullius*;" yet he requested that the information not come from the perspective of Church law, but "as understood by the priests of North Carolina." The archbishop called for a recommendation from Dennen, in anticipation of Haid's death, regarding whether the vicariate should be continued or a diocese erected. And he wondered if the *nullius'* territory—with "whatever number of counties"—would deprive the new bishop of necessary support. Finally he warned Dennen, "Think this matter over maturely...[and] leave personalities altogether out of consideration." Michael Curley also ordered the report to be submitted within thirty days.[58] Dennen, who did not consult with his Ordinary in preparing or filing this diocesan evaluation, needed less than half that time.[59] The effort was intended to prepare for a quick and effective attainment of their objectives as soon as Bishop Haid would die, and input from the Carolina Ordinary now, it was presumed, would only retard that objective.

While Dennen was working on his report for Curley, he received word that Leo Haid was sending Felix Hintemeyer to Rome the following year, as episcopal proxy for the fourth decennial visit *ad limina.* The bishop did not believe his own health could withstand the burdens of international travel, so the next ranking vicariate official, the Vicar General, had been appointed to take his place. "The Bishop's expression is in my opinion, evidence of feebleness and incapacity," Dennen advised the archbishop of Baltimore. "Please tell me what I should do."[60] The decision was that their report to the delegate should be prepared without delay.

In this case the priest's evaluation was readily substantiated. Leo Haid's health was declining, and his physical infirmity was inhibiting his work as a missionary bishop. The abbot's health had generally been good through the years, though the complaints increased with time. The most serious problem of his earliest prelatial years came in 1888, when "whilst laying out fences," he had suffered an unfortunate encounter with poison ivy, and found himself bedridden for four days and somewhat disfigured.[61] But such major episodes were rare, and he especially resisted any calls to rest or stay in bed. Yet time had brought rheumatism,[62] bouts of the grippe;[63] his teeth were never good;[64] he grew very sensitive to cold weather, and developed sciatica.[65] All of these were relatively minor burdens from which he could readily recover. In 1908, however, his physical deterioration began to accelerate. With only three teeth left in his upper jaw, he was annoyed to find even they hurt, so much indeed that travel had to be temporarily curtailed.[66] Then in 1909, two weeks before Falconio's visit, he fell ill—the malady pertained to his stomach, apparently, but was left unidentified in the official records—he was anointed, and reportedly almost died.[67] He was, however, sufficiently restored by the Solemnity of Benedict that he could preach as scheduled in the delegate's presence. Nevertheless, his doctor ordered him to take an extended rest that summer, which with great reluctance he endured in England and Scotland.[68] Haid was rejuvenated by this respite, nonetheless; he proved somewhat more prudent in his scheduling after that, and even accepted the necessity of having a traveling companion to assist him on longer journeys. Not until 1918, however, when he was weighted by the turmoils in Virginia as well as by his health, did he finally admit that "the burden is growing heavier and heavier," and resign himself to the necessity of a sempiternal retardation of his pace.[69] He was able to make only a fraction of his visitations in the missions that year,[70] and he never again resumed his full schedule. In 1920 he attended Peter Engel's jubilee in Minnesota;[71] then at the year's end he was ordered to bed. Yet he confided to Mark Cassidy, "I will not listen,"[72] and in the spring he was forcing himself to keep up appearances. He went to Baltimore for the Cardinal's funeral; in the vicariate he invested Christopher Dennen and others as monsignors—but he attended the dinner that followed that ceremony only after being promised there would be no speeches.[73] That year, Oestreich took charge of the burden of the bishop's correspondence, admitting to the archabbot at Saint Vincent that the heat too "is a little hard on him."[74] By 1922, Haid traveled only out of necessity, primarily for his episcopal duties. He even absented himself from the abbatial blessing of Engel's successor at Saint John,[75] the monastery that had given the bishop two such congenial spirits in Abbots Alexius and Peter. But both of those men were dead now. So were Wimmer, Zilliox, Gibbons,

Northrop, and Price. Saint Vincent had already buried two archabbots; three abbots of Saint John had gone to their reward; two had died in New Jersey. Before the year was over, Innocent Wolfe, the only abbot in the American Cassinese Congregation to persevere through a reign that exceeded the length of Haid's, would die. The old ways were changing; the faces were new. But the abbot-bishop of Carolina lingered. He became the "Dean", the longest reigning abbot in the Congregation; finally he became the longest reigning bishop in America, again the Dean. But he did not die. He was ill, but the release of death was denied him.

In Baltimore and Wilmington, the septuagenarian's decline seemed less the charge of a zealous apostolic career, than it was an opportunity for change. Dennen's report labeled progress through the last thirty-two years to be "slow." But had there been a "young, active Bishop with missionary zeal," he wrote, "we could be better advanced." The priest made no recommendation regarding the retention or dismemberment of the abbatial territory once Haid died, but the Benedictines should definitely be withdrawn from all the parishes outside that territory, he said; apparently, this included the counties from the 1891 grant, too, a right pertaining to the abbey's responsibilities in the state which Dennen did not elucidate for the archbishop. "Besides," he said, "all those places were founded by seculars." Dennen also accused Haid of misappropriation of funds. He had sent the delegate a copy of O'Donoghue's will, he said, to show how Saint Peter Church in Charlotte had been cheated. He did not mention, however, that he had failed to study the records of the estate, documents that showed the exactitude with which the will's provisions were met; he also neglected to advise the prelate regarding the Benedictines' possession of the parish under the provisions made by the Holy See in 1891; nor was there an explanation for the priest's failure to include the codicils to the O'Donoghue will among the materials forwarded.[76]

It was imperative that Haid's destructive hold on the Church in North Carolina be terminated, Dennen believed. But the Benedictines' power and influence in fighting this necessary restriction should not be underestimated. That, he believed, had been Price's error. Dennen told the archbishop,

> The year after the erection of the *Abbatia Nullius* Father Price induced all the bishops of the province to sign a protest to Rome[.] The late Cardinal Gibbons did not sign. The others received a rebuke from Rome. Cardinal Gibbons told Bishop Haid so, and he told me. So that part will have to be handled gingerly.[77]

The top priority for the moment, Dennen held, was to obstruct the plans that lay beneath Hintemeyer's journey to Rome. "The suspicion is," he explained, "that Felix will try and have the Holy See attach Charlotte and Mecklenburg County to the *Abbatia Nullius'* territory. This will cripple the work of the Secular Bishop[.] The Faith will suffer, and no progress can be made for the church."[78] "If Felix can get to Rome," he said, "without others being prepared, all previous work will be undone."[79]

Curley and Bonzano dined together a few days after Dennen filed his report. The archbishop warned the delegate that the Benedictines were in pursuit of Mecklenburg, and that they were prepared to offer Haid's episcopal resignation—in exchange for a compensatory appointment as a titular archbishop[80]—as their ultimate bargaining point for obtaining that territory. Michael Curley wrote the southern priest afterwards, "The Delegate gave me to understand very clearly that nothing of the kind would ever be done with his consent, but he added that as things are now, you can never tell when some influential person might bring the matter up in Rome and have something unforseen done." Dennen was advised to continue as he had been, and he should, Curley said, still be sure to "keep my name out of it."[81]

Quoting almost verbatim from the Dennen report, while appending some personal observations and signing his own name exclusively, the metropolitan filed his report concerning the Vicariate Apostolic of North Carolina and its abbot-bishop on 18 June 1923. This was his official recommendation:

> To my mind there is only one solution for the question and that is, on the death of the present Vicar Apostolic, to retain the *Abbatia Nullius* and to constitute the territory outside the eight counties of the *Abbatia Nullius* a Diocese. The Episcopal See might be placed in Wilmington, North Carolina, Asheville, or Charlotte.[82]

The report and recommendation were filed until their reactivation by the "death of the present Vicar Apostolic."

Felix Hintemeyer, carrying in his trunks the *relationes* for the visit *ad limina,* a draft for one thousand dollars intended for the Holy Father,[83] and reportedly a petition asking to amend the *abbatia nullius* with the territory of Mecklenburg County, left Belmont on 27 May and landed in Naples on 10 June 1924.[84] Supposedly he was authorized to bargain away all the other counties except Gaston, in exchange for Charlotte. Documentation of these instructions, however, apparently does not exist.

Before the prior left America, Curley had sent his Carolina cohort instructions to write the delegate immediately, should definite news of the Benedictines' ambitions for Mecklenburg be obtained. Bonzano was fully aware, Curley assured the priest, of "the whole situation of North Carolina." And it seemed already assured that once Leo Haid was dead the entire state, except for the abbatial territory, would be erected as a diocese.[85] Father Felix's itinerary called for him to journey from Naples to Montecassino where he would remain through 12 June. He was to spend four weeks in Rome, before visiting relatives in Bavaria.[86] In Naples he was met by Dom Mauro Inguanez, O.S.B., the guestmaster at the archabbey *nullius.* The Vicar General of Belmont "was so happy when he arrived," the Italian wrote, "but he looked tired already." Not planning to leave for Montecassino until three o'clock, the two monks stopped in a restaurant for luncheon. But in the midst of their meal, Hintemeyer fell ill, and Inguanez "took him in a motor to the nearest hospital," where the prior was diagnosed as having suffered a "light stroke," one that would necessitate less than a week being sacrificed for recovery. The archabbot of Montecassino was wired, and the prior of the archabbey went to Naples to oversee Father Felix's arrangements personally. A private room was secured. Inguanez took charge of those valuable trunks.[87] The patient even received a visit from the Duke and Duchess of Aosta,[88] who had heard of the presence of the illustrious invalid from America.

Hintemeyer did well during his first days of convalescence. He regained the use of the paralyzed right arm and leg quickly. His spirits were good. But nephritis set in, and eight days after the stroke the monks were still not permitted to move him to more private quarters either at the Duke's palace, another private residence, or the archabbey.[89] Then after two more days of hospitalization, the prior's condition began to deteriorate.[90] Conscious of what was happening, Hintemeyer urgently instructed the Cassinese monk to safeguard the trunks, "especially the *'Relatio'* of the Vicar of Belmont," and to sequester these items in the safety of Montecassino.[91] On Friday, 27 June, while attended by the prior and guestmaster of Montecassino, Hintemeyer received the Sacrament of Extreme Unction. "He was very calm," Inguanez wrote Belmont, "during his illness he never said a word of complaint. He told me more than once that he was happy to receive everything [that came] from the hands of Our Lord."[92] Indeed, Dom Mauro reported that Father Felix's "resignation to the will of God was really edifying. One of the servants who assisted him and for twenty years did not go to confession was so touched by the patience and good example of Father Felix that he went to confession and received Holy Communion."[93]

Hintemeyer was unable to speak after the twenty-sixth, but he did not lose comprehension until Saturday the twenty-eighth. That afternoon Dom Mauro Inguanez cabled the abbot-bishop of North Carolina, that at two o'clock the Very Reverend Dom Felix Michael Hintemeyer, O.S.B., D.D., age sixty-two, became the six hundred first monk of the American Cassinese Congregation to enter upon his eternal rest. The body was carried from Naples to Montecassino on Monday, 30 June. Felix Hintemeyer was entombed there at the motherhouse of the Order of Saint Benedict on Wednesday, 2 July 1924.[94]

At Belmont, Father Thomas, as the bishop's secretary, received the cable announcing the death of Father Prior, and it fell upon him to communicate the news to the abbot and friend of Felix Hintemeyer. Leo Haid received the announcement in silence; he did not even dictate a response to the cablegram. All the abbot ordered was a solemn requiem Mass to be sung in the Abbey Cathedral on the thirtieth, the day the body was to be taken to Montecassino, and presumably the day of interment. A stone in the prior's honor was later ordered for the Abbey Cemetery in Belmont.

Father Melchoir Reichert sang the requiem at Belmont; Father Nicholas Bliley served as deacon. The bishop assisted from the throne, attended by Fathers Thomas Oestreich and Maurus Buchheit as pontifical chaplains.[95] The abbot met the death of his friend with edifying peace and an uncompromised silence. He spoke only for the solemn absolution and blessing for his faithful coadjutor.

But if dignity prevailed at Belmont, with the abbot's silence and a succession of solemn liturgies on behalf of the deceased prior, there was considerable upheaval in Italy, where a variety of parties turned their attention toward the acquisition of Hintemeyer's luggage and the documents therein. According to Father Felix's instructions, the Montecassino monks had taken possession of the trunks, the two *relationes*, and the money for the Holy Father. Oestreich was aware of this, but failed to acknowledge the work of Inguanez.[96] That left the Italian monks unsure of Belmont's pleasure, and without direction for facing the interest that followed on the prior's death. Oestreich also did not inform Father Willibald Baumgartner, whom Haid appointed on 2 July to be Father Felix's successor as prior and Vicar General,[97] about the safety of the trunks. Apparently the new prior did not relinquish his parochial assignment in Winston and reach the abbey until three weeks after his appointment.[98] Then, in ignorance of where his predecessor's effects were, he wrote Father Gabriel Locher, O.S.B., at Sant' Anselmo in Rome, inquiring into the security of the luggage and its contents. For reasons that were not specified, he suggested that it was Oestreich rather than himself who was concerned regarding the whereabouts of these items. Locher replied that "no one here knows anything." One trunk, he recalled had reached Rome, but it had been removed to Montecassino after the death.[99]

Dennen too was interested in the luggage of the late Vicar General. He found that Curley was out of the country, however, so he addressed the delegate directly, asking that an effort be made to obtain the *Relatio* before it could be submitted to Rome by Haid's Benedictine agents. Dennen also wrote Curley, but only after his return to America. By this time, Father Dennen had inquired of Father Omer Matt, O.S.B., at the abbey, who "did the typing for Felix when he went to Rome and double crossed us as to the Vicariate." Thus he learned, as Fathers Willibald and Omer thought was true, that Sant' Anselmo possessed the precious documents.[100] Acquisition of those papers by the agents of the American hierarchy should effectively prevent their submission, it was thought, so appropriate investigations were initiated. Subsequently, as inquiries were so frequently being sent to Sant' Anselmo, the primate asked his secretary to implore from Montecassino an account of Hintemeyer's effects. But in the spirit of the Benedictine Order's treasured autonomy, the archabbot *nullius* of Montecassino instructed his guestmaster to advise the secretary to the Abbot Primate that "we did not care to write and give these informations [sic]."[101]

The American Consul at Naples also inquired into the destiny of Felix Hintemeyer's possessions, and the Italian government seems to have expressed its interest, too. It is unclear what influence was exercised for the luggage to receive so much attention from such divergent sources. But the inviolability of the Archabbey of Montecassino won a hasty retreat from each of the interested parties. Inquanez wrote Oestreich, "I answered and told [the American Consul] that Father Felix during his illness consigned to me all that belonged to him, with instructions to send everything to you at Belmont. In such way we [also] avoided troubles from the Italian Law."[102]

The trunks were not retired from prominence until the following year, however. In January, the two *relationes* were withdrawn from the luggage by Dom Mauro, and were finally delivered to the Vatican. The Holy Father received his honorarium, too.[103] The trunks did not reach Belmont until May of 1925,[104] a full year after Prior Felix's departure from America. But by that time interest in these bags and their contents had waned, as conditions in North Carolina had been significantly altered.

When the new prior had reached Belmont on the twenty-third, he found Bishop Haid seriously ill. Though the prelate had not been bedridden, he had consented to make only necessary public appearances. He had attended and granted an absolution at the requiem for his friend. A new, life-sized statue of Saint Benedict was blessed for the north courtyard at the abbey, and the abbot had received his last class of young men into the Order. But he did little else that required a public appearance.

By the third week of July, the abbot's deterioration had increased significantly. His gall-bladder was troubling him; there was the general infirmity old age had brought; and he had also faced the blow to his spirit, caused by the early death of his prior, his confrere, his friend, on another continent while in the service of Belmont Abbey.

In his last years, Abbot Leo had developed a theological precept that met the need for clearly focusing his spirituality on the Divinity. He adopted "this brief, but powerful motto: 'I go to the Father!' " That thought, that clarity of purpose, he said, enabled him to bear his cross and his crozier. He found that it helped him to "loosen the bonds which bind us to this world—It will sweeten our departure—make death less to be feared—even desirable as the separation of the veil which keeps us from the home prepared for us in our Father's mansion."[105]

On 23 July the Benedictine patriarch was confined to bed, and received the last Sacraments of the Church. They were administered by Vincent Taylor, the Benedictine pastor in Greensboro. Taylor had gone to the abbey to pay homage to his monastic father and reportedly had begged the prior for the privilege of anointing the abbot-bishop who had ordained him a priest and received his monastic vows.[106] The abbot was only semi-conscious after receiving the Sacraments.[107]

At thirteen minutes past nine, on the morning of 24 July, Father Nicholas Bliley, O.S.B., wired the three dependent priories, "Bishop critically ill. End expected any time. Received Sacraments."[108] Abbot Leo lingered through the day, attended constantly by the Benedictine monks of Maryhelp who were his children. He lived on while the monks recited Compline, and offered the canticle. He tarried in this life until at half past nine, on the evening of 24 July 1924, Leo Michael Haid, monk of the Order of Saint Benedict, became the six hundred second member of the American Cassinese Congregation to enter the rewards of eternal life.

He had written thirty years earlier: Upon his death there devolves on the deceased abbot the obligation to "pray for his widowed Abbey, and aid his former children. . . ."[109] Those children prayed that night at Belmont that this man whose great disappointment in life had been his creation by God with the propensity "to know [but] not to reach" his Lord, had finally found happiness, had finally fulfilled his aspiration, "I belong wholly to God;"[110] "I go to the Father!"[111]

The Widow Mourns

Brother George Poellath, O.S.B., sacristan of the Abbey Cathedral, spent the night preparing the testimonies proper to a "widowed" throne. On the morning of the twenty-fifth, the monks found the cathedral doors and the abbatial-episcopal throne draped in black cloth. The Missal was set for the first public requiem for the bishop. And Prior Willibald, now Apostolic Administrator of the abbey and of the vacant Sees of Belmont and North Carolina, appointed Father Vincent to offer that Mass.[112]

The body of the abbot was dressed in the vestment he had worn in December of 1893, when he celebrated that first Mass in the Abbey Church of Maryhelp. On Saturday, 26 July, at seven o'clock in the evening, the remains were translated to the cathedral, borne in procession to the place where they would lie in state. The Gastonia *Gazette* and Charlotte *Observer* gave daily coverage of the activities at Belmont, and speculated that Hintemeyer's untimely "death may have hastened Haid's."[113] Father Michael Irwin wrote Baumgartner expressing the same thought: "His sorrowful death [was] caused no doubt by a heart-breaking grief."[114]

On Monday, the monks gathered around their father's body and chanted the solemn Office of the Dead. Baumgartner then called for a Grand Silence in the monastery until after the funeral on the next day. The newspapers reported

> Daily, mourners have filed in and out of the large brick edifice, for a glimpse at a departed leader and to kneel for a few minutes in prayer at the altar. . . The only sounds have been the click of heels and now and then a suppressed sob.
> Outside the Cathedral, all has been quiet. The shuffle of feet on the sidewalks has been the only sound heard, as mourners have trod slowly forward along the walks leading to the church.

Inside the cathedral, Brother George sat vigil, and surveyed the strangers who had invaded his monastery's church to visit the Benedictine patriarch.

From Charlotte, Gastonia, even from distant points, have come women in silks and satins, not a few in tattered dresses, and men, some strong, others broken, who have moved silently past the candle-lighted bier in which rested the frail remains of a churchman so dear to the hearts of thousands. Dressed in purple robes, his bishop's mitre upon his head and a pectoral cross in his gloved hands, lay an American born of simple Pennsylvania parents who . . . rose to be Vicar Apostolic of the commonwealth of North Carolina and Dean of the Roman Catholic Hierarchy in the United States. In death as in life his face retained the serene calm of prelate and scholar.[115]

While the people processed, the monks too were busy. The priests offered Masses sequentially. Brothers prepared the bishop's grave, situating it beneath the figure of Christ on the huge crucifix which dominated the monastery's cemetery. As Vicar Apostolic, Leo Haid could have requested burial at the Pro-Cathedral in Wilmington, just as Gibbons had chosen to be laid in the crypt of his cathedral in Baltimore. As an abbot-*nullius*, Haid possessed the privilege of interment in the Abbey Cathedral. But Leo Haid, who had reminded his confreres years earlier that he was "a monk before I was either a priest or a Bishop,"[116] had asked to lie among his fellow monks. His grave was positioned so that the crucifix towered over his remains; his priests' graves were to his right, the brothers' to his left. The grave of Jeremiah Joseph O'Connell was at his feet, to the left. To adorn the bishop's grave, Michael McInerney designed a marble and granite tomb, inscribed with the abbot's dignities and the three coats-of-arms he had used. The insignia of his office, in relief, appeared on the body of the monument, crossed over the vault.[117] McInerney's design eloquently showed two croziers at odds.

For his funeral on Tuesday, 29 July, the Dean of the American hierarchy[118] was honored by the presence of his fellow bishops, Hugh Boyle of Pittsburgh and Patrick Barry from Florida. The Ordinaries of Richmond,[119] Charleston, Baltimore,[120] and Savannah, all Sees of the province, sent personal representatives. The abbots of Saint Mary, Saint Bernard, Saint Leo, Saint Procopius, and the archabbot of Saint Vincent attended, as did monks from New York and elsewhere. Thirteen vicariate priests, several from Charleston, and of course the monk-priests of Maryhelp, vested for the pontifical requiem and interment. Charles Mohr, abbot of Saint Leo and son by vow of the deceased prelate, pontificated at the Mass—it was thought that an abbot rather than a bishop should commend the soul of Leo Haid to God. Hugh Boyle delivered the eulogy, however. Father Subprior Melchoir served as archpriest of the Mass. Fathers O'Brien and Watkins, representing the vicariate clergy, served as deacon and subdeacon respectively. The *ceremoniarius* was Father Nicholas, assisted by Aloysius Wachter as prefect.[121]

The Solemn Pontifical Requiem Mass was sung at Maryhelp Cathedral by Abbot Charles, at ten o'clock that morning. As the privilege of the throne stood vacant, and was forbidden to the prelate of another jurisdiction anyway, Abbot Charles celebrated *ad faldistorium* while folds of black fabric occupied the *cathedra* alone.

> Into the beautiful Cathedral at the Abbey—the handsome brick pile about which the Bishop's life work revolved—poured prelates of equal rank, Benedictine priests and secular-clergy, nuns, monks and other members of his own flock. Hundreds stood in the aisles, unable to crowd into the seats occupied by hundreds of others, and in the rear and outside the Cathedral were hundreds [more], bareheaded who stood reverently for two hours while the Pontifical Requiem Mass was being sung.[122]

Boyle, Ordinary of the abbot's native See, spoke of this monk's "luxuriant mind" and his "wealth of character." He lauded Abbot Leo for, "His vivid and attractive personality and his altogether unusual gifts of mind and character, [which] have made him live in the affection and esteem of those from whom he has been parted [after] the long period of his ministry."[123] Then, at the conclusion of the Mass, Bishops Boyle and Barry, Archabbot Aurelius, and Abbots Ernest and Charles performed the solemn absolutions.[124] After that the great bell in the cathedral's major tower began the toll; it harmonized with the clock that just then struck noon.[125]

The *schola cantorum* of the monastery alternately sang the *Miserere* and the *Benedictus*,[126] while the six priestly pallbearers carried the bishop's remains from his cathedral to the monastic cemetery. There a simple interment service was conducted. Only the monks and the deceased's closest associates were permitted near the grave, but there were "hundreds of [other] mourners standing a short distance away, their eyes dimmed with tears and suppressed sobs choking the throat. The casket was [then] lowered to an early grave as it was sprinkled with holy water."[127] As the body descended, a monk intoned the *"Ultima,"* a hymn begging the intercession of the Mother of God at "the last hour." The chant was entered by the *schola cantorum* and all the monks.

And with that prayer to his highly favored "Virgin Most Faithful," Leo Haid was returned to dust. It marked the end of a life not without its monuments of success. His God had called him to be a monk first, then to the abbacy, and finally to be a missionary and bishop. The statistics verified the wisdom of that Divine commission. By 1924, the vicariate had more than eight thousand Catholics, more than sixty churches, more than fifty priests; there were three hospitals, two orphanages, parochial schools, academies, convents, all in North Carolina where prior to the appearance of Leo Haid the Church could not even maintain a bishop. This man was acknowledged as the father of five monasteries, each with a school; he was the only abbot-ordinary in the country, a Roman Count, Assistant at the Pontifical Throne, Dean of the American Abbots, Dean of the American Hierarchy; he had left behind him the separated territory that was the *abbatia nullius* and which to him was the most significant aspect of his legacy.

But Leo Haid did not die happy. That he did not achieve. And the reason lay not in the contentious spirit of his priests, the active interests of his monks, nor even in the loss of his friend just one month earlier. Leo Haid was not satisfied for reasons that were far more intimate to his spirit and the aspirations that had so strongly colored his character and his work. By the call of God he had lived as a bishop, an active missionary apostle for Christ and His Church. But he had never been able to tear his heart away from the cloister of his monastery. Leo Haid believed he had been "created to know [God]," yet he had found it was his destiny "not to reach [Him]." And "this," he said, is "to lose all. I belong wholly to God. I must serve Him with my whole soul and body. Have I done this? Am I doing it now?" And the answer, he feared, was negative, and "my end must be in keeping with my soul."[128]

Professionally too, he had been unable to find peace. He never understood how it could be that his efforts should attract such scorn. The last petition from Christopher Dennen, signed by all the secular priests of the vicariate, would have mystified him even further, and yet it was typical of how the subordinates of the abbot-bishop judged him, and how little they understood the Benedictine ethos that lived at the core of his values. The document accused the Vicar Apostolic of weakness, irresponsibility, lack of zeal, fiscal corruption, and selfishness. Yet the priests unanimously swore,

> Let me emphasize this fact. No expression in this testament is to be construed as a criticism of Bishop Haid or reflecting on him. No Bishop could be kinder to his priests than Bishop Haid; and the secular priests have frequently expressed this point.[129]

Michael Irwin recognized this dichotomy of response—the magnetic pull toward Abbot Leo's charisma and good intentions, the dissatisfaction with his episcopal reign and his monastic heart. Irwin wrote Father Willibald that the monk who was also a bishop had lived outside—or at least beyond—his own time.

> The late Abbot-Bishop was a marvelous man for his day and for what was expected of him in his time. He pressed forward and ran his appointed course as a giant. At the dawn of a new era God called him to his reward for his work was finished. We are now in a New Age. The old order changeth.

Despite that, however, Michael Irwin believed Leo Haid had erected a singular monument of success that would out-live the rancor of his time, and speak to later generations of a good man who had left behind him a true *opus dei* in the foothills of the North Carolina mountains. He said, "I cannot conceive of a place outside of Heaven itself where there was to be found a deeper spirit of holy joy than I [have] found at Belmont [Abbey], at first as a youth, then later as a mature man."[130]

Leo Haid had made much the same point when he reminded both those who praised him and those who criticized him, "The greatest merit belongs to others. I would have miserably failed without the Monastery, College, and Seminary. . . I speak these words [as] simple truth."[131] In the end, his body like his heart had found its only rest, its true support, in the precincts of his monastery.

At thirty-nine *anno regni* of his abbacy, and thirty-six *anno regni* of his episcopate, the aspiration finally bore fruit: "I go to the Father!"

> *Ultima in mortis hora,*
> *Filium pro nobis ora.*
> *Bonam mortem impetra,*
> *Virgo Mater Domina.*
> *Bonam mortem impetra,*
> *Virgo Mater Domina.*[132]

Epilogue:

The Crozier Turns Inward

Willibald Baumgartner was far too gentle a man to deal with the tempests that assaulted his brief and inglorious tenure as administrator.[1] Both the monastery and the vicariate suffered pangs of instability in the absence of the mitre, after its uninterrupted reign of more than three decades. Father Willibald lacked the personal and administrative character for taking charge and maintaining order. So his subordinates were generally left to their own devices, a situation of which they took full advantage. The prior's rather abstract approach to governance also left him unaware of the work of Christopher Dennen, who while sending regular reports to Belmont regarding his troublesome[2] fellow priests,[3] did not neglect to inform Baltimore of the "sad state of affairs" at the abbey.[4] Nevertheless, Father Dennen did send a sympathetic and percipient message to the beleaguered pro-vicar: "Uneasy lies the head that wears the crown."[5]

That, however, was a lesson learned early in his tenure as pro-vicar, and Baumgartner already looked forward to relinquishing his authority to whomever the Benedictines chose to succeed Leo Haid. So the election Chapter was convoked at Belmont less than a month after the bishop's death. In the apostolic mandate, the monks were called upon to name an abbot *nullius*, who would thus be nominated vicar according to the provisions of the *Bulla Erectionis* of 1910.

Five names dominated the pre-election scrutinies, the sixth obvious candidate, Thomas Oestreich, having been removed from contention by untimely ill health. There was still Alphonse Buss, age forty-seven, who was Master of Novices, Prefect of Clerics and Seminarians, and the monastery's artist and printer. Bernard Haas, age fifty-eight, the most broadly experienced of the five men, was a proven administrator, pastor, and educator. Michael McInerney, age forty-seven, showed talent for practical administrative duties, but had never served at the priories, held an executive position in the monastery or schools, nor given himself to a full schedule of either pastoral or educational duties. Vincent Taylor, age forty-seven, had spent his entire monastic life since ordination in parish work; he was well liked, but not well known. And Willibald Baumgartner, age seventy-one, experienced in the priories, pastoral work, and teaching, had acquired a reputation as a gentle, fatherly monk, of high virtue, but limited executive talent. All five of these monks were respected members of the Belmont cloister, and each—with the possible exception of Taylor, whose long absence rendered judgment uncertain—was considered a man of solid monastic values and observance; accordingly, the distinctions for each candidate tended to flow from other qualities.

Buss quickly fell from contention when complaints surfaced regarding his work with the novices.[6] Baumgartner's reticent leadership, in combination with his advanced age, served to eliminate him, as well. Taylor, a gracious, gentlemanly Virginian who represented the best aspects of pastoral concern coupled with devotion to Maryhelp, emerged as a strong factor in the election, and the obvious choice for those monks who urged the importance of pastoral commitments. McInerney was the candidate who represented the best chance for maintaining some of the prestige that the monastery had enjoyed under Haid. Father Michael's talents, his possession of a reputation that was already national in scope, the distinction of his work, all endorsed his abbatial potential. And as Buss informed Taylor, Father Michael was held in particularly "high esteem" in the monastery at this time.[7] McInerney also had the advantage of representing a reasonable compromise between the demands of the cloister and those of the apostolate. Finally, Bernard Haas was an outstanding candidate for a position of leadership. If Haid had died during the illness of 1909, Haas would have been a leading candidate to succeed him. But by 1924, with the years and a weak heart having cost him noticably, Haas was less promising, except as an interim abbot whose reign nature would be likely to characterize by brevity.

The second abbot-ordinary of Belmont was elected on 20 August 1924. Forty-five votes were cast, four of which were by proxy. By the second ballot, Buss and Baumgartner were no longer being considered. The next vote saw Haas drop from contention. On the fourth ballot, Vincent George Taylor passed Michael McInerney; he emerged as abbot-elect of Maryhelp and the *abbatia nullius*,[8] and as the nominee for the throne of the Vicariate Apostolic of North Carolina.

Since Roman approbation was required both for the monastic and the diocesan offices, the monks expected to have to await confirmation for at least six weeks. The Benedictines were not aware that Curley and the Delegate were petitioning for the erection of a North Carolina diocese; thus they were also ignorant of the fact that Vincent Taylor would not be confirmed in any position, until it had been determined whether the vicariate would continue or be erected as a diocese; whether the abbot-elect possessed the rights to the office even if the diocese were created; and whether Taylor should receive episcopal consecration even if he did not receive the throne of either the vicariate or the new North Carolina diocese.

The interregnum was an uneasy period, made worse by the prolonged wait for Rome's decision. The delay was lengthened not only by the efforts to have the vicariate terminated, but by the failure of the Benedictine agents to take immediate action. The primate's late entry into the confirmation effort, caused by some confusion of papers and communication, enabled Dennen, Curley, and the delegate to win a full hearing for their case, to register their requests and objections, and thus to initiate an inquiry into the apparent needs of the Church in North Carolina. Therefore, Belmont received no word from Rome in September; the wait continued through October, and into November. Then matters were further complicated when Willibald Baumgartner wrote one of his cordial letters to the *praeses*, Ernest Helmstetter of Saint Mary Abbey in New Jersey. Intending to speak from a perspective of humility more than fact or information, Father Willibald advised Abbot Ernest that "the whole Community prefers to have the care of the Vicariate given to somebody else."[9] Abbot Ernest communicated this surprising news to the primate at once, since Maryhelp's renunciation of its right to the vicariate paved the way for Taylor's immediate confirmation. Indeed Abbot Ernest speculated that the approval might be granted within two days. The primate informed the Curia that Belmont was no longer interested in retaining jurisdiction over the entire state and that the abbot-elect would be satisfied with being an abbot-ordinary without episcopal consecration.[10]

Rome was certainly surprised by this turn of events, but not as much as was the abbot-elect. Indeed perhaps no one was more surprised to hear of the renunciation than was Vincent Taylor, who was quick to disagree with the prior's belief that "the whole Community" was not interested in retaining the vicariate. Taylor was extremely interested in retaining the vicariate, and advised the *praeses* that he had no intention of renouncing the episcopacy. If Rome desired that he be only an abbot-ordinary, he would certainly resign himself to that dignity, but he refused to pretend that he preferred that resolution for the delay in his confirmation. Taylor reminded Helmstetter that Rome granted the Chapter at Maryhelp "'a free hand' in the appointment of a Vicar"; the election was held with that in mind, and he believed he had been properly nominated for the throne of the vicariate. "Our representatives in Rome," he judged, "have not handled the situation in a very intelligent manner."[11]

It was too late, however, for Baumgartner's work to be rectified. For the first time in the three months since the election, the Benedictine agents in Rome had acted promptly. The supposed abdication of the vicariate and episcopate had already been communicated to the Curia. In the first week of December, immediately following receipt of Maryhelp's renunciation, the decisions regarding North Carolina had been made. On 12 December Vincent Taylor's formal confirmation as abbot *nullius* of Belmont was issued and published, without granting him the right of episcopal consecration.[12] As Leo Haid had correctly predicted thirty-four years earlier, his "successor...would sway the crozier one way only—inward."[13]

Although Father Willibald had provided for the resolution of the more than sixteen weeks Taylor had awaited confirmation, his was not the only influence at work. Since Curley was still out of the country when Haid died, Dennen immediately wrote Pietro Fumasoni-Biondi, who had replaced Bonzano as Apostolic Delegate. The Pope's representative was advised of the contents of the several communiques to his predecessor; the Legation made further inquiries of Dennen; the priest replied immediately, and the process began for terminating the Benedictine domination of the Catholic Church in North Carolina.[14] After his return, Curley also was active in urging the step. Remarkably, all of these endeavors were undertaken without any inquiry being placed with the pro-vicar; not even a statistical report was requested. The ruse that made it possible to avoid consulting with, and thus alerting, the Benedictines was Archbishop Curley's specious insistence that he had never been informed who was serving as Apostolic Administrator of the vicariate; thus, it was reasoned, how could there be contact? And the Apostolic Delegate, noting Curley's solicitous concern for his suffragan See, was satisfied to deal directly with the Metropolitan.[15]

The prelate of Baltimore was, however, sufficiently aware of Father Willibald's administrative duties that he assisted the Benedictine's removal from office. As late as 5 December, Father Willibald still believed the vicariate's administration would be "left in our hands." He had sent that observation to Father Arthur Freeman, a vicariate priest who forwarded it by Special Delivery post to Dennen, who in turn sent the letter to Curley with the notation, "comment on my part is unnecessary."[16] Curley wrote to Christopher Dennen in response, on 9 December 1924, assuring him *sub secreto* that everything had already been decided. "North Carolina is to have a Bishop of its own," he said. The *abbatia nullius* "is to continue of course," the archbishop added, but its territory would not be changed.[17]

This last reference relates to Dennen's unsubstantiated charge of 1922, regarding the Benedictines' ambitions for Mecklenburg County. Haid never submitted a request for the expansion of the *nullius*, of course. Indeed there is no available documentation to authenticate the contention that the petition—supposedly carried by Father Felix—even existed. In support of the belief in the petition there may be cited the prior's extreme concern regarding the safety of his trunks and their contents; Haid's explicit statement of interest in changing the boundaries of the *nullius*; and the testimony of Nicholas Bliley who supposedly formulated the proposal, and of Omer Matt who supposedly typed it. But if Haid signed this petition, what was its fate? Obviously part, if not all, of Prior Felix's concern regarding his luggage related to the draft for one thousand dollars. He makes no reference to the supposed petition. Also, in all the correspondence from Inguanez, the man who was privy to the contents of Hintemeyer's trunks and responsible for them, reference is made to only two *relationes*. These were *both* finally submitted to Rome in January 1925, by agents familiar with their contents—*after* the new North Carolina diocese had already been created, and when a request by a deceased bishop to take a county from the defunct vicariate, now created but not erected as a diocese, would have been ludicrous at best. Haid had sent reports to Rome concerning the Vicariate Apostolic and the abbatial 'diocese'; but there is no proof of any petition, it seems, for revising the territory of the *nullius*. He did desire the acquisition of Mecklenburg County by the monks; it appears that he even had a petition to that effect drafted; but there is insufficient evidence to support the contention either that he did request the territorial change, or that the impetus for the two year effort by Dennen and Curley had proceeded from a foundation more solid than supposition.

The Diocese of Raleigh, erected to replace the Vicariate Apostolic of North Carolina, and embracing that body's former territory, was created on 12 December 1924, the same day as the confirmation of Vincent Taylor as abbot ordinary. On 17 December the Sacred Consistorial Congregation informed Archbishop Curley of the erection, and advised him of the unusual step to be taken regarding the territory's governance until the first bishop was appointed. The current administrator, Father Willibald, who did not reside in the new diocese but in the *abbatia nullius*, was to be removed. As his replacement the Sacred Congregation had selected Michael Curley, who lived in Baltimore.[18] This extraordinary step was confirmed by the *Bulla* when published.[19] Curley advised Baumgartner that the Benedictine should remain as administrator until the archbishop reached North Carolina and formally erected the new diocese with the public reading of the *Bulla*.[20] After that Curley would name his own vicar general to care for the diocese while the administrator resumed residence in Maryland. But Baumgartner was uneasy about continuing in his office for even that brief period of time, since he was unsure that Curley had the right to make such an appointment—before the documents had been read and thus before the archbishop actually became the administrator—and since Rome so obviously desired him to surrender the governance of the Catholic Church in North Carolina into other hands. Father Willibald was also concerned about the imbalance at Belmont resulting from his retaining administration of the vicariate after having transferred the reins of the monastery and *nullius* to Taylor. But Curley assured Baumgartner that the Benedictine was "still Administrator of the new Diocese in every sense of the word,"[21] and asked that the erection of the new Raleigh jurisdiction be scheduled for 12 March 1925.[22]

Taylor, unaware of Curley's activities regarding the Benedictines, asked the archbishop to be the prelate who granted him the abbatial blessing.[23] Father Willibald, also unconscious of the work of Curley, Dennen, Freeman, and others, cheerfully and naively wrote in his official report for the new administrator, "I am glad to state, that my relations with the Seculars were most pleasant."[24] In particular this rather incredible statement shows Baumgartner's ignorance regarding Father Dennen's work. That priest had recommended much more than the erection of a new diocese and the restrictions for the Benedictines. He also called for an investigation of the Benedictine priory in Richmond, since he was sure that vicariate monies had been sent there;[25] moreover, he advised that an inquiry be made into the O'Donoghue estate of two decades earlier, and into the conditions at the Benedictine parish in Charlotte, Saint Peter.[26] Dennen visited Curley in Baltimore on 19 January,[27] arranged the itinerary for the new administrator's tour of the North State,[28] and submitted in all humility to his appointment as the first vicar general of the Diocese of Raleigh.[29] Once the appointment of the new bishop, William Hafey, a member of the episcopal household in Baltimore, was announced, Dennen offered his first affront to Belmont's second abbot. He informed Vincent Taylor that the long-standing practice of "entertaining him and his blind sister at [Dennen's] cottage" would have to end. That summer Father Dennen replaced Abbot Vincent and Miss Mary Taylor with Hafey.[30]

Curley filed a lengthy report with the Apostolic Delegate on 10 April 1925, regarding the condition of the Catholic Church in North Carolina. The appraisal was based on the archbishop's observations during the twenty-one days he spent in the state, and information gathered at Belmont and from Dennen. Archbishop Curley expressed particular concern regarding the counties held by the Benedictines. These were largely Protestant, of course, but they were, he believed, wealthy and thus of interest to the new diocese. Curley also speculated that it might be possible to rest the 1891 counties out of the Benedictines' control. "If demands were made by the new Bishop on the Abbot for more Benedictine Fathers for the Counties," he reasoned, "the Abbot could not supply them. . . ." Vincent Taylor, Curley noted,

> has his own difficulties in the matter of his monastic regulations and the work. At the present time, he has twenty-four Priests at work in the Dioceses of Richmond, Savannah and Raleigh. The result is, that he is short of men at home in the Monastery, particularly for the work of teaching. As the result of the death of the Bishop and the Vicar General, the Monastic Seminary is at the present time very poorly equipped with Teachers of Philosophy and Theology. The new abbot is fully alive to all his difficulties, and is determined to start at once to improve conditions.[31]

And that is what Vincent Taylor did, restructuring commitments in order to maximize the abbey's strengths and utility. He also cultivated cordial relations with Hafey, and pretended not to notice the indignities that marked his relations with Curley.[32] He was, in many ways, the perfect man to follow the flamboyant success of Leo

Haid, and to administer the necessary reduction in the abbey's commitments. Taylor was a man of charm and courtly manners. In the post-bellum South, he was that highly prized quasi-patrician known as the "Southern Gentleman." He was gracious; his character was as strong as his accent was smooth and mellifluous. To women he was always "charmed;" men were heard with a nod of the head and a facade of interest. Expression of his own values, however, was often held discreetly in check—as the dichotomy between the recollections of his associates and the documents of his reign so clearly expresses. Nevertheless, Vincent Taylor earned a solid reputation as a "gentleman."[33]

The commencement of his tenure had been rough. His first act as abbot-elect had been to order improvements, new furnishings, and a thorough redecoration and renovation of the abbatial apartments. Even with Father Michael closely supervising the work, the cost neared two thousand dollars.[34] But after that first gesture of plutocratic inclinations, he settled into the economy of restructuring priorities at Belmont, and soon afterwards of facing the Great Depression.

Taylor withdrew the monks from Bristow (1927), made large expenditures in Richmond and Savannah, and definitively established the remaining Virginia project as a priory. At the abbey he permitted the construction of the Haid Gymnasium (1929) and of an annex to Jubilee Hall (1954), but beyond that he had little interest in brick edifices. Athletics interested him more; the playing field at the college was improved, the grandstands upgraded, the handball alleys and tennis courts made permanent. The library was finally given proper housing and staffing (1939). Having a better eye for practical matters than his predecessor, Taylor set the monastery personnel records in order, redesigned the abbey's corporate structure, and had all the deeds reissued according to the norms of contemporary legal clarity. He reigned until 1956 in the monastery and 1959 in the *nullius*.

Belmont Abbey College was the most striking success of Taylor's tenure. The abbot reorganized the school in 1928, making it a junior college and a preparatory school. These were accredited and then slowly enlarged while Abbot Vincent sent monks to prepare for teaching assignments by earning advanced degrees in the secular arts and sciences. Finally, in 1952, Belmont Abbey College became a full, four-year, liberal arts college. It won accreditation in 1957.

Taylor's successor was Walter Coggin, a Richmond native who held a doctorate in philosophy. Coggin, more than anyone else in the sixty years that followed the first abbot's death, ruled Belmont in the spirit of Leo Haid. While a man of deep spirituality who took no pleasure in issuing commands, but seriously pondered the paternity of his position, Abbot Walter was also a great builder. During his tenure as vicar to Abbot Vincent and then as abbot ordinary in his own right, he constructed a library building, science hall, three dormitories, a students' refectory, and a new athletic centre and natatorium. He closed the preparatory school and seminary, and focused the monks' work more clearly on the college. Coggin, as a reigning diocesan Ordinary, was a Father at the Second Vatican Council, and oversaw the adaptations that followed on the Conciliar pronouncements. The Savannah priory, which had first been voted independence in the 1950's, only to have that status denied by Abbot Vincent, finally acquired its autonomy in 1961, after Coggin had been elected to the throne at Belmont.

Abbot Walter was succeeded in 1970 by Edmund McCaffrey, by Jude Cleary in 1975, and Peter Stragand in 1978. It was with this succession of leaders that Belmont met the centennial of the arrival of the first monks in Carolina, and began reevaluating its parochial commitments, refocusing attention on affairs of the cloister and the demands of the educational apostolate. This was an effort specifically recommended by Rome.[35] In 1983, there were approximately fifty monks for the choir. Ten of these were in Richmond; three were in parishes, two in chaplaincies; the rest were in residence at the abbey or undertaking advanced studies.

The men of Haid's era should also be mentioned here. Of the ten monks who were the abbot's first associates, Melchior Reichert survived the longest. After a lengthy pastorate to the blacks, work in hospital ministry, and service as subprior of the abbey, he died in 1940. Father Willibald served as prior and vicar general until his death in 1930. Julius Pohl went to his grave six weeks after Leo Haid. William Mayer, Roman Kirchner, Patrick Donlon, George Lester, and Felix Hintemeyer preceded the bishop in death. Abbot Charles survived until 1931. In 1938, Walter Leahy died as a parish priest in New Jersey.

Bernard Haas suffered a heart attack in 1927, and was removed from his office as the Richmond prior. He survived until 1933. Ignatius Remke succeeded Father Willibald at the parish in Winston in 1924; then in 1927 he succeeded Bernard Haas in Richmond, his own home town. Remke died in 1944. Thomas Oestreich left the rectorship of Belmont Abbey College in 1924, but continued in teaching and seminary work. Finally his health required his removal to the chaplaincy of Saint Joseph Hospital in Asheville, where the Sisters of Mercy cared for him, while he tended to the spiritual needs of the patients. He died in 1943. Gilbert Koberzynski preceded Haid in death by four years; Francis Meyer passed away fifteen years before Brother Gilbert; Oswald Moosmueller died four years before Meyer; but Katharine Drexel lasted into the 1950's.

Michael McInerney survived until 1963. In his senior years, Saint Vincent awarded him an honorary doctorate in recognition of his artistic contributions to the Benedictine Order through a career of more than half a century. Joseph Tobin served two terms as prior of the monastery and one as Apostolic Administrator (during the interregnum of 1959-1960). When the Diocese of Charlotte was finally erected on 12 January 1972, in vindication of Gibbons' prediction, Father Joseph became its Vice Chancellor. He died in 1978. Bishop Hafey and his successor in Raleigh, Eugene McGuinness, were attentive to the Benedictines of Belmont; both were promoted to other Sees. Not until Vincent Waters, the third Ordinary of Raleigh and an alumnus of Belmont, did a prelate retain the office until death. Christopher Dennen enjoyed the respect of the people and prelates of North Carolina throughout his life. When he died in 1939, he was buried in the cemetery at Belmont Abbey, a few yards from the grave of Leo Haid.

Bishop Waters tried to introduce the cause for the beatification of Thomas Frederick Price, but found insufficient arguments to support a contention of sanctity. Monsignor Charles Gable, a priest of Raleigh who was first affiliated with the vicariate and had studied in the Belmont seminary, tried to collect "miracles" attributed to Leo Haid's Heavenly intercession. This project was preparatory to introducing the abbot's cause for canonization in Rome. Unfortunately, no miracles were ever reported.

Finally, there must be considered the true Haid legacy, the *abbatia nullius* of Belmont. Vincent Taylor took a greater interest in evangelization and parochial work within its precincts than had his predecessor, but his success was not outstanding and did not satisfy Rome. The Holy See suggested that the abbot-ordinary petition for the partition of his territory, so that the abbey's limited personnel might better serve their *nullius* 'diocese'.[36] Taylor acquiesced, and in 1944 the *nullius* was restricted to the three hundred fifty square miles of Gaston County. In 1960, the territory was partitioned again,[37] reducing it to the five hundred acres of the monastery grounds, an area generally lacking in permanent secular residents. Thus the abbey became the smallest 'diocese' in the world. This partition was particularly lamented in Belmont because it separated the Sisters of Mercy at Sacred Heart Convent—faithful coadjutors whose presence was greatly treasured—from the *abbatia nullius*, and placed them in the Diocese of Raleigh.

Then on 1 January 1977, by request of the American bishops, the *abbatia nullius* was suppressed. Ironically, the termination of the separated territory came at the conclusion of the monastery's first century, the point at which Haid had believed it would be most needed. Though still exempt, of course, Belmont Abbey became territorially a part of the Diocese of Charlotte. The Abbey Cathedral, the only one ever erected in the United States, returned to its original status as the 'Abbey Church of Maryhelp'; only the *National Register of Historic Places* continued to recognize it as a "cathedral". Yet the suppression of the *nullius* was greeted with surprising warmth at the abbey. There were three main reasons for this: 1) The pastoral obligations of the abbatial 'diocese' had already died with the partition of 1960; 2) the gracious first Ordinary of Charlotte, Michael Begley, then reigning, was a loving and benevolent friend to the Benedictines, and was convinced of the importance of the monastic witness in his territory; and 3) the monks realized that for the first time since 1887, their abbatial father would not be bound by the travels, obligations, and absences that followed on membership in the episcopal conference and visits *ad limina*. The suppression of the *abbatia nullius diocesis* was received with pacific resignation by the monks of Belmont, who saw therein fresh opportunities for actualizing Benedictine values. The suppression of the abbey's diocesan character was not taken as the termination of the dream of Leo Haid.

footnotes

AAB	Archdiocesan Archives of Baltimore (Maryland)
AAM	Archives of the Abbey of Maryhelp (North Carolina)
AANB	Archives of the *Abbatia Nullius* of Belmont (North Carolina)
ACFA	Archives of the American Cassinese Federation of the Order of Saint Benedict (Pennsylvania)
BACA	Archives of Belmont Abbey College (North Carolina)
BPA	Archives of Benedictine Priory (Georgia)
BSA	Archives of the Sisters of the Blessed Sacrament for Indians and Colored People (Pennsylvania)
CFMSA	Archives of the Catholic Foreign Mission Society of America (New York)
DCA	Archives of the Diocese of Charleston (South Carolina)
D.RAH.A.	Archives of the Diocese of Raleigh (North Carolina)
D.RICH.A.	Archives of the Diocese of Richmond (Virginia)
DSA	Archives of the Diocese of Savannah (Georgia)
D.SU.A.	Archives of the Diocese of Superior (Wisconsin)
NDUA	Archives of the University of Notre Dame (Indiana)
PAR	Provincial Archives of the Congregation of the Holy Redeemer (New York)
RB	*Regula Benedicti*
SAA	Archives of Sant' Anselmo Abbey (Rome)
SBAA	Archives of Saint Benedict Abbey (Kansas)
S.BE.A.	Archives of Saint Bernard Abbey (Alabama)
SBMA	Archives of Saint Benedict Motherhouse (Bristow, Virginia)
SBPA	Archives of Saint Benedict Priory (Virginia)
SCSA	Archives of Saint Charles Seminary (Maryland)
SJA	Archives of Saint John Abbey (Minnesota)

SLA	Archives of Saint Leo Abbey (Florida)
SMA	Archives of Saint Mary Abbey (New Jersey)
SPOA	Archives of Saint Paul Outside the Walls (Rome [microfilm at The Catholic University of America])
SVA	Archives of Saint Vincent Archabbey (Pennsylvania)

Special Notations

1. *Primate* indicates the reigning Abbot Primate of the Order of Saint Benedict:
   Hildebrand de Hemptinne, O.S.B. (1893-1913)
   Fidelis de Stotzingen, O.S.B. (1913-1947)
2. *Delegate* indicates the Apostolic Delegate to the Church in the United States at the time indicated:
   Francesco Satolli (1893-1896)
   Sebastiano Martinelli, O.S.A. (1896-1902)
   Diomede Falconio, O.F.M. (1902-1911)
   Giovanni Bonzano (1911-1922)
   Pietro Fumasoni-Biondi (1922-1933)
   Apostolic Delegation is used when the communication indicated was not issued over the Delegate's signature.
3. When a number is given after the designation for an archival repository, this indicates that a copy of the material cited is on file at Maryhelp, numbered as indicated.
4. For cataloged materials at Belmont, the official repository for the Haid papers, the filing designation is indicated in brackets following the reference. For subsequent references to cited material, the filing information is not ordinarily repeated.
5. Because of their shared repository, listings for AAM, AANB, and BACA have all been given ordinarily as AAM.
6. For compact reference, periodical citations are rendered here according to their place in the several volumes of *Publicity Files* in AAM whenever possible.

pROLOGUE:

the IÔeal Of BeneÔict Of nuRSIa

[1]Benedict lived from c. 480 to 547. Nursia is located about seventy-five miles northeast of Rome.

[2]Gregorius Magnus, *Dialogues*, ii, 1. (J.P. Migne, *Patrologia Latina*, 66 [Paris, 1847], 125-204).

[3]*Ibid*. Benedict had only about three years of solitude, before a priest, shepherds, and various others came to see the budding *vir dei*.

[4]*Ibid*., 3. This may have been Vicovaro, but certainty is lacking.

[5]*Ibid*.

[6]*Ibid*., 8.

[7]*Ibid*.

[8]Cf. *Regula Benedicti*, *caput* xlviii.

[9]*Ibid*., lxvii.

[10]Cf. *ibid*., xlviii.

[11]*Ibid*. xxxi, lv.

[12]"*Officina vero ubi haec omnia diligenter operemur claustra sunt monasterii et stabilitas in congregatione*." *Ibid*., iv.

[13]*Ibid*., liii.

[14]*Ibid*., ii, iii, lxi, lxiii.

[15]"*Christo omnino nihil praeponant*." *Ibid*., lxxii.

[16]Ideally, the will is perfected by obedience.

[17]*RB*, Prologue.

[18]The *horarium* is the daily schedule of the monks. Benedict gives instances when the hour is rearranged, for example, regarding work, prayer, and meals. Cf., for example, *RB*, xli.

[19]*RB*, xli.

[20]*Conversatio* includes, among other factors, poverty and celibate chastity.

[21]*RB*, xlviii.

[22]For example, *ibid*., xxxv.

[23]*Ibid*., ii, xxi, lxv.

[24]*Ibid*., lviii.

[25]*Ibid*., lvii.

[26]*Ibid*., viii-xix.

[27]*Ibid.*, xx.

[28]*Ibid.*, xi-xv, for example.

[29]*Ibid.*, xix.

[30]*Ibid.*, xx. "*Et non in multiloquio, sed in puritate cordis et compunctione lacrimarum nos exaudiri sciamus. Et ideo brevis debet esse et pura oratio. . .*"

[31]"*Nihil operi Dei praeponatur.*" *Ibid.*, xliii.

[32]*Ibid.*, xxii.

[33]Cf. *Ibid.*, xlii, xlviii., etc.

[34]Instances of these problems are highly varied in character and content. Three of the best known examples were the Maurists, Cluniacs, and Cistercians. The Maurists placed inordinate emphasis on scholarly work; Cluniacs led an extraordinarily liturgicized existence—even farm laborers proceeded to their toils in *statio*. And most importantly, the well-intentioned Cistercian "reform", created the observance that now serves as the popular notion of a monk.

[35]Gregory (c. 540-604), on his Sicilian estates, arranged the establishment of six monasteries that would follow the *Regula Benedicti*. His villa in Rome became the Monastery of Saint Andrew, and Gregory served as a monk of that house.

[35]Gregory (c. 540-604), on his Sicilian estates, arranged the establishment of six monasteries that would follow the *Regula Benedicti*. His villa in Rome became the Monastery of Saint Andrew, and Gregory served as a monk of that house.

[36]Wilfrid (634-709), though remembered as less than an ideal monk, did prove a leader for the role Benedictines were to play in the arts. He believed each new monastery needed its share of singers, masons, and artisans.

[37]Bede the Venerable (673-735) is the epitome of the monastic scholar.

[38]Though the schools favored, primarily, the members of the monastery, the learning was disseminated more extensively in these early days than the educational opportunities. In this, Benedict Biscop (628-690), who taught Bede (among others), is an example. It was Benedict Biscop who forcefully insisted on the importance of a scriptorium in the monasteries of the day.

[39]Pope Gregory II (d. 731).

[40]Boniface was killed in 754(5) when natives objected to the loss of a sacred arbor at the good Bishop's hand.

[41]Here, as in England, the schools were firstly for the monks, or in a larger sense were seminaries. These eventually broadened into wider forms of educational activities.

[42]The five were: Saint Vincent (Pennsylvania, 1855), Saint John ([originally "Saint Louis"] Minnesota, 1866), Saint Benedict (Kansas, 1876), Saint Mary (New Jersey, 1884), and Maryhelp (North Carolina, 1884).

[43]Boniface Wimmer (1809-1887) was not the first Benedictine to labor in the Americas, but his was the first permanent Benedictine settlement in North America.

Chapter I:

michael hite

[1]Details of this journey were given in various contemporary newspaper and journal accounts. See "Falconio at Belmont," The Charlotte *Daily Observer* (18 October 1910), 1. Also, "Pomp and Ceremony at Belmont Abbey: Pope Confers Honor," The Charlotte *News* (18 October 1910), 1, 7. Also, "America's Only *Abbatia Nullius*," *The News Letter* (November, 1910), 2. Also, "Apostolic Delegate's Reception," *The News Letter* (November, 1910), 4.

[2]"Falconio at Belmont," and "Apostolic Delegate's Reception," *ibid.*

[3]*Ibid.* This distinction, known as an *abbatia nullius diocesis* (an abbey of no diocese), exceeds other titles because it creates a jurisdictional independence (of a quasi-diocesan character), and thus a significant form of ecclesiastical exemption. Most other distinctions, such as the title "archabbey," are merely honorific. Cf. Chapter VII, *infra.*

[4]"Falconio at Belmont," 18 October 1910.

[5]"Apostolic Delegate's Reception," November, 1910.

[6]"Falconio at Belmont," 18 October 1910.

[7]AAM. *Publicity Files*, Volume v. "Distinction Won by Former Pittsburgher," [unlabeled press clipping] c. June 1910.

[8]Haid was ordained a titular bishop after being named head of the Vicariate Apostolic of North Carolina.

[9]Haid was *praeses* of the American Cassinese Congregation of the Order of Saint Benedict for two terms, 1890-1896.

[10]For most of the materials in the history of the Haid/Hite family, I am indebted to the efforts and generosity of Arthur Hite, the genealogist of Bishop Haid's family. A documents and correspondence file, courtesy of Mr. Hite, is maintained in the Abbey Archives at Belmont. As of this writing, the file is active and has not been catalogued into the collection. The only known source for the Unity Township location is in the archives of Saint Vincent Archabbey, Latrobe, Pennsylvania.

[11]SVA.

[12]Census reports are inconsistent in citing her age. The family name is sometimes spelled *Stader,* also.

[13]AAM. Hite file. Cf. *supra*, no. 10.

[14]*Ibid.*

[15]SVA. Baptismal Register for Saint Vincent Church, 17 February 1848 entry.

[16]*Ibid.*, 17 August 1849.

[17]Mr. Hite's work, accomplished in the 1970's and 1980's, has graciously been placed at the disposal of this volume's needs.

[18]Sebastian Doris, *Belmont Abbey: Its Origin, Development, and Present State* (Belmont, North Carolina: [privately published] 1971 [revised edition]), 46.

[19]AAM. Hite file, and 1870 Census Report.

[20]*Ibid.*

[21]SVA.

[22]SVA.

[23]Photographs reveal that Haid did not start his beard until some some time between 1877 and 1879. In a photograph at Belmont (dated 1877) he is clean-shaven; in one dated 18 March 1879, there is a beard (though not a long one).

[24]The Abbey Archives at Belmont has only one photograph showing the Haid profile, and that is a candid shot.

[25]In addition to his nose, Haid seems to have had some pause regarding his lack of height. In photographs he ordinarily posed seated. When he stood, he ordinarily donned a tall hat, or at least a biretta.

[26]By tradition, Haid was given his religious name out of fond memory for Father Leo Rau, OSB. SVA. *Seminarists' Symposium,* Volume v, 102. See also, Felix Fellner, *Abbot Boniface and His Monks* [unpublished typescript], 634, and 641, n. 53. Haid told of the origin of his name in an interview with Fellner on 5 October 1904.

[27]Jerome Oetgen's biography of Wimmer is the only complete source published regarding the Abbot. This is an indispensible volume for all American monastic studies. Jerome Oetgen, *An American Abbot* (Latrobe, Pennsylvania: The Archabbey Press), 1976.

[28]Wimmer even hired a layman in order to secure the quality of music at Saint Vincent Archabbey. He also sent a monk who later served at Belmont, Father Gerard Pilz, OSB, to study art in Europe. For further information, cf. Fred J. Moleck, "Music At Saint Vincent Archabbey Under Boniface Wimmer," *The American Benedictine Review* (June, 1963), 248-262.

[29]Saint Vincent had Wimmer's largest seminary, but other independent monasteries of the Federation, at various times, also maintained a faculty to educate at least their own members who were preparing for ordination.

[30]Of course, there is no way of knowing how Wimmer would have handled that point, supposedly reached a century into the missionary monastery's existence, when the character of the house begins the transition toward the more traditional formulae of cenobitic values. Archabbot Boniface did his part. He established these monasteries, gave from his own bountiful supply the first breath of spirit, a spirit that was a perceptive amalgamation of a fourteen centuries old monastic *modus vivendi* with a distinctly American—some would say, *too* American—*modus operandi.* It was an uncomfortable union at times, but his legacy nonetheless. And each of his foundations, throughout their first century and beyond, was bound to deal with it, understand it in light of new times and changing visions, exercise it under leaders who never knew Boniface Wimmer, and live it with integrity in a manner recognizable as monastic, Benedictine, and authentic to the particular, autonomous monastery. The traditions of Benedict and Wimmer do not always seem compatible on the surface, yet

Wimmer did see that the Benedictine missionaries succeeded in their initial, and primarily priestly, endeavors, before the task of engendering a pervading spirit of monasticism fell to the Archabbot's successors. Leo Haid, and the four abbots who followed him in the first century of Belmont Abbey, were all charged with reconciling the vision of Wimmer with the tradition of Benedict, but only Haid carried with him the experience of having served Wimmer himself.

[31]Novices tend to have their visions of spiritual integrity challenged by any number of issues. Among the more common ones are the sight of their abbot as a fallible being, monks as weak; brothers seem holier than the priest-monks; there seems too little time for prayer; educational apostolates are distracting; some monks seem lax; the *Regula* is adapted and perhaps compromised; the liturgy becomes repetitive and may seem an occasion of drudgery; and countless other threatening "realities."

[32]Oetgen's biography [cf. *supra*] is the best source for surveying Wimmer's theories of monasticism.

[33]He was particularly vocal on behalf of Wimmer in the upheavals of 1882.

[34]Haid's vows are preserved in the monastery archives at Belmont. (M1, No. 1 Vows) Actually his first vows have a misspelling, "Heaid"; his solemn vows have "Haid", written clearly and precisely.

[35]Fellner, *Abbot*, 634.

[36]SVA. Archivist's file regarding Haid.

[37]*Ibid.*

[38]*Major John Andre* went through several printings before the plates were destroyed in the Great Fire of Baltimore (7-8 February 1904). A subsequent edition was published by the Belmont Abbey Press.

[39]Haid declined to volunteer for any of the monasteries which were elevated to abbatial status, including Belmont.

[40]Oetgen, *American*, 258.

[41]ACFA. Minutes of the General Chapter, 1881. Cf. also, discussion in Fellner, *Abbot*, 662.

[42]ACFA.

[43]SJA. Letter from Wimmer to Alexius Edelbrock, 9 March 1883.

[44]Newark and North Carolina became independent in 1884; Alabama in 1891. Foundations in Chicago and Wetaug were refounded, moved, and reorganized through the years; eventually there were two abbeys (Saint Procopius [Lisle, Illinois] and Saint Peter [Canada]) which at least traced their roots to these cities. As for Baltimore, Richmond, Saint Mary's, and Erie, none produced an independent monastery.

[45]Cf. Fellner, *Abbot*, 625.

[46]SBAA. Letter from Wimmer to Wolf, 27 May 1883.

[47]SVA. Letter from Wimmer to Joseph Amberger, 25 January 1885 (misdated "1886").

[48]SBAA. Letter from Wimmer to Wolf, 27 May 1883.

[49]SVA. Letter from Wimmer to Utto Lang, 3 November 1883 (copy).

[50]SVA. Letter from Wimmer to Amberger, 20 August 1884.

[51]SVA. Letter from Wimmer to Amberger, 25 January 1885.

[52]*Ibid.*

[53]SBAA. Letter from Wimmer to Wolf, 27 May 1883.

[54]Cf. *ibid.*

[55]SVA. Letter from Wolf to Wimmer, 31 May 1883.

[56]SVA. Letter from Wimmer to Henry Northrop, 8 June 1883.

[57]SVA. Letter from Northrop to Wimmer, 13 June 1883.

[58]SVA. Letter from Wimmer to Cardinal Simeoni, 7 July 1884.

[59]Cf. Fellner, *Abbot*, 627-628.

[60]SVA. Letter from Wimmer to Augustine Pucci-Sisti, 3 July 1884.

[61]SVA. Letter from Wimmer to Simeoni, 7 July 1884.

[62]SVA. Letter from Wimmer to Amberger, 25 January 1885.

[63]SVA. Letter from Pucci-Sisti to Wimmer, 17 October 1884.

[64]Cf. Fellner, *Abbot*, 628.

[65]SAV. Letter from Wimmer to Amberger, 25 January 1885.

[66]AAM. Bull of Erection for Maryhelp Abbey, 19 December 1884.

[67]SVA. Letter from Northrop to Wimmer, 31 January 1885.

[68]SVA. Notice to capitulars from Wimmer, 20 January 1885.

[69]ACFA. Protocol of election, 11 February 1885.

[70]It is interesting that each of these men eventually became abbots: Zilliox and Pfraengle in New Jersey, and Hintenach at Saint Vincent.

[71]Fellner, *Abbot*, 631. And ACFA. Protocol of election, 11 February 1885.

[72]ACFA. *Ibid.*

[73]*Ibid.*

[74]Some years later, Leo Haid recalled this story from the departure of the capitulars: "As some of the Fathers were walking to Latrobe to take the evening train, they met two neighbors, who never were friendly to Saint Vincent and its activities. As they passed them, one of them remarked rather loudly to the other: 'God be praised, the priest factory is breaking up.' However, one of the Fathers in a happy frame of mind quickly retorted: 'By no means, we are only swarming.'" Fellner, *Abbot*, 632.

[75]Oetgen, *American*, 256.

[76]Cf. Jerome Oetgen, "Oswald Moosmueller: Monk and Missionary," *The American Benedictine Review* (March, 1976), 1-35.

[77]Wimmer had no way of knowing either what Moosmueller was about to do or that Zilliox would reign for barely more than one year.

[78]SVA. Letter from Wimmer to Lang, 22 March 1885.

[79]Fellner, *Abbot*, 632. Cf. Letter from Wimmer to Bruanmueller, 23 March 1885.

[80]SVA. Letter from Wimmer to Lang, 22 March 1885.

[81]SBAA. Letter from Wimmer to Wolf, 17 February 1885 [translator unidentified].

[82]SVA. Cf. also letter from Wimmer to Bruanmueller, 23 March 1885.

[83]SVA. Letter from Wimmer to Amberger, 20 August 1884.

[84]Cf. Fellner, *Abbot*, 632.

[85]Cf. Oetgen, *American*, 281.

[86]Fellner, *Abbot*, 632.

[87]Cf. SBAA. Letter from Wimmer to Wolf, 20 February 1885 [translator unidentified].

[88]*Ibid.*

[89]AAM. Letter from Moosmueller to Pohl, 14 February 1885. [Al.O, No. 1. Julius Pohl, OSB, RP—Correspondence]

[90]SVA. Letter from Wimmer to Lang, 22 March 1885.

[91]SBAA. Letter from Wimmer to Wolf, 18 April 1885.

[92]*Ibid.*

[93]SVA. Letter from Wimmer to Bernard Smith, undated (summer, 1885).

[94]SVA. Letter from Wimmer to Bernard Smith, 20 June 1885. Smith's papers are preserved at Saint Paul Outside the Walls (Rome).

[95]Cf. SVA. Letter from Wimmer to Lang, 20 June 1885.

[96]*Ibid.*

[97]AAM. Letter from Wimmer to Pohl, 7 July 1885. [M8, No. 1. Abbatial Election Materials]

[98]Cf. SBAA. Letter from Wimmer to Wolf, 11 April 1885.

[99]Cf. SVA. Letter from Wimmer to Amberger, 15 July 1885.

[100]SBAA. Letters from Wimmer to Wolf, 11 April and 2 June 1885.

[101]*Ibid.*

[102]SVA.Letter from Wimmer to Lang, 21 December 1885.

[103]SBAA. Letter from Wimmer to Wolf, 11 April 1885.

[104]Two capitulars were at Maryhelp that summer: Placidus Pilz, who was prior, and Julius Pohl, the rector of the college. Only the latter was interested in attaching himself permanently to Maryhelp.

[105]ACFA. *Elenchus*, 14 July 1885.

[106]The brothers had no voice in Chapter, and were not enumerated with the ten founders.

[107]ACFA. *Elenchus*, 14 July 1885.

[108]AAM. Julius Pohl's election calendar, entry for 14 July 1885. [M8, No. 1. Abbatial Election Materials]

[109]ACFA. *Elenchus*, 14 July 1885.

[110]AAM. Pohl's calendar, 14 July 1885.

[111]*Ibid.*

[112]Fellner, *Abbot*, 634.

[113]AAM. Pohl's calendar, 14 July 1885.

[114]*Ibid.*

[115]*Ibid.*

[116]*Ibid.*

[117]Fellner, *Abbot*, 634.

[118]AAM. Pohl's calendar, 14 July 1885.

[119]*Ibid.*

[120]*Ibid.*, 15 July 1885.

[121]Fellner, *Abbot*, 635.

Chapter II:

a Dream of Slight Promise

¹SVA. Letter from Jeremiah O'Connell to Wimmer, 15 July 1885.

²SVA. Letter from Wimmer to Utto Lang, 24 September 1876.

³Cf. discussion *infra.*

⁴O'Connell died in 1894, one month short of his seventy-third birthday.

⁵AAM. William F. O'Brien, "Doctor Jeremiah O'Connell: Author of *Catholicity in the Carolinas and Georgia.*" Unpublished typescript, p.1. [B5, No. 1. O'Brien, William F., Reverend] Valuable biographical information and corroboration is also found in Jeremiah Joseph O'Connell, *Catholicity in the Carolinas and Georgia: Leaves of Its History* (New York: Sadlier, 1879).

⁶O'Connell, *ibid.*, 244.

⁷*Ibid.*, 245.

⁸*Ibid.*, 247.

⁹*Ibid.*, 248-249.

¹⁰*Ibid.*, 477.

¹¹Cf. John Tracy Ellis, *The Life of James Cardinal Gibbons, Archbishop of Baltimore, 1834-1921,* Volume I (Milwaukee: Bruce, 1952), 78.

¹²O'Connell, 290.

¹³Bill Sharpe, "Gaston," *A New Geography of North Carolina,* Volume II (Raleigh: Sharpe Publishing Company, 1958), 765.

¹⁴*Ibid.*, 766.

¹⁵Robert F. Cope and Manly Wade Wellman, *The County of Gaston: Two Centuries of a North Carolina Region* (Charlotte, North Carolina: Gaston County Historical Society, 1961), 26. And Minnie Stowe Puett, *History of Gaston County* (Charlotte, North Carolina: Observer Printing House, 1939), 110 and 113.

¹⁶Cope, 69.

¹⁷AAM. Assignment of Bid, 18 December 1871, John F. Wooten to Jeremiah O'Connell. [J3, No. 2. Land: O'Connell, J.J.]

[18]*Ibid.* The deed mistakenly notes 536 acres being transferred.

[19]O'Connell, 478.

[20]*Ibid.*, 479.

[21]Cope, 106.

[22]Cf. Sharpe, 771.

[23]The 1870 census showed 12,602 people in Gaston County; 18,430 were white; 4,172 were black.

[24]The county had deposits of ceramic quartz; the clay would be good for bricks; there was iron, tin, and even gold. Sharpe, 761.

[25]Cope, 1.

[26]*Ibid.*, 160.

[27]Sharpe, 765.

[28]*Ibid.*, 763.

[29]"Gaston never knew agricultural prosperity. The small farms ordinarily were self-sufficient; . . . and the yield was low." Sharpe, 765.

[30]*Ibid.*

[31]Cope, 8.

[32]John Walker, a dairy farmer, reportedly owned the area's first slave. She served him as a domestic, and was purchased around 1763, in Charleston. Cf. Cope, 18.

[33]O'Connell, 478.

[34]Blackwell P. Robinson, *The North Carolina Guide* (Chapel Hill: University of North Carolina Press, 1955), 385.

[35]O'Connell, 478-479.

[36]Cf. Ellis, *Life*, I, 62.

[37]"I retain jurisdiction over the Vicariate of N[orth] Carolina, till the H[oly] F[ather] is pleased, at the suggestion of the B[isho]ps of this Province, to appoint a B[isho]p for N[orth] C[arolina]." D.RAH.A. James Gibbons, Diary (*Acta Episcopalia*), entry for 29 August 1872.

[38]O'Connell, 479.

[39]AAB. Gibbons' diary, 26 June 1875.

[40]SVA. Letter from Gibbons to Wimmer, 1 August 1875.

[41]*Ibid.*

[42]AAB. Gibbons' dairy, 26 June 1875.

[43]*Ibid.*, 3 April 1875.

[44]Records of the reasons for the refusal have not been retained by the Redemptorists. Their archivist, Father Alfred C. Rush, C.SS.R., theorized that the reason was this: "At that time the C.SS.R. work was completely confined to the urban centers of the East in our province. Many a year would pass before we moved into the South." AAM. Letter from Rush to Paschal Baumstein, 25 May 1983. [uncatalogued materials]

[45]O'Connell, 472.

[46]SVA. Letter from Gibbons to Wimmer, 1 August 1875.

[47]SVA. Letter from Wimmer to Lang, 24 September 1876.

[48]O'Connell claims to have been offered $50,000 for the mine. Cf. O'Connell, 479.

[49]Bishop Lynch had already tried to secure the Benedictines for South Carolina. Cf. discussion in Oetgen, *American*, 148, 219.

[50]AAM. O'Brien's transcription of Gibbons' remarks at the dedication of Maryhelp Abbey Church in 1894. William F. O'Brien, "Early History of the Origin of Belmont Abbey College and the Coming of the Fathers of the Ancient Order to North Carolina" (unpublished typescript, six pages), 3. [B5, No. 1. O'Brien, William F., Reverend]

[51]Cf. SVA. Note by Wimmer of 17 August 1875, on letter from Gibbons of 1 August 1875.

[52]SVA. Letter from Benno Hegele to Wimmer, 17 January 1876.

[53]SVA. Chapter Minutes, Saint Vincent Archabbey, 19 January 1876.

[54]SVA. Letter from Hegele to Wimmer, 20 January 1876.

[55]SVA. Letter from Hegele to Wimmer, 26 January 1876.

[56]SVA. Copy of letter (with translation) from Wimmer to Amberger, 20 August 1884.

[57]SVA. Official file on Herman Wolfe. Cf. also, Fellner, *Abbot*, 523, n.9. And AAM. Letter from Michael Irwin to Sebastian Doris (?), 8 March 1928, quoted in Doris, *Belmont*, 19. Also AAM. Letter from Philip Hurley to Ambrose Keefe, 1 March 1976. [uncatalogued materials]

[58]SVA. Letter from Wolfe to Wimmer, 26 January 1876.

[59]*Ibid.*

[60]AAB. Gibbons' diary, 25 March 1876.

[61]SVA. Letter from Wolfe to Wimmer, 26 January 1876.

[62]O'Connell, 479.

[63]He would not have them until April.

[64]SVA. Letter from Wolfe to Wimmer, 5 April 1876.

[65]Various dates apply, as described *infra.*

[66]AAM. Will of Herman Wolfe, 29 March 1876, and the later will of 26 August 1876.

[67]These are all the known documents of the period dealing with the original five hundred six acres and its conditions of transfer. Given the complexity of these negotiations, it is not inconceivable that additional versions were considered, also.

[68]AAM. Deed from O'Connell to Gibbons, 11 October 1875. [J3, No. 1. Land: O'Connell, J.J.]

[69]AAM. Contract from "Wolfe"/Gibbons to O'Connell, 11 October 1875. [J3, No. 2. Land: O'Connell, J.J.]

[70]AAM. Deed from Gibbons to Wolfe, 13 March 1876. [J3, No. 1. Land: O'Connell, J.J.]

[71]AAM. Will of Herman Wolfe, 29 March 1876. [E10, No. 1. Vows and Documents (W-Z)]

[72]AAM. Deed from O'Connell to Gibbons, 11 October 1875.

[73]AAM. Contract from "Wolfe"/Gibbons to O'Connell, 11 October 1875.

[74]AAM. Deed from O'Connell to Wolfe, 17 July 1876. [J3, No. 1. Land: O'Connell, J.J.]

[75]AAM. Will of Herman Wolfe, 26 August 1876. [E10, No. 1. Vows and Documents (W-Z)]

[76]AAM. Deed/Document from O'Connell to Wolfe, 15 November 1877. [J3, No 1. Land: O'Connell, J.J.]

[77]AAM. Deed from O'Connell and Wolfe to Wimmer, 3 December 1877. [J3, No. 4. Land: O'Connell, J.J.]

[78]AAM. Letter from Wimmer to Haid, 2 May 1886. [J3, No. 4. Land: O'Connell, J.J.]

[79]Cf. SVA. Letter from Philip Cassidy to Wimmer, 27 October 1876.

[80]Letter from Michael Irwin to Sebastian Doris (?), 8 March 1928; quoted in Doris, *Belmont*, 22.

[81]SVA. Personnel files. And O'Connell, 481-482. And AAM. Letter from Hurley to Keefe, 9 March 1876.

[82]SVA. Letter from Wimmer to Michael Regen (?), 7 August 1876. Gibbons actually apologized for the poor crops: AAM. Letter from Gibbons to Wolfe, 13 October 1876. [AO.O, No. 1. Gibbons, James Cardinal]

[83]SVA. Letter from Wolfe to Wimmer, [date unclear] July 1876.

[84]Doris, *Belmont*, 10.

[85]SVA. Personnel File on Cassidy.

[86]O'Connell, 481.

[87]As Wolfe phrased it, "It was difficult at my age to work with the old gentleman." SVA. Letter from Wolfe to Wimmer, 11 October 1880.

[88]SVA. Letter from Cassidy to Wimmer, 27 October 1876.

[89]SVA. Letter from Wolfe to Wimmer, 14 September 1876.

[90]SVA. Letter from Joseph Keller to Wimmer, 4 March 1877.

[91]O'Connell, 488-489.

[92]SVA. Letter from Wolfe to Wimmer, 5 July 1876.

[93]O'Connell, 481.

[94]SVA. Letter from Keller to Wimmer, 4 March 1877.

[95]SVA. Letter from brothers to Wimmer, 8 April 1877.

[96]It has been suggested that this was his second visit, but that appears to be unsubstantiated.

[97]Oblates are non-monastic affiliates of the Order, who accept special pious responsibilities but take no vows.

[98]Cf. Fellner, *Abbot*, 519. Brother Altman Alt had been added to the menage.

[99]AAM. Letter from Wimmer to Pohl, 1 January 1878. [M8, No. 1. Boniface Wimmer]

[100]Cf. Oetgen, *American*, 266 ff.

[101]AAM. Letter from Wimmer to Pohl, 6 August 1879. [M8, No. 1. Boniface Wimmer]

[102]*Ibid.*

[103]SBAA. Letter from Wimmer to Innocent Wolf, 23 May 1883.

[104]SVA. Letter from Wimmer to Lang, 3 November 1883.

[105]SVA. Letter from Edwin Pierron to Wimmer, 14-15 September 1883.

[106]*Ibid.*

[107]SVA. Letter from Moosmueller to Wimmer, 10 March 1877.

[108]AAM. Personnel records on Pohl. And Doris, *Belmont*, 18-19.

[109]SVA. Personnel Files on Stephen Lyons. Also ACFA. Correspondence regarding Lyons. Cf. also, SVA. Letter from Wolfe to Wimmer, 11 October 1880.

[110]SVA. Letter from Pohl to Zilliox, 3 July 1879.

[111]SVA. Letter from Wimmer to Zilliox, 29 July 1879.

[112]SVA. Letter from Wolfe to Wimmer, 11 October 1880.

[113]AAM. Annual Statement for calendar year 1880, signed by Wolfe. [J1, No. 1. Abbey (1881)]

[114]SVA. Letter from Wolfe to Wimmer, 21 August 1877 (enclosure).

[115]SVA. Letter from Wolfe to Wimmer, 11 November 1877.

[116]SVA. Letter from Wimmer to Lang, 21 December 1880.

[117]AAM. Annual Statement for calendar year 1880.

[118]SVA. Letter from Wimmer to Lang, 9 March 1880.

[119]AAM. Letter from Wimmer to Pohl, 1 November 1880. [A1.O, No. 1. Julius Pohl, OSB, RP—Correspondence]

[120]Cf. Fellner, *Abbot*, 625-626.

[121]AAM. Annual Statement for calendar year 1880.

[122]Enrollment sources differ appreciably. Whenever possible, enrollment figures in this volume are taken from the transcript records. Figures vary, of course, within each year. Whenever possible, the maximum number enrolled has been used, without regard to the period of any particular student's perseverance.

[123]AAM. Letter from Irwin to Doris (?), 8 March 1928; quoted in Doris, *Belmont*, 20.

[124]SVA. Letter from Wimmer to Wolfe, 18 April 1885.

[125]SVA. Letter from Wimmer to Wolfe, 11 April 1885.

[126]AAM. Letter from Northrop to Pohl, 9 October 1882. [A1.O, No. 1 Julius Pohl, OSB, RP—Correspondence]

[127]D.RICH.A. Letter from Lawrence O'Connell to Bishop Keane, 27 June 1879.

[128]SVA. "Saint Mary's Boarding School For Boys" (four page brochure). Cf. also, SVA. Letter from Wolfe to Wimmer, 17 July 1877.

[129]AAM. Letter from Wimmer to Pohl, 6 August 1879. [M8, No. 1. Boniface Wimmer]

[130]AAM. Letter from Irwin to Doris (?), 8 March 1928; quoted in Doris, *Belmont*, 20.

[131]Saint Mary's College *Catalogue*, 1880-1881 (1881).

[132]SVA. Letter from Lyons to Wimmer, 26 July 1881.

[133]SVA. Personnel File on Cyprian Moncton Creagh.

[134]SVA. Letter from Creagh to Wolfe, 6 February 1878.

[135]SVA. Letter from Creagh to Wimmer, 15 April 1884.

[136]Cf. AAM. Letter from Wimmer to Pohl, 7 August 1884; also Wimmer to Pohl, 21 August 1884. [M8, No. 1. Boniface Wimmer]

[137]AAM. Pohl's calendar, 15 July 1885.

[138]*Ibid.*

[139]*Ibid.*, 20 July 1885.

[140]*Ibid.*, 27 July 1885.

[141]*Ibid.*, 26 July 1885.

[142]At this point the monks were distributed thusly: Willibald, Richmond; Melchior, Savannah; Julius, Carolina; Leo, George, Patrick, Walter, and Charles, *en route* from Virginia to North Carolina; Felix, Bernard, Francis, and Benedict, Saint Vincent. Roman and William have escaped mention in any known reputable sources.

[143]SVA. Personnel files.

[144]AAM. Pohl's calendar, 27 July 1885.

[145]AAM. *Publicity Files*, Volume i. "Right Reverend Bishop Leo Haid Completes His Fiftieth Year As a Benedictine," Pittsburgh *Observer* (Thursday, 4 December 1919), 1 and 16 [quoting Charles Mohr].

[146]AAM. Address by Haid, 17 October 1910. Reprinted in *The Jubilee Book of Belmont Abbey* (Belmont: Abbey Press, 1910), 26.

[147]AAM. Pohl's calendar, 28 July 1885.

[148]"The Benedictine Abbey of Belmont, North Carolina," *American Ecclesiastical Review* (December, 1910), 720-721.

Chapter III:

a Mitred Abbot

[1]SVA. Letter from Boniface Wimmer to Joseph Amberger, 25 January 1886.

[2]*RB,* Prologue.

[3]*Ibid.*, xlviii.

[4]AAM. Julius Pohl's election diary, entries for 29 and 31 July 1885.

[5]*Ibid.*, 6 August 1885.

[6]*Ibid.*

[7]SVA, No. 5. Letter from Leo Haid to Boniface Wimmer, 13 August 1885.

[8]AAM. Cf. Pohl's diary, entries for 10-20 August 1885.

[9]*Ibid.*, 19 August 1885.

[10]*Ibid.*, 2 August 1885.

[11]*Ibid.*, 4 August 1885.

[12]*Ibid.*, 8 August 1885.

[13]"Without congregation," sometimes known as "private Mass".

[14]AAM. Pohl's diary, 19 August 1885.

[15]J.S. Bassett, "A North Carolina Monastery," *Magazine of American History* (February, 1893), 132-133.

[16]AAM. Pohl's diary, 8 August 1885.

[17]*Ibid.*, 26 August 1885.

[18]On 23 August, for example, Pohl counted sixteen visitors, fourteen of whom had journeyed from Charlotte. There were so many guests that Haid was obliged to request donations after serving dinner to so many people. *Ibid.*, 23 August 1885.

[19]*Ibid.*, 25 August 1885.

[20]*Ibid.*, 26 August 1885.

[21]AAM. Letter from A.L. Rives to Leo Haid, 29 August 1885. [A1.O, No. 1. Railroad]

[22]AAM. Letter from William J. Wright to Leo Haid, 29 October 1885. [A1.O, No. 1. Wright, William J. (Railroad Company)]

[23]SVA. No. 5. Letter from Leo Haid to Boniface Wimmer, 15 September 1885.

[24]SVA. No. 5. Letter from Haid to Wimmer, 4 September 1885. Cf. also Robert Lee Stowe, Sr., *Early History of Belmont and Gaston County, North Carolina* [(no publisher indicated) 1951], 49. According to this recollection, Haid paid one fourth of the total expense. The road is described as "about the worst in the county."

[25]Cope, 149.

[26]AAM. Insert for school *Catalogue*. Also, AAM, Chapter Minutes, 26 August 1885 (first meeting). These were the fields in which the men were to be prepared to function:

> *Leo Haid:* president; English literature, bookkeeping, commercial law, political economy, elocution, arithmetic, Spanish, moral and dogmatic theology
>
> *Julius Pohl:* Director (Rector) of the College; phonography, violin, vocal music, religion, and liturgy
>
> *William Mayer:* doctrine, Latin, German, geography, history, liturgy, English grammar and composition, arithmetic, spelling, reading, and bookkeeping
>
> *George Lester:* French, German, penmanship, reading, spelling, history (American and Bible), and geography
>
> *Patrick Donlon:* algebra, geometry, trigonometry, English grammar, reading, spelling, and Latin
>
> *Walter Leahy:* rhetoric, composition, arithmetic, bookkeeping, chemistry, natural philosophy, English grammar and literature, elocution, geography, and history
>
> *Roman Kirchner:* prefect of students; Latin, Greek, and German
>
> *Charles Mohr:* prefect of students; Latin, German, piano, telegraphy, arithmetic, bookkeeping, and Bible history

[27]AAM. Pohl's diary, 26 August 1885.

[28]College *Catalogue* (1885-1886), 7.

[29]AAM. An open letter "To Our Patrons." This was published in advertisements in 1885, and was included in the 1884-1885 *Catalogue* (p. 5). Haid wrote the text himself on 15 July 1885.

[30]AAM. Haid's handwritten text for the charter. [A1.0, No. 3. Writings]

[31]*Ibid.* The charter was approved 1 April 1886.

[32]AAM. Letter from Haid to Father Chrysostom (Saint Vincent), 11 April 1886. [A1.O, No. 3. Writings]. The Saint Benedict's Dramatic Association had been founded by Pohl in the spring term of 1884.

[33]Cf. AAM. Recollections of students collected in 1928 by Bernard Haas, for the golden jubilee celebration of the College. In particular, note the Chronology compiled by Haas from these recollections. [B5, No. 1. Golden Jubilee—Testimonials]. Cf. also, "Saint Mary's College," *Our Southern Home* (July, 1887), 1.

[34]AAM. *Publicity Files*, Volume i. "College Chit-Chat," McAdenville *Times* (17 March 1887), n.p.

[35]The books still exist (AAM). On the same page on which he drafted the text for the invitation to his abbatial benediction, Haid noted the need to order three volumes in leather and cloth, of 300-350 pages each. The first was for the Debating Society (the only one to need a second volume during Haid's life); the second was for the *Acta Capituli* (for minutes of the monastic Chapter); the third was to be the *Index Monachorum* (the official catalogue of the abbey's monks).

[36]AAM. Letter from Jerome Schmitt to Haid, 12 October 1885. [A1.O, No. 1. Jerome Schmitt, OSB, RP]

[37]Cf., Fellner, *Abbot*, 636-637.

[38]SVA, No. 5. Letter from Pohl to Wimmer, 25 October 1885.

[39]Cf., SVA, No. 5. Letter from Haid to Wimmer, 2 September 1885.

[40]Wilmington, North Carolina, was the See of the Vicariate.

[41]Cf. SVA, No. 5. Letter from Haid to Wimmer, 23 October 1885.

[42]Cf. SVA, No. 5. Letter from Haid to Wimmer, 1 November 1885.

[43]*Ibid.*

[44]SVA. Letter from Wimmer to Amberger, 25 October 1885.

[45]SVA. No. 4. Letter from Haid to Wimmer, 19 November 1885.

[46]AAM. The handwritten text with corrections is preserved in the abbey's archives. [A1.O, No. 3. Writings]

[47]The cathedral proper had been a victim of fire in 1861.

[48]The impropriety of his timing has already been mentioned.

[49]SVA, No. 5. Letter from Haid to Wimmer, 1 November 1885.

[50]AAM. Guest list in Haid's handwriting. [A1.O, No. 3. Writings]

[51]SVA, No. 4. Letter from Haid to Wimmer, 19 November 1885.

[52]AAM. Letter from Wimmer to Innocent Wolf (unlabeled transcript and translation), 13 November 1885. [B8, No. 2. Boniface Wimmer]

[53]AAM. *Publicity Files*, Volume i, includes several newspaper articles. The best are "The Benediction of an Abbot," Charleston *News and Courier*, 27 November 1885. And "Abbot Leo Haid, O.S.B.", Pittsburgh *Dispatch*, 27 November 1885.

[54]AAM. List "Presents to Right Reverend Abbot Leo, OSB", 11 November 1885. [A1.O, No. 1. Jubilees]

[55]SVA, No. 4. Letter from Haid to Wimmer, 19 November 1885.

[56]Pittsburgh *Dispatch*, 27 November 1885.

[57]*Ibid.*

[58]SVA. Letter from Wimmer to Amberger, 15 January 1886.

[59]SVA. No. 5. Letter from Haid to Wimmer, 2 September 1885.

[60]SVA, No. 5. Letter from Haid to Wimmer, 4 September 1885.

[61]BPA. Amendments approved in corporate meeting of 4 December 1885, signed by Haid, Moosmueller, and Reichert.

[62]SVA. Letter from Wimmer to Amberger, 15 January 1886.

[63]SVA. Letter from Edward Cafferty to Wimmer, 26 February 1886.

[64]*Ibid.*

[65]*Ibid.*

[66]*Ibid.*

[67]SVA, No. 4. Letter from Haid to Wimmer, 18 July 1886.

[68]SVA. Letter from Moosmueller to Wimmer, 27 July 1886.

[69]SVA. Letter from Moosmueller to Wimmer, 3 August 1886.

[70]SVA, No. 4. Letter from Haid to Wimmer, 18 July 1886.

[71]SVA. Letter from Moosmueller to Wimmer, 5 August 1886.

[72]SVA. Letter from Moosmueller to Wimmer, 11 August 1886.

[73]SVA. No. 4. Letter from Haid to Wimmer, 14 August 1886.

[74]SVA. No. 4. Letter from Haid to Wimmer, 25 August 1886.

[75]SVA. Letter from Moosmueller to Wimmer, 22 December 1886.

[76]SVA, No. 4. Letter from Haid to Wimmer, 23 July 1887.

[77]Cf. SVA, No. 4. Letter from Haid to Wimmer, 30 August 1886.

[78]SVA. Letter from Haid to Wimmer, 23 July 1887.

[79]*Ibid.*

[80]SVA, No. 4. Letter from Haid to Wimmer, 29 July 1887. There was also a problem on Skidaway concerning the Sisters. They had been a constant annoyance to the new bishop and to Haid. In this visit, Haid also accomplished the closing of the Sisters' property and the final removal of the ladies' presence on the island. Only their debts remained. "As long as I am superior," Leo Haid resolved, "no Sister will be permitted to live on the Island."

[81]SVA, No. 4. Letter from Haid to Wimmer, 25 August 1886.

[82]Cope, 143.

[83]*Ibid*., 132.

[84]Cf. SVA, No. 4. Letter from Haid to Wimmer, 6 September 1886; and Stowe, *Early*, 30-31.

[85]Cope, 124.

[86]AAM. Haas' Chronology.

[87]O'Connell, 482.

[88]SVA, No. 5. Postscript on letter from Haid to Wimmer, 23 October 1885.

[89]SVA, No. 4. Letter from Haid to Wimmer, 3 February 1887.

[90]SVA, No. 4. Letter from Haid to Wimmer, 31 December 1885.

[91]SVA, No. 5. Postscript on letter from Haid to Wimmer, 23 October 1885.

[92]SVA, No. 5. Letter from Haid to Wimmer, 2 September 1885.

[93]*Ibid.*

[94]SVA, No. 5. Letter from Haid to Wimmer, 18 September 1885.

[95]SVA, No. 5. Letters from Haid to Wimmer, 2 September, and 4 September 1885.

[96]SVA, No. 4. Letter from Haid to Wimmer, 10 January 1886.

[97]SVA, No. 4. Letter from Haid to Wimmer, 13 January 1886.

[98]*Ibid*., and letter from Haid to Wimmer, 10 January 1886. Also, AAM. Haas' Chronology.

[99]SVA, No. 4. Letter from Haid to Wimmer, 13 January 1886.

[100]*Ibid.*

[101]*Ibid.*

[102]SVA, No. 4. Letter from Haid to Wimmer, 10 January 1886.

[103]SVA, No. 4. Letter from Haid to Wimmer, 13 January 1886.

[104]SVA, No. 4. Letter from Haid to Wimmer, 10 January 1886.

[105]SVA, No. 4. Letter from Haid to Wimmer, 13 January 1886.

[106]AAM. O'Brien, "Doctor", 1-2.

[107]SVA, No. 4. Letter from Haid to Wimmer, 29 January 1886.

[108]NDUA. Letter from Felix Hintemeyer to Ludwig-Missionsverein, 10 November 1902.

[109]SVA, No. 5. Letter from Haid to Wimmer, 23 October 1885. "I am not over fond of farming . . ."

[110]SVA, No. 4. Letter from Haid to Wimmer, 11 February 1886.

[111]SVA, No. 5. Letter from Haid to Wimmer, 13 October 1885.

[112]SCSA, No. 1. Letter from Haid to Zilliox, 24 May 1886.

[113]AAM. Letter from Haid to Father Chrysostom, 11 April 1886.

[114]SCSA, No. 1. Letter from Haid to Zilliox, 24 May 1886.

[115]SVA, No. 5. Letter from Haid to Wimmer, 1 October 1885.

[116]SCSA, No. 1. Letter from Haid to Zilliox, 24 May 1886.

[117]AAM. Conference notes by Haid, 1885. [A1.O, No. 1. Sermons and Retreats]

[118]AAM. Homily notes, 1885. [A1.O, No. 1. Sermons and Retreats]

[119]AAM. "Questions for Manifestation," dated "188-" [sic]. [A1.O, No. 1. Sermons and Retreats]

[120]SVA, No. 5. Letter from Haid to Wimmer, 1 October 1885.

[121]SVA, No. 4. Letter from Haid to Wimmer, 18 July 1886.

[122]SVA, No. 5. Letter from Haid to Wimmer, 13 October 1885.

[123]Cf. Sadliers' *Catholic Directory*, 1884, 1885, 1886, 1887, 1888. The quantity of missions listed expands irregularly because of the month-long missionary circuit that could not always be staffed. For a description of the sequence and conditions of this circuit, cf. AAM. "Reminiscences of a Year's Work in North Carolina" by Walter Leahy [M15, No. 1. Personal Papers]. Regarding Saint Benedict Church, Leo Haid wrote, "I must enlarge the [Maryhelp Abbey] Chapel at once: every Sunday some must stand and then the colored people go out for fear of offending the whites." (SVA, No. 4. Letter from Haid to Wimmer, 6 September 1886)

[124]AAM. Notes by Leo Haid regarding 17-19 December 1885. [A1.O, No. 3. Writings]

[125]SJA, No. 3. Letter from Haid to Alexius Edelbrock, 21 July 1886.

[126]SVA, No. 4. Letter from Haid to Wimmer, 25 August 1886.

[127]SCSA, No. 1. Letter from Haid to Zilliox, 24 May 1886.

[128]NDUA. Letter from Hintemeyer to Ludwig-Missionsverein, 27 March 1911.

[129]AAM. Letter from Haid to Father Chrysostom, 11 April, 1886.

[130]SVA, No. 4. Letter from Haid to Prior Michael Hofmayer, OSB (Saint Vincent), 4 March 1886.

[131]SVA, No. 5. Letter from Haid to Wimmer, 15 September 1885.

[132]SVA, No. 5. Letter from Haid to Wimmer, 11 September 1885.

[133]SVA, No. 5. Letter from Haid to Wimmer, 1 October 1885.

[134]SVA, No. 5. Letter from Haid to Wimmer, 13 August 1885.

[135]SVA, No. 5. Letter from Haid to Wimmer, 4 September 1885.

[136]SVA, No. 5. Letter from Haid to Wimmer, 11 February 1886.

[137]SVA, No. 5. Letter from Haid to Wimmer, 19 November 1885.

[138]SVA, No. 5. Letter from Haid to Wimmer, 6 January 1887.

[139]Cf. SVA, No. 5. Letters from Haid to Wimmer, 13 August, 15 September, 1 October 1885, etc.

[140]SVA. Copy of letter from Wimmer to Bruanmueller, 12 April 1886.

[141]SVA, No. 4. Letter from Haid to Wimmer, 29 January 1886.

[142]SVA, No. 4. Letter from Haid to Wimmer, 26 January 1886.

[143]SVA, No. 4. Letter from Haid to Wimmer, 8 February 1886.

[144]SVA, No. 4. Letter from Haid to Wimmer, 6 September 1886.

[145]SVA, No. 4. Letter from Haid to Wimmer, 29 January 1886.

[146]SVA, No. 4. Letter from Haid to Wimmer, 6 September 1886.

[147]Cf. SVA, No. 5. Letters from Haid to Wimmer, 18 September, 1 October 1885.

[148]SVA, No. 4. Letter from Haid to Wimmer, 26 December 1885.

[149]AAM. Deed, Saint Vincent to Maryhelp, 7 June 1886. [J3, No. 8. Land: Gaston County]

[150]SCSA, No. 1. Letter from Haid to Zilliox, 24 Mary 1886.

[151]SVA, No. 4. Letter from Haid to Hofmayer, 4 March 1886.

[152]Quoted in Colman Barry, *Worship and Work: Saint John Abbey and University, 1856-1945* (Collegeville, Minnesota: North Central Publishing Company, 1956), 223. This was said at the abbatial election of Peter Engel, 28 November 1894.

[153]SVA, No. 4. Letter from Haid to Wimmer, 31 December 1885.

[154]SVA, No. 5. Letter from Haid to Wimmer, 1 October 1885. Cf. also Fellner's discussion of Haid's loneliness. Fellner, *Abbot*, 636.

[155]SVA. Some sample closings:

> "obediently" (23 October 1885)
> "your most humble servant" (25 October 1885)
> "yours" (13 August 1885)
> "with sincere affection" (25 August 1885)
> "your son" (2 September 1885)
> "rejoicing in the hope of seeing you soon" (19 November 1885)
> "with deep affection" (31 December 1885)
> [variations on] "sincerely" (March 1886)
> "Fraternally yours" (14 August 1886; 30 August 1886)

N.B., as Haid grows in confidence he abandons images of subservience ("obediently," "your son") for equality ("fraternally").

[156]SCSA, No. 1. Letter from Haid to Zilliox, 6 November 1886.

[157]For a discussion of the *crescat* story, its validity, and its aftermath, cf. Paschal Baumstein, "Variations in Heraldic Insignia at Maryhelp Abbey," *The American Benedictine Review* (March, 1983), 62-73. Cf. especially, n.4.

[158]SVA, No. 5. Letter from Haid to Wimmer, 25 August 1885.

[159]SVA, No. 4. Letter from Haid to Wimmer, 13 January 1886.

[160]*Ibid.*

[161]SVA, No. 4. Letter from Haid to Wimmer, 11 February 1886.

[162]SVA, No. 4. Letter from Haid to Wimmer, 26 February 1886.

[163]Much of what follows is adapted from the history of the College Building, published in 1982: Paschal Baumstein, "The First Sign of Permanence," *Crescat* (Summer, 1982), 1-6.

[164]When Haid finally built this wing, it was not made to join the three storey monastery, after all.

[165]SVA, No. 4. Letter from Haid to Wimmer, 11 February 1886.

[166]AAB. Letter from Haid to Gibbons, 17 February 1886.

[167]AAM. *Publicity Files,* Volume i. "Another Mark of Southern Progress," McAdenville *Times*, May 1886, 1.

[168]Psalm 126.

[169]AAM. Letter from John J. Cox (former student) to Bernard Haas, 30 April 1926. [B5, No. 1. Golden Jubilee—Testimonials]

[170]SCSA, No. 1. Letter from Haid to Zilliox, 24 May 1886.

[171]SJA, No. 3. Letter from Haid to Edelbrock, 21 July 1886.

[172]SVA, No. 4. Letter from Haid to Wimmer, 14 August 1886.

[173]SCSA, No. 1. Letter from Haid to Zilliox, 25 December 1886.

[174]*Ibid.* And SVA, No. 4. Letter from Haid to Wimmer, 6 January 1887.

[175]AAM. Letter from John J. Cox to Bernard Haas, 30 April 1926.

[176]Cf. AAM. *Publicity Files*, Volume i. "Enlargement of the College Chapel," McAdenville *Times* (February 1887).

[177]SVA, No. 4. Letter from Haid to Wimmer, 13 September 1887.

[178]SVA, No. 4. Letter from Haid to Wimmer, 17 October 1887.

[179]SVA, No. 4. Letter from Haid to Wimmer, 27 January 1887.

[180]SVA, No. 4. Letter from Haid to Wimmer, 3 February 1887.

[181]SVA, No. 4. Letter from Haid to Wimmer, 7 February 1887.

[182]SVA, No. 4. Letter from Haid to Wimmer, 13 January 1886.

[183]SVA, No. 5. Letter from Haid to Wimmer, 13 October 1885.

[184]AAM. *Publicity Files*, Volume i. "College Chit-Chat," McAdenville *Times*, article dated 17 March 1887.

[185]SJA, No. 3. Letter from Haid to Edelbrock, 20 May 1887.

[186]SVA, No. 4. Letter from Haid to Wimmer, 13 September 1887.

[187]*Ibid.*

[188]AAM. Haas' Chronology.

[189]AAM. *Publicity Files*, Volume i. "A Southern Benedictine Abbey," New York *Sun*, 7 March 1886.

[190]AAM. Reminiscences collected by Dom Paul Milde, OSB, from the original brothers at Maryhelp, 1927. [B5, No. 1. Reminiscences (Father Paul)]

[191]There are many available sources of this story. These are a few: AAM. Letter from Sebastian Doris to Robert Brennan, undated (1961). [M137, No. 1. Correspondence] And BPA. "Belmont Abbey Aids Church in South," by John B. Ebel, 2 October 1953. And Doris, *Belmont*, 9, n.4.

[192]Ebel, *ibid.*, thinks it was for Belmont England. And in discussions with members of a local historical society in Gaston County, I found the Belmont Abbey of England story to be the only one commonly considered reputable.

[193]AAM. Letter from Miriam Rabb, of the North Carolina Department of Conservation and Development, to Robert Brennan, 20 November 1961. [M137, No. 1. Correspondence]

[194]AAM. Letter from Bird S. Coler to Haid, 23 December 1912. [A1.O, No. 1. Correspondence, 1911-1915]

[195]AAM. Copy of letter from Haid to Bird S. Coler/Perry Belmont, 25 December 1912. [B1, No. 1. Belmont Township]

[196]Perry Belmont, *An American Democrat: The Recollections of Perry Belmont* (New York: Columbia University Press, 1940).

[197]*Ibid.*, 276.

[198]Cf., New York *Times* (7 June 1928), 15.

[199]Letter from Vincent Taylor to Perry Belmont, 1 June 1928. [Quoted in Belmont, 275.]

[200]AAM. Letter from Agnes Regan to Vincent Taylor, 21 June 1928. [A2.O, No. 1. Belmont, Perry]

[201]AAM. Letter from Thomas Oestreich (secretary to the abbot) to Agnes Regan, 1 July 1928. [A2.O, No. 1. Belmont, Perry] As a typical example of the various confused versions of the story that appeared subsequently, see "Plant and Facility Report: Sacred Heart College" (March, 1970), a disquisition submitted to the Southern Association of Colleges and Schools:

> Belmont was first incorporated in 1895 and again in 1945. Belmont was originally called Garibaldi but changed to Belmont when the Southern Railroad objected to the name. The name was changed to honor Augustus P. Belmont of New York City. At the time, Mr. Belmont was a close friend of Bishop Leo Haid, administrator of Saint Mary's College (later Belmont Abbey College). It is not clear as to whether Bishop Haid had sufficient influence to effect the choice of a name but history indicates that Bishop Haid was by no means a "back seater" in Garibaldi Town.

[202]AAB. Letter from Mark Gross to Gibbons, 10 November 1886.

[203]AAB. Letter from Mark Gross to Gibbons, 16 June 1887.

[204]*Ibid.*

[205]SVA, No. 4. Letter from Haid to Wimmer, 18 July 1886; and AAM. Haas' Chronology.

328

[206]New York *Sun*, 7 March 1886.
[207]SCSA, No. 1. Letter from Haid to Zilliox, 24 May 1886.
[208]AAM. Letter from Haid to Father Chrysostom, 11 April 1886.
[209]SVA, No. 4. Letter from Haid to Hofmayer, 4 March 1886.
[210]SJA, No. 3. Letter from Haid to Edelbrock, 21 July 1886.

Chapter IV:

a Second Jurisdiction

[1]D.RAH.A. James Gibbons, Diary *(Acta Episcopalia)*, entry for 29 August 1872. "I retain jurisdiction over the Vicariate of N[orth] Carolina, till the H[oly] F[ather] is pleased, at the suggestion of the B[isho]ps of this Province, to appoint a D[isho]p for N[orth] C[arolina]."

[2]AAB. Letter from John Cardinal Simeoni to Gibbons, 11 June 1881.

[3]AAB. *Terna* for Vicariate Apostolic of North Carolina, 1879. See also Ellis, *Life*, I, 186. Janssens was later named an archbishop.

[4]AAB. Letter from Mark Gross to Gibons, 16 September 1879.

[5]Sadliers' *Catholic Directory*, 1880. "Vicariate Apostolic of North Carolina."

[6]AAB. Letter from Mark Gross to Gibbons, 20 September 1880.

[7]AAB. Letter from Simeoni to Mark Gross, 10 October 1880.

[8]AAB. Letter from Mark Gross to Gibbons, 26 October 1880.

[9]AAM. Letter from Northrop to "Reverend Benedictine Fathers, Saint Mary's College," 22 September 1881. [AO.O, No. 1. Northrop, Henry, Bishop]

[10]AAM. Letter from Edwin Pierron to Haid, 16 July 1885. [A1.O, No. 1. Edwin Pierron, OSB, RP]

[11]AAB. Gibbons' diary, entries for 25 and 29 May. It is of interest that the next entry in his diary, 7 June, records his elevation to the cardinalate.

[12]AAB. Letter from Mark Gross to Gibbons, 16 June 1887.

[13]AAB. Letter from De Propaganda Fide to Gibbons, 23 July 1886.

[14]AAB. Letter from Gibbons to De Propaganda Fide, 31 August 1886.

[15]SCSA, No. 1. Letter from Haid to Zilliox, 25 December 1886. Becker was the bishop who actually received the prestigious appointment to Savannah.

[16]Cf. Ellis' discussion, *Life*, II, 440-441.

[17]Cf. SBAA. Letter from Wimmer to Innocent Wolf, 2 February 1887. The letter from Rome to Wimmer (SVA) is dated 7 January 1887.

[18]SVA, No. 4. Letter from Haid to Wimmer, 3 February 1887.

[19]SVA, No. 14. Letter from Mark Gross to Wimmer, misdated 6 February 1888 (should be "1887").

[20]SJA, No. 3. Letter from Haid to Edelbrock, 20 May 1887.

[21]SVA, No. 4. Letter from Haid to Wimmer, 17 October 1887.

[22]Cf. discussion in Fellner, *Abbot*, 635.

[23]AAB. Letter from Haid to Gibbons, 7 April 1888.

[24]SJA, No. 3. Letter from Haid to Edelbrock, 7 April 1888.

[25]Cf. AAB. Letter from Haid to Gibbons, 12 April 1888.

[26]SJA, No. 3. Letter from Haid to Edelbrock, 17 April 1888.

[27]SJA, No. 3. Letter from Haid to Edelbrock, 30 April 1888.

[28]SJA, No. 3. Letter from Haid to Edelbrock, 15 May 1888.

[29]SJA, No. 3. Letter from Haid to Edelbrock, 1 June 1888.

[30]The formal invitations are preserved: AAM. [B7, No. 1. Leo Haid—Episcopal Ordination], 5 June 1888.

[31]AAB. Letter from Haid to Gibbons, 17 April 1888.

[32]AAB. Letter from Haid to Gibbons, 18 June 1888.

[33]AAB. Letter from Haid to Gibbons, 17 April 1888.

[34]AAM. The *Publicity Files* at AAM contain several items regarding the ceremony. The best are: "Consecrated Bishop: Abbot Leo Haid Elevated," Baltimore *Sun* (2 July 1888). And "Consecrated Bishop," *Catholic Mirror* (7 July 1888).

[35]*Ibid., Sun.*

[36]AAM. *Publicity Files*, Volume i. "Interesting Services," *The Daily Messenger* (Wilmington), 15 July 1888. And "Cardinal Gibbons Arrives," *The Daily Messenger* (Wilmington), 13 July 1888. And "A Prominent Visitor," Charlotte *News and Observer*, (?) July 1888. And "Bishop Haid Installed," Wilmington *Morning Star*, 17 July 1888. And "Our Eminent Visitor," *The Daily Messenger* (Wilmington), 14 July 1888. And "Personal," *The Daily Messenger* (Wilmington), 15 July 1888.

[37]Cf. AAM. "Reminiscences of a Year's Work in North Carolina," by Walter Leahy. [M15, No. 1. Personal Papers]

[38]SJA, No. 3. Letter from Haid to Edelbrock, 5 January 1888.

[39]AAM. *Publicity Files*, Volume i, 62. Letter to the Editor from Leo Haid, Gastonia *Gazette* (24 May 1888).

[40]AAM. *Publicity Files*, Volume i, 63. "Bishop Haid's Letter", Gastonia *Gazette* (24 May 1888).

[41]SJA, No. 3. Letter from Haid to Edelbrock, 9 November 1888.

[42]SVA, No. 9. Letter from Haid to Hintenach, 26 October 1888.

[43]SJA. Letter from Haid to Edelbrock, 10 December 1888.

[44]Ignatius Remke, *Historical Sketch of Saint Mary's Church, Richmond, Virginia, 1843-1935* [cf. listing in bibliography, *infra*], 17.

[45]SVA, No. 9. Letter from Haid to Hintenach, 11 September 1888.

[46]SVA, No. 9. Letter from Haid to Hintenach, 3 November 1888.

[47]SJA, No. 3. Letter from Haid to Edelbrock, 9 November 1888.

[48]SVA, No. 9. Letter from Haid to Hintenach, 26 October 1888.

[49]SJA, No. 3. Letter from Haid to Edelbrock, 22 August 1888.

[50]SJA. Letter from Haid to Bernard Locnikar, 10 January 1891.

[51]SJA, No. 3. Letter from Haid to Edelbrock, 10 December 1888.

[52]SAA, No. 3. Letter from Haid to Primate, 8 October 1909.

[53]SJA. Letter from Haid to Peter Engel, 6 April 1909.

[54]SVA, No. 9. Letter from Haid to Hintenach, 3 August 1888.

[55]SAA, No. 3. Letter from Haid to Primate, 1894 (page one, with precise date, is missing).

[56]AAM. Informal sacramental register kept by Haid.

[57]BSA, No. 1. Letter from Haid to Katharine Drexel, 30 May 1900.

[58]SAA, No. 3. Letter from Haid to Primate, 15 October 1894.

[59]Cf. AAM. Letter from Bernard Smith to Haid, 11 June 1892. [A1.O, No. 1. Smith, Bernard]

[60]SJA. Letter from Haid to Engel, 22 April 1920.

[61]SVA, No. 9. Letter from Haid to Father Adalbert (Prior of Sant' Anselmo), 17 August 1893.

[62]ACFA. Letter from Vincent Huber to Haid, 15 June 1892.

[63]SVA, No. 9. Letter from Haid to Father Adalbert, 17 August 1893.

[64]Ibid.

[65]SAA, No. 3. Letter from Haid to Primate, 30 June 1896.

[66]SVA, No. 1. Letter from Haid to Hintenach, 11 September 1888.

[67]Cf. discussion in Fellner, Abbot, 697-698.

[68]SVA, No. 9. Letter from Haid to Hintenach, 4 October 1888.

[69]SVA, No. 14. Letter from Haid to Bernard Smith, 6 June 1891.

[70]SVA, No. 9. Letter from Haid to Father Adalbert, 3 March 1891.

[71]AAB. Letter from Simeoni to Gibbons, 20 December 1890.

[72]SVA, No. 9. Letter from Haid to Hintenach, 27 December 1890.

[73]SVA, No. 9. Letter from Haid to Hintenach, 23 April 1891.

[74]AAB. Letter from Gibbons to Simeoni, 8 January 1891.

[75]SVA, No. 14. Letter from Haid to Bernard Smith, 6 June 1891.

[76]Ibid.

[77]AAM. Letter from Gibbons to Haid, 12 September 1892. [A1.O, No. 1. Gibbons, James Cardinal]

[78]Decree of De Propaganda Fide, 4 December 1891. [Both AAM and D.RAH.A. have copies.]

[79]SVA, No. 10. Letter from Haid to Leander Schnerr, 22 December 1893.

[80]SVA, No. 9. Letter from Haid to Hintenach, 6 June 1889.

[81]By the time the fifty years had expired part of the territory had already been granted in perpetuity; the rest was ceded to the Diocese of Raleigh, which had been created in 1924. Saint Peter Church in Charlotte was granted in perpetuity, however, on 9 June 1942. Vincent Waters, who later served Raleigh as bishop, and whose love for the Abbey was noteworthy for its extraordinary moderation, succeeded in 1969, in securing Belmont's withdrawal from the Charlotte church [cf. D.RAH.A. Letter from Waters to Walter Coggin, 10 November 1969].

[82]AAM. Letter from Haid to Drexel, 24 June 1893. [A1.O, No. 1. Correspondence (1885-1889)]

[83]SJA, No. 5. Letter from Haid to Locnikar, 24 July 1890.

[84]The Collegian (May, 1894), 162-163. Also "The Grotto at Belmont Abbey," Bulletin (February, 1939).

[85]AAM. Milde, "Reminiscences."

[86]AAM. Publicity Files, ii, 1. "A Splendid Function," Catholic Mirror (May, 1891), 8.

[87]AAM. Program for dedication of the Lourdes Grotto at Belmont [uncatalogued materials].

[88]AAM. "Splendid Function."

[89]AAM. Program.

[90]AAM. "Splendid Function."

[91]Ibid.

[92]AAM. Program.

[93]AAM. *Publicity Files*, i, 107. "Saint Mary's College," Mount Holly *News* (c. 1 June 1891).

[94]Cf. Oetgen's comment, *American*, 321-322, n.81.

[95]Mark Gross had tried in 1887 to get the Benedictine Sisters of Richmond to establish a convent in Charlotte. Cf. AAB. Letter from Mark Gross to Gibbons, 16 June 1887.

[96]Records at the Sisters' Motherhouse are imprecise on this point. I am following here the learned assumption of Mr. Hite, letter of 29 March 1983.

[97]AAB. Letter from Haid to Gibbons, 8 April 1892.

[98]There is, in the oral tradition of the Abbey, a story so commonly reported that it must be mentioned. According to this version, the Abbot decided he would take Mercies over Benedictines because he wanted "Sisters who will *work*." I have been unable either to substantiate or disprove this pericope. In terms of the inference the story projects against the Benedictine Sisters, I must note, however, that the Bishop seems to have greatly loved the Virgins of the Order, and he did choose them to share soon afterwards in his foundation in northern Virginia, where they proved far more successful and responsible than did their male counterparts.

[99]AAM. Speech by Anselm Biggs, 24 September 1969.

[100]D.RAH.A., No. 3. Annals of the Sisters of Mercy, 1841-1892, by Sister Mary Charles Curtin, R.S.M., 62-63.

[101]*Ibid.*, 63.

[102]*Ibid.*

[103]*Ibid.*, 64-65.

[104]D.RAH.A., No. 2. Annals of the Sisters of Mercy, 1892-1910, by Sister Agatha Ryan, 71.

[105]*Ibid.*, 72.

[106]AAM. *Publicity Files*, i, 133. "The Dedication Exercises." Charlotte *Observer* (9 September 1892).

[107]D.RAH.A., No. 2. Ryan Annals, 72.

[108]*Ibid.*, 73.

[109]Most notable in this period was the new Saint Peter Church in Charlotte. Father Francis Meyer raised the money through Katharine Drexel and other sources, and apparently ran such an efficient operation that the cornerstone was laid 3 September 1893, and the church was blessed on Christmas Eve that same year.

[110]AAM. *Publicity Files*, i, 151. "The New Catholic Church," Charlotte *Observer* (27 December 1893).

[111]Sources differ for many of the dates, and there sometimes is confusion regarding which wing was under construction at any particular time. This list is presented with confidence, if not certainty, in its accuracy. It was compiled through elaborate checks between correspondence and dated photographs. I usually trusted newspapers and periodicals only if they said construction was at that time in progress, or if they were covering a groundbreaking, cornerstone blessing, or opening ceremony; they were never trusted when they merely recited dates on which something had or would happen. There are some financial records which helped in the dating, too, but since brickmaking in particular was constant, and the Bishop would buy supplies comfortably in advance or at the last moment, depending on when money appeared, these were of little help on the whole. Whenever possible, since interest here is in construction more than use, the date given is the year in which construction began.

[112]SVA, No. 9. Letter from Haid to Hintenach, 27 December 1890.

[113]SJA, No. 5. Letter from Haid to Locnikar, 30 December 1890.

[114]*Ibid.*

[115]SVA, No. 9. Letter from Haid to Hintenach, 5 February 1891.

[116]SJA. Letter from Haid to Locnikar, 10 January 1891.

[117]*Ibid.*

[118]*Ibid.*

[119]SVA, No. 9. Letter from Haid to Hintenach, 5 February 1891.

[120]SJA. Letter from Haid to Locnikar, 10 January 1891.

[121]SJA. Letter from Haid to Locnikar, 1 February 1892.

[122]AAM. Contract of 9 February 1892. [A1.O, No. 1. Church—Construction]

[123]AAM. *Publicity Files*, i, 121. "The Feast of Saint Benedict," Charlotte *Observer* (22 March 1892).

[124]AAM. *Publicity Files*, i, 122. "Items from Saint Mary's College," Mount Holly *News* (1 April 1892).

[125]AAB. Letter from Haid to Gibbons, 8 April 1892. At best this is a half-hearted invitation to the Cardinal. It appears, at least, that Haid was "resigned" to taking prominence in the ceremonies even before His Eminence was advised of the event.

[126]By the 1890's dramatics had replaced forensics as the most prestigious campus activity for students. In the 1930's, athletics moved into prominence, but because of the personal interest of the Abbot, the precedence of the theatre stood unquestioned prior to Leo Haid's death.

[127]When there were two theatre presentations, one was usually executed by the young ladies at Sacred Heart Academy. Father Felix would sometimes write their scripts.

[128]AAM. *Publicity Files*, i, 127. "The New Abbey Church," Charlotte *Chronicle* (5 May 1892).

[129]*Ibid.*

[130]*Ibid.*

[131]AAM. *Publicity Files*, i, 130. "New Abbey Church," *The Church News* [Washington], (14 May 1892).

[132]AAM. *Publicity Files*, i, 129. "At Saint Mary's," Charlotte *News* (4 May 1892).

[133]AAM. *Church News.*

[134]AAM. "Abbey," Charlotte *Chronicle*, 5 May 1892. This article includes the text of the Bishop's speech.

[135]AAM. The entire document is reprinted *ibid.*

[136]AAM. *Publicity Files*, i, 128. "Mary Help Abbey," Raleigh *News and Observer* (7 May 1892).

[137]AAM. *Publicity Files*, i, 128. "Festivities at Saint Mary's College," Charlotte *News* (5 May 1892).

[138]AAM. *Publicity Files*, i, 128. "A Strange Visitor in Paw Creek—The Negroes Terribly Alarmed." [Unlabeled newspaper clipping]

[139]BSA, No. 1. Copy of Letter from Haid to Drexel, 24 June 1893.

[140]D.RAH.A. Document between Haid and Drexel, 1 July 1893. Cover letter is dated 28 December 1893.

[141]Cf. discussion in Consuela Marie Duffy, *Katharine Drexel: A Biography* (Cornwells Heights, Pennsylvania: Sisters of the Blessed Sacrament, [1965] 1972), 73-75.

[142]Cf., for example, BSA, No. 1. Letter from Haid to Drexel, 8 May 1900; with notation by Drexel, dated 16 May 1900.

[143]AAM and BSA. Haid and Drexel correspondence for 1914.

[144]BSA, No. 1. Letter from Haid to Drexel, 24 June 1893.

[145]AAM. Letter from Drexel to Haid, undated (1893). [A1.O, No. 1. Correspondence to Leo Haid from Katharine Drexel]

[146]D.RAH.A. Document between Haid and Drexel, 1 July 1893.

[147]AAM. Letter from Drexel to Haid, 16 October 1893. [A1.O, No. 1. Correspondence to Leo Haid from Katharine Drexel]

[148]BSA, No. 1. Letter from Haid to Drexel, 20 October 1893. In 1904, Mother Drexel visited Belmont. She attended what she admitted to be a magnificent Cathedral Vespers, matched only by the loveliness of the church itself. She found there a row of pews running the entire length of the church, front to back, reserved for blacks. Unfortunately the entire row of pews was unpopulated. Abbot Leo was still trying to explain the situation in letters as late as 1910. Cf. for example, letter from Haid to Drexel, 18 July 1910 [BSA, No. 1].

[149]BSA, No. 1. Letter from Haid to Drexel, 18 December 1893. The vestment the Bishop wore for that first Mass was used again for his corpse in 1924. Cf. Doris, *Belmont*, p. 36, n. 19.

[150]Leo Haid tried to get Katharine Drexel to provide new Stations, but failed. AAM. Letter from Haid to Drexel, 20 January 1894. [A1.O, No. 1. Correspondence from Leo Haid to Katharine Drexel]

[151]The church is still standing, and much of what follows is taken from critical evaluation and observation, as well as comparison with period photographs and descriptions. There are four other principal sources used in dealing with the church here: AAM. *Publicity Files*, ii, 3-4. "An Historic Event," *Catholic Mirror* (21 April 1894), 1; also *Catholic News*. AAM. Donna Alyn Hollar, "Maryhelp Abbey Cathedral: Analysis and Interpretation of Gothic Revival," unpublished typescript (University of North Carolina at Charlotte, 19 April 1982) [B5, No. 1. "Maryhelp Abbey Cathedral" (architectural study)]. And Paschal Baumstein, "Chapel, Church, Cathedral," *Crescat* (Summer, 1983), pp. 1-8.

[152]*Ibid., Mirror.*

[153]*Ibid.*

[154]Regarding the windows, cf. *Mirror*, Hollar, and Baumstein [no. 151, *supra*]. Also AAM. *Bulletin*, (January, 1939). [B6, No. 1. Cathedral Windows].

[155]The records of the fair document Mayer's awards, of course, but since the prize was the manufacturer's rather than the owner's, no record acknowledges which of the Belmont windows were on exhibit in Chicago. The oral tradition claims the windows of Saints Patrick and Placid were the medalists; this cannot be proven on the basis of known records, though on the basis of quality, artistry, and workmanship these would have been appropriate selections from the Belmont windows for the exhibit.

[156]Cf. AAM. Letter from Francis Mayer to Haid, 30 December 1903. [A1.O, No. 1. Mayer and Company] *N.B.*, This is Francis Mayer of Munich, not Francis Meyer the monk-priest of Belmont.

[157]AAM. "Historic Event."

[158]Cf. Letter from Michael Irwin to Sebastian Doris, 8 March 1928, quoted in Doris, *Belmont*, 21-22.

[159]William O'Brien, "Early," 3.

[160]AAM. "Historic Event."

[161]P.G. Marion and William F. O'Brien were the future priests.

[162]The two future monks of Maryhelp would be known as Father Eugene Egan, O.S.B., and Father James Buchholz, O.S.B.

[163]The future abbot was George Taylor, who would take the name "Vincent" in religion. Taylor was in virtually all the plays presented during his school days. His two sisters, Mary and Lucie, who were enrolled at Sacred Heart Academy, matched his level of devotion to dramatics. Mary in particular participated in dramatics and forensics.

[164]Ganss was a priest of the Diocese of Harrisburg. Cf. Oetgen, *American*, 225.

[165]This cast included the two sisters of the future abbot, Vincent Taylor. Mary gave the introductory address and played Mina, Queen of West Saxony; Lucie portrayed Princess Ethelinda.

[166]SVA, No. 9. Letter from Haid to Hintenach, 11 July 1888.

[167]SJA, No. 5. Letter from Haid to Locnikar, 11 January 1891.

[168]Brother Meinrad, an Austrian native born in 1872, went to Saint Leo's in the fall of 1893. He made his profession at the point of death on 13 July 1894, but lingered then until the next month, dying on 19 August.

[169]Frater Lawrence Wiegand was a parishoner at Saint Mary's in Richmond before entering the Order. He was born in 1873, and entered the monastery in 1892. He accompanied Buechling to Florida in 1893, but later was permitted to spend his declining months with his family in Virginia. He died in Richmond on 12 March 1897.

[170]Metzger was born of Protestant parents in Saxony in 1871. After his mother's death in 1889, he went to Baltimore where he was adopted by August Brock and converted to Catholicism. He entered Belmont as a candidate for the brotherhood. A subsequent decision in favor of priesthood required that he enter a different monastery where he could become a clerical novice. Bishop Haid sent him to Florida. While supervising a school outing and picnic there in December 1891, an accidental discharge of a rifle resulted in the Frater's untimely death.

[171]SVA, No. 9. Letter from Haid to Hintenach, 10 October 1888. And AAM. Chapter Minutes, 10 October 1888.

[172]SVA. Letter from Gerard Pilz to Wimmer, 12 April 1886.

[173]Cf. Fellner, *Abbot*, 697.

[174]SVA, No. 9. Letter from Haid to Hintenach, 5 November 1889.

[175]SVA, No. 9. Letter from Haid to Hintenach, 9 November 1889.

[176]SVA, No. 9. Letter from Haid to Hintenach, 17 November 1889.

[177]SVA, No. 9. Letter from Haid to Hintenach, 2 December 1889.

[178]The exact course of Judge Dunne's life is shaded in obscurity—or at least concealed by the burden of his successive adventures. I have assembled his story primarily from: "Obituary: Judge E.F. O'Dunne [sic]," *Catholic Mirror* (Baltimore: October 1904). And Edmund Francis Dunne, "The Sicily of America: The Catholic Colony of San Antonio, Florida—Where They Grow the Genuine Sicily Lemon," (San Antonio, Florida: [1883] 1885). And H.H. Walker Lewis, "Eugene O'Dunne," *The Lawyers' Roundtable of Baltimore and Its Charter Members* (Baltimore: Paul M. Harrod Company, 1978), 50-66 [originally printed in the *American Bar Association Journal* as "Baltimore's Judicial Bombshell," in July, 1970].

[179]Lewis, *ibid.*, 52.

[180]"Obituary"

[181]Dunne.

[182]*Ibid.*

[183]SVA. Letter from John Moore to Wimmer, 1 February 1886.

[184]SLA. Diary of Joseph Kast (sacristan of Saint Anthony Church, Florida).

[185]Eugene later dropped the "Viscount," but altered his patronym to "O'Dunne," by which name he too became a judge and enjoyed a long career in Baltimore, noteworthy for its eccentricity and flamboyance. Cf. Lewis, *supra.*

[186]Brian was later well known in New Mexico as a journalist. The two sisters entered the convent.

[187]AAM. Document, between Haid and Judge Edmund F. Dunne, 18 October 1888. [S5, No. 1. Dunne, E.F.] See also AAM. Chapter Minutes, 10 October 1888.

[188]AAM. Disquisition entitled "Judge Edmund F. Dunne, Counted by Pope Pius IX: His Relations with the Benedictines of Saint Leo, Florida," with the notation: "an interesting experience: interesting but expensive." [S5, No. 1. Dunne, E.F.]

[189]AAM. Letter from Edmund F. Dunne to Charles Mohr, 10 January 1893. [FF1.O, No. 1. Dunne, E.F.]

[190]AAM. Disquisition. See also *ibid.* See also AAM. Chapter Minutes, 21 January, 16 February, and 29 March 1893.

[191]AAM. Disquisition.

[192]Judge Dunne died in Baltimore in 1904.

[193]SVA, No. 9. Letter from Haid to Hintenach, 23 April 1891.

[194]SVA, No. 9. Letter from Haid to Hintenach, 2 December 1889.

[195]SJA, No. 3. Letter from Haid to Edelbrock, 6 April 1890.

[196]SVA, No. 9. Letter from Haid to Father Adalbert, 3 March 1891.

[197]AAM. Letter from Charles Mohr to Haid, 2 January 1894. [A1.O, No. 1. Florida Apostolate]

[198]SAA, No. 3. Letter from Haid to Primate, 28 June 1894.

[199]AAM. Letter from Moore to Haid, 22 May 1894. [A1.O, No. 2 Florida Apostolate]

[200]AAM. Petition from founders of Saint Leo Priory to Haid. [A1.O, No. 3. Florida Apostolate]

[201]The document is preserved ACFA.

[202]SLA. Letter from Haid to Mohr, 4 October 1894.

[203]SAA, No. 3. Letter from Haid to Primate, 15 October 1894.

Chapter V:

the linton legacy

[1]The most readily accessible description of the advent of the Lintons is: Helen Johnston, *The Fruit of His Works: A History of the Benedictine Sisters of Saint Benedict's Convent, Bristow, Prince William County, Virginia* (Bristow: Linton Hall Press, 1954), 37 ff.

[2]*Ibid.*, 37.

[3]*Ibid.*, 38.

[4]*Ibid.*, 39.

[5]*Ibid.*, 39-40.

[6]*Ibid.*, 40.

[7]*Ibid.*

[8]*Ibid.*, 38-41.

[9]*Ibid.*, 47.

[10]*Ibid.*

[11]AAM. Letter from M.J. Colbert to Haid, 4 June 1894. [A1.O, No. 1. Saint Joseph Institute, Bristow, Virginia]

[12]Johnston, 47.

[13]AAM. Letter from Pohl to Haid, 23 March 1903. [A1.O, No. 1. Julius Pohl, OSB, RP—Correspondence] And Letter from Thomas H. Lion to Pohl, 4 August 1917. [A1.O, No. 1. Saint Joseph Institute, Bristow, Virginia]

[14]AAM. Letter from Pohl to Haid, 15 July 1917. [A1.O, No. 1. Bristow Mineral Rights]

[15]AAM. Letter from Lion to Pohl, 4 August 1917. And Will of Anne Cecilia Phillips, 2 May 1917. [A1.O, No. 1. Saint Joseph Institute, Bristow, Virginia]

[16]AAM. Deed, from Anne C. Phillips to Martin F. Morris, Emily V. Mason, Imogen B. Lyons, and Nannie Lomax Green, for 1736 acres in Prince William County, Virginia, 14 January 1893. [A1.O, No. 1. Bristow Mineral Rights]

[17]AAM. Letter from Colbert to Sister Mary Baptista Linton, V.H.M., 13 January 1893. [A1.O, No. 1. Saint Joseph Institute, Bristow, Virginia]

[18]AAM. Letter from Linton to Haid, 29 March 1893. [A1.O, No. 1. Saint Joseph Institute, Bristow, Virginia]

[19]AAM. Letter from Colbert to Linton, 13 January 1893.

[20]AAM. Letter from Linton to Haid, 29 March 1893.

[21]AAM. Deed from Phillips to Trustees (Morris, Mason, Lyons, and Green), 14 January 1893.

[22]AAM. Letter from Linton to Haid, 29 March 1893. [A1.O, No. 1. Saint Joseph Institute, Bristow, Virginia]

[23]Johnston, 47-48.

[24]AAM. Chapter Minutes, 29 March 1893.

[25]AAM. Letter from M. Cardinal Ledochowski to Haid, 20 June 1893. [A1.O, No. 1. Saint Joseph Institute, Bristow, Virginia]

[26]AAM. Charter of the Benedictine Society of Linton Place, Prince William County, Virginia, 1 August 1893. [A1.O, No. 1. Saint Joseph Institute, Bristow, Virginia]

[27]Cf. AAM. Letter from Colbert to Haid, 4 June 1894.

[28]The convent later became Saint Benedict Motherhouse.

[29]Cf. Johnston, 48-49.

[30]AAM. Copy of letter from Haid to Pohl, 6 September 1893. [A1.O, No. 1. Bristow Monks—Correspondence]

[31]AAM. Copy of letter from Haid to Pohl, 13 September 1893. [A1.O, No. 1. Bristow Monks—Correspondence]

[32]AAM. Cf. copies of letters from Haid to Pohl, of 30 April 1894, 7 May 1894, 9 June 1894. [A1.O, No. 1. Bristow Monks— Correspondence]

[33]AAM. Copy of letter from Haid to Pohl, 30 April 1894.

[34]AAM. Copy of letter from Haid to Pohl, 9 June 1894.

[35]AAM. Letter from Colbert to Haid, 4 June 1894.

[36]AAM. Chapter Minutes, 6 June 1894.

[37]AAM. Copy of letter from Haid to Pohl, 20 December 1896. [A1.O, No. 1. Bristow Monks—Correspondence]

[38]AAM. Chapter Minutes, 6 June 1896.

[39]AAM. Indenture between the Trustees (Morris, Mason, Lyons, and Green) and the Benedictine Society of Linton's Ford. [A1.O, No. 1. Bristow Mineral Rights]

[40]Johnston, 51-52.

[41]Ibid., 11-15.

[42]AAB. Gibbons' diary, entry for 13 November 1875.

[43]Johnston, 55.

[44]SBMA. Sisters' Chapter Minutes, 4 October 1893.

[45]Johnston, 53.

[46]Ibid., 57.

[47]Ibid., 95.

[48]Ibid., 62.

[49]SBMA. Day Book kept by Father Julius, entry for 18 May 1897.

[50]Ibid., entry for 22 August 1897.

[51]Ibid., 23 September 1895.

[52]Ibid., 5 July 1895.

[53]Ibid., 20 April 1899.

[54]Johnston, 67.

[55]SBMA. Day Book, 21 November 1901.

[56]Ibid., 21 August 1900.

[57]Ibid., 22 September 1900.

[58]AAM. Cf. in particular, letters from Father Edward [no further identification is in evidence] to Pohl, of 2 March 1897 and of 11 March 1897. [A1.O, No. 1. Julius Pohl, OSB, RP—Correspondence]

[59]Johnston, 95-96.

[60]Cf., for example, AAM. Letter from Zilliox to Pohl, 19 October 1879. [A1.O, No. 1. Julius Pohl, OSB, RP-Correspondence]

[61]SBMA. Day Book, 7 August 1898.

[62]Johnston, 74.

[63]AAM. Letter from Pohl to Haid, 8 August 1898. [A1.O, No. 1. Julius Pohl, OSB, RP—Correspondence]

[64]SBMA. Day Book, 7 August 1898.

[65]*Ibid.*, 9 August 1898. And Johnston, 74.

[66]AAM. Letter from Pohl to Haid, 21 August 1898. [A1.O, No. 1. Bristow—Diocesan Issues] And Johnston, 74.

[67]AAM. Letter from Pohl to Haid, 8 August 1898.

[68]Johnston, 74.

[69]SBMA. Day Book, 8 August 1898.

[70]*Ibid.*, 9 August 1898.

[71]Johnston, 75.

[72]AAM. Letter from Pohl to Haid, 21 August 1898.

[73]AAM. Letter from Pohl to Haid, 26 August 1898. [A1.O, No. 1., Julius Pohl, OSB, RP—Correspondence]

[74]AAM. Letter from Pohl to Haid, 21 August 1898.

[75]SBMA. Day Book, 15 August 1898.

[76]*Ibid.*, 16 August 1898.

[77]*Ibid.*, 18 August 1898.

[78]*Ibid.*, 5 September 1898.

[79]*Ibid.*, 6 September 1898.

[80]*Ibid.*, 11 September 1898.

[81]AAM. Letter from Major J.K. Weaver to Pohl, 14 September 1898. [A1.O, No. 1. Julius Pohl, OSB, RP—Correspondence]

[82]Cf. SBMA. Day Book, 3 September 1898. The photograph is preserved in AAM.

[83]AAM. Letter from Pohl to Haid, 21 August 1898.

[84]Johnston, 49.

[85]AAM. Letter from Pohl to Haid and capitulars, undated (1914). [A1.O, No. 1. Bristow—Diocesan Issues]

[86]SBMA. Day Book, 22 February 1895.

[87]*Ibid.*, 13 March 1895.

[88]*Ibid.*, 16 April 1895.

[89]*Ibid.*, 5 May 1895.

[90]AAM. Letter from Pohl to Haid, 20 July 1898.

[91]SBMA. Day Book, 3 June 1898.

[92]*Ibid.*, 8 April 1899.

[93]*Ibid.*, 10 May 1899.

[94]*Ibid.*, 11 May 1899.

[95]*Ibid.*, 28 October 1899.

[96]*Ibid.*, 16 July 1900.

[97]*Ibid.*, 7 September 1900.

[98]*Ibid.*, 30 September 1900.

[99]Cf., for example, AAM. Letters from Pohl to Haid of 20 July 1898 [A1.O, No. 1. Julius Pohl, OSB, RP—Correspondence]; 12 July 1917 [A1.O, No. 3. Saint Joseph Institute, Bristow, Virginia]. See also SBMA. Day Book, 14 September 1900.

[100]SBMA. Ledger: Saint Jospeh Institute. [This ledger contains a complete set of financial statements covering Belmont Abbey's years in Bristow. Most of the reports from Pohl's years also include the statistics regarding personnel, students, livestock, etc.]

[101]Ibid.

[102]AAM. Notation by Haid on letter from Pohl to Haid, 12 December 1897. [A1.O, No. 1. Julius Pohl, OSB, RP— Correspondence]

[103]SBMA. Ledger.

[104]SBMA. Day Book, 3 June 1898.

[105]Cf. AAM. Letter from Pohl to Haid, 4 April 1914. [A1.O, No. 1. Bristow—Diocesan Issues]

[106]AAM. Letter from Pohl to Haid and capitulars, undated (1914).

[107]AAM. Letter from Pohl to Haid, 10 June 1898. [A1.O, No. 1. Julius Pohl, OSB, RP—Correspondence]

[108]AAM. Letter from J.T. O'Farrell to Felix Hintemeyer, 7 May 1914. [A1.O, No. 1. Bristow—Diocesan Issues]

[109]AAM. Resolutions of the Diocesan Consultors of Richmond, as communicated to Bishop O'Connell (authenticated copy sent to Haid), following on meeting of 9 April 1914 [the document itself is undated (1914)], signed by Thomas E. Waters, secretary.

[110]AAM. Letter from Pohl to Haid, 4 April 1914.

[111]Ibid.

[112]Cf. division of Benedictine personnel in Virginia listed in Joseph Magri, The Catholic Church in the City and Diocese of Richmond (Richmond: Whittet and Shepperson), 1906, 124.

[113]AAM. Letter from Pohl to Haid, 4 April 1914.

[114]AAM. Letter from Pohl to Haid and capitulars, undated (1914).

[115]SBMA. Day Book, 4 July 1895.

[116]Cf., for example, AAM. Letter from Sister Mary Zita Zimmerman, OSB, to Haid, 10 October 1900. [A1.O, No. 1. Bristow Sisters]

[117]SBMA. Day Book, 3 October 1896. Also cf. Johnston, 64.

[118]SBMA. Ibid., 2 July 1897.

[119]Ibid., 26 May 1897.

[120]Ibid., 27 May 1897.

[121]Ibid., 2 July 1897.

[122]AAM. Letter from Pohl to Haid, 6 December 1900. [A1.O, No. 1. Bristow—Diocesan Issues]

[123]AAM. Indult from Propaganda Fide to Maryhelp Abbey, 20 June 1893. [A1.O, No. 1. Bristow—Diocesan Issues]

[124]AAM. Letter from Augustine Van de Vyver to Pohl, (7) March 1910. [A1.O, No. 13. Saint Joseph Institute, Bristow, Virginia]

[125]AAM. Letter from Van de Vyver to Haid, 9 March 1910. [A1.O, No. 13. Saint Joseph Institute, Bristow, Virginia]

[126]AAM. Letter from Pohl to Haid, 1 September 1910. [A1.O, No. 14. Saint Joseph Institute, Bristow, Virginia]

[127]AAM. Letter from Pohl to Haid, 9 March 1910. [A1.O, No. 1. Julius Pohl, OSB, RP—Correspondence]

[128]Cf. AAM. Letter from Pohl to Haid, 14 March 1910. [A1.O, No. 1. Julius Pohl, OSB, RP—Correspondence]

[129]AAM. Letter from Pohl to Haid, 1 September 1910.

[130]AAM. Letter from Pohl to Haid, 28 November 1917. [A1.O, No. 4. Saint Joseph Institute, Bristow, Virginia]

[131]AAM. Letter from Pohl to Haid, 14 March 1910. [A1.O, No. 1. Julius Pohl, OSB, RP—Correspondence]

[132]AAM. Letter from Pohl to Haid, 8 July 1917. [A1.O, No. 3. Saint Joseph Institute, Bristow, Virginia]

[133]AAM. Chapter Minutes, 15 June 1917.

[134]AAM. Letter from Pohl, Raphael Arthur, and John Smith to Haid and capitulars, 12 June 1917, appended to Chapter Minutes, *ibid.*

[135]AAM. Chapter Minutes, 15 June 1917.

[136]*Ibid.*

[137]AAM. Letter from Pohl to Felix Hintemeyer, 20 June 1917, appended to Chapter Minutes, *ibid.*

[138]AAM. Letter from Bernard Haas to Haid, 14 September 1917. [A1.O, No. 2. Bernard Haas, OSB, RP]

[139]AAM. Letter from Mother Edith, OSB, to Haid, Holy Thursday, 1893. [A1.O, No. 1. Bristow Sisters]

[140]The Abbey did not assign a trained archivist until The Reverend David Kessinger, OSB, was appointed in 1973. This document was catalogued c. 1981.

[141]AAM. Letter from Pohl to Haid, 28 November 1917.

[142]AAM. Letter from Pohl to Haid, 31 December 1917. [A1.O, No. 4. Saint Joseph Institute, Bristow, Virginia]

[143]AAM. Letter from Haid to Pohl, 26 December 1887. [A1.O, No. 1. Julius Pohl, OSB, RP—Correspondence]

[144]AAM. Letter from Pohl to Haid, 25 July 1898. [A1.O, No. 1. Julius Pohl, OSB, RP—Correspondence]

[145]AAM. Letter from Pohl to Haid, 16 June 1898. [A1.O, No. 1. Julius Pohl, OSB, RP—Correspondence]

[146]AAM. Letter from Pohl to Haid 22 May 1900. [A1.O, No. 1. Julius Pohl, OSB, RP—Correspondence]

[147]SBMA. Day Book, 3 August 1901.

[148]AAM. Letter from Pohl to Haid, 17 January 1897. [A1.O, No. 1. Julius Pohl, OSB, RP—Correspondence]

[149]AAM. Letter from Pohl to Haid, 9 August 1897. [A1.O, No. 1. Julius Pohl, OSB, RP—Correspondence]

[150]SBMA. Day Book, 31 May 1900.

[151]AAM. Letter from Pohl to Haid, 3 November 1900. [A1.O, No. 1. Julius Pohl, OSB, RP—Correspondence]

[152]SBMA. Day Book, 28 December 1902.

[153]AAM. Letter from Haid to Priors and Fathers in Savannah, Richmond, and Bristow, 10 September 1908. [A1.O, No. 1. Apostolates: Priories]

[154]Cf. AAM. Letter from Pohl to Haid, 9 March 1910. [A1.O, No. 1. Julius Pohl, OSB, RP—Correspondence]

[155]Leo Haid continued to stress these monastic requirements in his three other houses, but for Bristow there is no further mention of their importance.

[156]These centered on the brothers, but priests and clerics also were involved.

[157]Of course he was never in residence at Bristow to test his effect there.

[158]Those who took this approach were small in number, but they caused the Prior disproportionate difficulty.

[159]This is an abridged chronicle of the Brothers' *conversatio* and stability, offered as an illustration of the conditions with which the Prior was dealing:

On 15 November 1895, Brother Wolfgang left in the night and tried to find a wife in Maryland.(a) Brother Herman departed on 14 September 1896, that being the best alternative to suicide.(b) In 1897, a particularly busy year, Brother Joseph, "who came here in rags—without anything whatsoever—and proved a traitor," was expelled;(c) Brother John a former Trappist went to Bristow,(d) stayed three months, and returned to the Trappists;(e) Brother Leonard, the cook, abandoned his post, so Bishop Haid sent Brother Willibald to replace him, but Brother Leonard returned the day before his successor appeared, and Father Julius, in the interest of peace, had to dispatch the former cook in a way that would prevent him and the new appointee from encountering one another.(f) Later that same year, Brother Bernard, who was so filthy and odoriferous that Pohl could not even bear to enter the man's cell, was writing illicit letters.(g) And before the year was completed, Brother Cook "left without a word,"(h) and returned again—to "a cold reception."(i) Conditions worsened the next year. In front of the students, two Brothers "created quite a scene. . .the one *biting*, the other *scratching* and inundating each other with water."(j) Another cook left and Father Julius hired his own mother in an effort to stabilize the kitcheners. Mrs. Pohl, however, was severely upbraided in altercations with Brothers,(k) and died before finishing a single year on the job.(l) Through the years, the kitchen continued to be the center of Pohl's troubles. In 1904, the cook and another brother came to blows,(m) then a third brother "boxed" the Cook.(n) Brother Vincent, the cook mentioned in the two previous incidents, was still in prime vigor in 1920, when he caused

> quite an eruption. He chased boys with clubs and cornered them even into the very toilet-rooms, slapping them, etc., which though often forbidden him, is of frequent occurrence. Even the sight of blood does not cause him to halt. The loud and scandalous talk—disedifying all within reach of hearing . . . is such that if by chance any guests were here—and could *not* fail to understand—would force me to claim ill-health. The humiliation would simply be overwhelming! A few hours after this he tackled Reverend Father Florian and Frater Denis, before all the boys, calling both "bums", ignorant fellows, dirty lazy men, incapable of teaching or prefecting. ...Clubs (not card-clubs) are the usual resort; stones to hurl at the Prefect—apparently (of this I would not be oversure) he went to his room; indications point to a knife. Needless to say parents will soon hear of this.(o)

Brother Vincent was replaced as cook, but was kept at Saint Maur. Then Father Julius learned that the new cook was the man who had actually instigated his predecessor's last rampage.(p) Had only the brothers disrupted Bristow, Pohl might have survived on better terms. But one priest in particular proved so abrasive, and succeeded in causing sufficient scandal, that he actually earned abbatial intervention. He was the worst problem among the monk-priests, but he was not alone. Many were as motley as so many brothers had proven, although most of the clerics were at least less violent. Their offenses which got them sent to Saint Maur ranged from the refusal of a newly ordained priest to preach, to a drug addiction acquired while on assignment in Richmond. This last man was one of Polh's greatest successes. Being completely rehabilitated, he returned to Belmont where he became one of the College's foremost educators. He was also an unfailing proponent of the wisdom of leadership and the paternal charity of Leo Haid, whose judgment had placed him in what at first seemed the wild and burdensome world of Julius Pohl's Priory.

(a) SBMA. Day Book, 15 November 1895.

(b) *Ibid.*, 14 September 1896.

(c) *Ibid.*, 2 May 1897.

(d) *Ibid.*, 12 May 1897.

(e) AAM. Letter from Pohl to Haid, 4 August 1897. [A1.O, No. 1. Julius Pohl, OSB, RP—Correspondence]

(f) SBMA. Day Book, 12 July 1897, and 13 July 1897.

(g) AAM. Letter from Pohl to Haid, 10 November 1897. [A1.O, No. 1. Julius Pohl, OSB, RP—Correspondence]

(h) SBMA. Day Book, 30 November 1897.

(i) *Ibid.*, 1 December 1897.

(j) AAM. Letter from Pohl to Haid, 10 June 1898. [A1.O, No. 1. Julius Pohl, OSB, RP—Correspondence]

(k) AAM. Letter from Pohl to Haid, 16 June 1898. [A1.O, No. 1. Julius Pohl, OSB, RP—Correspondence]

(l) SBMA. Day Book, 24 January 1899.

(m) AAM. Letter from Pohl to Haid, 23 May 1904. [A1.O, No. 1. Julius Pohl, OSB, RP—Correspondence]

(n) AAM. Letter from Pohl to Haid, 3 June 1904. [A1.O, No 1 Julius Pohl, OSB, RP—Correspondence]

(o) AAM. Letter from Pohl to Haid, 26 May 1920. [A1.O, No. 7. Saint Joseph Institute, Bristow, Virginia]

(p) AAM. Letter from Pohl to Haid, 27 May 1920. [A1.O, No. 7. Saint Joseph Institute, Bristow, Virginia]

[160]Although Saint Maur was never really put in order, the proximate cause of the removal of Pohl from office in 1922 was supposedly the Prior's ill health, not his incompetence.

[161]SBMA. Day Book, 26 November 1900.

[162]*Ibid.*, 28 October 1900.

[163]AAM. Letter from Mrs. A.J. Barnes to Haid, 3 August 1922. [A1.O, No. 8. Saint Joseph Institute, Bristow, Virginia]

[164]*Ibid.*

[165]*Ibid.*

[166]*Ibid.* Father Julius had always thought his health delicate, and he complained frequently. People were so accustomed to this feature of his personality, that even in his final illness there was some reluctance to indulge him.

[167]AAM. Letter from Mrs. F.M. Kane to Haid, 16 August 1922. [A1.O, No. 9. Saint Joseph Institute, Bristow, Virginia]

[168]AAM. Letter from Pohl to Haid, 12 July 1917. [A1.O, No. 3. Saint Joseph Institute, Bristow Virginia]. And Letter from Pohl to Haid, 12 June 1919 [A1.O, No. 6. Saint Joseph Institute, Bristow, Virginia]. And SBMA. Ledger.

[169]Cf. AAM. Letter from Raphael Arthur to Haid, 8 January 1917. [A1.O, No. 3. Saint Joseph Institute, Bristow, Virginia]. And Letter from Pohl to Haid, 19 January 1920. [A1.O, No. 6. Saint Joseph Institute, Bristow, Virginia]

[170]AAM. Letter from Pohl to Haid, 12 June 1919.

[171]AAM. Letter from Pohl to Haid, 12 July 1917.

[172]AAM. Letter from Pohl to Haid, 19 January 1920.

[173]AAM. Letter from John O'Grady to Bishop O'Connell, 19 August 1922. [A1.O, No. 9. Saint Joseph Institute, Bristow, Virginia]

[174]*Ibid.*

[175]*Ibid.*

[176]AAM. Letter from Mrs. F.M. Kane to Haid, 16 August 1922.

[177]AAM. Letter from Mrs. A.J. Barnes to Haid, 3 August 1922.

[178]Cf. AAM. Letter from Joseph Tobin to Haid, 4 August 1922.

[179]*Ibid.* Abbot Leo never did deal with Smith; and Pohl's successor was saddled with the man, too—but only for the time required to choreograph the expulsion.

[180]*Ibid.* And AAM. Letter from Tobin to Haid, 6 August 1922. [A1.O, No. 8. Saint Joseph Institute, Bristow, Virginia]. And Letter from O'Grady to Bishop O'Connell, 19 August 1922.

[181]AAM. Letter from Tobin to Haid, 4 August 1922.

[182]*Ibid.*

[183]AAM. Letter from Tobin to Haid, 6 August 1922.

[184]AAM. Letter from Pohl to Haid, 14 August 1922. [A1.O, No. 8. Saint Joseph Institute, Bristow, Virginia]

[185]AAM. Letter from Pohl to Haid, 20 August 1922. [A1.O, No. 9. Saint Joseph Institute, Bristow, Virginia]

[186]Cf. AAM. Letter from Zilliox to Pohl, 28 January 1886. [A1.O, No. 1. Julius Pohl, OSB, RP—Correspondence]

[187]AAM. Letter from Pohl to Haid, 10 June 1919. [A1.O, No. 6. Saint Joseph Institute, Bristow, Virginia]

[188]AAM. Letter from Bishop O'Connell to Haid, 22 August 1922. [A1.O, No. 9. Saint Joseph Institute, Bristow, Virginia]

[189]AAM. Letter from O'Grady to Bishop O'Connell, 19 August 1922.

[190]SBMA. Ledger.

[191]*Ibid.* And AAM. Twenty-Ninth Annual Statement: Saint Joseph Institute, 19 August 1922. [A1.O, No. 9. Saint Joseph Institute, Bristow, Virginia]

[192]AAM. Letter from Ignatius Remke to Haid, 10 January 1923. [A1.O, No. 10. Saint Joseph Institute Bristow, Virginia]

[193]AAM. Letter from Remke to Haid, 22 January 1924. [A1.O, No. 12, Saint Joseph Institute, Bristow, Virginia]

[194]AAM. Letter from Remke to Haid, 11 September 1922. [A1.O, No. 10. Saint Joseph Institute, Bristow, Virginia]

[195]SBMA. Ledger.

[196]AAM. Letter from Remke to Haid, 10 January 1923.

[197]AAM. Letter from Wilfrid Foley and John Smith to Leo Haid, 20 July 1924. [A1.O, No. 1. Bristow Monks—Correspondence]

[198]AAM. Letter from Remke to Haid, 11 September 1922.

[199]AAM. Letter from Remke to Haid, 26 September 1923. [A1.O, No. 1. Bristow Monks—Correspondence]

[200]AAM. Letter from Remke to Haid, 22 January 1924.

[201]AAM. Letter from Remke to Haid, 11 September 1922.

[202]AAM. Letter from Remke to Haid, 30 October 1922. [A1.O, No. 10. Saint Joseph Institute, Bristow, Virginia]

[203]AAM. Letter from Remke to Haid, 10 January 1923.

[204]AAM. Letter from Remke to Haid, 16 February 1923. [A1.O, No. 11. Saint Joseph Institute, Bristow, Virginia]

[205]*Ibid.*

[206]AAM. Letter from Remke to Haid, 23 February 1923. This letter is marked *"Destroy!"* [A1.O, No. 11. Saint Joseph Institute, Bristow, Virginia]

[207]Cf. Chapter VIII.

[208]AAM. Letter from Remke to Haid, 23 February 1923.

[209]*Ibid.*

[210]AAM. Copy of the decision of the Circuit Court of Prince William County, Virginia (undated [February, 1923]). [A1.O, No. 1. Saint Joseph Institute, Bristow, Virginia]

[211]Johnston, 88 and 115.

[212]Maryhelp also reserved an option on some of the livestock, but on 11 July 1927 the Abbey announced its decision not to withdraw the animals. Cf. SBMA. Letter from Vincent Taylor to Mother Agnes, 11 July 1927.

[213]Taylor elaborated on the points in: SBMA. Letter from Taylor to Mother Agnes, 18 May 1927.

[214]Cf. SBMA. Letter from Taylor to Mother Agnes, 4 June 1927.

[215]AAM. Petition from Taylor to Camillus Cardinal Laurenti, Prefect of the Congregation for Religious, 1 July 1927. [A2.O, No. 1. Saint Joseph Institute, Bristow, Virginia]

[216]SBMA. Letter from Taylor to Mother Agnes, (dated 24 October 1924, should be:) 24 October 1927.

Chapter VI:

The Mitre Exceeds the Crozier

[1]AAM. Volume i of the Abbey's *Publicity Files* contains a set of press clippings regarding the appointment. These are the most important: "Two New Bishops Selected," New York *World*, 22 January 1897. "Surprise From Rome," Baltimore *Sun*, 23 January 1897. "Surprise From Rome," Pittsburgh *Post*, 23 January 1897. "New Catholicism Loses," New York *Journal*, 24 January 1897. "Wilmington's New Bishop," New York *Herald*, 24 January 1897.

[2]*Sun, ibid.*

[3]*Ibid.*

[4]*Journal.*

[5]*Herald.*

[6]*World.*

[7]Cf. discussion in Ellis, *Life*, II, 447.

[8]*Sun.*

[9]AAB. Minutes of the Meeting of the Bishops of the Province of Baltimore, 24 September 1896.

[10]AAB. Gibbons' diary, entry for 9 October 1896.

[11]AAB. *ibid.*, entry for 24 September 1896. And AAB. Letter from Haid to Gibbons, 3 September 1896.

[12]AAB. Letter from Haid to Gibbons, 26 September 1896.

[13]AAB. Gibbons' diary, entry for 15 February 1897.

[14]*Ibid.*, entry for 9 May 1897.

[15]AAM. Chapter Minutes, 11 June 1898.

[16]*Ibid.*, 26 June 1897.

[17]SAA, No. 2. Letter from Hintemeyer to Primate, 27 October 1897.

[18]AAM. Publicity Files, Volume i. "Item of Interest From a Centre of Apostolic Work," *Catholic Mirror*, October, 1897.

[19]AAM. *Publicity Files*, i, contains much of the newspaper coverage of the festivities. In particular see: "Silver Jubilee at Belmont: Cardinal Gibbons Will Be There," Charlotte *Observer*, 19 November 1897. "Departure of Cardinal Gibbons," Baltimore *Sun*, 24 November 1897. "Cardinal Gibbon's Party," Charlotte *Observer*, 24 November 1897. "Silver Sacerdotal Jubilee," *Catholic Mirror*, November 1897. "Notable Day at Saint Mary's," Charlotte *Observer*, 25 November 1897.

[20]*Ibid*. Also, Invitation for 25 November 1897. [M11, No.1. Haid's Jubilee]

[21]"Notable Day at Saint Mary's."

[22]"Silver Sacerdotal Jubilee."

[23]SAA, No.3. Letter from Haid to Primate, 29 November 1897.

[24]AAM. *Publicity Files*, i, p. 204. "A Spiritual Retreat," (unlabeled newspaper clipping, 1898).

[25]AAM. Most of the description comes from Paschal Baumstein, "The First Sign of Permanance," *Crescat* (Summer, 1982), pp. 1-6,

[26]AAM. *Publicity Files*, i, 203. "North Carolina Benedictines," *Catholic Standard and Times*, [19] September 1898.

[27]AAM. *Publicity Files*, i, includes many articles covering the conflagration. "Catholic College a Mass of Ruins," *Catholic Standard and Times*, [undated]. "College Burned," Latrobe *Clipper*, 20 May 1900. "Catholic College Destroyed," Pittsburgh *Dispatch*, 20 May 1900. "College Burned," Columbus *Enquirer*, 20 May 1900. "Fire at Saint Mary's Monastery," Richmond *Dispatch*, 20 May 1900. "Saint Mary's College Burned," Washington *Post*, 20 May 1900. "Belmont College Fire," Johnstown *Democrat*, 20 May 1900. "Parents in Pittsburgh Anxious Over a Fire," Pittsburgh *Post*, 20 May 1900. "Saint Mary's College Burns," Atlanta *Constitution*, 20 May 1900. "Fire at Saint Mary's: Well Known College Suffers Heavily," [unlabeled]. "Saint Mary's College Burned, Charlotte *Observer*, 20 May 1900. "Saint Mary's College Burned," Gastonia *Gazette*, 23 May 1900. "The Burning of Saint Mary's" Norfolk *Landmark*, [undated]. "The Situation at Belmont," Charlotte *Observer*, 22 May 1900. "Saint Mary's College, Belmont, Partially Burned Today," Charlotte *News*, 19 May 1900. Felix Hintemeyer, "Catholic College in Ruins," *Catholic Standard and Times*, (undated).

[28]Newspapers differ regarding whether or not there was sufficient water to justify the journey from Charlotte. Hintemeyer argued that water was "abundant."

[29]SBSA, No.1. Letter from Haid to Drexel, 30 May 1900.

[30]SJA, No.1. Letter from Haid to Peter Engel, 24 May 1900.

[31]SJA, No.1. Letter from Haid to Engel, 9 June 1900.

[32]AAM. Chapter Minutes, 19 May 1900.

[33]AAM. *Publicity Files*, i, 225. "Saint Mary's College Burned."

[34]AAM. Haas' chronology.

[35]AAM. *Publicity Files*, i, 226. "The Situation at Belmont."

[36]SJA, No.1. Letter from Haid to Engel, 24 May 1900.

[37]AAM. Letter from Primate to Haid, 25 June 1900.

[38]SJA, No.1. Letter from Haid to Engel, 9 June 1900.

[39]SJA, No.1. Letter from Haid to Engel, 24 May 1900.

[40]AAM. Letter from Haid to Francis Meyer, 26 May 1900. [Al.0, No.1. Fire (1900)].

[41]*Ibid*.

[42]Cf., Paschal Baumstein, "A Divine Practice," The North Carolina *Architect* (July-August, 1983), pp. 14-19.

[43]AAM. *Catalogue* of Saint Mary's College. Cf. honors listing for 1900-1901 and 1901-1902.

44"Salute to Our Master Builder," *Abbey: News, Views,* (Spring, 1957), p. 1.

45"A Church Should Make People Mindful of God," [New Subiaco] *Abbey Message* (October, 1951), p. 1.

46Nevertheless, the dating of his exeat and testimonials indicates that his initial attendance at Belmont was not for clerical or religious purposes.

47"A Church Should . . ."

48AAM. Circular letter over the signatures of Bernard Haas and Leo Haid, undated (August, 1900). [B6, No.1. Fire (1900)]

49AAM. Letter from Haid to Mark Cassidy, undated (Spring, 1919 ?). [M102, No.2. Leo Haid, O.S.B., Abbot]

50AAB. Letter from Haid to Gibbons, 7 December 1907.

51Cf. BSA.

52SJA, No.1. Letter from Haid to Engel, 3 December 1909.

53AAM. [A1.0, No.7. Sermons and Retreats]

54AAM. [A1.0, No.4. Sermons and Retreats]

55SJA, No.1. Letter from Haid to Engel, 10 September 1907.

56AAM. Notes for opening address of retreat at Saint Vincent Archabbey, 30 July 1919. [A1.0, No.2. Sermons and Retreats]

57AAM. Notes for retreat for novices, 12 June 1918 conference. [A1.0, No.2. Sermons and Retreats]

58AAM. "Lecture to Myself and Superiors," by Leo Haid, 29 June 1913 (second day of four of conferences). [A1.0, No.7. Sermons and Retreats]

59AAM. The Ludwig-Missionsverein was signed into existence by Ludwig, King of Bavaria, on 12 December 1838. Two-thirds of its monies were to support missionaries in Asia and the New World; the rest was to assist Franciscans at the Holy Sepulcher in Jerusalem. Cf. Theodore Roemer, *The Ludwig-Missionsverein and the Church in the United States (1838-1918),* (Washington, D.C.: The Catholic University of America Press, 1933 [published dissertation]). Much of the correspondence from Belmont was written by Felix Hintemeyer, and is preserved on microfilm at NDUA.

60The Society of the Propagation of the Faith was founded in Lyons in 1822. It sought to organize spiritual and financial aid to Catholic missionaries.

61Much of what follows is from Baumstein, "Divine."

62Cf. AAM. Mrs. W.R. Stowe, three page typescript later published in the Charlotte *Observer* and the Georgia *Bulletin*. [M91, No.2. Newspaper Coverage]

63Cf. BPA. Letter from Michael McInerney to Eugene Egan, 29 November 1923.

64AAM. Cf. official file on Michael McInerney. [A3.0, No.1 ff. Michael McInerney, OSB, RP]

65AAM. Two page typescript, undated (1950's?). [B5, No.1. Michael McInerney, OSB, RP—Career Review]

66*Ibid.* Also vita in official file.

67SJA, No.3. Letter from Haid to Alexius Edelbrock, 25 August 1888.

68AAM. Letter from Haid to Sister Mary de Ricci, 10 September 1908. [A1.0, No.1. Correspondence, 1906-1910]

69AAM. Letter from Father Thomas Stemler, O.S.B., to Haid, 13 May 1916. [A1.0, No.1. Correspondence, 1916-1920]

70AAM. Letter from Julius Pohl to Haid, 9 August 1897. [A1.0, No.1. Julius Pohl, OSB, RP—Correspondence]

71SVA, No.9. Letter from Haid to Hintenach, 2 December 1889.

72SJA, No.3. Letter from Haid to Edelbrock, 17 September, 1889.

73AAM. "Lecture to Myself and Superiors," by Haid, 18 June 1913 (first day of four of conferences). [A1.0, No.7. Sermons and Retreats]

[74]AAM. Notes for retreat conferences for novices, 12 June 1918. [A1.0, No.2. Sermons and Retreats]

[75]AAM. Letter from Leo Panoch to Haid, 18 June 1895. [A1.0, No.1. Correspondence, 1884-1899]

[76]ACFA. Letter from Haid to Engel, 26 October 1902.

[77]AAB. Letter from Haid to Gibbons, 20 August 1892.

[78]AAB. Letter from Haid to Gibbons, 5 June 1889.

[79]Cf. Ellis, *Life*, I, 83.

[80]SVA, No. 11. Letter from Haid to Aurelius Stehle, 22 May 1924.

[81]SAA, No. 3. Letter from Haid to Primate, 30 December 1895.

[82]ACFA. Letter from Haid to Innocent Wolf, 16 February 1900.

[83]SVA, No. 14. Letter from Hintemeyer to Prior of Saint Vincent, 1 July 1909.

[84]AAM. Letter from Locnikar to Haid, 6 April 1894.

[85]SAA, No. 3. Letter from Haid to Primate, 30 December 1895.

[86]SAA, No. 3. Letter from Haid to Primate, 4 November 1903. And SVA, No. 10. Letter from Haid to Leander Schnerr, 7 April 1917.

[87]SAA, No. 3. Letter from Haid to Primate, 6 November 1904.

[88]SAA, No. 3. Letter from Haid to Primate, 17 December 1903, and 30 July 1905.

[89]SJA. Letter from Haid to Locnikar, 25 January 1891.

[90]SJA. Letter from Haid to Engel, 13 April 1916. And BSA, No. 1. Letter from Haid to Drexel, 22 January 1916.

[91]SVA, No. 14. Letter from Haid to Prior of Saint Vincent, 24 June 1910.

[92]SJA. Letter from Haid to Engel, 13 April 1916.

[93]Cf., for example, SAA, No. 3. Letter from Haid to Primate, 14 October 1906.

[94]AAM. Conference notes by Haid, 1912. [A1.0, No. 6. Sermons and Retreats]

[95]AAM. Conference notes by Haid for priests' retreat, 1912. [A1.0, No.6. Sermons and Retreats]

[96]"Memories," part two (uncatalogued at AAM), by Sebastian Doris, OSB, 29 September 1979.

[97]SJA, No. 3. Letter from Haid to Edelbrock, 1 November 1889.

[98]AAM. Petition from parishoners at Saint Mary Church (Richmond), January 1901. [A1.0, No. 1. Willibald Baumgartner, OSB, RP—Saint Mary's Petitions]

[99]AAM. Notice (10 January 1901) for meeting (13 January 1901), Saint Mary Church (Richmond). [A1.0, No. 1. Willibald Baumgartner, OSB, RP—Saint Mary's Petitions]

[100]AAM. Minutes of parishoners' meeting, 13 Janaury 1901. [A1.0, No. 1. Willibald Baumgartner, OSB, RP—Saint Mary's Petitions]

[101]*Ibid.*

[102]AAM. Letter from Van de Vyver to Haid, 11 January 1901. [A1.0, No. 1. Willibald Baumgartner, OSB, RP—Saint Mary's Petitions]

[103]AAM. Letter from Baumgartner to Haid, 17 April 1901. [A1.0, No. 2. Willibald Baumgartner, OSB, RP]

[104]*Ordo* of the American Cassinese Congregation of the Order of Saint Benedict (issued annually).

[105]*Ibid.*

[106]*Ibid.*

[107]*Ibid.*

[108]*Ibid.*

[109]BPA. Corporation Minutes, 3 October 1902.

[110]*Ibid.*, 7 December 1902.

[111]*Ibid.*, 9 December 1902.

[112]*Ibid.*, 14 February 1904.

[113]*Ibid.*, 4 August 1904.

[114]BPA. Letter from Haid to Haas, 1 November 1904.

[115]BPA. Letter from McInerney to Egan, 26 October 1923.

[116]BPA. On 18 December 1901, Bishop Keiley addressed Father Aloysius Hanlon, OSB, confirming the parish boundaries from Oswald Moosmueller's time. But in 1919, when Blessed Sacrament Parish was given its borders, territory was taken—understandably and appropriately—from Sacred Heart (cf. notice from Keiley, 12 July 1919). In 1920, Benedictines were continuing to protest the partition of their territory in Savannah (see letter from Haas to Keiley, 28 June 1920).

[117]BPA. Letter from Keiley to Haas, 26 October 1902.

[118]BPA. Letter from Keiley to Aloysius Hanlon, 3 July 1908.

[119]BPA. Letter from Keiley to Haas, 12 September 1915.

[120]BPA. Letter from Keiley to Haas, 28 October 1919.

[121]Cf. for example, AAM. Letters from Keiley to Haid, 6 February and 12 February 1919.

[122]Cf. BPA. Letter from Haas to Egan, 20 July 1921.

[123]Cf. McGraw.

[124]Robert Brennan, *A History of Saint Mary's Church, Richmond, Virginia* (Belmont: Abbey Press, 1962), 21.

[125]Margaret Meagher, *History of Education in Richmond* (Richmond: Works Progress Administration [Federal Writers' Project], 1939), 125.

[126]Cf. SAA No. 3. Letter from Haid to Primate, 8 October 1909.

[127]AAM. Letter from Haid to Mark Cassidy, undated (Spring, 1919 ?). [M102, No. 2. Leo Haid, OSB, Bishop]

[128]AAM. Letter from Pohl to Haid and capitulars, undated (1914).

[129]D.RICH.A. Consultors' Minutes, 1909-1910.

[130]Cf. McGraw.

[131]SAA, No. 3. Letter from Haid to Primate, 23 January 1911.

[132]D.RICH.A. Roman documents files, 10 June 1910.

[133]Cf. AAM. Letter from Haid to Mark Cassidy, 25 March 1919. [M102, No. 1. Leo Haid, OSB, Bishop]

[134]AAM. Letter from Haid to Mark Cassidy, undated (Spring, 1919).

[135]Cf. AAM. Letters from Haid to Mark Cassidy, 28 April 1919, 2 December 1920, 8 July 1921, 21 July 1921. [M102, No. 1 and No. 2. Leo Haid, OSB, Bishop]

[136]BPA. Notice from Haid, 17 September 1902.

[137]BPA. Letter from Haid to Haas, 17 February 1902.

[138]AAM. Letter from Haid to Priors and Priests at Saint Maur, Sacred Heart, and Saint Mary (Richmond), 10 September 1908.

[139]Cf., for example, the Savannah catalogue (1908) and Richmond catalogue (1912-1913). The daily horarium was

8:30 a.m.	doors opened
8:45	flag ceremony
9:00	military drill
9:20	class recitations
11:30	recess
12:00 p.m.	class recitations
2:00	flag ceremony

[140]Richmond catalogue, *ibid.*

[141]BPA. Letter from Haid to Haas, 27 October 1921.

[142]Savannah Catalogue, 1906.

[143]AAM. Letter from Haid to Mark Cassidy, undated (c. 1920). [M102, No. 3. Leo Haid, OSB, Bishop]

[144]*Ibid.*

[145]Richmond catalogue, 1913-1914.

[146]AAM. Letter from Haid to Mark Cassidy, undated (c. 1920).

[147]SLA. Diary of Joseph Kast.

[148]AAM, Letter from Haid to Mark Cassidy, undated (c. 1920).

[149]SJA, No. 1. Letter from Haid to Engel, 11 February 1904.

[150]AAM. "With Bishop Leo Haid, OSB, in North Carolina," unsigned work [by a lay student ?], undated (c. 1928 [sic]). [B5, No. 2. Golden Jubilee—Testimonials]

[151]AAM. Letter from Father George Bornermann to Haid, 27 November 1891. [A1.0, No. 1. Correspondence 1884-1899]

[152]College *Catalogue*, 1885-1886.

[153]Cf. *Publicity Files*, v, 7. "At Belmont College: Gratifying Prospects for Bright Opening Thursday," unlabeled newspaper article (1915 or 1916).

[154]College *Catalogue*, 1917-1918.

[155]*Ibid.*, 1920-1921.

[156]*Ibid.*, 1917-1918.

[157]*Ibid.*

[158]*Ibid.*, 1916-1917.

[159]*Ibid.*, 1909-1910.

[160]*Ibid.*, 1920-1921.

[161]Cf. *ibid.*, 1879-1880.

[162]*Ibid.*, 1916-1917.

[163]*Ibid.*

[164]Cf. *ibid.*, 1920-1921.

[165]*Ibid.*, 1922-1923.

[166]AAM. *Publicity Files*, i, 107, "Saint Mary's College," Mount Holly *News*, dateline 25 May 1891.

[167]AAM. Letter from Thomas Oestreich to Haid, 21 March 1891. [A1.0, No. 1. Thomas Oestreich, OSB, RP]

[168]AAM. Will of Henry G. Ganss, 3 January 1909. [A1.9, No. 1. Ganss, H.G.—Estate]

[169]AAM. Visitation Reports from 1910, 1914, and 1920. [A1.0, No. 1. Visitation (1910) (1914) (1920)]

[170]Most of what follows is taken from Paschal Baumstein, "The Tradition of Saint Leo's," *Crescat* (Autumn, 1981), 1-6.

[171]AAM has McInerney's floor plans, original drawing, and other materials.

[172]AAM. The Q1 collection contains photographs, both interior and exterior, of Saint Leo Hall.

[173]AAM. Text reprinted in *Souvenir of the Alumni Reunion*, 27 November 1913.

[174]AAM. Notes for retreat for novices, 11 June 1918.

[175]AAM. Letter from Haid to Mark Cassidy, undated (c. 1920).

[176]AAM. Notes for retreat for novices, 11 June 1918.

[177]AAM. "Lecture to Myself and Superiors," 1913.

[178]AAM. "Some Hints—Prefects and Professors," by Leo Haid, undated (c. 1915). [A1.0, No. 1. Hints for Prefects and Professors]. These instructions were posted for the faculties of all four schools.

[179]SJA, No. 1. Letter from Haid to Engel, 3 December 1909.

[180]The prize is preserved in AAM.

[181]*Souvenir.*

[182]*Ibid.*

[183]*Ordo.*

[184]SAA, No. 3. Letter from Haid to Primate, 10 May 1903.

[185]AAM. Letter from Haid to Hintemeyer, 11-12 June 1903. [M11, No. 2, Leo Haid, Abbot]

[186]SAA, No. 3. Letter from Haid to Primate, 4 November 1903.

[187]AAM. Letter from Haid to Hintemeyer, 13 August 1903.

[188]Cf., for example, AAM. Letter from Haid to Hintemeyer, 6 June 1903.

[189]Cf., for example, AAM. Letter from Haid to Hintemeyer, 22 August 1903.

[190]AAM. This correspondence fills seven folders. [M11, Nos.1-7. Leo Haid, Abbot]

[191]AAM. Letter from Haid to Hintemeyer, 8 June 1903. [M11, No. 2. Leo Haid, Abbot]

[192]SAA, No. 2. Letter from Hintemeyer to Primate, 20 June 1904.

[193]AAM. Letter from Haid to Hintemeyer, 8 June 1903.

[194]SAA, No. 3. Letter from Haid to Primate, 4 November 1903.

[195]SAA, No. 3. Letter from Haid to Primate, 17 April 1904.

[196]SAA, No. 2. Letter from Hintemeyer to Primate, 20 June 1904.

[197]AAM does not have full estate files for Brown, but some of the letters from the niece, Mrs. Annie Devereaux of Boston, are still extant. [A2.0, No. 1. Devereaux, Annie]

[198]Most of the files from the O'Donoghue settlement are contained in AAM. [A1.0, No. 1. O'Donoghue Estate]

Chapter VII:

A Grasp on Security

[1] The best discussion of the juridical aspects of being an *abbatia nullius* is: Matthew Benko, *The Abbot 'Nullius'*, in The Catholic University of America Canon Law Studies, no. 173 [published doctoral dissertation] (Washington, D.C.: The Catholic University of America Press, 1943).

[2] *Ibid.*, 27.

[3] Maria Einsiedeln, which may have been created an abbey *nullius* as early as 934, and thus would be the oldest existing abbatial 'diocese' in the world, has today no territory beyond its monastery grounds. When Maryhelp's *nullius* territory was subjected to its second partition (1960), and reduced to the grounds of the abbey, it became the smallest 'diocese' in the universal Church. For a concise statement of the origins of abbeys *nullius*, cf. *ibid.*, 9-13.

[4] Cf. *ibid.*, xiii and 1-2. Canons 319-327 in the 1917 Codex reflect the fact that "the Code has evolved almost a new legislation in this respect." Whereas, the old Code evaluated abbeys *nullius* from their hierarchial status, and thus was mostly concerned with their existence as sub-diocesan entities, the 1917 Code approached them from the perspective of the role of the Abbot-Ordinary, which was on a par with that of a bishop, except in matters pertaining to powers exclusive to episcopal Orders.

[5] AAM. Letters from Haid to Hintemeyer, 16 and 18 June 1903. [M11, No. 1. Apostolic Delegate (vicariate/*Nullius*)]

[6] AAM. Financial Statement, 1 January 1899. [J1, No. 1. Abbey (1898)]

[7] AAM. Letter from Hintemeyer to Delegate, undated (1909). [M11, No. 1. Apostolic Delegate (Vicariate/*Nullius*)]

[8] AAM. Letter from Haid to Primate, 8 November 1909. [A5.0, No. 6. Abbatial Confirmation/*Nullius* Change, 1975, etc.]

[9] AAM. Letter from Hintemeyer to Haid undated (May 1908). [A1.0, No. 1. *Nullius*]

[10] *Ibid.*

[11]SAA, No. 2. Letter from Hintemeyer to Primate, (14 ?) May 1908.

[12]AAM. Letter from Hintemeyer to Haid, undated (May 1908).

[13]SAA, No. 2. Letter from Hintemeyer to Primate, (14 ?) May 1908.

[14]AAM. Letter from Hintemeyer to Haid, undated (May 1908).

[15]AAB. Letter from Haid to Gibbons, 24 June 1908.

[16]*Ibid.*

[17]SAA, No. 2. Letter from Hintemeyer to Primate, 22 March 1909.

[18]*Ibid.*

[19]SAA, No. 4. Letter from Haid to Primate, 8 April 1909.

[20]SAA, No. 2. Letter from Hintemeyer to Primate, 10 April 1909.

[21]SAA, No. 4. Letter from Haid to Primate, 8 April 1909.

[22]SAA, No. 2. Letter from Hintemeyer to Primate, 10 April, 1909.

[23]AAM. Copy of petition of 11 April 1909. [A1.0, No. 1. *Nullius* Erection—Petition]

[24]AAM. Letter from Haid to Primate, 8 November 1909. [A5.0, No. 6. Abbatial Confirmation/*Nullius* Change, 1975, etc.]

[25]AAB. Letter from De Lai to Gibbons, 16 December 1909.

[26]AAB. Letter from Haid to Gibbons, 24 June 1908.

[27]AAB. Letter from Gibbons to De Lai, 25 January 1910.

[28]*Ibid.*

[29]Cf. SAA, No. 2. Letter from Hintemeyer to Primate, 19 April 1910.

[30]AAM. Letter from Delegate to Haid, 20 March 1910. [A5.0, No. 6. Abbatial Confirmation/*Nullius* Change, 1975, etc.]

[31]AAM. Letter from Hintemeyer to Primate, undated (March, 1910, No. 2). [A5.0, No. 6. Abbatial Confirmation/*Nullius* Change, 1975, etc.]

[32]AAM. Letter from Hintemeyer to Primate, undated (March, 1910, No. 1). [A5.0, No. 6. Abbatial Confirmation/*Nullius* Change, 1975, etc.]

[33]AAM. Letter from Hintemeyer to Primate, undated (March, 1910, No. 2).

[34]SAA, No. 2. Hintemeyer to Primate, 22 March 1910.

[35]AAM. Letter from Hintemeyer to Primate, undated (March, 1910, No. 2).

[36]AAM. Letter from Hintemeyer to Primate, undated (March, 1910, No. 1).

[37]AAM. Letter from Hintemeyer to Primate, undated (March, 1910, No. 2).

[38]AAM. Letter from Delegate to Haid, 24 March 1910. [A5.0, No. 6. Abbatial Confirmation/*Nullius* Change, 1975, etc.]

[39]SAA, No. 2. Letter from Hintemeyer to Primate, 22 March 1910.

[40]SAA, No. 2. Letter from Hintemeyer to Primate, 28 March 1910.

[41]SAA, No. 2. Letter from Hintemeyer to Primate, 19 April 1910.

[42]AAM. Letter from Hintemeyer to Delegate, undated (1910). [M11, No. 1. Apostolic Delegate (Vicariate/*Nullius*]

[43]SAA, No. 2. Letter from Hintemeyer to Primate, 19 April 1910.

[44]Cf. SAA, No. 4. Letter from Haid to Primate, 4 June 1910.

[45]SAA, No. 4. Letter from Haid to Primate, 12 May 1910.

[46]SAA, No. 4. Letter from Haid to Primate, 24 June 1910.

[47]AAM. Letter from Apostolic Delegation to Haid, 23 June 1910. [A5.0, No. 6. Abbatial Confirmation/*Nullius* Change, 1975, etc.] And AAB. Letter from Apostolic Delegation to Gibbons, 23 June 1910.

[48]"America's Only *Abbatia Nullius,*" *Newsletter* (November, 1910), 2.

[49]The Bulls are preserved in AAM. (+ E, No. 1. Ecclesia] The Bull of Erection was published in: "Erectio Abbatiae Belmontensis in *'Abbatiam Nullius'*", *American Ecclesiastical Review* (December, 1910), 690-695.

[50]*Ibid.*

[51] Cf. note from Anselm Biggs, O.S.B., in AAM. [E10, No. 1. *Nullius* Erection (Translation of Bull)]

[52] AAM. *Bulla Erectionis*, 8 June 1910. This is quoted from the translation by Biggs, *ibid.*

[53] Cf. AAM. Letter from Christopher Dennen to Hintemeyer, 26 October 1910. [A1.0, No. 1. Dennen, Christopher, Reverend]

[54] AAM. *Bulla Erectionis*, 8 June 1910.

[55] AAM. Letter from Delegate to Haid, 21 September 1910. [A1.0, No. 2. *Nullius* Erection Ceremony]

[56] "Falconio at Belmont." The Charlotte *Daily Observer* (18 October 1910), 1.

[57] "America's Only *Abbatia Nullius*." *Newsletter* (November 1910), 3-4.

[58] "Belmont Cathedral Abbey Erected With Impressive Catholic Ceremony," The Charlotte *Daily Observer* (19 October 1910), 1-3.

[59] "Pomp and Ceremony at Belmont Abbey: Pope Confers Honor," The Charlotte *News* (18 October 1910), 7.

[60] Cf. *The Jubilee Book of Belmont Abbey* (Belmont: Abbey Press, 1910), 27.

[61] "Belmont Cathedral . . .", 3.

[62] AAM. Invitation for 18 October 1910. [A1.0, No. 2. Silver Jubilee (Abbatial)]

[63] SAA, No. 2. Letter from Hintemeyer to Primate, 29 October 1910.

[64] SAA, No. 2. Letter from Hintemeyer to Primate, 19 April 1910.

[65] AAM. Letter from Gibbons to Haid, 22 September 1910. [A1.0, No. 1. Gibbons, James Cardinal]

[66] AAM. Letter from Gibbons to Hintemeyer, 18 October 1910. [M11, No. 2. Correspondence—Official]

[67] "Pomp . . .", 7.

[68] SJA. Letter from Haid to Peter Engel, 6 April 1909.

[69] AAM. Letter from Dennen to Hintemeyer, 26 October 1910.

[70] SJA, No. 1. Letter from Haid to Engel, 22 November 1910.

[71] AAB. Letter from Michael Irwin to Gibbons, 3 November 1910.

[72] AAM. Letter from Dennen to Haid, 26 October 1910.

[73] Cf. AAB. Letter from Irwin to Gibbons, 3 November 1910.

[74] *Ibid.*

[75] *Ibid.* Dennen, however, places the story later—1901. Cf. AAB, No. 3. Letter from Dennen to Delegate, 30 May 1922, also signed by secular clergy of the Vicariate Apostolic of North Carolina.

[76] *Ibid.*

[77] AAM. Letter from Dennen to Hintemeyer, 30 October 1910. [A1.0, No. 1. Correspondence (1910)]

[78] *Ibid.*

[79] Cf. Raymond Lane, *The Early Days of Maryknoll* (New York: David McKay Company, 1951), 58.

[80] Cf. (Priest of Maryknoll), *Father Price of Maryknoll: A Short Sketch of the Life of Reverend Thomas Frederick Price* (Maryknoll, New York: Catholic Foreign Mission Society of America, 1923), 11-12.

[81] AAB. Letter from Mark Gross to Gibbons, 10 November 1886.

[82] Nazareth, the orphanage, was constituted in 1897, and by 1899 was in full operation. Sister Catherine, R.S.M., of the Belmont Mercies, one of two of Price's sisters who entered the convent, was his chief assistant. The Mercies also conducted the girls' asylum, Saint Anne, at Belmont.

[83] The first copy of *Truth* appeared in April of 1897. *Our Lady's Orphan Boy* entered publication in 1903, seeking funds to support the orphanage.

[84]Lane, 126.

[85]Cf. Robert E. Sheridan, *The Founders of Maryknoll: Historical Reflections* (Maryknoll, New York: Catholic Foreign Mission Society of America, 1980), 6.

[86]CFMSA. Letter from George Woods to James Anthony Walsh, 18 August 1921.

[87]D.RAH.A. "Memoirs," (galley proofs) by William F. O'Brien.

[88]Robert E. Sheridan, editor *Very Reverend Thomas Frederick Price, M.M., Co-Founder of Maryknoll: A Symposium* (Privately published at Maryknoll, New York, 1956), interview with Louis Bour, 26 October 1955.

[89]Sheridan, Founders, 6.

[90]*RB*, chapter vii.

[91]CFMSA. Letter from Woods to Walsh, 18 August 1921.

[92]Sheridan, *Symposium*, testimony of Michael Irwin.

[93]*Ibid.*, testimony of Vincent Taylor (October 1955).

[94]This account comes from the paper Price placed in the cornerstone of the building on 21 April 1902. It was recovered after the building burned in 1906.

[95]CFMSA. Price's Diary, entry for 5 July 1910.

[96]Cf. Canonist's opinions requested by Haid on the proposed ordination in AAM. [DV1.0, No. 1. Woods, George, Reverend—Deafness Impediment] Woods was ordained a priest on 18 December 1910.

[97]CFMSA. Letter from Woods to Walsh, 18 August 1921.

[98]CF. Sheridan, *Symposium*.

[99]Lane, 66. And CFMSA, Price's diary, entry for 14 October 1908.

[100]Sheridan, *Founders*, 11.

[101]CFMSA, Price's diary, entry for 6 October 1909.

[102]Cf. *ibid.*, 20 October 1909.

[103]*Ibid.*, 2 May 1910.

[104]AAB. Letter from Price to Gibbons, 31 May 1910.

[105]*Ibid.*

[106]CFMSA. Price's diary, entry for 17 June 1910.

[107]*Ibid.*, 4 July 1910.

[108]*Ibid.*, 15 July 1910.

[109]*Ibid.*, 22 August 1910.

[110]*Ibid.*, retreat observations between entries for 22 and 23 August 1910.

[111]Cf. SAA, No. 4. Letter from Haid to Primate, 4 June 1910.

[112]CFMSA. Price's diary, entry for 4 October 1910.

[113]*Ibid.*, 12 October 1910.

[114]*Ibid.*, 16 October 1910.

[115]CFMSA. Letter from Price to Walsh, 16 October 1910.

[116]CFMSA. Price's diary, entry for 19 October 1910.

[117]*Ibid.*, 22 October 1910.

[118]*Ibid.*, 21 October 1910.

[119]AAB, No. 6. Letter from Price to Gibbons, 27 October 1910.

[120]*Ibid.*

[121]AAB, No. 5. Petition, November 1910, from the secular clergy of the Vicariate Apostolic of North Carolina to Gibbons, Metropolitan of the Province of Baltimore.

[122]These were Thomas Griffin, William O'Brien, Michael Irwin, Patrick Marion, William Whearty, Robert Barton, W.B. Hannon, Joseph Gallagher, Francis Gallagher, Thomas P. Hayden, and William J. Dillon.

[123]AAB, No. 5. Petition, November 1910. SCSA also has a copy.

[124]Cf. Sheridan, *Founders*, 56-57.

[125]Sheridan, *Symposium*, document of 16 January 1911.

[126]CFMSA. Price's diary, entry for 1 April 1911.

[127]AAB. Minutes of the Meeting of the Archbishops of the United States, 27 April 1911.

[128]AAM. Letter from Woods to Haid, 27 June 1911. [DV1.0, No. 1. Woods, George Andrew, Reverend]

[129]AAM. Letter from Price to Haid, 7 October 1911. [A1.0, No. 1. Price, Thomas Frederick, Reverend]

[130]CFMSA. Price's diary, entry for 18 and 23 January 1912.

[131]*Ibid.*, 8 April 1912.

[132]CFMSA. Letter from Irwin to Father Browne at Maryknoll, 22 October 1919.

[133]CFMSA. The letter from Woods to Walsh, 18 August 1921, consists largely of Father Woods' assessment of Price. The letter was submitted by Woods to Leo Haid for comment. On 22 August he appended the paragraph quoted.

[134]AAM. *Bulla Erectionis,* 8 June 1910.

[135]Cf. *Souvenir of the Alumni Reunion,* 27 November 1913.

[136]Cf. for example, SCSA, No. 1. Letter from Haid to Herman J. Heuser (editor of the *American Ecclesiastical Review*), undated (1911).

[137]AAB, No. 2. Letter from Haid to Gibbons, 28 January 1911.

[138]Cf. *ibid.*

[139]Cf. AAB. Letter from Father M. O'Keefe (to Gibbons ?), 5 January 1872.

[140]AAM. Letter from Gibbons to Haid, 23 January 1911. [A1.0, No. 2. Gibbons, James Cardinal]

[141]AAB, No. 2. Letter from Haid to Gibbons, 28 January 1911.

[142]Cf. CFMSA. Price's diary, entry for 25 February 1911.

[143]AAB. Letter from Dennen to Gibbons, 16 February 1911.

[144]AAM. Letter from W.J. Dillion to Haid, 17 February 1911. [A1.0, No. 1. Correspondence (re: Vicariate)]

[145]AAM. Letter from Woods to Haid, 27 February 1911. [A1.0, No. 1. Correspondence (re: Vicariate)]

[146]AAM. Letter from Robert Barton to Price, 23 December 1911. [A1.0, No. 1. Barton, Robert, Reverend]

[147]AAM. Letter from Barton to Haid, 27 March 1911. [A1.0, No. 1. Barton, Robert, Reverend]

[148]AAM. Letter from William F. O'Brien to Haid, 31 March 1911. [A1.0, No. 1. Correspondence (re: Vicariate)]

[149]AAM. Letter from Price to Haid, 14 April 1911. [A1.0, No. 1. Conference of Archbishops]

[150]In addition to the Minutes (AAB), see: SAA, No. 4. Letter from Haid to Primate, 10 May 1911.

[151]SAA. *ibid.*

[152]AAM. Letter from Delegate to Haid, 13 May 1911. [A1.0, No. 1. Vicariate]

[153]AAM. Letter from Gibbons to Haid, 18 May 1911. [A1.0, No. 2. Gibbons, James Cardinal]

[154]AAB. Petition from Gibbons to Pius X, 31 May 1911.

[155]Cf. SJA, No. 1. Letter from Haid to Engel, 30 May 1911.

[156]AAB. Letter from Delegate to Gibbons, 1 September 1911. And AAM. Letter from Delegate to Haid, 1 September 1911. [A1.0, No. 1.Vicariate]

[157]AAM. Letter from Gibbons to Haid, 2 September 1911. [A1.0, No. 2. Gibbons, James Cardinal]

[158]CFMSA. Price's diary, entry for 23 September 1911.

358

[159]*Ibid.*, 2 October 1911.

[160]AAM. Letter from Price to Haid, 7 October 1911. [A1.0, No. 1, Price, Thomas Frederick, Reverend]

[161]SVA, No. 9. Quoted in letter from Haid to Hintenach, 3 November 1888. Haid said this originally at the Pontifical High Mass with students in attendance on the occasion of the first solemn profession (Gregory Windschiegel's) at Belmont, 1 November 1888.

[162]AAM. From poem by Mary Taylor, 1910. [A1.0, No. 1. Silver Jubilee (Abbatial)]

[163]From statistics in *Jubilee Book*, 46.

[164]SVA. Letter from Haid to Felix Fellner, 19 January 1922.

Chapter VIII:

the dean

[1] AAM. "Virgin Most Faithful," May conferences by Leo Haid, first delivered at Saint Vincent Abbey in 1878. [Al.O, No.1. Mary, Saint—Conferences]

[2] SVA, No. 9. Letter from Haid to Hintenach, 2 December 1889.

[3] AAM. May Conferences.

[4] AAM. Notes for retreat conference by Haid, delivered at Saint Vincent Archabbey, 22 June 1920. [Al.O No.10. Sermons and Retreats]

[5] Cf. for example, D.RAH.A. Letter from Hintemeyer to Joseph Gallagher, 18 July 1913.

[6] Cf. for example, AAM. [M11, No. 1. Correspondence—Official]

[7] AAM. *Publicity Files*, Volume xiii, 14. "Father Felix Dies on Trip to Rome," [Georgia] *Bulletin*, June) 1924.

[8] For example, *Pontia, the Daughter of Pilate*, c. 1895.

[9] Quoted in *Souvenir*, 27 November 1913.

[10] Cf. reference in AAM. Letter from Dennen to Hintemeyer, 26 October 1910.

[11] The details of the offer have not been preserved either at AAM or D.SU.A. Cf. AAM. Letter from Jean Myers (archivist) to Paschal Baumstein, 21 December 1983. [uncatalogued materials]

[12] AAM. Chapter Minutes, 18 January 1915.

[13] SVA, No. 14. Letter from Haid to Prior of Saint Vincent, 18 December 1916. The revised horarium:

4:15	rising
4:30	Matins and Lauds
	followed by an interval
5:35	Priests: individual Masses
	Clerics: common meditation in chapel
6:00	Conventual Mass

6:30	Prime and thanksgiving
7:00	breakfast
7:30	recreation or walk
8:00	study and class preparations
8:30	classes
10:45	music, etc.
11:40	Minor Hours and Particular Examen.
12:00	luncheon
	followed by Vespers
	followed by recreation
1:30	study, *lectio*, etc.
2:00	classes
4:15	music, etc.
6:00	supper
	followed by thanksgiving, *lectio*, devotions,
	recreation, etc.
7:30	Compline
	followed by study, etc.
9:00	dormition

[14]Cf. AAM. Visitation Reports, especially 1907, 1910, 1914, 1917, 1920, and 1923. [Al.O, No. 1, Visitation (1907), (1910), (1914), (1917), (1920), (1923)]

[15]*Ibid.*, Report to the Community, 1923.

[16]*Ibid.*, Report to the Community, 1920.

[17]*Ibid.*, Report to the Abbot, 1920.

[18]AAM. Conference notes by Haid, 1912. [Al.O, No. 6. Sermons and Retreats]

[19]*Ibid.*

[20]*Ibid.*

[21]AAM. Notes for retreat for novices, 12 June 1918. [Al.O, No. 2. Sermons and Retreats]

[22]AAM. "Seat of Wisdom," May Conferences.

[23]AAM. Notes for a conference concerning "Destiny," undated (c. 1920).

[24]AAM. Notes for retreat for novices, 12 June 1918.

[25]AAM. Notes for retreat for novices, 11 June 1918. [Al.O, No. 2. Sermons and Retreats]

[26]AAM. Lecture notes by Haid, December 1888. [Al.O, No. 2. Sermons and Retreats]

[27]AAM. May Conferences.

[28]AAM. Notes for retreat for novices, 11 June 1918.

[29]*Ibid.*

[30]*Ibid.*

[31]AAM. Document of 25 July 1914. [Al.O, No. 1. Assistant at the Pontificial Throne]

[32]This was on 25 May 1914. Copies of the commemorative photographs are preserved in AAM. Cf. also, letters from Haid to Hintemeyer, spring and summer 1914. [M11, No. 8, No. 9, No. 10. Leo Haid, Abbot]

[33]AAM. Letters from Haid to Hintemeyer, spring and summer 1914.

[34]AAM. Letter from Haid to Hintemeyer, undated (May 1914). [M11, No. 8, Leo Haid, Abbot]

[35]AAM. Letter from Benedict XV to Haid, 15 October 1919. [B7, No. 1. Leo Haid—Golden Jubilee (Profession) (Papal Missive)]

[36]AAM. Letter from Gregory Diamare to Haid, 13 November 1919. [Al.O, No. 1. Golden Jubilee (Profession)]

[37]SJA. Letter from Haid to Engel, 27 June 1917.

[38]Cf. AAM. Letter from Denis O'Connell to Haid, 5 September 1917. [A1.0, No. 1. Correspondence (1917)]

[39]Cf. AAM. Letter from Dennen to Haid, 25 May 1917. [Al.O, No. 1. Correspondence (1917)]

[40]Cf. for example, AAM. Letters from Eugene Egan to Haid, of 2 May 1918 and 13 August 1918. [Al.O, No. 1. Eugene Egan, OSB, RP]. And letter from Francis Underwood to Haid, bearing notation by Haid, 23 August 1917. [Al.O, No. 1. Francis Underwood, OSB, RP]

[41]Cf. AAM. Letter from Apostolic Delegation to Haid, 11 January 1923. [Al.O, No. 1. Correspondence (1923)]

[42]Cf. Ellis, *Life*, II, 632.

[43]Cf. Vincent de Paul Fitzpatrick, *Life of Archbishop Curley: Champion of Catholic Education* (Baltimore: [no publisher listed], 1929).

[44]"Fogarty calls him "the truculent successor to Gibbons." Cf. Gerald P. Fogarty, *The Vatican and the American Hierarchy From 1870 to 1965* (Stuttgart: Anton Hiersemann, 1982), 314.

[45]Cf. John Tracy Ellis, *Catholic Bishops: A Memoir* (Wilmington, Delaware: Michael Glazier, 1983), 47.

[46]*Ibid.*, 51.

[47]AAM. Sermon delivered by Haid at Silver Jubilee of Christopher Dennen, 14 November 1916. [Al.O, No. 9. Sermons and Retreats]

[48]AAM. Remnants of official papers. [DV1.O, No. 1. Dennen, Christopher, Reverend]

[49]Cf. for example, AAM. Letter from Dennen to Haid, with enclosures, 20 October 1914. [DV1.O, No. 1. Saint Mary Pro-Cathedral (Wilmington, North Carolina)]

[50]AAB holds the complete files of the Dennen/Curley correspondence. For this struggle the years 1922-1925 are the most significant.

[51]SJA. Letter from Haid to Engel, 17 April 1921.

[52]SVA, No. 14. Letter from Hintemeyer to Priests of the Vicariate Apostolic of North Carolina, 7 December 1922, to be read at Masses of 17 December 1922.

[53]AAB. Letter from Curley to Dennen, 14 May 1922.

[54]SVA, No. 14. Letter from Hintemeyer to Priests of the Vicariate, 7 December 1922. Despite the transfer of the official celebration to the following year, the priests were "hereby directed on the coming twenty-first day of December to observe the following:"

1. To expose the Blessed Sacrament to the public adoration for one hour from eight a.m. to nine a.m.;
2. To offer the Holy Mass *"Pro Ordinario"*;
3. To let the children recite the Holy Rosary aloud;
4. To give the Solemn Benediction at the end of the hour of adoration;
5. Lastly, to sing the hymn, "Holy God, We Praise Thy Name".
   Thus everyone will join in spirit in the Jubilee Mass which the Right Reverend Jubiliarian will personally celebrate at Belmont Abbey at the above mentioned hour.

⁵⁵AAM. Menu for banquet tendered the jubilarian, 11 April 1923. [B7, No. 1. Leo Haid—Golden Jubilee (Priesthood)]. And, Invitation to the jubilee Mass, 11 April 1923. [B7, No. 1. Leo Haid—Golden Jubilee Invitation (1923)]

⁵⁶AAM. Letter from Remke to Haid, 23 March 1923.

⁵⁷AAB. Letter from Curley to Dennen, 10 May 1923.

⁵⁸*Ibid.*

⁵⁹AAB. The request was dated 10 May 1923; the response, 24 May 1923.

⁶⁰AAB. Letter from Dennen to Curley, 24 May 1923.

⁶¹SVA, No. 9. Letter from Haid to Hintenach, 4 October 1888.

⁶²SJA. Letter from Haid to Bernard Locnikar, 10 January 1891.

⁶³SVA, No. 10. Letter from Haid to Leander Schnerr, 19 February 1893.

⁶⁴SVA, No. 10. Letter from Haid to Schnerr, 6 August 1894.

⁶⁵BSA, No. 1. Letter from Haid to Katharine Drexel, 21 December 1898.

⁶⁶SJA. Letters from Haid to Engel, 14 April 1908 and 9 May 1908.

⁶⁷SAA. No. 2. Letter from Hintemeyer to Primate, 22 March 1909.

⁶⁸SJA. Letter from Haid to Engel, 11 June 1909.

⁶⁹SJA. Letter from Haid to Engel, 18 August 1918.

⁷⁰AAM. Letter from Haid to Mark Cassidy, 28 April 1919. (M102, No.2. Leo Haid, OSB, Bishop]

⁷¹SJA. Letter from Haid to Engel, 22 April 1910. Also cf., Barry, *Worship*, 252.

⁷²AAM. Letter from Haid to Mark Cassidy, 2 December 1920. [M102, No. 1. Leo Haid, OSB, Bishop]

⁷³SJA. Letter from Haid to Engel, 17 April 1921.

⁷⁴SVA, No. 11. Letter from Haid to Aurelius Stehle, 4 August 1921.

⁷⁵SJA. Letter from Haid to Alcuin Deutsch, 11 April 1922.

⁷⁶AAB. Letter from Dennen to Curley, 24 May 1923.

⁷⁷*Ibid.*

⁷⁸*Ibid.*

⁷⁹*Ibid.*

⁸⁰Anselm Biggs, the Abbey's chronicler, giving Father Nicholas Bliley (who was Haid's canonist at Belmont) as the source, says that the plan of 1924 called for the *Nullius'* territory to be changed to include only Mecklenburg and Gaston Counties, and to have Haid named a titular archbishop. According to Biggs' recollection, Bliley claimed to have prepared the *Relatio* for this appeal. [Interview with Anselm Biggs, 22 February 1984]

⁸¹AAB. Letter from Curley to Dennen, 26 May 1922.

⁸²AAB. Letter from Curley to Delegate, 18 June 1923.

⁸³Cf. AAM. Letter from Mauro Inguanez to Thomas Oestreich, 8 July 1924. [M59, No. 1. Thomas Oestreich]

⁸⁴AAM. Letter from Inguanez to Oestreich, 11 June 1924. [M59, No. 1. Thomas Oestreich]

⁸⁵AAB. Letter from Curley to Dennen, 24 March 1924.

⁸⁶Cf. AAM. [M59, No. 2. Thomas Oestreich]

⁸⁷AAM. Letter from Inguanez to Oestreich, 11 June 1924.

⁸⁸AAM. Letter from Inguanez to Oestreich, 1 July 1924. [M59, No. 1. Thomas Oestreich]

⁸⁹AAM. Letter from Inguanez to Oestreich, 18 June 1924. [M59, No. 1. Thomas Oestreich]

⁹⁰AAM. Letter from Inguanez to Oestreich, 23 June 1924. [M59, No. 1. Thomas Oestreich]

⁹¹AAM. Letter from Inguanez to Oestreich, 1 July 1924.

[92]*Ibid.*

[93]AAM. Letter from Inguanez to Oestreich, 8 July 1924. [M59, No. 1. Thomas Oestreich]

[94]AAM. Letter from Inguanez to Oestreich, 1 July 1924.

[95]AAM. *Publicity Files*, xiii, 14. "Father Felix Dies On Trip to Rome," (Georgia) *Bulletin*.

[96]AAM. Letter from Inguanez to Oestreich, 14 August 1924. [M59, No. 1. Thomas Oestreich]

[97]AAM. Letter from Haid to Baumgartner, 2 July 1924. [M59, No. 1. Thomas Oestreich]

[98]Cf. Doris, *Belmont*, 49.

[99]AAM. Letter from Gabriel Locher to Baumgartner, 7 November 1924. [A1.5, No. 1. Gabriel Locher, OSB]

[100]AAB. Letter from Dennen to Curley, 5 December 1924.

[101]Cf. AAM. Letter from Inguanez to Oestreich, 14 August 1924.

[102]AAM. Letter from Inguanez to Oestreich, 8 July 1924.

[103]AAM. Letter from Inguanez to Oestreich, 4 January 1925. [M59, No. 2. Thomas Oestreich]

[104]AAM. Letter from Thomas Cook and Son World-Wide Travel Service to Oestreich, (May, 1925). [A2.0, No. 1. Felix Hintemeyer, OSB, RP—Estate (local)]

[105]AAM. Speech by Haid, undated (post 1910). [A1.0, No. 12, Sermons and Retreats]

[106]Cf. also, Doris, *Belmont*, 49-50, n.1.

[107]Cf. AAM. *Publicity Files*, xiii, 18. "Death Came at 9:30 p.m.," (unlabeled newspaper clipping).

[108]BPA. Telegram from Nicholas Bliley to Eugene Egan, 24 July 1924.

[109]SJA, No. 5. Letter from Haid to Norbert Hofbauer, 8 November 1894.

[110]AAM. Notes for retreat for novices, 11 June 1918.

[111]AAM. Speech by Haid, undated (post 1910).

[112]Cf. Doris, *Belmont*, 49-50, n.1.

[113]"Bishop Leo Haid, Abbot of Belmont Abbey, Succombs After Lingering Illness," Gastonia *Gazette* (25 July 1924), 1.

[114]AAM. Letter from Michael Irwin to Baumgartner, undated (1924). [A1.5, No. 1. Irwin, Michael, Reverend]

[115]AAM. *Publicity Files*, xiii, 22. Taylor Glenn, "Final Mass for Bishop Haid at Ten A.M. Today," Charlotte *Observer*, 29 July 1924.

[116]AAM. Speech by Haid, 1892. Reprinted in "The New Abbey Church," The Charlotte *Chronicle*, 5 May 1892.

[117]McInerney's sketches are preserved in AAM.

[118]Cardinal O'Connell of Boston also claimed this title, since he was the longest reigning member of the highest strata (the Cardinalate) of the American hierarchy.

[119]Denis O'Connell sent Felix Kaup as his representative, both to the funeral and to the abbatial benediction of Leo Haid's successor at Belmont.

[120]Archbishop Curley was still in Ireland.

[121]AAM. Notice of Mass assignments for Pontifical *Requiem ad Faldistorium*, 29 July 1924. [B7, No. 1. Leo Haid—Funeral Mass]

[122]AAM. *Publicity Files*, xiii, 23. Taylor Glenn, "Many Dignitaries Present," Charlotte *Observer*, 30 July 1924.

[123]AAM. *Publicity Files*, xiii, 10. Bishop Boyle's eulogy is printed in "Bishop Haid's Luxuriant Mind and Wealth of Character Eulogized."

[124]AAM. Notice of Mass assignments, 29 July 1924.

[125]AAM. Glenn, "Many."

[126]AAM. Notice of Mass assignments, 29 July 1924.

[127]AAM. Glenn, "Many."

[128]AAM. Notes for retreat for novices, 11 June 1918.

[129]AAB, No. 3. Letter from Dennen to Delegate, 30 May 1922, also signed by secular clergy of Vicariate.

[130]AAM. Letter from Irwin to Baumgartner, undated (1924).

[131]AAM. Speech by Haid, 17 October 1910, quoted in *Jubilee Book*, 27.

[132]"In the last hour,
Pray to thy Son for us.
May we enter well upon death,
O Virgin, Mother, Lady.
May we enter well upon death,
O Virgin, Mother, Lady."

This prayer is still (1984) sung at burials at Maryhelp. It is also offered as part of the cemetery services each November. The monks also sing it randomly at various special occasions, especially jubilees.

epilogue:

the Crozier turns inward

[1]Cf. AAM. Letter from Stephen Webber to Vincent Taylor, 7 December 1924. [A2.0, No. 4. Correspondence (1924)]

[2]Cf. AAM. Letter from Dennen to Baumgartner, 16 December 1924. [A2.0, No. 1. Correspondence (1924)]

[3]Cf. AAM. Letter from James Gallagher to Baumgartner, 19 December 1924. [A2.0, No. 1. Correspondence (1924)]

[4]Cf. AAB. Letter from Dennen to Curley, 5 December 1924.

[5]AAM. Letter from Dennen to Baumgartner, 16 December 1924.

[6]Cf. AAM. Letter from Alphonse Buss to Taylor, 18 September 1924. [A2.0, No. 1. Correspondence (1924)]

[7]Ibid.

[8]ACFA. Protocol of the election of 20 August 1924.

[9]AAM. Letter from Baumgartner to Helmstetter, 25 October 1924. [A1.5, No. 1. Anthony Meyer, OSB, RP]

[10]AAM. Letter from Gabriel Locher to Baumgartner, 7 November 1924. [A1.5, No. 1. Gabriel Locher, OSB]

[11]AAM. Letter from Taylor to Helmstetter, 30 November 1924. [A2.0, No. 3. Abbatial Confirmation]

[12]The Bull of Confirmation as Abbot Ordinary is preserved in AAM.

[13]AAM. Chapter Minutes, 22 February 1890.

[14]AAB. Dennen summarizes his activities for Curley in: Letter from Dennen to Curley, 5 December 1924.

[15]Cf. AAB. Letter from Delegate to Curley, 26 January 1925 ["As your Grace is aware, we knew nothing of this appointment" of Baumgartner]. Also cf. AAB. Letter from Curley to Baumgartner, 28 January 1925.

[16]AAB. Letter from Baumgartner to Arthur R. Freeman, forwarded to Dennen, then forwarded to Curley, 4 December 1924; with letter from Freeman to Dennen, 5 December 1924.

[17]AAB. Letter from Curley to Dennen, 9 December 1924.

[18]AAB. Letter from Sacred Consistorial Congregation to Curley, 17 December 1924.

[19]D.RAH.A. Bull of Erection of Pius XI for Diocese of Raleigh, 22 December 1924.

[20]AAB. Letter from Curley to Baumgartner, 28 January 1925.

[21]AAB. Letter from Baumgartner to Curley, 12 February 1925. And AAB. Letter from Curley to Baumgartner, 13 February 1925.

[22]AAB. Letter from Curley to Baumgartner, 27 February 1925.

[23]AAB. Letter from Taylor to Curley, 30 January 1925.

[24]AAB. Letter from Baumgartner to Curley, 10 February 1925.

[25]D.RAH.A. Letter from Dennen to Curley, 3 February 1925.

[26]AAB. Letter from Dennen to Curley, 14 January 1925.

[27]AAB. Letter from Curley to Dennen, 15 January 1925.

[28]AAB. Letter from Curley to Dennen, 7 February 1925.

[29]Cf. AAB. Letter from Dennen to Francis Gallagher, 13 March 1925.

[30]D.RAH.A. Letter from Dennen to William Hafey, 27 May 1925.

[31]AAB, No. 4. Report from Curley to Delegate, 10 April 1925.

[32]The most significant of these related to Curley's reluctance to invite Taylor, who as head of the *Abbatia Nullius* was one of the Archbishop's suffragans, to the Provincial meetings. An appeal for an official clarification had to be made before that situation was resolved. The oral tradition at Belmont also records that Taylor was publicly humiliated for wearing a livery that was supposedly inappropriate to his rank, at a meeting of the Ordinaries of the United States. The problems regarding the status of the abbatial 'diocese' in the Province were raised again for Taylor's successor when the archiepiscopal See of Atlanta was erected in 1962. Apparently, Rome did not officially assign the *nullius* to the new Province (as it did concerning Raleigh, Charleston, etc.), yet Baltimore also declined to recognize the *nullius* diocese as a suffragan territory. The Delegate had to resolve the situation.

[33]Numerous interviews with monks of Belmont Abbey and employees of Belmont Abbey College, 1974-1984. Also AAM. Necrology for "The Most Illustrious and Most Reverend Lord, The Lord Vincent George Taylor, O.S.B.", prepared by Anselm Biggs, 1959. And Anselm Biggs, "A Remembrance of Abbot Vincent Taylor," *Crescat* (Winter, 1978), 4.

[34]AM. Annual Statement, signed by Father Nicholas Bliley, Procurator, 30 June 1925. [J1, No. 1. Abbey (1925)]

[35]It is significant in terms of Haid's legacy that the several reminders Belmont received, regarding the necessity of a cloistered orientation over a missionary emphasis, were issued in conjunction with statements regarding the burden of the *Nullius*. In advising the second Abbot of Belmont to request that the abbatial 'diocese' be partitioned in the 1940's, the Apostolic Delegate said

> While your abbey has been successful in scholastic projects, it is inevitable that the missionary phase of the priests' life has to be foregone. Indeed, it does not seem possible for the abbey to work the territory as it should be worked to provide for the greater spread of the Faith there.
>
> —Letter from Delegate to Vincent Taylor
> 23 October 1943

That same theme marked the second parition, which occured in 1960.

> To the end that the Fathers of the Order of Saint Benedict living there, long renowned in the estimation of all for their religious observance, the splendor of their piety and the cultivation of the arts and sciences, may better contribute to the good of souls and the advancement of Catholicism, and in order that, having been freed from external duty of whatever other sort, they may devote their entire efforts to the education and formation of youth [the *Nullius* is partitioned].
>
> —Decree of the Sacred Consistorial Congregation
> 26 March 1960

Paul VI addressed the need for re-evaluating the service performed by abbeys *nullius* in his Apostolic Letter of 23 October 1976, seeking to remind all monks affiliated with abbatial 'dioceses' of the necessary return to priorities:

> Hence, since "the principal duty of monks is to present to the Divine Majesty a service at once humble and noble within the walls of the monastery, whether they dedicate themselves entirely to divine worship in the contemplative life or have legitimately undertaken some apostolic or charitable activity," it has seemed good to revise some of the canonical rules pertaining to abbeys *nullius*.

And the revision of Paul VI was a decree that no new abbatial 'dioceses' should be erected, and that as feasible those already existing should have their 'diocesan' character suppressed.

When the time came for Belmont to relinquish its *abbatia nullius*, the Holy See reiterated the values it had been commending to the monastery's attention for more than thirty years:

> This Sacred Congregation for Bishops regards the educational work of the College as the chief pastoral help for the entire region and hence while it rejoices greatly over the past activity, it offers every good wish for the future that the work of this distinguished College may flourish from day to day and be perfected in accord with the norms and statutes which old and new documents of the Church commend for Catholic Schools.
>
> —Letter from the Sacred Congregation
> for Bishops to Jude Cleary, 31 January 1976

Thus Belmont's mandate to replace missionary commitments with monastic and educational work and emphasis was particularly clear, and its values and objectives in this regard were obvious.

[36]*Ibid.*, letter of 23 October 1943.

[37]AAM. Decree of the Sacred Consistorial Congregation, 26 March 1960.

Bibliography

Part I:

Major Published Sources

Bassett, J.S. "A North Carolina Monastery." *Magazine of American History* (February, 1893), 131-135.

Baumstein, Paschal. "Chapel, Church, Cathedral." *Crescat* (Summer, 1983), 1-8.

_____. "The First Sign of Permanence." *Crescat* (Summer, 1982), 1-6.

_____. "The Tradition of Saint Leo's." *Crescat* (Autumn, 1981), 1-6.

_____. "Variations in Heraldic Insignia at Maryhelp Abbey." *The American Benedictine Review* (March, 1983), 62-73.

"The Benedictine Abbey of Belmont, North Carolina." *American Ecclesiastical Review* (December, 1910), 720-721.

Benedict of Nursia. *Regula.* [available in any number of editions. Cf. in particular, the Editio critico-practica (1912), edited by Cuthbert Butler].

Brennan, Robert. "Benedictines in Virginia." *The American Benedictine Review* (March, 1962), 25-40.

_____. *A History of Saint Mary's Church*. Belmont, North Carolina: Abbey Press, 1962. [The edition in AAM is annotated and corrected]

Chaignon la Rose, Pierre. "Arms of the Vicar Apostolic of North Carolina." *The American Ecclesiastical Review* (July, 1911), 9-11.

"Erectio Abbatiae Belmontensis in 'Abbatiam Nullius' ". *The American Ecclesiastical Review* (December, 1910), 690-695.

Hintemeyer, Felix. "The Maryhelp Abbey." *The Catholic Church in the United States of America*, Volume I. New York: The Catholic Editing Company, 1912, 50-54.

_____. "The Vicariate Apostolic of North Carolina and Abbatial Diocese of Belmont." *The Catholic Church in the United Church of America*, Volume III. New York: The Catholic Editing Company, 1914, 260-274.

Johnston, Helen. *The Fruit of His Works: A History of the Benedictine Sisters of Saint Benedict's Convent, Bristow, Prince William County, Virginia.* Bristow: Linton Hall Press, 1954.

O'Connell, Jeremiah Joseph. *Catholicity in the Carolinas and Georgia: Leaves of Its History.* New York: Sadlier, 1879.

Oetgen, Jerome. *An American Abbot: Boniface Wimmer, O.S.B., 1809-1887.* Latrobe, Pennsylvania: The Archabbey Press, 1976.

_____. "Boniface Wimmer and the American Benedictines: 1877-1887." *The American Benedictine Review* (March, 1974), 1-32.

_____. "The Origins of the Benedictine Order in Georgia." *Georgia Historical Quarterly* (June, 1969), 165-183.

Remke, Ignatius. *Historical Sketch of Saint Mary's Church, Richmond, Virginia, 1843-1935.* [gives no publication information, probably should be: Belmont, North Carolina. Abbey Press, c. 1935]

Part II:

Partial Listing Of Published Sources Regarding Secondary Concerns

Ahern, Patrick H. *The Life of John J. Keane, Educator and Archbishop.* Milwaukee: Bruce, 1955.

Bailey, James Henry. *A History of the Diocese of Richmond.* Richmond, Virginia: Diocese of Richmond, 1956.

Barry, Colman J. *The Catholic University of America 1903 1909: The Rectorship of Denis J. O'Connell.* Washington: The Catholic University of America Press, 1950.

_____ *Worship and Work: Saint John Abbey and University,* 1856-1956. Collegeville, Minnesota: North Central Publishing Company, 1956.

Baumstein, Paschal. "A Divine Practice." *The North Carolina Architect* (July-August, 1983), 14-19.

Belmont, Perry. *An American Democrat: The Recollections of Perry Belmont.* New York: Columbia University Press, 1940.

Benko, Matthew. *The Abbot 'Nullius'.* The Catholic University of America Canon Law Studies, No. 173. Published Doctoral Dissertation. Washington, D.C.: The Catholic University of America Press, 1943.

Cope, Robert F. and Manly Wade Wellman. *The County of Gaston: Two Centuries of a North Carolina Region.* Charlotte, North Carolina: Gaston County Historical Society, 1961.

Duffy, Conseuela Marie. Katharine Drexel: A Biography. Cornwells Heights, Pennsylvania: Sisters of the Blessed Sacrament, (1965) 1972.

Dunne, Edmund Francis. *The Sicily of America: The Catholic Colony of San Antonio, Florida — Where They Grow the Genuine Sicily Lemon.* [pamphlet] San Antonio, Florida: ([1883] 1885).

Ellis, John Tracy. *Catholic Bishops: A Memoir*. Wilmington, Delaware: Michael Glazier, Incorporated, 1983.

_____. *The Life of James Cardinal Gibbons, Archbishop of Baltimore, 1834-1921*. Two Volumes. Milwaukee: Bruce, 1952.

Fellner, Felix. "Father Oswald Moosmueller: The Pioneer Benedictine Historian of the United States." *Records of the American Catholic Historical Society of Philadelphia* (March, 1923), 1-16.

Fitzpatrick, Vincent de Paul. *Life of Archbishop Curley: Champion of Catholic Education*. Baltimore: (privately published), 1929.

Fogarty, Gerald P. *The Vatican and the American Hierarchy From 1870 to 1965*. Stuttgart: Anton Hiersemann, 1982.

Hilpische, Stephanus. *Benedictinism Through Changing Centuries*. Collegeville, Minnesota: Liturgical Press, 1958.

Lane, Raymond. *The Early Days of Maryknoll*. New York: David McKay Company, 1951.

Lewis, H.H. Walker. "Eugene O'Dunne." *The Lawyers' Roundtable of Baltimore and Its Charter Members*. Baltimore: Paul M. Harrod Company, 1978, 50-66. [This chapter was originally published as an article, in virtually the same form, in *American Bar Association Journal* as "Baltimore's Judicial Bombshell," in July, 1970.]

Magri, Joseph. *The Catholic Church in the City and Diocese of Richmond*. Richmond: Whittet and Shepperson, 1906.

Miller, Miriam. *A History of the Early Years of the Roman Catholic Diocese of Charlotte*. Charlotte: Laney-Smith, 1984.

Moleck, Fred J. "Music at Saint Vincent Archabbey Under Boniface Wimmer." *The American Benedictine Review* (June, 1963), 248-262.

Oetgen, Jerome. "Boniface Wimmer and the Founding of Saint Vincent Archabbey." *The American Benedictine Review* (June, 1971), 147-176.

_____. "Boniface Wimmer and the American Benedictines: 1856-1866." *The American Benedictine Review* (September, 1972), 283-313.

_____. "Boniface Wimmer and the American Benedictines: 1866-1876." *The American Benedictine Review* (March, 1973), 1-28.

_____. "Oswald Moosmueller: Monk and Missionary." *The American Benedictine Review* (March, 1976), 1-35.

Powers, George. *The Maryknoll Movement*. Published dissertation (M.A.), The Catholic University of America. Maryknoll, New York: Catholic Foreign Mission Society of America, 1920 (1926).

Price, Thomas Frederick. *Collected Letters of Thomas Frederick Price, M.M.* Robert Sheridan, editor. Maryknoll, New York: Maryknoll Fathers, 1981.

(Priest of Maryknoll). *Father Price of Maryknoll: A Short Sketch of the Life of Reverend Thomas Frederick Price*. Maryknoll, New York: Catholic Foreign Mission Society of America, 1923.

Puett, Minnie Stowe. *History of Gaston County*. Charlotte, North Carolina: Observer Printing House, 1939.

Reger, Ambrose. *Die Benedictiner im Staate Alabama*. Baltimore: Drud von Kreuzer Brothers, 1898.

Robinson, Blackwell P. *The North Carolina Guide*. Chapel Hill: University of North Carolina Press, 1955.

Roemer, Theodore. *The Ludwig-Missionsverein and the Church in the United States (1838-1918)*. Published Dissertation. Washington, D.C.: The Catholic University of America Press, 1933.

Separk, Joseph H. *Gastonia and Gaston County, North Carolina (1846-1949)* Gastonia: J.H. Separk, 1949.

Sharpe, Bill. "Gaston." *A New Geography of North Carolina*, Volume II. Raleigh: Sharpe Publishing Company, 1958, 761-786.

Sheridan, Robert E. *The Founders of Maryknoll: Historical Reflections.* Maryknoll, New York: Catholic Foreign Mission Society of America, 1980.

Stowe, Robert Lee, Sr. *Early History of Belmont and Gaston County, North Carolina.* [No publisher indicated] 1951.

Worsley, Stephen C. "Catholicism in Antebellum North Carolina." *North Carolina Historical Review* (October, 1983), 399-430.

Part III:

Unpublished Sources

Doris, Sebastian. *Belmont Abbey: Its Origin, Development, and Present State.* Belmont, North Carolina: [privately issued], 1971 (revised edition). [N.B., the original was an unpublished Master's thesis.]

Fellner, Felix. *Abbot Boniface and His Monks.* Saint Vincent Archabbey Archives: typescript, n.d.

Hollar, Donna Alyn. "Maryhelp Abbey Cathedral: Analysis and Interpretation of Gothic Revival." Unpublished graduate research paper (University of North Carolina at Charlotte, 19 April 1982).

McGraw, Walter John. "Saint Benedict's Parish of Richmond, Virginia." Unpublished thesis. University of Richmond, 1949-1950.

Meagher, Margaret. *History of Education in Richmond.* Richmond: Works Progress Administration (Federal Writers' Project), 1939.

Sheridan, Robert E., editor. *Very Reverend Thomas Frederick Price, M.M., Co-Founder of Maryknoll: A Symposium.* Privately issued at Maryknoll, New York, 1956.

Sherry, Agnes. "The Development of Catholic Education in North Carolina." Unpublished Master's thesis. Fordham University, April 1930.

part IV:

archival Repositories

Archives of the *Abbatia Nullius* of Belmont (North Carolina). The Right Reverend Peter N. Stragand, O.S.B., Sixth Abbot of Belmont and successor to the Abbots Ordinary.

Archives of the Abbey of Maryhelp (North Carolina). The Right Reverend Peter N. Stragand, O.S.B., Abbot.

Archives of the American Cassinese Federation of the Order of Saint Benedict (Pennsylvania). The Right Reverend Martin Burne, O.S.B., Abbot-President; The Very Reverend Omer Kline, O.S.B., Archivist; Brother Philip Hurley, O.S.B., Assistant Archivist.

Archives of the Archdiocese of Baltimore (Maryland). The Most Reverend William Borders, Ordinary; Sister Felicitas Powers, R.S.M., Archivist.

Archives of Belmont Abbey College (North Carolina). The Right Reverend Peter N. Stragand, O.S.B., Chancellor; The Honorable Basil Whitener, Chairman of the Board of Trustees; Dr. John R. Dempsey, President.

Archives of Benedictine Priory (Savannah, Georgia). The Right Reverend Leopold Krul, O.S.B., major superior; The Very Reverend Conan Feigh, O.S.B., Prior.

Archives of the Catholic Foreign Mission Society of America (Maryknoll, New York). The Reverend Delbert Robinson, M.M., Archivist; The Reverend Robert Sheridan, M.M., Historian.

Archives of the Diocese of Charleston (South Carolina).*

Archives of the Diocese of Raleigh (North Carolina). The Most Reverend Joseph Gossman, Ordinary; Mrs. Robert Leary, Archivist.

Archives of the Diocese of Richmond (Virginia). The Most Reverend Walter Sullivan, Ordinary.

Archives of the Diocese of Savannah (Georgia).*

Archives of the Diocese of Superior (Wisconsin).*

Archives of Saint Benedict Abbey (Kansas).*

Archives of Saint Benedict Motherhouse (Bristow, Virginia). Mother Andrea Verchuck, O.S.B., Prioress; Sister Damien Tambola, O.S.B., Archivist.

Archives of Saint Benedict Priory (Richmond, Virgina). The Right Reverend Peter N. Stragand, O.S.B, major superior; The Very Reverend Benedict McDermott, O.S.B., Prior. [N.B., This collection includes the records of the Benedictine Military Institute, also. At the time the current work was being researched, this repository had not yet been organized]

Archives of Saint Bernard Abbey (Alabama).*

Archives of Saint Charles Seminary [Sulpician House of Studies] (Baltimore, Maryland).*

Archives of Saint John Abbey (Collegeville, Minnesota). The Right Reverend Jerome Theissen, O.S.B., Abbot; The Reverend Vincent Tegeder, Archivist.*

Archives of Saint Mary Abbey (New Jersey).*

Archives of Saint Leo Abbey (Florida). The Right Reverend Fidelis Dunlap, O.S.B., Abbot; The Reverend Henry Riffle, O.S.B., Archivist.*

Archives of Saint Paul Outside the Walls (Rome). [For this project, microfilm at the Catholic University of American (Washington) was used]

Archives of the University of Notre Dame (Indiana). Dr. Wendy Schelerth, Archivist.

Archives of Saint Vincent Archabbey (Latrobe, Pennsylvania). The Right Reverend Leopold Krul, O.S.B., Archabbot; The Very Reverend Omer Kline, O.S.B., Archivist; Brother Philip Hurley, O.S.B., Assistant Archivist.

Archives of Saint' Anselmo Abbey [International House of Studies for the Order of Saint Benedict] (Rome).*

Archives of the Sisters of the Blessed Sacrament for Indians and Colored People [Saint Elizabeth Convent] (Cornwells Heights, Pennsylvania).*

Provincial Archives of the Congregation of the Holy Redeemer (New York).*

*Indicates repositories which supplied information without personal research privileges.

PART V:

Types Of Works Not Listed In The Bibliography

1. In most cases the bibliography excludes works consulted within the larger environment of the various archival collections named.
2. Standard and general reference works have not been included.
3. Minor sources not directly employed in this work, and of little value to researchers are not listed.
4. Newspapers and use of their morgues are not cited in the bibliography.

Index

1. Ordinarily, churches, parishes, and missions are indexed according to their location. They are found under the name of the county in which they are situated.

2. Ordinarily, schools and apostolates are indexed under name of the sponsoring monastery, convent, or religious order.

3. Because poor recordkeeping has obscured the identity of many of the Benedictine brothers, most references to the non-ordained monks are included under the listing for Maryhelp Abbey.

ML   10/11